Pat Dolenc

Economic Development

ECONOMIC DEVELOPMENT

THEORY, POLICY, AND INTERNATIONAL RELATIONS

A Twentieth Century Fund Book

Ian M. D. Little

Basic Books, Inc., Publishers

New York

The Twentieth Century Fund is an independent research foundation which undertakes policy studies of economic, political, and social institutions and issues. The Fund was founded in 1919 and endowed by Edward A. Filene.

Board of Trustees of the Twentieth Century Fund

Morris B. Abram	Georges-Henri Martin
Peter A. A. Berle, Chairman	Lawrence K. Miller
Jonathan B. Bingham	Don K. Price
Hodding Carter III	James Rowe
Benjamin V. Cohen	William D. Ruckelshaus
Brewster C. Denny	Arthur M. Schlesinger, Jr.
Charles V. Hamilton	Harvey I. Sloane, M.D.
Patricia Roberts Harris	Charles P. Taft
August Heckscher	David B. Truman
Matina S. Horner	Shirley Williams, M.P.

M. J. Rossant, Director

Library of Congress Cataloging in Publication Data
Little, Ian Malcolm David.
   Economic development.

   "A Twentieth Century Fund study."
   Bibliography: p. 425
   Includes index.
   1. Economic development. 2. Underdeveloped areas.
3. International economic relations. I. Title.
HD82.L49 1982   338.9   82-71366
ISBN 0-465-01787-8 (cloth)
ISBN 0-465-01793-2 (paper)

Copyright © 1982 by the Twentieth Century Fund, Inc.
Printed in the United States of America
Designed by Vincent Torre
10 9 8 7 6 5 4 3 2 1

Contents

FOREWORD *vii*

PREFACE *ix*

PART I
Basic Notions
Chapter 1   *The Meaning of Development*   3
Chapter 2   *On Different Kinds of Economics*   16

PART II
Theorizing, 1943–60
Chapter 3   *Planning and Industrialization*   29
Chapter 4   *Planning and Foreign Trade Regimes, 1945–60*   60
Chapter 5   *Structuralism and Monetarism: The Latin American Debate*   77
Chapter 6   *The Dual Economy: Surplus Labor and Resources for Industrialization*   86
Chapter 7   *Other Elements and Areas of Neglect*   98
Chapter 8   *Interim Summary and Forward Linkage*   118

PART III
A Resurgence of Neoclassical Economics After 1960

Chapter 9	*Planning, Trade, and Labor Markets After 1960*	*125*
Chapter 10	*New Topics*	*159*

PART IV
The New Radicalism

Chapter 11	*Equality, Poverty, Labor Demand, and Basic Needs*	*209*
Chapter 12	*Dependency and Underdevelopment*	*218*

PART V
Description and Record of Less Developed Countries

Chapter 13	*Description and Record*	*269*

PART VI
International Systems and Confrontation

Chapter 14	*The Old International Economic Order—The Trade Regime, 1945–73*	*285*
Chapter 15	*The Old International Economic Order—The Monetary System, 1944–73*	*305*
Chapter 16	*Distributive Justice and the New International Economic Order*	*322*
Chapter 17	*The New International Economic Order and the Events of 1973–80*	*334*
Chapter 18	*International Systems: A Summary View*	*371*

NOTES	*385*
BIBLIOGRAPHY	*425*
INDEX	*441*

Foreword

The demands of the developing countries for a so-called new international economic order have become something of a ritual incantation in recent years, gaining some credence from constant repetition. There had been critical studies of the new order, but none that placed it in perspective in terms of either economic theory or political reality. Thus, the Twentieth Century Fund was receptive when Ian M. D. Little, the British economist, expressed an interest in exploring the pattern of economic development in the postwar era.

All during that era, both the theory and the practice of economic development were subject to changes, sometimes abrupt, often costly. The theory, originating for the most part in the West and influenced by the pattern of the advanced industrialized countries, has been substantially revised; the practice, carried out in the developing countries, has been erratic, characterized by drastic shifts in economic policies and entrepreneurial activities. In general, the economies of these countries have changed less than their policies. Perhaps the most notable shift in recent years has been the increasing unity, at least in rhetoric, of the developing countries, commonly banded together as the Third World. They have made use of the variety of international institutions to press their demands and influence public opinion.

Foreword

In his proposal to the Fund, Little, a fellow of Nuffield College and formerly professor of the Economics of Underdeveloped Countries at Oxford, proposed to undertake a major study dealing with the economics and politics—as well as myths and realities—of development. It was his view that the developing countries opposed the present system, although it was not necessarily operating to their disadvantage, largely because they saw it as having been foisted on them. It was his intention to suggest a system that both sides would find more satisfactory. The Fund, which has long been involved in economic development studies and international affairs, decided to support Little's project.

In his book he analyzes the three major periods of development planning: the early postwar years, dominated by ambitious planning for large-scale investment in industry and maximum economic growth; the 1960s, when planning was less detailed and the emphasis switched from industry to agriculture; and today's demand for a new order, with controls of trade and complex and discriminating preference systems, which he strongly opposes.

Little champions the formulations of younger American and British economists, and some Third World economists trained in the United States and Britain, who reject planning in favor of decentralization and the freeing up of market forces. Bringing his accumulated wisdom and critical intelligence to bear on the recent course of development, he has provided recommendations that are as significant as they are controversial. It is always pleasing when a proposal lives up to the expectations we had for it, and we are delighted that this one has managed to do so.

M. J. ROSSANT, DIRECTOR
The Twentieth Century Fund
March 1982

Preface

This is a rather comprehensive, critical survey of development economics, including the main international economic issues that have given rise to North-South confrontation. It is not written in the style of a textbook, and may contain too much personal judgment to be considered as such. While some professors may nevertheless find it useful in graduate courses, it is intended to be read by nonacademics and noneconomists who are interested in less developed countries. Probably 90 percent of the book is accessible to anyone with only a smattering of economics. There is no algebra and no geometry. In some parts, however, the analysis gets intricate, and economic concepts are occasionally used without the very full explanation that a noneconomist might need for total understanding. The reader who finds himself almost out of his depth should persevere, as he will quickly find his footing again.

A full bibliography would have left no room for the text. The nearly five hundred works cited bear close relevance to the text, but the list is far from comprehensive and is not intended even as a select bibliography. However, reference is often made to other authors' specialized bibliographies, so that a lead-in is provided for more intensive study of most of the topics treated.

Despite its broad coverage, there are limits. Much of development economics is policy oriented. Economic policies serve both political and moral ends; but means and methods are shaped also by prejudices associated with different histories, value systems, and intellectual influences. I touch upon these interfaces, so that the book contains some elements of political economy. But it is more superficial in this respect than I once hoped. In common with almost all the development literature, the centrally planned economies are largely ignored. Little is known outside about those countries that would rank as less developed by normal criteria, and the more developed centrally planned economies have negligible trade and aid relations with all but a very few LDCs; and they also play little part in North-South dialogues or confrontation on trade and payments systems. The omission of China will be regarded by some as lamentable, but I decided that in the present state of knowledge I would have little confidence in the validity of anything I wrote about the economy.

Even within the above disciplinary and territorial bounds there are gaps. Apart from defense expenditure, I deal with almost all topics that have excited interest in the literature or in the North-South debates. Some of these are, however, of less importance than topics that I omit. The short- and medium-term macroeconomic management of LDCs was a much neglected subject until very recently, when some work began to appear. But this is too recent, and perhaps as yet too tentative, for me to have been able to absorb it. Another important topic that has given rise to relatively little research, and that I ignore, is the international migration of workers. Finally, I should say that I have consulted only the English language literature.

Part II concerns the first wave of thinking about development. The difference between this and post-1960 work on LDCs is marked. A person in a hurry could omit Part II (and also the section on planning in chapter 9, which makes little sense except as a continuation of chapter 3). But this would be a pity because the older thinking, although I argue it was mostly wrong, still casts a shadow. Part V consists of a description of some features of the Third World in the late 1970s and changes in previous decades. Some may prefer to read it earlier, either before Part II or Part IV. Finally, the reader interested only in international

Preface

systems and confrontation will find Part VI reasonably self-contained, although some of the judgments rely on earlier discussion.

I come to acknowledgments. The following have read or otherwise contributed to some part of the text: S. Anand, H. Bull, C. Diaz Alejandro, V. Joshi, P. Oppenheimer, A. Premchand, T. King, L. Scandizzo, M. FG. Scott, A. K. Sen, R. Skidelsky, T. N. Srinivasan, E. Thorbecke, J. von Pischke, and M. Yudelman. I am very grateful to them. But, apart perhaps from members of the Twentieth Century Fund and its referees, no one has read it all, and some parts have been seen by no one but the author. The usual disclaimers apply. Some of the ideas were presented in seminars given at the Woodrow Wilson School, Princeton University, in 1980; I am grateful to members of the seminar for comments and to the Woodrow Wilson School for support. Boston University; Nuffield College, Oxford; and the Institut für Weltwirtschaft, Kiel, also provided facilities for my work. I am further grateful to audiences at the Department of Overseas Development in London, the Université Libre de Bruxelles, Hamburg University, the Institute for International Economic Studies, Stockholm, and the Graduate Institute for International Studies, Geneva.

I thank the Oriel Press for permission to republish excerpts from my contribution to P. Oppenheimer (ed.), *Issues in International Economics*, 1980, in chapter 16 of this book; and the American Enterprise Institute for permission to publish excerpts from my contribution to R. C. Amacher, G. Haberler, and T. D. Willett (eds.), *Challenges to a Liberal International Economic Order*, 1979, in chapter 4.

Finally, I am indebted to my wife for acting as research assistant throughout and for typing all preliminary drafts. Another draft was typed, with great speed and efficiency, by Ruth Saxe, and sent to the Twentieth Century Fund in early June 1981. A few amendments were made between then and the beginning of September, mainly in response to anonymous referees. With rare exceptions, literature appearing after early 1981 is ignored.

Ian M.D. Little

PART I

Basic Notions

Chapter 1

The Meaning of Development

In the past decade, the idea that economic development could be identified with the growth of national income per head has been under heavy attack. For example, an article by Dudley Seers called "The Meaning of Development" has twice been published, (in 1969 and 1977)[1] in the *International Development Review*, the organ of the Society for International Development. This article sought to dethrone the target growth rate of 5 percent in the national incomes of developing countries set by the United Nations for the First Development Decade, the 1960s. It sought instead to concentrate attention on equality and the reduction of unemployment and poverty, though wisely without actually defining the meaning of development.

Discussion of this issue leads one back to first principles and to problems of social values. What is the meaning of an increase in national income? Measuring it at marginal cost, and given some very strong assumptions and a suitable quantity index, it implies that the set of goods and services of some earlier period could be made available in a later period with something to spare. This is usually called an increase in real product. If we use market prices rather than resource costs, we get, again with very strong assumptions, a utility measure telling us that the real product of the first period would not have sufficed to give everyone as much utility as he has in the second period—not, of course, that everyone is actually better off. Why not call one or another of these indices a measure of economic growth or of economic development?

The trouble is that even the more neutral term "economic growth" is not wholly neutral. To quote myself of thirty years ago: "To say 'the real income of the community is greater' is not much different from saying 'the income of the community is really greater' which is again not much different from 'the community is better off.'"[2] If these welfare implications are to be avoided, the fact that they are not intended must be reiterated to the point of tedium. Even that does not work. Let me illustrate from Harvey Leibenstein (1957), who says, "we shall utilize per caput output or per capita income as our index of development."[3] He goes on to explain that a rise in per caput output merely means that the community has the *possibility* to achieve a higher standard of life.[4] He calls per caput output an "observation index" and adds that "an index of observation is bereft of welfare implications."[5] Whether this latter statement is true depends on what it is called. An index of development certainly has welfare implications because "development" is a word that undoubtedly carries value overtones, just as do words like "welfare" and "optimum."[6]

If the above were false, Seers would not repeatedly write about the meaning of "development," which he rightly recognizes to be a normative word. With such words, there is liable to be a competitive struggle to get one's own definition accepted. Those who struggle, wishing to influence policy, are right to do so. If a definition gets accepted, it tends to deemphasize considerations not included in the definition. If, for instance, "development" were measured by poverty, equality, and employment, somehow combined, the potentiality of the economy for future achievement, even in these self-same dimensions, would tend to be ignored. If one were just tracking past achievement this might not matter; but an index of development also becomes an objective, and it would clearly be tragic not to provide for the future.

Anyone who writes that such-and-such a policy would further economic development is making a value judgment. But surely, it will be protested, one can discuss the causes of the growth of national income per head (that is, a series of numbers concocted by government statisticians) in a neutral way. If, in so doing, it is shown that some policy change would make this series grow faster in the future, that is not to say that the policy change should be made. I agree that verbal neutrality is possible. I am saying only that it is very difficult where the description of the change studied normally carries overtones of approval or disapproval. The author has to go to great lengths to neutralize such overtones. If, as so often happens, he does the opposite and substitutes words like "progress" or "development," then he has very clearly, even if unintentionally, entered the realm of persuasion.

I differ from Gunnar Myrdal, whose views on value judgments in the social sciences are well known. He and some others take the view that it is wrong to try to exorcise the value overtones that cling to many social science concepts.[7] Rather, the value judgments should be brought out into the open.[8] But what of the person who wants to explain changes in national income per head without taking a position on whether a rise is bad or good? He has no intentional value judgment to make explicit, and must therefore exorcise the overtones of his subject matter to avoid any unintentional implicit judgment. Alternatively, of course, the writer may want to promote policies to increase national income per head. In this case, I agree that he does best to make an explicit statement in favor of increasing income per head, which will involve him in making value judgments.

In some areas of study, the economist has little difficulty in being positive. He may study the elasticity of the supply of tea from Assam. The values that lead him to this work might include the view that the Assamese are nice people and should be helped. We can easily suppose that the most likely way his study will help them is to produce a correct answer. His conclusion that the elasticity is 1.3 does not look like a value judgment, nor is it. This would not seem worth saying if Myrdal did not seem to argue that value judgments are all-pervasive in the social sciences if only because writers and researchers have motives for doing what they do that are inevitably influenced by society. This is true, but it does not follow that they inevitably make value judgments. Nor does it even follow that their positive statements are biased, though this is often the case, especially with work on developing countries. My point is that one should make a clear distinction between false or biased positive statements and value judgments. There is nothing morally wrong with preaching; but it is wrong to mislead people knowingly about what is true or false. Finally, I should add that whether a proposition is true or false is not itself dependent on the choice of a value system, for even this abhorrent proposition has been advanced by some social scientists.

My discussion of value judgments implies that there can be no objective definition of development and therefore no universally acceptable indicator. The best one might hope for would be to get some rough consensus on objectives and hence on how progress toward these objectives can be measured. But I very much doubt whether this can be achieved.

Development or Welfare?

There is a definition that I believe to be acceptable to most liberal economists. I think one could almost call it the liberal economic definition. It integrates economic development with welfare economics. Economic development (or economic progress or real economic growth) occurs if there is a rise in the present value of average (weighted) consumption per head. The future starts now, and consumption is measured at market prices or at the maximum prices people would be willing to pay for what they consume.

This definition is open in that the weights to be attached to each individual's consumption are left open. Everyone can attach his own weights, in the light of his views about inequality and poverty now and in the future. Or, if he believes there is sufficient consensus in society, he can attach what he believes to be social weights. This openness will enable us, I hope, to see how various authors and governments have differed in the course of time in their views about poverty, equality, and the amount by which the future should be discounted. One limit is to attach the same weight to a marginal unit of consumption, whosoever and whensoever the consumer. Another limit is suggested by John Rawls.[9] His anti-utilitarian theory implies that the welfare of society increases only if the welfare of the poorest person increases. This is extreme even for the author, and he substitutes the poorest class for the poorest person. This view can be incorporated in the liberal economists' welfare definition by giving a weight of unity to each member of this class and zero to all other persons.[10]

Although the welfare definition of development is open, it is not completely open. It would be futile if it were. In effect, our economic welfare function is defined in terms of the consumption of individuals.[11] This seems to imply that all collective goods are excluded. But this need not be so if they can be validly imputed to individuals. Whether such an imputation is valid depends on two considerations: first, on the nature of the public good, some public goods being much more like consumption than others; and, second, on how the collective decision is taken.

Let us take two rather extreme cases: a municipal public park and military expenditure. The first is surely consumption for those who use it. But to say that individuals consume the services of the armed forces sounds farfetched, although one could argue that military expenditure is a cost of consumption; thus, in assessing the likelihood of future levels of consumption, one might want to take military expenditure into account. But this is not satisfactory either, for defense is probably more a cost of independence than of consumption. Nor can we assume, because it is euphemistically given that label, that all military expenditure is defensive.

Let us turn now to the nature of the collective decision. If a kibbutz, say, decides to provide itself with a discothèque, the participatory nature of the decision makes one more inclined to say that even the elderly members of the community who dislike loud noises benefit by being pleased to know that their children can dance themselves deaf. But if a mad dictator decreed that 90 percent of the country was a game reserve, although farming land was scarce and the people poor, then we would be less inclined to argue that this devotion of resources to animals was part of the people's consumption.

In between such extreme examples lies a large number of difficult cases. It is clear that values, not only about what affects persons' individual welfare but also about the nature of desirable decision-making processes (that is, political values), enter in. Arthur Lewis in his excellent appendix on "Is Economic Growth Desirable?"[12] says firmly, "The case for economic growth is that it gives man greater control over his environment, and thereby increases his freedom." But suppose that decisions are increasingly taken for him, as some index number of consumption mounts? If participation in decision-making is an element in individual economic welfare because it determines whether a person would want to call the collective consumption his own, then economic and political values are not even conceptually distinct.

Individual economic welfare (the very definition of which presupposes some liberty to choose) is not all we care for. This has always been recognized. Liberty in a wider sense than the choice of a consumption basket is a political value that many would insist on. The Indian electorate seemed, when it overthrew Mrs. Gandhi in 1977, to be setting political values before economic ones—or negative freedom before positive freedom. But, even if we can separate the two conceptually, economic values are, as we have seen, not independent of political values. Thus, in the last analysis, the economist cannot claim, "Look! This is what I mean by economic development—political and social development is something else." No one can decide objectively just what shall be counted in individual standards of living. Even less can he decide what are basic human needs.

Moreover, in some philosophies individual welfare may not enter into a criterion of development. Alec Nove says of the USSR in the year following the First Five Year Plan, "1933 was the culmination of the most precipitous peacetime decline in living standards known in recorded history."[13] From figures of food supply, it seems probable that the consumption standards of 1913 were not reached again until around 1960.[14] But it may seem paradoxical to say that there was no economic development in the USSR from 1913 to 1960. (Certainly this would be the case if one assumed Bolshevik values.) But why fuss about the use of a single word? After all, it is fairly easy to describe the "development" of the USSR, without being very misleading, by saying that its productive capacity for making producers' goods and armaments increased enormously, but its capacity to satisfy personal consumption demands increased very little.

Unfortunately, in a world of statistics, targets, and propaganda, careful description leaves problems unresolved. Suppose that the United Nations and the World Bank decided to produce only indices of the consumption of the poorest 40 percent when tracking development, or imagine getting targets for the Third Development Decade written only in such terms. The thunder of protest would be deafening. So perhaps, after all, it is growth of the gross national product (GNP) per caput that governments want. If that is what they want, they will want it to be called development.

Let us turn to the problem of valuing investment. In the liberal economists' welfare function, investment is included insofar as it provides for future consumption. Depending on one's views as to the rate at which the future should be discounted, one might want to count a rise in investment as more, or less, valuable than a rise in average consumption now. This will depend on (1) how fast one thinks people are going to get better off anyway, (2) how much future consumption that extra investment will yield, and (3) when it will yield it. Let me elaborate on these three points.

1. The main reason, or so economists think, why one wants to discount future consumption is that it is expected that people will be richer then. This is intimately connected with ideas about income distribution, although inequality between contemporaries may seem more displeasing to some people than intergenerational inequality. It is clear that the faster people get richer, the less weight one will want to give to marginal

investment—or, to put it another way, the greater the required yield in terms of future consumption. A high stress on equality implies a desired low rate of investment. If the present discounted value of the future consumption yielded by an extra investment of one dollar is more than one dollar, then investment is worth more than average consumption, assuming that the dollar comes from average consumption.

2. Some investments yield much, others little; and still others have a negative yield, meaning that they decrease the capacity of the country to provide consumption in the future. This is important, for in the earlier days of the postwar period there was certainly a tendency to assume that all investment was good. It later became clear that much investment in developing countries yielded little or nothing in terms of either future potential output or future consumption. Either mistakes were being made, or growth of GNP was not the idol some have made it out to be.

3. The time that elapses before an investment, or the whole investment program, yields extra consumption is important. The limiting case is that it never yields any consumption, even if it has a high yield in terms of output. Soviet investment in the 1920s and 1930s was devoted to building up heavy industry that would produce mainly weapons. In the light of Hitler's invasion in 1941, one cannot say it was wasted. (The same is true of Japan, but this investment *was* wasted.) But even if the investment is intended to yield consumption, the delay can be great. In the postwar period, Mahalanobis argued that it was better for India to import fertilizers than food grains. Delay— one year. Then he argued that it was better still to build fertilizer plants. Delay—five years. His final triumph was to argue that it was better still to build heavy machine-making plants to make fertilizer plants (fertilizer-plant plants). Delay—ten years or more.[15]

There comes a point at which one must say that the apparently revealed values of the leaders of a country are inconsistent with the liberal economists' welfare function, elastic as it is. This, as we have just seen, may be because the government pays very little attention to poverty now, giving an unacceptably high priority to the growth of the industrial structure, with the promise of more consumption long delayed. Or it may be that the elite of a country esteems objectives that cannot all plausibly be inserted into individual utility functions. We may call these national objectives. They include the desire to be militarily powerful, to be able to exercise influence on international relations, to be independent and maybe nonaligned. They include the accoutrements that some may think are necessary for a proper nation—a conference center, some luxury hotels, and a national airline.

I think it has become clear in recent international debates, for example in speeches before the General Assembly of the United Nations, that the leaders of many developing countries set more store by these national objectives than most economists have realized. They seem to take a more collective, more nationalist view of development than do most Western liberals. The poverty of the nation may be put before the poverty of poor people. In addition, certain kinds of populist economic development may play a political role. They may serve as symbols that help in the process of nation building. Many less developed countries (LDCs) are pluralist or multicommunity societies, and the need to establish a sense of nationalism, of belonging to the nation rather than to a tribe or ethnic group within a state, could, in some cases, be a reason for such projects as a national airline. But it is hard to separate national values that one may respect from those urban elitist values that have come under attack, most especially from Michael Lipton.[16]

Then again, a national leader may feel that certain projects help to establish his legitimacy. Taiwan, which started no steel plant until the death of Chiang Kai-shek, provides an example. The generalissimo saw that a steel plant was undesirable on strategic grounds. Not only was it a good target for a bomb, but it also took more shipping to bring in the coking coal and iron ore than to bring in steel. But after his son took over, the next plan featured ten great projects, including a large steel plant. In earlier plans, particular projects had never been featured. It seems clear that Chiang Ching-kuo, the son, felt that a featured set of large projects somehow strengthened his regime. It has to be added that he could hardly have been right unless the mass of the people felt, for good or bad reasons, that such things were a good idea. Such feelings having nothing to do with any economic cost-benefit analysis. One could find plenty of "men in the street" in England who thought the Concorde was a splendid venture.

Some of these national virility symbols clearly reduce national income per head. But their creators believe that they are developmental.

It is not only ruling elites who may quarrel with the liberal economists' view of development. Some radical economists and sociologists of a neo-Marxist persuasion appear to define "underdevelopment" entirely in terms of the dependence of an economy on foreign capitalist economies, this in turn depending very much on its productive structure. They would doubtless argue that development—that is, increasing independence and a "balanced" industrial structure including basic industry—is necessary for long-run welfare increases; but welfare is certainly no part of the definition. There are still more radical approaches of a mystical revolutionary and nihilistic character. "Development" is held to have become a bad word, and it is suggested that "liberation" be substituted. What is demanded is freedom from everything the revolutionary feels to be oppressive: freedom, for instance, from aggression, elitism, inequality, alienation, and materialism.[17]

At the other end of the spectrum, a number of liberal economists, mostly but not all of the Chicago school, would object to my definition of the liberal economists' welfare function on the grounds that income distributional considerations should not be muddled up with efficiency. I have never understood this argument, for efficiency surely has to be defined in terms of some end. If that end is defined in utilitarian terms, then it is impossible to separate income distribution from efficiency.

Throughout this book I shall make frequent use of such expressions as "social profit" and "social rate of return." The word "social" implies that profits and returns are calculated using shadow prices, not actual or predicted market prices. Some economists, including those of the Chicago school, define the shadow price of a resource as the opportunity cost in terms of the market value of goods and services. I shall be using the shadow price of a resource to mean the opportunity cost in terms of welfare; and similarly, the shadow price of a final output is its marginal contribution to welfare. The shadow price is expressed as so many units of a monetary numeraire, but each unit of the numeraire has an identical welfare value. This definition leaves open the form and the arguments of the welfare function (sometimes also called the objective function). This openness does not matter. Logically, all that matters is that there should be some set of objectives in the light of which a policy, project, or state of affairs can be judged. There is no more difficulty, and no less, in the concept of social profitability than there is in any evaluative judgment concerning society.

The attack on growth as an objective was at least partly misdirected. Most LDC policymakers were not simply aiming at growth of output per head. If they had been, a more efficient use of their country's labor resources would have been a high priority, and a more labor-intensive growth would have resulted. They were trying to satisfy many other objectives, of both a national and a sectional character. It is up to the reader to decide what objectives he regards as admissible arguments in an acceptable welfare function.

Difficulties of Measurement and Social Indicators

Apart from the moral problems relating to the use of national income per head as an indicator of development, there are others of a more positive nature. First, national income statistics were conceived more as a measure of activity (for short-run Keynesian purposes) than as a measure of "real income." Thus, economic "bads," like travel to work, are included. Less remediably, the actual consumption of many services is hard to measure, so that inputs are used as a surrogate for outputs. What it all amounts to is that national income statisticians are not always measuring the quantities most relevant to answering the question of whether or not people are better off. One should add that, even when they aim to measure the right thing, the actual figures produced are often closer to guesses than measurements. This is especially true of LDCs, some more than others.

Such has been the dissatisfaction with income per head as a measure of development, or objective of development, that many people have argued for the substitution of a number of so-called social indicators, or, if not the substitution, at least the supplementation of national income figures by such social indicators. Indeed, a whole industry has grown up to produce and compare such social indicators as, for example, infant mortality rates, other death rates, the incidence of various diseases, the number of doctors per head, hospital beds per head, school enrollment rates, literacy rates, and dietary statistics.

No one would want to fasten on any single indicator, such as suicides, as a good measure of current social welfare. But if more than one indicator is to be used, then one is forced to weight the different indicators in order to get a summary measure. Such weighting is as subjective as the weighting for people's consumption by their income levels. A recent example of an attempted welfare measure along these lines is the "quality of life" index developed by the Overseas Development Council and Morris D. Morris. It combines with equal weights the expectation of life at age 0, at age 1, and literacy. I find this a rather narrow conception of the quality of life.

The following points need to be made about social indicators:

1. They are concerned mainly with current welfare, and in this respect are comparable to national income accounting measures of consumption. (Some, however, are also indicators of human capital formation.)
2. Many of them are as flawed as national income accounting figures in that they measure inputs not outputs, for example, doctors per head, school enrollment rates. But this does not apply to measures of literacy or mortality. (This is part of the reason for their choice of the "quality of life" index.)
3. Many are as flawed as the concept of average consumption in that they ignore distribution. The number of doctors per head tells one nothing about the sort of heads these doctors tend. An increase in the number of hospital beds does not imply an increase in the number of poor people who lie there. On the other hand, rises in some indicators, if at all substantial, are less likely to be accounted for by changes applying only to the relatively rich than is consumption in general. Calories per head is an obvious example.

Social indicators are undoubtedly useful to contemplate, especially when national accounts are very poor. But most liberal economists would probably prefer to look at current consumption when assessing welfare, especially if it were well measured and if it could be divided up between different income classes or other social groupings so that distributional weights could be attached. This is because consumption measured at market prices reflects the satisfaction of people's wants. On the other hand, some may prefer to see basic needs rather than wants satisfied, and social indicators are more suitable for this purpose.[18] One must reiterate that social indicators give little indication for the future. Finally, they take no account of national or political objectives.

The discussion of social indicators has clearly landed us back in the realm of values—something that must be discussed in order to interpret and understand the changing ideas about economic development that we shall be reviewing. One aspect of these changes is the accusations that are often leveled against those who wrote and lectured about development in the previous decade or decades. As we have seen, one of the main accusations is an undue concentration on the growth of GDP, or national income, with the implied neglect of poverty, equality, and unemployment. If substantiated, the neglect could clearly spring either from a difference in values or from a different understanding of how in fact benefits would get distributed.

Chapter 2

On Different Kinds of Economics

Development Economics

Before trying to classify different kinds of theorizing about economic development, we have to ask what development economics is. One approach is to say that it is what development economists do. And what do they do? They study the economics of less developed countries (LDCs) as defined, say, by the United Nations. But this answer presupposes some common issues and problems among LDCs, and we are increasingly aware of differences. As the differences mount, perhaps the term will disappear, and we shall speak only of economists specializing in particular groups of countries that do have a lot in common. Development economics will then have ceased to exist. But in the past, there has been a perception of sufficient homogeneity, even if it was sometimes misleading.

But cannot development economics be distinguished in some other way than by subject matter? One may ask whether it is not distinguished by objectives—the objective of growth, for instance. Although growth was for a century a neglected subject in mainstream economics, a recrudescence of interest in the growth of the more developed countries (MDCs) occurred at about the same time as development economics was born, say, in 1944. So development must mean something different from growth, if development economics is to be distinguished by objective. In chapter 1, I introduced the liberal economists' objective function, but this would serve equally well for MDCs and LDCs. Why should it not? We are all human beings. But I also said that nationalist objectives in fact played a considerable role. Without suggesting that such objectives are not also of some importance in developed countries, it could be argued that the specifically nation-building objectives are of special importance in LDCs, since not only are many of them young nations with as yet very unsettled political systems, but many are also plagued by the special problems of tribal and plural societies. But this is not true of all. Moreover, development economists, with rare exceptions, have paid little or no attention to such matters. They have not been active in exploring the political consequences of different economic policies, although most, when in the role of advising governments, will have been very conscious of political constraints. So I do not think one can say that development economics has been distinguished by objectives.

It is, however, true that the work of development economists has concentrated on the medium and long run to an extent that is not true of the work of economists focusing on developed countries. One of the main consequences has been that problems of managing the economy in the short run, handling fluctuations and shocks, whether they are caused internally or externally, were neglected. (An exception to this is the International Monetary Fund [IMF], which sees, for instance, the work of the International Bank for Reconstruction and Development [IBRD] as essentially concerned with *long-run* development.) This concentration is at last beginning to dissolve, as students of the LDCs have begun to realize that the long run is an integral of short runs.

Finally, we can ask whether development economics has been distinguished by a different style of analysis, which may or may not have been required by the different actors, different institutions, and indeed the very poverty of developing countries. I believe that the answer is yes. But justification for this answer will come later from our description and analysis of development ideas.

GENERAL CLASSIFICATIONS OF ECONOMIC THEORIES

Economic theory and analysis can be classified, often dichotomized, in various ways. The common distinctions made in textbooks on development have been between classical, neoclassical, and Marxist. The dichotomies include normative/positive, static/dynamic, equilibrium/disequilibrium, general/partial, and so on. Often these distinctions are not clearly defined, and all too often one branch of the dichotomy is used as a term of abuse. Who likes to have his work called partial, static, and neoclassical? Only a few such distinctions are, I think, going to be essential for our purpose of analyzing development theory. All the above dichotomies apply to any branch of economics. In discussing the meaning of development I have, in effect, already said a lot about the normative/positive distinction.

MAGNIFICENT DYNAMICS

The term is William Baumol's.[1] As with all dynamic analysis, it is characterized by the functional dependence of the quantities of one period on those of another. It is magnificent because of its boldness, the sweeping nature of its generalizations, and the fact that the subject matter is the development of the whole economy over long periods. Baumol applies the term to the classical economists (including Marx), to Schumpeter, and to Harrod.

I shall apply this term rather differently, to those who seek to go behind the normal economic concepts of savings, investment, techniques, and productive efficiency—which may be said to be the standard components of a purely economic explanation of growth and change—in a comprehensive manner, and thus try to explain growth in terms of institutional, political, cultural, and psychological variables in a broad historical context.

The classical economists Marx and Schumpeter fit my description. But in my play, they will be largely offstage, the father figures who influence my cast. The contributions that I shall describe as "magnificent dynamics" are those of Rostow, Hagen, and the dependency and neo-Marxist theorists. In doing so, I associate myself with Baumol's remark that the use of the word "magnificent" is not meant to prejudge the quality of the analysis.

This brings me to the main categorization I have decided to adopt, which is structuralism versus neoclassical economics. Hollis Chenery has also seen this as an essential antithesis.[2] (He classifies approaches to economic development as neoclassical, neo-Marxist, and structuralist.) The proof of the pudding will be in the eating. In other words, the test will be whether this dichotomy enables us to bring out, without too much distortion of individual positions and contributions, the essential differences in styles of thought and analysis, and indeed the conflicts, that have certainly permeated thinking about economic development in our period. Another possible antithesis would be between classical and neoclassical. I think this is less enlightening and I shall deal with it only en passant in chapter 6.

Structuralism

While the phrase "neoclassical" has been in common use for a long time, this is not true of "structuralism." One does not find the word at all in the earlier writings about development. It first came into use in the 1950s with reference to structuralist explanations of inflation in Latin America, as opposed to the monetarist explanations and policies largely identified with the IMF. Even in recent textbooks, its use is mainly confined to this context.

It may therefore seem odd to include as structuralists writers who have never used the term. But this need not be so. M. Jourdain spoke prose for more than forty years without knowing it.[3] Chenery does not hesitate to say that "the initial set of structural hypotheses was formulated in the 1950s by writers such as Paul Rosenstein Rodan, Ragnar Nurkse, W. Arthur Lewis, Paul [sic] Prebisch, Hans Singer and Gunnar Myrdal."[4]

I think I can recall Isaiah Berlin once remarking that great thinkers always have very simple ideas about the universe, and that behind important schools of thought there also lurk very simple models. The complexity and sometimes impenetrability of the conceptual structure created, and the argumentative cleverness exhibited, arise only from the need to defend their homely positions against the attacks of those who look at things differently. With this in mind, I shall loosely define structuralism and neoclassical economics in terms of such simple visions of the world.

The structuralist sees the world as inflexible. Change is inhibited by obstacles, bottlenecks, and constraints. People find it hard to move or adapt, and resources tend to be stuck. In economic terms, the supply of most things is inelastic. Such general inflexibility was thought to apply particularly to LDCs. Peasants were hardly economic men and were stuck in the mud; people were ruled by custom and authority; entrepreneurs were lacking; and communications were poor. There was little choice as to what to produce from the land. As a result of poverty, demands, too, were inflexible, especially for food. If there was to be any development, the demand for imports would be highly inelastic, since capital goods must come from abroad. Demands also were inelastic, especially for food, for imports into developing countries, and for their exports. Such general inflexibility was thought to apply particularly to developing countries, but not exclusively so, for, as we shall see, there was much structural thinking about the adaptation of European countries to the situation in which they found themselves in the early postwar period.

This alleged inflexibility was married to the evident fact that the production structure of developing countries was very different from that of developed countries. To achieve development, this structure had to be changed, and to achieve rapid development it had to be changed rapidly. The direction of the structural change required could be discerned by cross-country studies of the structure of production and trade. As development proceeds, these structures must approximate more closely to those of the MDCs.[5]

The structuralist view of the world provides a reason for distrusting the price mechanism and for trying to bring about change in other ways. If supplies and demands are very inelastic, large price changes are needed to achieve small quantitative adjustments. Large price changes are disturbing, both directly and also because they result in changes in income distribution. These may or may not in themselves be desirable; but if the losers are powerful, they may in any event be able to resist the change through organized industrial or political action. Supply and demand generally are more elastic the longer one waits. But if short-run reaction can negate the required price change, the long run never arrives. It follows from what we have said that there is no such thing as a structuralist theory of growth; it may be called into play to explain why other theories do not work very well, but it primarily seeks to provide a reason for managing change by administrative action.

We have said that the structuralist view provides a reason for distrusting the price mechanism. But in interpreting the development of ideas about development, we shall have to be on our guard against assuming that it has been a reason rather than a rationalization. For there are other reasons for distrusting the price mechanism; and, indeed, it has long been in the socialist tradition to do so, while structuralism is of recent origin.

On the plane of analysis, it is not so much a matter of mistrusting prices as of ignoring their influence. This is consistent with the supposition that quantities are highly price inelastic or will not change. Thus, structuralist models assume fixed relationships (or ones that change exogenously) between quantities or between values with prices assumed constant.

In line with most economic writing, in this preliminary sketch we have treated structuralism in the limited sense of being about the structure of economic flows—that is, the relative magnitudes of the inputs and outputs of different economic activities, and not about the institutional, moral, and legal framework of these activities, nor about the power relationships functioning within that framework. This is in line with the structuralists themselves, who were not much given to interdisciplinary analysis.

Neoclassical Economics

Neoclassical economics has been "mainstream" economics for more than a century. Its birth was the marginalist revolution of the 1870s. It has been associated particularly with the concept of marginal utility and the explanation of prices as exchange values. Marginal productivity as a theory of distribution is in fact earlier. Schumpeter ascribes it to Longfield in 1853, and von Thünen around the same date.[6]

In certain circles, especially those influenced by the postwar school of Cambridge (England) economists, "neoclassical" has become a term of abuse. The emotional reasons, in the case of the Cambridge school, stem from the fact that its members believe that neoclassical economics purports, at least partly, to explain wages and interest (and profits) in terms of marginal productivities, and even that it seeks to justify the existence of profits as stemming from the scarcity (that is, high marginal productivity) of capital.

It is true that many neoclassical writers have used a production function, with constant returns to scale, and have assumed perfect competition. In such models, the real wage is equal to the marginal product of labor, and the rate of interest is equal to the marginal product of capital. On the other hand, many economists, for whom marginalism is a stock in trade, have made contributions to theories of monopoly and monopsony in which there is no such equation of real wages with marginal physical product. Many, even of those who pen such algebraic anathemas as $\frac{\partial P}{\partial K} = r$, and $\frac{\partial P}{\partial L} = w$, would argue that monopoly, power conflicts, and institutions—even class conflicts—play a role in the share of labor in the national income. It is possible both to believe this and to think that models assuming perfect competition (largely for mathematical simplicity) can also be enlightening in revealing real world influences.

The capital theory controversy has been in the vanguard of the attack on neoclassicism, and the emotionalism of the attack certainly suggests that the attackers are basically concerned with demolishing a theory that seems to suggest that distribution is determined by natural economic forces and not by social conflict. But the weapons used appear to have the sharpness of logic. They have centered on the possibility of measuring capital but also on the erstwhile esoteric notion of "reswitching" ("erstwhile" because young economists are now born with it at their fingertips).

Measuring capital is a backward-looking activity. It plays a necessary role in historical research into the statistical explanation of growth known as "growth accounting." Within our period, such neoclassical attempts to explain growth have had considerable influence on thinking about development, although there has been rather little application to developing countries, no doubt largely because available figures are too poor for this approach to be very plausible. The influence mainly took the form of encouraging people to believe in the importance of human capital (see chapter 10).

But nonhistorical models of growth, dubbed neoclassical, also abound. Unlike structuralism one can thus say that there is a body of neoclassical growth theory. The main corpus of the work has concentrated on full employment models and the achievement and properties of golden ages in which all magnitudes grow at the same rate. There is no duality, no underemployment, no structural adjustment. Golden-age models have not much interested development economists. However, a number of dualistic models, starting with that of D. W. Jorgenson,[7] also use neoclassical production functions.

The use of neoclassical production functions may, as Robert Solow has stressed, be a mere elucidatory convenience and play no necessary part in the story of capital accumulation and the adjustment to changing factor prices.[8] It is this latter part of the story that is going to have particular relevance for us.

Consider the following propositions. As investment proceeds, the demand for labor rises. Eventually, provided it proceeds fast enough to more than cope with a growing population, this will cause a rise in real wages and a fall in the rate of profit, which in turn will cause the introduction of more capital-intensive techniques. These propositions are the essence of a neoclassical theory of growth. They look like a very reasonable description of the history of the developed countries, and more recently of South Korea, Taiwan, Hong Kong, Singapore, and possibly others.[9] They seem to presuppose only profit maximization, and not necessarily perfect competition. It does not require any statement to the effect that the rate of interest is equal to the marginal productivity of capital, for the amount of capital and changes in it can be left undefined.

The theory of reswitching, prima facie, seems to put a spoke in the wheel. It is possible that a rise in real wages would result in a lower value of capital per man. The newly favored technique could, after the rise in real wages, have a higher operating cost, that is, employ more men per unit of output. This might happen because the relative cost of capital equipment was lower with the new technique—this being because the machinery itself had a lower labor cost component and a higher profit rate component (remember that the rate of profit is now lower). This shows that the adaptation to higher real wages cannot necessarily be described as an increase in capital intensity.[10] But it appears to be a curiosum that flies in the face of history and direct observation.[11] Nor would its importance be obvious even if it occurred, for it does not show that labor in the economy as a whole is not saved, since the switch would be to a technique that uses less labor in its construction.

Returning to developing countries, in many there have been large real wage increases in the industrial sector that no one would ascribe to increasing scarcity of labor. No one would suggest, or has suggested, that the distribution of income in such cases is primarily determined by the "natural" economic forces of neoclassical growth. But, of course, the effect of higher wages on the choice of technique may remain.

After this very brief excursion into growth theory, we must return to our search for a definition of neoclassical economics. Despite the influence of Cambridge (England), I feel justified in thinking that the attack on the concept of capital, and its use in some growth models, does not go to the heart of the hostility to neoclassical economics. Thus, neoclassical economics may be defined as the result of a vision of the world that is the opposite of the structural vision. I think this is more useful than producing a shibboleth, such as declaring anyone who cannot mouth the phrase "marginal productivity of capital" to be a structuralist.

Thus, a neoclassical vision of the world is one of flexibility. In their own or their families' interests, people adapt readily to changing opportunities and prices, even if they do not like doing so and even though they may take their time. Businesses pursue objectives roughly consistent with the assumption that they maximize risk- and time-discounted profits. (One should be on the lookout for other objectives that might make this assumption misleading, such as those that arise from a divorce of management and ownership.) There is usually a wide variety of ways of making things such that production methods can be expected to shift when input prices change. Demand schedules are consequently curves, neither kinked nor vertical. Supply schedules are also smooth and rarely vertical. Although demand and supply always depend to a greater or lesser extent on expectations of an uncertain future, nevertheless most markets usually tend to achieve an equilibrium without wild price fluctuations. In short, the price mechanism can be expected to work rather well.

It is not a central tenet of a neoclassical outlook that the price mechanism will achieve Pareto-optimality in production (no more of one thing can be produced without less of another). Many economists, considered to be in the neoclassical tradition, have contributed much to the subject of market failure and price distortions. Many in the field of development have been concerned with shadow prices, a concern that implies a belief that actual prices fail to reflect social costs and benefits closely enough. Admittedly, some authors seem to tie "neoclassical economics" to the assumptions required for Pareto-optimality—perfect competition and foresight. There are certainly neoclassical *models* in this sense. But no economist believes they are such exact descriptions of reality that he need not look out for explanations of the workings of markets that include monopoly, oligopoly, and ignorance of both the present and the future, and be on the watch for policies that take account of such matters. Neoclassical economics can thus be described as a paradigm that tells one to investigate markets and prices, perhaps expecting them often to work well, but also to be on the watch for aberrations and ways of correcting them. Perhaps the single best touchstone is a concern for prices and their role.

We have given the names "structuralist" and "neoclassical" to two ends of a spectrum. There is no point in drawing a line. This implies that many analyses, and policy prescriptions, have elements of both. A fortiori this applies to economists themselves. For instance, an economist may be mainly neoclassical in his thinking, while also maintaining that there are important areas where the market fails to achieve a tolerable equilibrium, whether for institutional or more fundamental reasons.

PART II

Theorizing, 1943–60

Chapter 3

Planning and Industrialization

Varieties and Means of Planning

INTRODUCTION

The 1940s and 1950s were the years of maximum enthusiasm for "planning," in some sense. But the concept of planning is complex, and it is essential to embark on an analysis of the meanings of the term, and of different kinds of planning.

Planning, by definition, is about the future; but, also by definition, the future is unknown and uncertain. Every economic agent plans, except when he acts on the spur of the moment. An individual plans his expenditure and his income. Since the future is unknown, his plans may turn out to be good or bad.

A father may plan the whole family's expenditure; but more likely he will decentralize or delegate some of it, in which case the wife and children also plan. There is a problem of coordination. The family plans have to be consistent, in the sense that budgetary limits are not overstepped. If the family has collective objectives, there is also the problem of efficiency: do the budgetary allocations and the individual plans serve these ends as well as possible? Not all planning need have budgetary implications, but the same problems of consistency and efficiency will arise. The homely example makes the point that the basic issues in planning are (1) who plans and, if many plan, (2) how consistency is achieved, and (3) how the individuals' plans are influenced in order to achieve possible collective objectives.

We are concerned with governmental planning. Any government that consciously intervenes in the economy with some end in view may be seen as planning. Accepting this definition implies that all governments plan, even if they merely raise money to preserve law and order. We have here a spectrum, ranging from Hong Kong to the USSR. There is also a spectrum in the dimension of the efficiency of coordination of revenues and expenditures. For instance, a government comprises many ministries and often other spending agencies as well. Their expenditures may be well or badly coordinated from the point of view of serving overall governmental objectives, which may themselves be more or less precisely defined or agreed on. In the end, there may be no discernible rationale to the outcome of a politico-bureaucratic struggle; and expenditures may also outrun revenues to a disastrous extent. It then becomes a matter of choice whether one says that the government plans exceedingly badly or fails to plan at all. Much the same is true of nonbudgetary interventions.

THE INSTRUMENTS OF PLANNING

The basic distinction is between guiding or controlling by means of negative controls and positive commands on the one hand, and using the price mechanism on the other. That this was as important a distinction as that between public and private ownership was brought out long ago in the debate on how to run a socialist economy.

One way is to decentralize decisions, telling managers to maximize profits in the light of the price mechanism, modified by taxes and subsidies in order to correct for its failings,[1] a solution developed by E. Barone in 1908[2] and elaborated by others including Lange[3] and Lerner.[4] It was wholly rejected by socialist planners until the 1960s and has been rather fully adopted only by Yugoslavia, though the Yugoslavian "model" differs from the

Barone model because of workers' ownership and participation in management. Hungary also has gone some way in reintroducing the function of the price mechanism in allocating resources. The Soviet Union and other Eastern European countries began some tentative moves in this direction in the 1960s, but the movement toward "market socialism" was slowed down when it was realized that such reforms would reduce the power of the bureaucracy and the Communist party. Here we have probably the primary reason for the rejection of market socialism.

But the above view would not be accepted by structuralists. In their opinion, even a "doctored" price mechanism (doctored to allow for various alleged failings of market prices) either cannot achieve required structural changes or cannot achieve them fast enough or in an acceptable manner. So we have the essential distinction between a command economy, which is planned by directives and controls, and a "market socialist" economy, which induces change through the general instruction to maximize profits in the light of a set of prices that may be influenced by the government. While this is an essential distinction, no system of planning wholly abjures controls, and none wholly abjures the price mechanism: for instance, most consumer goods are allocated by the price mechanism even in highly planned economies.

In mixed systems of public and private ownership, the manner in which the private sector can be planned is limited, for the private sector cannot be commanded. Admittedly, it may be possible for a ministry to lean on particular companies in such a way that the pressure comes very close to being a directive. Such persuasion is most prevalent in Japan, but it is also significant in South Korea and Taiwan, and probably exists to some extent in many countries. But even in these countries, the government cannot force a company to do something the management believes will be unprofitable.

The private sector can, however, be prevented from doing things. In peacetime, such negative control has probably been most pervasive in India. Permission has been required, during most of the period since World War II, to export, import, invest, buy or sell foreign assets, obtain power and many raw materials, and manufacture many products. Other countries have taken a more positive approach, developing close relations between government and industry, which may make it possible for a government not only to consult with particular firms but also to influence them in a manner both parties find acceptable. Where credit is rationed and the banking system is mainly public, as in France and many developing countries, then the government can also see that favored sectors or firms have easy access to credit, and others do not.

The behavior of private actors, and decentralized public actors, may also be influenced by the government publishing predictions of the future state of the economy. This gives rise to the theory of indicative planning invented by the French. The essential idea is to get more rational and less risky investment decisions made than under a wholly decentralized system. In the latter case, many decision-makers would be making different guesses about the likely rate of growth of the economy and its main sectors, and also about the expansion plans of their competitive rivals and complementary suppliers. A central plan would inform these decision-makers about likely trends in quantities and perhaps also in prices.[5] Consultative committees for different industries would provide much more detailed information and an exchange of views. This kind of system is likely to be most relevant where there is a population of large firms with oligopolistic connections.

The central plan is essentially a set of targets and predictions. A target is an objective that the government intends to aim at with some weapon it can use; a prediction is a prediction. According to the theory of indicative planning, the central plan is itself a direct instrument of planning: that is, it is itself an influence acting on decentralized decisions. More generally, however, the central plan is supposedly a guide to the use by public authorities of the more direct levers of budgets, taxes, directives, and controls. But the plan document seldom contains statements of the way in which such levers will be used to try to achieve the targets.

The chief differences between less developed countries and more developed countries are: (1) most LDCs publish plans (often at the behest of aid donors), (2) LDCs, with few exceptions, use quantitative controls much more extensively, and (3) government expenditure is less effectively controlled and planned in LDCs.

DEGREES OF CENTRAL PLANNING AND PLANNING HORIZONS

At a minimum, every government plans its own expenditure and designs a revenue system. Beyond this, almost all governments try to equalize supply and demand for a few key aggregates, such as labor and foreign exchange. Many also try to influence the level of savings and investment—and the overall level of prices. Such macroeconomic planning is in principle comprehensive, taking into account the whole economy. It may or may not be supported by a detailed and sophisticated planning model. But comprehensiveness and detail are very different.

The above sketch applies to almost all MDCs, among which only Japan now goes much further. In addition, most LDC governments try to plan the structure of the economy and in particular to promote industrialization. Most have also tried to accelerate the rate of growth of gross domestic product. Some, most notably India, go in for more detail and attempt to plan the supply and demand for some particular products. Even in India, however, the supply of, and demand for, the vast majority of things is a by-product of market forces and those particular controls that happen to impinge on them, rather than a matter of conscious planning. It is only in the USSR that almost everything is planned (apart from the quite high proportion of food that comes from small private plots).

Whether or not a country relies heavily on the market mechanism, institutions are important. The price mechanism cannot work well without at least a suitable set of monetary institutions, and a legal framework. Moreover, certain products and services are essentially public goods for which quantitative planning is the only solution. (What is essentially a public good is always arguable at the margin, which is perhaps where the argument should lie.) Quantitative planning in turn requires its own institutions and expertise.

In most MDCs, institutions largely evolved in response to demand. But LDCs are trying to grow, and are actually doing so, far faster than the MDCs did even in the period when their basic institutional structure was formed. A strong case can be made for saying that evolution is too slow, and institutional development has to be promoted by the government.

The time horizon adopted depends very much on whether the main emphasis is on comprehensive macroplanning or on structural and institutional planning. The former is associated with annual budgets or plans, frequent adjustments of monetary and fiscal levers, and until recently, occasional changes in exchange rates. The finance ministry and the central bank are the short-term planning agencies involved. Structural planning is associated with longer-term plans, from three to ten years, although five years is most commonly chosen. A planning commission or ministry is normally responsible. Its planners will generally attempt to see that the Five Year Plan is consistent and comprehensive, so that if implemented it should not result in those serious disequilibria of supply and demand for aggregate foreign or domestic resources that are the normal short-run concerns of the finance ministry or central bank. But in practice, five years is far too long for consistency. Few if any Five Year Plans have both avoided serious crisis and mapped the future course of the economy without very large errors. A conflict between short- and medium-term plans is usually unavoidable and results in difficult relations between planning ministries and finance ministries.

In general, LDCs have opted for published Five Year Plans, which are supposed to serve as guidelines for public expenditures and for economic policies, in the light of an attempt to project the main national income and foreign accounts of the country. Few MDCs publish plans, and many do not officially attempt medium- or long-term projections.

LEVELS OF PLANNING—PROJECTS AND SECTORS

We have given a sketch of "central" planning, or planning at the highest level. Planning at the lowest level is project planning. In the private sector, investment projects are planned for profit in the light of anticipated prices (which may, however, be influenced by the government). In the public sector, this may not be the case; and there is then an issue of what investment criteria should be used.

Ministries and other public agencies are likely to be concerned with many investment projects over a long period, and these may influence one another. Planning at this level is termed sectoral planning, and such planning will usually include more than investment projects. For example, a ministry of agriculture will also be concerned with institutional matters, such as research, extension services, conditions of tenure, and so on.

Theoretical Debates

THE POSTWAR PLANNING DEBATE IN THE UNITED KINGDOM

The United Kingdom was the main stage for the academic planning debate, which deserves attention for two reasons. First, the main structural arguments for planning became clear. These were the presence of large disequilibria and inflexibility of response to price incentives. These arguments have carried over to the LDC context, it being frequently claimed that resources are peculiarly immobile in LDCs. Second, many economists who concerned themselves with development, both those who took part in the planning debate and others, were in England during and immediately after World War II.*

The United Kingdom achieved a high degree of planning in the course of World War II. Virtually all consumer goods were rationed, some on a points (or equally distributed second-currency) basis. Virtually all producers' goods were allocated. All foreign transactions, and also shipping space, were controlled. There was a 100 percent excess profits tax, and the price mechanism played

---

*Those who were already, or became, almost exclusively development economists include Arndt, Rosenstein Rodan, Mandelbaum (later Martin), Lewis, Singer, Frankel, and Bauer. Others who have at times concerned themselves with developing countries include Balogh, E. A. G. Robinson, and Kaldor. There is no doubt that this was a potentially influential group, both because of their writing and because of the influence some had on a slightly younger group who became prominent later in the 1950s. There is also little doubt that views formed at the time influenced their approach to LDC problems.

very little role in allocating anything. There were, of course, some loopholes; but the compression of standards of living was remarkable, and they were compressed toward a level that nevertheless left almost everyone's "basic needs" satisfied. The effect on people's thinking lasted for some years. The allocation of materials and productive capacity for the war effort pointed up some of the deficiencies of planning that have since become familiar.[6] Nevertheless, it was a model, albeit one that could probably never be repeated except in the case of a major war, and with an almost wholly committed population.

No one questioned that such control and planning were essential. To take a simple example, the greatly reduced level of consumption could have been achieved by the price mechanism only by causing gross and unacceptable inequality. It would have been impossible to levy taxes sufficiently powerful to prevent too much inequality of consumption.

In the early postwar years, it seemed that recovery, and the new structural transformation required, was too much to ask of the price mechanism. The basic elements apparently favoring a structuralist approach[7] were:

- Continuing shortages of many goods, which could not be relieved by imports because of a balance-of-payments constraint. Since this balance-of-payments constraint was common to all of Europe, it could be identified as a "dollar gap."
- Rectification of the balance of payments would, in view of the loss of external assets and worsened terms of trade, require large changes in the productive structure to produce more exports (or import substitutes, but exports were emphasized).
- A number of industries, especially coal and textiles, for whose products there was excess external demand, had capacity to spare but lacked labor. It was felt that labor was immobile and that the productive structure lacked adequate flexibility.

There was a violent debate on the role of planning for several years. The philosopher-administrator Lord Franks published a powerful plea for peacetime planning, based more, as befitted his background, on the platonic idea of guardians who would oversee and somehow direct the broad outlines of the development of the economy in accordance with some unity of purpose, which, in peacetime, would admittedly have to be created.[8] However, while his plea could be seen as groping for the idea of indicative planning (for he did not want compulsion), it was not based on any appreciation of the merits and demerits of the price mechanism. He was not an economist. It derived, it seems, rather from a nostalgia, shared by many, for the shared national objectives and harmony of a people fighting a just war. This is an idea that many have subsequently hoped would apply to the new nations, and it finds an echo in frequent assertions of the need for informing the people of those nations of the reasons for planning, and for harnessing public support and cooperation. Indeed, this is one of the major reasons for publishing plan documents.

The economists stressed inflexibility, especially labor immobility, and the fact that there were large disequilibria in this period. The main implication was that wartime controls could not be quickly eliminated, and that even in the long run controls might be required from time to time to deal with major disturbances. Few contributors seemed to envisage that pervasive controls might continue for an indefinite period.[9] The two most notable books on planning published in this period were essentially pleas for somewhat greater government intervention, but in the form of planning through influencing prices.[10] Some economists were even more deeply attached to the price mechanism and showed greater distrust of government.[11] Most prominent economists of the time (many more than those mentioned) took part in this controversy.[12]

As we have seen, some of these postwar arguments for central planning and controls carried over to the LDC context. But the planning literature that was explicitly related to LDC development was almost exclusively concerned with industrialization. We now turn to this literature.

A great deal of the theoretical argument for planning industrialization is closely related to protectionism (see chapter 4). Here we are concerned with arguments that would be valid in a closed economy. These arguments, all involving external economies of various kinds, stem mainly from three authors—P. N. Rosenstein Rodan,[13] T. Scitovsky,[14] and A. D. Hirschman.[15] The influence of these authors is clear from the subsequent reference to their ideas and to the adoption of their phrases, "big push," "pecuniary external economies," and "linkages." Sometimes these ideas have been misapplied, and it will be convenient at this point to examine them from a more critical standpoint than that so far adopted.

EXTERNAL ECONOMIES AND INDUSTRIALIZATION

The basic Rosenstein Rodan idea is simple. If you set up a shoe factory, not much of the demand resulting from the expenditures on shoemaking will be spent on shoes. Thus, isolated new ventures will be unprofitable. But if a large number of factories making different kinds of consumer goods (in proportion to marginal propensities to consume) are simultaneously established, then Say's law—that supply creates its own demand—will operate, and the resultant industrial complex will be viable. This idea can be called that of demand complementarity. The argument was applied to south and southeast Europe, where social overhead capital was assumed to be adequate, and where massive disguised unemployment in agriculture was also assumed. Later, for still more backward areas, Rosenstein Rodan developed the idea of the "big push"—bringing in required investment in social overheads, by which he meant primarily the required nontradable capital-intensive inputs common to all industrial production, mainly power and transport.[16] Basic capital-intensive tradable producers' goods, steel, chemicals, and oil products including petrochemicals were excluded for reasons of comparative disadvantage. But externalities of all kinds, not always precisely defined but clearly of the "pecuniary" character, soon to be defined by Scitovsky, received great stress. Indivisibilities were also stressed, for it would not have been so plausible to suggest that a tiny shoe factory could not sell its output. It is tempting to relate the idea of a "big push" to theories of "critical minimum effort," although Rosenstein Rodan did not himself do so.

The demand complementarity argument seems to require a closed economy; otherwise, import substitution and exports are possibilities. However, Rosenstein Rodan did *not* assume a closed economy. Since he advocated "light" labor-intensive consumer good production, capital goods and "basic" capital intensive intermediates would have to be imported. Weaknesses in the argument were that substitution for handicrafts was neglected (there was surely some such indigenous production in southeastern Europe and most other places). In addition, indivisibilities, and hence the risks of having to initiate production on a very large scale, are not very prominent in most of the consumer good industries Rosenstein Rodan had in mind. The argument seems also to fly in the face of history insofar as one interprets it to mean that the only way to start is with a big push. There was *some* industrialization not only in southeast Europe but also in many developing countries. It seems more relevant to ask why it did not go faster, rather than to produce reasons that respond more to the question of why it could not get off the ground at all.

Scitovsky distinguished technological or direct externalities (Meade's bees and fruit farmers),[17] which could hardly be very important, from externalities operating through the price mechanism, which he calls "pecuniary." Here again, a further distinction is really needed, although he did not make it. Such externalities can arise because the price mechanism is distorted—it does not reflect marginal costs or benefits. This is either because of mistaken policies on the part of the government or for more natural reasons. For example, the wage cannot reflect the opportunity cost of labor in a labor surplus economy. The correction of such errors by the use of shadow prices has come to be an essential feature of social cost-benefit analysis; and trying to make shadow prices coincide with actual prices is what we mean by "doctoring the price mechanism." But this was not what Scitovsky was really after. He was concerned that present prices, in the light of which it was assumed that private investment decisions were taken, would not be the equilibrium prices appropriate to the postinvestment situation for the very reason that the investment itself would shift the equilibrium prices. Assuming no distortions of the kind already mentioned, the equilibrium prices would be the shadow prices appropriate to an optimal solution. The investment decision would thus be optimal only if the coincidence were achieved. This goes to the heart of the distrust shown toward the price mechanism by many development economists, particularly those who decry what they call "static comparative advantage," and also by the central planning enthusiasts who equally decry partial analysis. It was also an argument used by French indicative planners: How can one plan investment for the future in the light of market prices when future prices do not, or seldom, exist?

When dealing with a single particular investment, the argument may seem tenuous.[18] We may take Scitovsky's own example. Investment in industry A cheapens its product, which increases profits in industry B, which uses that product. As a result, industry B increases its investment, which in turn increases demand for A's product. Scitovsky then assumes implicitly that the entrepreneurs in industry A will not have allowed for this effect, and so will have invested too little. Of course, they will then adjust, and A and B will reach equilibrium by a sequence of adjustments to each other's demands and prices.

It is fair enough to assume that a once-and-for-all jump would be better if there are the economies of scale implied by the first step in the above analysis. But it is much less reasonable to assume, if industry B is a very significant customer for industry A, that the latter will not take into account industry B's likely demands when planning its own expansion.[19]

If we extend the Scitovsky analysis to a very large investment program, then it is clear that the planners, if they use prices at all, should estimate the shadow prices that would prevail after taking their program into account. The earliest attempt to program investment in this way was by Chenery for Italy in the early 1950s, using an input-output matrix and linear programming.[20] This work took into account both price distortions (using a shadow price for labor) and the effect of the program on the shadow price of foreign exchange.

This work rested on the prior development of input-output analysis and of linear programming. The influence of these techniques themselves was considerable. To make their use easy or possible, internal demand is made independent of prices, and external demand is also either fixed or a linear function (usually inelastic) of the exchange rate. Input and capital coefficients are fixed, even for quite broadly defined sectors, and for the planning period of up to ten years. These are typically structuralist assumptions: the various ways in which adjustment might be made to varying scarcities, as reflected in prices, are ruled out. The great computational and model-making simplicities introduced by such assumptions have surely made proponents of planning techniques want to believe that these rigidities represent reasonable approximations to reality.

We have now come quite a long way from the planning debate of the early post-World War II United Kingdom. Techniques have become inflexible, but resources flexible. Labor flows easily to where it is wanted. The same was apparently assumed to be true of capital, even in a mixed economy like that of Italy.

Indeed, we seem now to be concerned with an entirely different reason for planning investments. Only if it is simultaneously and centrally planned can output demands (and shadow prices) be correctly anticipated. "Intersectoral relations are the essence of the problem"[21] and so is the "inability [of partial analysis] to determine how much of a given commodity will be required and the omission of external economies due to investment in other sectors. The first type of error is probably of greater quantitative significance."[22] The implied claim that central planners can correctly estimate demands is breathtaking; experience has shown that their errors are monumental. (We shall have more to say concerning the unreality of plans in chapter 9.) As already remarked, the Chenery model also allowed for a distortion in the labor market, using a fixed shadow price for labor. Such a distortion is, however, much less closely related to any need for simultaneous central planning of investment than are the arguments stemming from Scitovsky's pecuniary externalities.

The actual plans of developing countries in the 1950s (and later) have been much less sophisticated than the Chenery model. Most were only plans for a few major macroeconomic variables, without the links between the two being spelled out. Where a more comprehensive model was attempted, it was based on Harrod's analysis, relating rates of growth to required investment via assumed capital/output ratios (for which almost no appropriate data then existed). Harrod's growth model was essentially structural. It showed that there was only one rate of growth—the warranted rate of growth—which could reconcile a fixed capital/output and a fixed savings ratio. But there was another growth rate, the sum of productivity rises due to exogenous technical progress and the growth of the labor force—the "natural" rate of growth. This has been called a knife-edge theory, for, if the warranted rate of growth were not equal to the natural rate, there was what might be called a contradiction in capitalism.[23] But this contradiction arose only because of the assumption of fixed coefficients, as T. Swan,[24] R. M. Solow,[25] and N. Kaldor[26] later showed.

Harrod's problem could be ignored by planners as long as it was assumed that a "reserve army" of unemployed would last throughout the planning period. In effect, this was always assumed. No subtraction from the extra output from new investment was made on the grounds that labor was used, which would have had a positive product elsewhere in the economy. With a few exceptions, there was no planning for full employment, which was implicitly assumed to be impossible.

However, the implications of a natural rate of growth in the face of fixed capital coefficients were brought out by R. S. Eckaus in an influential article.[27] While examining all possibilities, he clearly considered that fixed coefficients were a cause of labor redundancy (and the article thus belongs to the structural school). The implication that there could be conflict between employment and output has also given rise to a lasting debate between the structuralists and those more inclined to make neoclassical assumptions. Since this work was not, however, explicitly linked to planning, we shall defer discussion of the substantive issues. It has given rise to both much empirical work based on assumed fixed coefficients and numerous articles showing them to be flexible.

We turn now to Hirschman's most influential contribution, the concept of linkages.[28] As in the case of pecuniary external economies, the interdependence of the productive system is seen as very important. Investment in industry A may cause something to happen in B. How is this different from pecuniary external economies (or diseconomies)? It is distinguishable only if the causative link is nonpecuniary. Hirschman assumed that one of the most important shortages in developing countries was in decision-making, particularly to produce. So if Hirschman's linkages are to be distinct, they have to galvanize an actual or potential supplier or client of the investing industry to do something that he would not have done, even though it would have been adequately profitable—for if it would *not* previously have been sufficiently profitable, the linkage is a pecuniary externality.

The importance of distinguishing Hirschman from Scitovsky will emerge later. We here consider only production relations, and not the more generalized concept that Hirschman introduced later.[29] First, take backward linkages. Firms often integrate backward, for various reasons—because they believe their suppliers are in a monopolitic position, making high profits, or are unreliable suppliers with respect to quality or delivery; or because they wish to reduce the risk of excessive price fluctuations; or because they want to expand, and their own market is not expanding fast enough. If the last reason is dominant, the result may also be diversification (sideways linkage). This kind of "inside linkage," to use Hirschman's own later phrase,[30] does not fit too well with the idea of galvanizing decision-making, for such insiders would seem to be already prone to decision-making. Turning to outside backward linkages, a new demand for inputs may result in new decisions being made by suppliers. But, as is also true of the inside backward linkage, it is difficult to distinguish this from a pecuniary externality. Conceptually, the distinction is possible. The new demand could suggest to the supplier that he should make some improvement that he could profitably have made anyway but had not considered. One need not further belabor the point, which applies equally to forward linkages.

The clearest case in which Hirschman's linkages can be distinguished from pecuniary externalities is where the linkage is created by the government or planning authority. This is common. Production is started with an assembly plant, and the government then creates backward linkages by insisting that components be produced or purchased locally, rather than imported. For example, the weaving of synthetic yarn suggests to the planners that they should promote the production of synthetic yarn, then fiber, and so back to a petrochemical complex. An alternative way of putting the point is to say that the linkage does not exist but has to be created. Hirschman's followers tended to as-

43

sume that any linkage was good. But administratively created linkages have been one of the main causes of very high capital intensity in manufacturing and sometimes of value subtracted at world prices.

What has this all to do with planning industrialization? It is most convenient to consider this in the course of a brief discussion of the concept of balanced growth.

THE BALANCED GROWTH CONTROVERSY

This controversy was the most prominent of all in the development literature of the 1950s. It was also one of the most futile ever extensively conducted in the pages of major journals. It was beset by misunderstandings of what others meant by the phrase. More important, the extent to which production should or should not be balanced (in some sense) must be a fallout from good planning or good policies. This planning or these policies should take account of various arguments that may lead toward or away from balanced growth, but concentration on the concept itself is like asking what is the optimum number of legs for an insect.

In a closed economy, the relative size of different industries must depend on final demand. However, within limits, the government can manipulate such demand (and the limits are wide in the case of an economy such as the USSR's). Central planners generally see it as their business to equate supply and demand. In 1954, Hirschman already thought, for some very good reasons, that this was an overrated activity, especially for economists.[31] He advocated project and sectoral planning and did not think it mattered much if supply and demand got out of line, for this would correct itself. But how to choose the sectors and projects to emphasize?

This answer (or anyway, part of the answer) was later given by his development of the theory of linkages. Special emphasis should be put on industries with most forward and backward linkages. In a closed economy, this must lead to excess capacity in the chosen industry and excess demand for its inputs. These disequilibria would stimulate "upstream" suppliers, while new undertakings would be stimulated "downstream" to make use of the excess capacity.

The industries with maximum linkages, in terms of potential sales to or purchases from other industries, could be discovered from input/output tables for more advanced economies (since *potential* interindustry transactions would be important for planning). The required work had been done by Chenery and Watanabe.[32] This criterion gave a high ranking for intermediates, as one might expect. Such industries are mostly very capital intensive. As a criterion, it flew in the face of comparative advantage and favored steel plants, which are, anyway, the darlings of nationalistic planners seeking modernity and prestige. Agriculture and services have the lowest linkages.

We can now see the importance of distinguishing between Hirschman and Scitovsky. With Scitovsky, pecuniary externalities should be allowed for to avoid harmful disequilibria, resulting from inadequate foresight. With Hirschman, linkages should be allowed for in order to create beneficial disequilibria.[33] The former leads toward central planning; the latter, toward project and sector planning, with deliberate benign neglect of the consistency central planners strive for and fail to achieve.[34] Since, as we have seen, it is very difficult indeed to distinguish pecuniary externalities from linkages, it is ironical that so much should appear to hang upon the distinction.

To the charge that inconsistency surely implies waste, Hirschman replied that this assumes that resources are fixed, while, as he saw it, disequilibria would call into being extra investment by stimulating entrepreneurship. With most countries struggling to save enough to support their investment programs, this may seem odd. The reply has to be that, in LDCs, investment (private investment, anyway) creates its own savings. The growth orientation of the argument also has to be noted, for the argument finally implies that savings are worth more than consumption.

On first looking into Hirschman's theory, after experience in India, at the end of the 1950s, the assumption that a key shortage was the ability to make investment decisions struck me as odd. India's Second Five Year Plan had just been swamped by a surge of private investment far exceeding the planners' expectations and the savings capacity of the country. Subsequent events suggest that there is no such shortage, at least in most of Asia.[35] How far it applies anywhere is debatable, but an inappropriate trans-

45

PLANNING AT THE PROJECT LEVEL: CHOICE OF TECHNIQUES AND INVESTMENT CRITERIA

Choice of techniques and investment criteria, although they have a somewhat independent literature, are of course the same; or rather, the former is subsumable under the latter.

It was widely accepted that LDCs were particularly short of capital, so that they should choose projects with low capital-output ratios, which normally also implies low capital-labor ratios (labor intensity). But soon such criteria were recognized as too crude;[36] the right answer must involve proper valuation of all inputs and outputs. The question also arose quite early of whether dynamic effects should enter into the calculation. This was the contribution of Walter Galenson and Harvey Leibenstein, who argued in favor of capital intensity on the grounds that the most capital-intensive projects would produce the most savings (they should have argued for the most profitable, not the most capital intensive).[37] Many critics suggested that the implied objective of maximum growth was extremist. At the same time, investment criteria *may* need to pay some regard to the future. This was all analyzed by A. K. Sen.[38] The subject was later swallowed up by the cost-benefit analysis literature, which is examined in chapter 9. While Galenson and Leibenstein were rightly criticized for their criterion of maximizing the investible surplus, some of the critics were not always sufficiently aware that their own position also favored capital intensity. The linkage doctrine did so. All those who pushed import substitution policies and balanced growth (extending beyond consumer goods industries) were pushing in the direction of capital intensity and an inadequate demand for labor.

At the time, this "choice-of-technique" literature—only one among many elements in planning at the project level—was not integrated with the general planning literature, which was dominated by arguments about central planning. The former concentrated on the issue of employment (and consumption) now, versus profits, which might promise more employment (and consumption) in the future. It neglected the possibility that prices other than wages might be giving wrong signals, especially those of foreign exchange and credit, and that this could be more important. It also did not face the issue of how projects were and should be planned in the public sector, or how private planning might best be influenced. At the same time, sectoral planning seems to have been wholly neglected.

The issue of the present versus the future had been addressed in 1928, at the level of the central allocation of resources, by the Soviet economist Feldman.[39] He showed that, even if investment goods industries are relatively capital intensive, total consumption will eventually be greater, the greater their share of new investment. In this model it was simply assumed that savings would equal investment (in real terms it had to, since one cannot eat machinery). With both Galenson/Leibenstein and Feldman, the purpose of investing in capital intensive projects or industries was to get more investment: with the former it was to produce more savings and hence investment; with the latter it was to produce more investment and hence savings. In India in 1953, Mahalanobis produced a model identical to that of Feldman. Mahalanobis was head of the Indian Statistical Institute, a member of the Planning Commission, and Nehru's most trusted economic adviser. There is thus no doubt that his model helped to determine the shape of the Indian Second Year Plan and later plans.[40] The dilemma was posed mainly in terms of consumption and how long higher consumption should be delayed. But given the rigid coefficients assumed, there was also an employment dilemma.

The Parting of the Ways—The Decline of Structural Planning in Europe and Its Evolution in LDCs

The European recovery program (1948–52) had required countries to produce plans showing that expenditures, approved under the aegis of the Organization for European Economic Cooperation, which was formed for the purpose, would require dollar assistance. These plans were hastily drawn up, and were mostly far short of the comprehensive attempts at consistency that were later to be made. The famous Monnet Plan for France was, for instance, a set of sectoral reconstruction and development plans for basic industries, with virtually no attempt to trace the macroeconomic implications.

But they served their purpose, which was to get an agreed division of Marshall Aid. They also provided the example that was to be followed under the Alliance for Progress, and by the International Bank for Reconstruction and Development and other aid agencies—namely that countries should be persuaded to have a plan in order to qualify for aid.

The Marshall Plan was a success. European recovery was dramatic, and the dollar shortage turned into a glut far sooner than economists had anticipated (see chapter 4). Yet the investment financed by Marshall Aid was a small proportion of the total. Its greatest effect may have been due to the small amount allocated to support the European Payments Union, which permitted the freeing of intra-European trade from quotas and thus served to uncork many supply bottlenecks. The disequilibria, and inflexibility of response to prices, proved to be ephemeral, not chronic. Thus, the more neoclassical economists saw their views prevail. Before the planning debate in the United Kingdom was over, Harold Wilson had lit "a bonfire of controls." By the mid-1950s, there was little left of comprehensive planning, other than the then conventional Keynesian macromanagement, and its brief revival in the 1960s was not a success. Even in France, the most dirigiste of the European economies, central planning withered in the 1960s and was virtually dead by the 1970s. However, the planning of extensive and increasing government expenditure began to extend beyond annual budgets and became more purposeful.

The LDCs took a different path. Outside Communist countries, India was for a long time the leader in attempting comprehensive plans, and in its wholehearted acceptance of the need to plan by controls. As early as 1934, Sir M. Visvesvarayya, an engineer, published his *Planned Economy for India*. It envisaged a growth of industrial production of 17.5 percent per annum for ten years (not impossible, as this was later achieved by South Korea and Taiwan!). He became a member of the Congress Party's National Planning Committee, founded in 1938 and promoted by Nehru and Subhas Chandra Bose (who later founded the Indian National Army, which fought with the Japanese during World War II). Despite conflict between Gandhians and those like Nehru who favored comprehensive planning and basic industries, the National Planning Committee's resolutions pointed toward the highly regulated Indian economy of the future, with a strong emphasis on basic industries. There were various other unofficial plans, produced by businessmen, Gandhians, and socialists, all notable for their optimism.

The Imperial Government itself began to plan for India's future during and after the war. A Planning and Development Department was founded whose Reconstruction Committee produced a document called *The Second Report on Reconstruction Planning 1945*. This adumbrated a First Five Year Plan and a fifteen-year perspective plan. It emphasized direct provision of new services for the poor. While favoring the extension of small-scale industry—to be dispersed and located in small towns and villages—it also recognized a need to give some priority to important capital goods industries. It emphasized popular participation and pinpointed administration as the potential Achilles heel of any Indian development program. In the words of A. H. Hanson, on whom I have relied for the above account, "in short, one may look in vain for any fundamental objective or method of the five year plans of the 1950s which is not foreshadowed in this remarkable documentary product of the later days of British rule."[41]

There was a not surprising delay after independence and partition in August 1947. The Planning Commission was founded in 1950. Its First Five Year Plan (1951–56) is often castigated as a mere collection of projects (which had mostly been dreamed up by the British Raj!). But full powers to control everything and anything were taken. It was not until the Second Five Year Plan that comprehensive investment planning was initiated, and an attempt made at overall consistency for the whole economy. It was then also that the heavy industry syndrome became firmly rooted (for fifteen years at least), backed up by Mahalanobis's models.

In all this, there is no sign of the influence of Western economists. To quote Hanson again, "What emerges with the greatest clarity from the 'prehistory,' however, is the decisive role played by one man: Jawaharlal Nehru. It was he who converted Congress to the idea of planning, and he who continued to insist on its importance at times when other, specifically more immediate, questions were tending to push it into the background,"[42] and "up to 1964, India's plans were Nehru's plans. For both their successes and their failures, therefore, he and the men he personally selected must be held largely responsible."[43] The last quotation, however, seems to reduce too much the role of others in the design of the plans.

Some commentators have pointed to the influence of Fabian socialism in LDCs.[44] This can be pushed too far in the case of India. It was certainly the socialist wing of the Congress Party that pointed India in the direction of planning; and it was this socialism, doubtless allied to the nationalist desire to make a clean break with what was thought to be the economic philosophy of the British Raj, that imposed the basic mistrust of the price mechanism that permeates Indian intellectual society to this day. But there was nothing particularly Fabian about this. Nehru did not spend his time in England at the London School of Economics, but first at Harrow and then as a law student. He seems to have become a quasi-Marxist as a result of organizing and participating in the International Congress against Colonial Oppression and Imperialism in Brussels in 1927, a Communist-front affair.[45] Of his Marxism, Sarvepalli Gopal writes:

> He was not well read in Marxism but was persuaded of its validity and emotionally inclined towards it. He also had a deep admiration for the achievements of the Soviet Union. Russia was the land of the future.... He hoped that some variation of the political and economic system prevalent in Russia would extend to India, but he was not prepared to have this by coercive methods.... Civil liberties were to Jawaharlal of absolute value, and the com-

munists had to reckon with this. Jawaharlal was not a Marxist in the normal sense of the word. He accepted the Marxist interpretation of history and its vision of a classless society, but he certainly did not believe in revolutionary dictatorship. Conditioned under Gandhi, he hated violence even if he did not in theory reject it, and stood for democratic and peaceful though not for constitutional means. But with these reservations, Jawaharlal, according to Palme Dutt, promised he would, as President of the Congress, do all he could to promote the Communist Party in India, and he even gave a series of specific undertakings as to what he would try to do.[46]

While he was too much in love with liberty to be a thoroughgoing Marxist, Nehru's economics, insofar as he could be said to have any, were Marxist in character. His attachment to planning was very firm. But there was probably a more direct Russian influence on the Indian plans. Mahalanobis used to visit Moscow, and the coincidence of his model with that of Feldman has already been noted. The emphasis on heavy industry was clearly inspired by the Russian example.

The style of Indian planning and development owed nothing to the Western and Latin American debates that I have reviewed. When I arrived to work in India in 1958, the key words that were being bandied about in Latin America and the West, such as "import substitution," "external economies," "linkages," and "structuralism," were never used. The key word was rather "self-reliance," including self-reliance in capital goods. Thus, although India was in fact planning for almost total import substitution whenever possible, in a highly structuralist manner, her planners were not influenced by any import of these concepts.

As rapid industrialization as possible was taken for granted, and was not thought to need justification. Certainly, quite rapid industrialization was the only way to achieve a target rate of growth of 6–7 percent per annum, for agriculture could not grow that fast. But it was also thought that there was no problem about which industries to choose. This can be rationalized in terms of export pessimism, a feature of Indian thinking that coincided with, but was not influenced by, that of the Economic Commission for Latin America. Thus, export pessimism, India's lack of many minerals, the idea that she must become independent of aid (and pay her debts) showed structurally that *all* manufactures must be made in India.⁴⁷ There seemed to be no possibility of choice, and so world prices were irrelevant. So far as industry was concerned the pattern would be determined almost entirely by domestic demand. Thus, "balanced" growth was also taken for granted and no allowance was made here for the role of prices—the typical structuralist assumption of almost total inelasticity.

J. N. Bhagwati and P. Desai have suggested that export pessimism was more of a rationalization than a reason. They write,

> It is interesting to note that the Second Plan did not explicitly state the rationale of the shift to heavy industries in terms of foreign trade constraints, so that the later justification of this strategy by alluding to "stagnant world demand" for Indian exports comes somewhat close to *post facto* rationalization. Indeed, the Second Plan's examination of export earnings through the Plan is so cursory that it is difficult to believe that the "stagnant world demand for Indian exports" assumption, by virtue of which the shift to heavy industries was later sought to be justified, was seriously made: such a crucial assumption, if made, would surely have been examined more intensively.⁴⁸

What then was the real reason for copying the USSR? There is some evidence that defense was uppermost in Nehru's mind;⁴⁹ and, in general, self-reliance and independence of other countries in case of another major war. Already in the 1930s, Nehru was a great dependency theorist. It is fair to add that there was no strong reason to believe that some heavy industry, especially steel, was not to India's comparative advantage, although it became clear later that the social returns, given the particular choices made of size, technique, output mix, and collaborators, were low or negative.

Although Bhagwati and Desai were probably right to regard the economic arguments as rationalizations, visiting economists, myself included, wrongly tended to agree with the planners that export possibilities, including those for manufactures, were very limited. The "two-gap" theory, which claims that foreign exchange may be a constraint on investment, even if savings are not, was implicit in this Indian thinking. Basic industry was required because India would not be able to export enough, on account of foreign demand limitations, to import the capital goods she needed, or the basic metals required to make them. Given that already only "essential" consumer goods were being imported, the corollary of this was that domestic savings could not substitute for foreign exchange, since less consumption would not be transformed into more foreign exchange either by import savings or releasing goods for export. I explicitly stated this in 1960: "A large element of foreign aid is, for a decade at least, indispensable. This is not so much because it is impossible to increase savings in India, but because savings cannot be translated into the kind of capital development which will later permit India to grow without continued reliance on foreign aid."[50] This two-gap idea, which was modeled and developed by Chenery and Bruno in the early 1960s, played a large role,[51] and will be referred to again.

Indian planning has been treated at some length, for several reasons.[52] It was the first to be based on a comprehensive framework or model. The ideas that it raised have been the subject of continuing debate. As we have seen, it owed nothing to Western influence. Finally, it was influential elsewhere. Almost every Asian country in the 1950s established some planning machinery. The resultant plans were not, in the 1950s, based on any comprehensive model. They were less pretentious and less doctrinaire. Heavy industry received less emphasis, mainly, no doubt, because, unlike India, there was plenty of import substitution, especially in textiles, still to be done in the consumer goods field. Despite this negative praise, it also appears to be true that these planning efforts were wholly ineffective in most countries. Pakistan, whose efforts were closely modeled on those of India, was something of an exception.[53]

Elsewhere it was often the need to justify aid that produced plans. In British Africa and the British Caribbean, colonial governments were of necessity doing some planning during World War II. After the war, the British government insisted on colonial plans under the Colonial Development and Welfare Act of 1945. The French, Portuguese, and Belgians themselves made development plans for their colonies. These were medium-term plans for government expenditure on development and did not aspire to be comprehensive. Thus, the African and Caribbean countries did not need to invent planning when they became independent, though they would doubtless have done so.

Latin America was the slowest region to embrace formal planning on the basis of a comprehensive view of the economy and to publish any plans.[54] This does not, of course, imply that no planning went on. Import substitution itself was a consciously adopted government strategy and was in that sense planned, even if haphazard in execution. But planning in the sense of a reasoned coordination of governmental expenditures was weak. Rather, more attention seems to have been paid to sectoral and project planning, and less to central consistency planning, than was the case in Africa or Asia. The Economic Commission for Latin America (ECLA) was a strong proponent of planning but made rather little headway, although its *Introduction to the Technique of Planning* (1955) was influential.[55] It was only with the foundation of the Alliance for Progress that most countries rushed out formal plans to qualify for aid (shades of the European plans under Marshall Aid).[56]

The Reasons for the Acceptance of Planning in LDCs, and the Influence of Economists

It is clear from the above account that almost all LDC governments enthusiastically accepted the idea that they should play a large role in the economy, sometimes by extensive public ownership, but more usually by direct intervention in the private sector.

Part of the explanation for this was the poor performance of the world economy from 1913 to 1945. Many of the now developing countries had grown rapidly from 1870 to 1913, especially those most dependent on international trade. Arthur Lewis has done more than anyone else to show this.[57] In the late 1940s and early 1950s, many references to stagnation suggest that few realized this. However, memories are short, and from 1913 to 1930 the growth of these countries had slowed down mainly because it slowed down in North America and Europe, during and after World War I. Then came the Great Depression, with a disastrous fall in the terms of trade of most developing countries, and massive unemployment in Europe and North America. Then came World War II, which disrupted their trade.

In the United Kingdom, and to a lesser extent in Continental Europe, it was widely believed that Keynesian remedies made it possible to avoid anything more than minor recessions in the future, provided that the United States did not have a major crisis. Consequently, only a small minority of economists saw the poor performance of the 1920s and 1930s as a reason for structural planning in Western Europe or North America.

In the developing countries it was different, for it was believed that inadequate industrialization was the reason for lagging performance. In addition to protective measures, a need to plan industrialization, with the government taking a major role, was widely perceived. It was also quickly understood that Keynesian remedies for unemployment and underemployment were inappropriate. Rapid structural change, and the idea that full employment, and even agricultural growth itself, depended on a massive shift of people out of agriculture, seemed to argue for a strong element of central direction.[58] In conflict with this latter argument, many governments showed a preference for heavy industry. Prestige and uncritical imitation of the USSR was, no doubt, a reason in some cases; in others, the desire for an independent armaments industry may have contributed.

In colonies, poor performance was blamed not only on the relatively free-trading policies of the colonial powers but also on a deliberate stifling of industrialization and the stimulation of export crops—from which the major gains were held to be reaped by the colonial power. Political independence was therefore expected to confer larger economic benefits, as was promised by their new governments, and by a few LDC economists. In these circumstances, governments had to be seen to be promoting development. This was part of their legitimacy. Widespread government help was expected, and the call to extend this in a rationally planned manner was inescapable. Moreover, fiddling with the price mechanism did not seem sufficiently purposive, and probably would have been considered too similar to the methods of colonial economic regimes. In some countries, it may also have been believed that physical planning would result in greater capacity use than would the price mechanism. So quantitative planning and direct promotion of investments were favored. It is notable that planning caught on immediately among the newly independent countries of Asia, Africa, and the Caribbean; whereas in Latin America, after a century of independence, it was slow to take root and still has not done so at all deeply.

Just as planning was needed to dissociate new nations from the relatively laisser faire economic systems of the colonial powers, so was "socialism" needed to dissociate them from the latter's political systems. These two aspects reinforce each other. There are few new nations in Asia, Africa, and the Caribbean that do not claim to be socialist; and few that do in Latin America. The socialist route to development was perceived to be supported by the apparent and continuing success, up to about 1960, of the Soviet five-year plans. The massive and successful effort to build up heavy industry enabled the USSR to survive Hitler's onslaught. After World War II, very rapid industrial growth continued, a growth more rapid than anywhere else until Japan got into its stride. Moreover, the USSR achieved full employment without inflation. Little was known outside the USSR of the cruelties of collectivization or of the famine of 1932, which together with Stalin's purges probably caused the death of upwards of 10 million people.[59] The fact that this rapid growth resulted in little or no improvement in the standard of living was also not appreciated. The influence on such countries as Egypt and India, and partly through India on other developing countries, was manifest. But even among those who would never have accepted either Russian aims or methods, their achievement certainly helped to make planning (somehow modified to suit more democratic systems) an acceptable concept.

At the same time as the apparatus, symbols, and rhetoric of planning were accepted for political reasons, so the discipline of a central plan was often rejected for another set of political reasons. The construction of the plan, and the plan document itself, should in theory be an instrument for rational decision-making in the economic sphere, especially as far as government expenditure is concerned; and it might, because of its longer-term nature, provide continuity in expenditure plans and economic policies when governments change. But these supposed advantages are also disadvantages. The plan may constrain the shorter-run economic choices that are essential in an unstable and uncertain world, choices politicians see as their prerogative. And governments will not be bound by their predecessors' plans. Even in a stable world, the best laid and most implementable five-year plans are unlikely to stick without a high degree of political centralization, consensus, and continuity. This helps to explain why planning was accepted, and also at the same time rejected.

Our account also suggests that those economists who were also planning enthusiasts had little influence on the acceptance of planning. They probably had more influence on the directions it took (though not in India). Planning for growth at the macroeconomic level was their specialty. They were armed with their Harrod/Domar equation,* and with linear programming, and they demanded input/output tables, which, albeit full of holes, were sometimes supplied. With these aids they concocted supposedly consistent plans of mainly empty boxes. Sectoral and subsectoral investment totals were targeted or projected when there were no projects, no levers to influence their creation, and no analysis to show that investment in that sector would be a good use of scarce funds. Thus, economists contributed to the excessive emphasis on central paper planning, although many other interests influenced the shape and size of the plan. There was no theoretical work on sectoral planning, while cost-benefit analysis and its application to projects was in its infancy. The essential iteration between levels of planning also went unanalyzed. There was no real possibility of designing a pattern of industrialization that would realize the externalities and scale economies that had been argued to be the reasons for planning.

* The GNP growth rate equals the savings rate times the marginal productivity of capital.

The early proponents of planning started from the negative proposition that laisser faire policies and the price mechanism were faulty. But they got no further than that. They had few positive ideas as to how planning could be beneficially implemented in LDC economies that were and would remain predominantly private, and in which the vast majority of economic decisions were made in response to market forces. Nor did they take much notice of the fact that governments were not all-powerful monoliths, even if not democratic, and that therefore planning would have to come to terms with political realities. The basic political assumption was that the LDC governments—indeed, all governments—were strong, wise, and undivided, and that their sole objective was the welfare of their people. This did not turn out to be true.

By the end of the 1950s, some but not all of the difficulties were realized by some economists. Myrdal is an interesting example. The third of his Cairo lectures[60] is an encomium of overall central planning and also a remarkable oratorical flight of thesis and antithesis. The thesis was that the great advantage of decolonization was that there was a new nation-state that could fill the role of guardian and plan for development. The antithesis was, in his words:

> Central Economic planning is always a difficult thing and, where it has been tried, it has not been much of a success in the advanced countries. Now, what amounts to a sort of super planning has to be staged by underdeveloped countries with weak political and administrative systems, and a largely illiterate and apathetic citizenry.[61]

Myrdal elaborated on the "difficult thing" as follows:

> *A whole cumulative expansion process has to be blueprinted in real terms* of the concrete investment projects, their effects on the volume of production in various lines and on consumption, on employment of workers and natural resources, the induced changes in health education and productiveness of labour, et cetera, in various sectors and different years, with main attention focussed on the circular causal interactions between all the factors in the system.[62]

Twenty-five years later, with much greater skills at his command, the most dedicated planner would not claim to be able to compete with such a program, even in the best statistically documented economy. Yet Myrdal's synthesis was:

> But the alternative to making the heroic attempt is continued acquiescence in economic and cultural stagnation or regression which is politically impossible in the world of today.[63]

It is small wonder that the 1960s saw conferences and books on the "Crisis in Planning." But there was no relation between the degree and effectiveness of central planning and the success of the economy, so the alternative was not the slough of despond that Myrdal prophesied.

Chapter 4

Planning and Foreign Trade Regimes, 1945-60

The postwar debate on the rules that should govern international trade and payments began with the negotiations for the International Trade Organization (ITO), which was never created.[1] Briefly, and ignoring some qualifications, the cornerstones of the Havana Charter of 1948 (which the United States failed to achieve) were:

1. The removal of quantitative restrictions.
2. Most-favored nation treatment (MFN) for any other barriers, including tariffs, except in the case of common markets.
3. A commitment to reciprocal negotiation of tariff reductions.

The less developed countries (LDCs) were shocked by this program, receiving some support from a number of more developed countries. They argued that quota restrictions were essential in order to establish the import priorities required to implement development plans. They demanded the right to discriminate between commodities (implying in effect the right to discriminate between countries). The MFN principle was also attacked on the grounds that LDCs would want to establish new preferences, apart from common markets. Geographical, political, and ethnic grounds were all mentioned. They rejected reciprocal tariff reductions. They wanted the charter to recognize that protection on their part would, in the long run, increase trade. They tried hard to get the principle that LDCs were entitled to use any and all forms of protection incorporated in the charter.

Why did the LDCs want to opt out of all obligations? Would they not benefit by nondiscrimination, by an agreement on the part of others to abjure protection, or at least some kinds of protection? Their response can be rationalized as follows. First, and this was a grave mistake, they never expected to be able to export manufactures to the industrialized countries; but they might export a little to their neighbors, especially if they were ethnic as well as geographic neighbors, hence the desire to be able to create new preferences. Second, they presumed that the industrialized countries would not protect against raw materials. Third, on competing farm products (sugar being the most important), the cause was probably lost anyway, for the United States itself proposed to exempt farm products from the ban on quotas. The determination to use industrialization through import substitution as the main feature of development planning is clearly implicit in their pre-Havana and Havana attitudes. The belief in the need to use import quotas to help steer the pattern of development, rather than necessarily to protect, also emerged.

Australia acted as the leader of the LDCs at the preparatory conference for the ITO. She had industrialized behind high protection and exported few manufactures. Australia had her own theory of protection. It was to provide high wages for a growing population by indirectly taxing the rich pastoralists. The aim was redistributory, and first-best means were regarded as politically impossible. It did not matter much if income per head were reduced.[2] Australia is thought to have been the richest country in the world in the second half of the nineteenth century, and she has remained one of the richest in this century. Australia's reasons for protection may have applied to a few Latin American countries, especially Argentina and Chile, and nowhere else.

61

The situation of the European countries was different. The United Kingdom took the lead on the need for discrimination against particular countries—the United States, of course. As the "owner" of the second major world currency, she was most conscious of the very large excess demand for dollars that would materialize if currencies were convertible into dollars (especially after the disastrous attempt at convertibility in 1947). Until production in Europe recovered, North America was the only source of supply for the demand that was pent up in the form of European currency balances, mostly sterling.

There was a large external disequilibrium, as well as inelasticities of supply, that could be expected to last for some years, just the sort of situation for which, as was seen in chapter 3, there are very good reasons for not relying wholly on the price mechanism. Discriminatory import controls and inconvertibility were accepted as essential by all the commentators mentioned there. Differences arose concerning how quickly they might be removed. But few agreed with Balogh, who argued strongly for permanent controls and trading blocks outside the dollar area.[3] However, even when Europe had begun to rebuild its dollar reserves, unease remained. Until at least the mid-1950s, many economists were awaiting the supposedly inevitable postwar United States slump. It was also thought that productivity rose faster in the United States than elsewhere and that this would cause further difficulties. Despite a large devaluation of sterling and other currencies in 1949, many economists and officials were very wary of embracing convertibility and eliminating controls. In 1957 G. D. A. MacDougall could still entitle a book *The World Dollar Problem*.[4] The powers of the European economies to restructure and grow were greatly underestimated. Nevertheless, by the end of the 1950s, virtually all import controls were eliminated, and all major European currencies were convertible on current account. From then on, Bretton Woods worked fairly well—until it was overthrown by a kind of dollar problem very different from that envisaged. Tariff protection was greatly reduced under General Agreement on Tariffs and Trade (GATT) auspices.

Things went differently in the Third World. During World

War II, imports were controlled everywhere. Indeed, in the case of some Latin American countries control had started earlier—during the Depression. After the war, controls were relaxed (but not eliminated) in many LDCs, until there was a balance-of-payments crisis. Controls were almost invariably instituted to deal with such a crisis and not for protective reasons (Mexico was an exception). For some, the crisis occurred in the 1930s as a result of greatly reduced export earnings. But for most, the cause was increased spending for development since World War II. In a few, for example Brazil, the reason was more that an overvalued exchange rate was a legacy of the war, and there was reluctance to change it. In some others, there was a total disruption of export markets and war damage—especially in Korea and Taiwan. Once controls were instituted they tended to stay, and often they were intensified.

There is a familiar progression that has occurred and remained in most LDCs. The government spends so much in the name of development that the balance of payments suffers. Some foreign assistance may be obtained, but imports must still be cut. Inflation results, and the development program has to be cut back. But inflation once started is hard to stop, and even if there is a devaluation, or a series of devaluations, the currency tends to remain overvalued, creating a requirement for controls to keep imports in check. We have seen that trade controls were already being linked to development at and before the Havana Conference. But is the sort of sequence described beneficial for development?

Let us sort out the arguments for protection and for trade controls, which are supposed to apply particularly to LDCs. We shall pay special attention to the question of whether such arguments are really for tariffs, other taxes or subsidies, or quantitative restriction. We can then relate these to the positions taken by leading economists and also examine the question of whether such arguments have determined the commercial policies of developing countries.

There were four basic arguments in the literature of the 1940s and 1950s:

1. Capital formation can be speeded up by limiting consumption goods imports.
2. Maximum development requires there to be a tendency for investment to outrun savings, with consequent pressure on the balance of payments, which will in turn necessitate import controls.
3. Fluctuations in export earnings necessitate import controls.
4. Industry must be protected.

The first of these was probably most prominent in the minds of the LDC Havana negotiators. Ragnar Nurkse thought it a hot topic, since he devoted much of one of his six lectures in Rio de Janeiro in 1951 to pouring cold water on it.[5] His argument can be paraphrased as follows.[6] If consumption goods imports are limited, people will divert expenditure to domestic goods (though they might save some more as a result of their favored foreign goods not being available), which must be presumed to be in inelastic supply. As a result, prices rise and pull resources out of domestic investment (construction, earth moving) into making consumption goods. If there is to be any real rise in investment, domestic savings thus have to rise (unless aid increases). The inflation caused may result in some "forced" savings, but this is unreliable. The pattern of investment is also likely to be unfavorably influenced both by the controls and the inflation they generate. Domestic investment will be diverted to making the luxury goods no longer imported, and basic overhead capital formation will suffer. Nurkse here pointed to several effects that were going to make themselves felt in many countries and had presumably already started to do so in Latin America. His diagnosis, it may be noticed, differed from that of Hirschman—with Nurkse a shortage of savings dominated, with Hirschman a shortage of investment.

Some will believe that there is a weakness in Nurkse's argument—the assumed inelastic supply of domestic consumption goods. This is the core of many arguments about development. There has been a tendency to assume that parts, at least, of the domestic economy could always produce more, without investment. This was, for instance, a feature of one of Mahalanobis's early Indian models. Agriculture, and what would now be called the informal sector, would look after consumption, while the planners planned machines to make machines. To take another example, project planners are often accused of neglecting the multiplier effects of projects (that is, the increased output that the critics claim would result from spending the incomes generated by the project).

No one supports the extreme Keynesian case of perfectly elastic supply. On the other hand, many might claim that there is always some excess capacity. This would modify Nurkse's argument to the extent that some part of the increased savings might come as a result of a real increase in output, and the rest from his "inflation tax."

Before turning to the second basic reason for trade controls, it is important to note that there is a price mechanism way of dealing with luxury imports, which is to tax them heavily by a high tariff while at the same time taxing the domestic production, or potential production, of substitutes by excise taxes. This is likely to do more to raise domestic savings, and so permit more capital goods imports, for two reasons. First, the high tariff on the residual imports results directly in government income and savings; and second, domestic substitutes for luxury imports often have a high import component. It is hard for government to restrict these latter imports because that results in unemployment.

We now turn to the second argument—that one will get more "development" if there is always excess demand. There are two strings to this bow: (1) since the excess demand is ex hypothesi created by increasing investment, higher *growth* is implied, and (2) *current* output will be higher with excess demand.

It should be noticed that higher current output is generated, if at all, only by excess demand for domestic output. One can have excess demand for domestic output, but not for imports. This has been the case for a number of oil exporting LDCs in recent years. It would be argued, however, that for most LDCs such a position was unattainable, because high investment necessitates high capital goods imports. If export receipts cannot be increased, then so little is left for materials, components, and final consumption goods that the price mechanism cannot be relied on.

In short, it is advocated that the government forces the pace to the extent that it creates such a disequilibrium that the price movements implied would be more damaging than controls. This is the wartime economy solution to development that was quite widely advocated in our period. From 1940 to 1948 either the USSR or the United Kingdom was the model. We saw in chapter 3 that the United Kingdom was then an almost totally controlled economy. As we shall see, import (and exchange) controls alone cannot do the trick. Clearly everything depends on the validity of the two arguments that (1) more investment and (2) more output can be achieved from existing productive capacity.

We have already dealt with (1) in discussing Nurkse's arguments. More investment must have its counterpart in more savings. If more savings are achieved by taxes and other inducements, then there is no overall disequilibrium. We shall assume that, in these circumstances, a viable balance of payments can be achieved by some combination of exchange rate, tariffs, or export subsidies. If sufficient savings are not achieved via the price mechanism, then they may be achieved either by inflation or by extensive price controls, rationing, and queuing.

Inflation can be considered as having the dual role of increasing the level of investment and of getting more output from existing capacity. We know more about inflation now than when Nurkse was writing. I shall draw on these later ideas. That there is some trade-off between output and a reduction of inflation parallels the Phillips curve concept, dating from the 1950s, which traces a relation between inflation and employment and output. In any country, there will always be some underutilized capacity. Increasing demand will thus always result in some increased production, as well as inflation to the extent that increased production is impossible in the short run.

The weakness of the above argument is the tendency for inflation to accelerate. In an inflationary situation, total demands being greater than supply, someone has to end up being disappointed. As people learn this, and learn to expect inflation, they increase their monetary demands, thus accelerating inflation. This must happen, unless there are some members of the economy who are too weak to be able to defend their position. (There is a permanent savings gain only if these are the nonsavers, so that income distribution is shifted in favor of the wealthy.) In technical jargon, the long-run Phillips curve may become vertical, and inflation then does no good at all, either for investment or output. Indeed, it does harm because of the manifest inefficiencies and social dislocation to which it gives rise. In particular, the distortions of investment, in a situation in which prices inevitably cease to be good signposts, can easily begin to outweigh the increased level of investment, so that a smaller, more efficient program could well yield higher total returns.

This theory of accelerating inflation is highly plausible. Inflations always have accelerated, until there has been either an explosion or a deflationary reversal of policies by the government when the rate of inflation becomes intolerable. As we shall see in chapter 5, this was neglected by the Latin American structuralists. Nowadays, one hears little of the idea that inflation promotes growth.

Excess demand can be controlled without inflation if there is extensive price control. This involves quantitative allocation of raw materials and components, whether imported or domestic, the rationing of consumer goods, and queuing for those things that are not rationed. The price mechanism becomes highly distorted, and its allocative functions are overtaken by bureaucratic planning. Very high rates of investment have been achieved by these means in the USSR (comparable rates have also been achieved in Japan without excess demand or much inflation). But probably no developing country has the administrative ability to operate sufficiently effective price controls.

Fluctuation in export earnings was the third argument for import controls. Fluctuations in import prices, or import needs arising from a harvest failure, may also give rise to quite sudden pressures on the balance of payments, though they were less often mentioned, especially in the 1940s and 1950s. This needs little comment. It is widely accepted that such fluctuations may on occasion be a good reason for controls. A large temporary fluctuation in the exchange rate might be more disruptive than control of imports. It might even be completely inefficacious in stemming a loss of reserves. The alternative is large holdings of reserves or large variations in borrowing. Controls may be difficult to institute quickly, and it is expensive to keep in being an apparatus of control if it needs to be used only occasionally. Since borrowing may also be expensive, and reserves expensive in terms of some better investment opportunity, it is clear that there is room for compromise. Finally, we must note that large fluctuations in foreign exchange availability, which are not due to clear mismanagement of the economy, plague relatively few, mostly small, economies. It is rational for them to hold relatively large reserves. So this is a reason for import controls only on occasion and only for a limited number of economies.

The fourth argument for import controls is the need to protect industry—to favor industrialization. There was an overwhelming consensus within LDCs in the 1940s and 1950s that industry had been neglected or actually discouraged by colonial rulers, or inhibited by a malign system of laisser faire, imposed even on politically independent countries by the United States or the United Kingdom, and that it must be protected. Protection was also overwhelmingly thought of as protection of the home market only.

The economically rational arguments as to why economic growth might be accelerated by favoring industry boil down to (1) the infant industry argument, (2) that the price mechanism is distorted in LDCs in a way that handicaps industry, and (3) interindustrial externalities of the Scitovsky or Hirschman variety, as already discussed in chapter 3.

Essentially, the name "infant industry" implies that we can restrict ourselves to reasons that will vanish in time. In the case of a new industry, costs can be expected to decline over time. If the industry is to be worthwhile, from a private (or social) point of view, the later profits (or social profits) must outweigh the earlier losses (or social losses) by enough to result in an adequate private (or social) rate of return. There is thus no good reason to encourage the industry, unless there is a divergence of private and social profit, or unless the social rate of return is sufficiently lower than acceptable private rates of return. A divergence of private and social profit may arise because the private entrepreneur cannot capture the benefit of cost reductions for himself.

But cost reduction alone is neither a sufficient nor necessary reason for protecting or otherwise favoring an industry. Cost reductions without externalities do not constitute a good reason. And if there are external economies, there is no need for cost reduction. Essentially an infant industry is one that generates a special kind of externality, "learning by doing," where some of the learning escapes. This seepage must also be supposed to peter out, or else there would be a permanent reason to give the industry some special favors. "Infant industry" arguments may apply as strongly, or more strongly, to the introduction of new techniques in agriculture as they do to any industry. An "infant industry" is a dated concept that should be abandoned; but this is not to deny that the extension of favors to certain activities may sometimes be justifiable on the ground that they have important external effects.

Industrial wages higher than the opportunity cost of labor is the distortion of the price mechanism most likely to reduce the level of industrialization below what it should be. This case will be discussed later. Other distortions also exist, especially in the capital market; but these have usually favored modern industry, at least in the postwar period.

We must next recognize that industry is not homogeneous. This enables one to reintroduce interindustry externalities, of the Hirschman, Scitovsky, or even Pigou-Meade varieties, which may require a planner to favor some industries more than others. But then this is also true of infant industries, for some may be more subject to learning by doing and suffer more seepage. It is also true of the need to favor on the grounds that wages exceed the opportunity cost of labor (or, more strictly, exceed the shadow wage).

These alleged externalities and distortions would ideally require a very elaborate system of taxes and subsidies for their correction. But this was hardly perceived in the 1940s and 1950s. Economists thought mostly in terms of tariffs as the major method of favoring an industry. This was hardly logical, for industries that produce nontraded goods may be very strong candidates for special treatment for any or all of the above reasons. This failure to see that many of the supposed reasons for encouragement applied to industries that certainly needed no protection seems to need some explanation. It could have arisen because economists were trying to find good reasons for tariffs, rather than asking what industries should receive special assistance and what form that assistance should best take.

Few questioned the idea that restricting imports was a royal road to industrialization. But while most economists thought in terms of tariffs, most protection was given by import controls. It will later emerge that tariffs are not a very good method of encouraging industry and that import controls are much worse.

The "Singer-Prebisch" thesis, although largely foreshadowed in the ITO debates, has pride of place in the academic literature in challenging the liberal view of what constitutes a desirable set of international trade rules. H. W. Singer's main 1949 thesis was that LDCs had not got much out of international investment and trade—above all not much industrialization.[7] There were hints that they might have got less than nothing out of it, as a result of diverting resources away from the industrialization, which would have had major external economies. He took up the alleged secular worsening of the terms of trade from a United Nations document (which he probably wrote).[8] He explained this "indisputable fact" essentially by an ever increasing degree of monopoly shared by labor in the production of manufactures, but he made little of this so far as balance-of-payments management was concerned. He used it to cast general doubt on the value of trade and foreign investment for LDCs.

Raul Prebisch and the Economic Commission on Latin America emphasized the same "indisputable fact" from 1949 onward.[9] It was disputed by several economists, but for a decade it remained plausible as a result of the worsening in LDC terms of trade after the peak in commodity prices at the time of the Korean War. It became enshrined in the United Nations Conference on Trade and Development (UNCTAD) and among many development economists as a result of constant repetition. Subsequent events and more research have shown convincingly that it was not merely disputable but was counterfactual, at least in this century.[10]

The primary conclusion was the need to industrialize. But why does not the change in the terms of trade against primary commodities itself cause industrialization? Singer has explained this by saying that when times were good there was no incentive, and when they were bad there was no money. This was (necessarily for the argument) allied to the view that "all private activity tends to be governed by the price relations of the day"—a view that may do some injustice to the intelligence of entrepreneurs. While this argument may have some force in explaining the relatively slow growth of LDC industrialization between 1913 and 1939, it would not be very apposite in the face of a trend caused neither by war, stagnation, nor slump in the industrialized countries.

More than the theory of declining terms of trade was, or should have been, needed to make ECLA and Prebisch believe that trade must be controlled. Nevertheless, elaborations of the theme seemed to add plausibility to this conclusion. It was held that the foreign income-elasticity of demand for LDC exports was lower than that for imports—especially if domestic demand was to be steered toward investment goods for development. To this was added the acceptable argument that the price elasticity was very low (at least for developing countries taken together). This all added up to the thesis that exports of LDCs were virtually exogenous. Therefore, total imports were also exogenous. Import controls or other restrictions were therefore not restrictive of trade.[11] They served only to control the pattern of imports in the interest of development. Also, given the declining terms of trade, balance-of-payments trouble would be endemic, and frequent devaluation would result with consequent inflation. Moreover, devaluation would further worsen the terms of trade in the face of an inelastic foreign demand. All this begins to look rather plausible.[12]

Even if we accept the elasticity assumptions, however, it still does not add up to a case. Export taxes could be used to prevent devaluation from reducing export proceeds. Luxury taxes can prevent low-priority imports. The externalities (if they exist) inherent in industrialization could be dealt with by taxes and subsidies. The idea that controlling imports does not reduce the volume of trade neglects its discouraging effect on manufactured exports, which should certainly not have been presumed to be in inelastic demand. It also neglects the fact that LDCs were losing their share of world markets in many primary commodities as a result of inability to supply.[13] Finally, it is probably an illusion that reducing real consumption is less inflationary if it is done by the price rises that result from controls than if it is done by price rises resulting from other policies. The argument could thus be fully convincing only to those who had acquired faith in planning by controls rather than the price mechanism.

Myrdal was one of the few economists who directly addressed the question of controls versus encouraging industrialization through the price mechanism.[14] He wrote:

> My argument so far has led to the conclusion that *import restrictions in underdeveloped countries are primarily necessitated by the effects on the foreign exchange balance of the increased demand for imported goods. This, in turn, is the direct or indirect result of the increased investment implied by an economic development policy.*[15]

If Myrdal had written "caused" instead of "necessitated," this would have been correct. As we have seen, controls were generally instituted when there was a balance-of-payments crisis. If governments had been merely intent on encouraging industrialization, they would surely have preferred tariffs for fiscal reasons, as many had done in the interwar period. Thus, tariff protection had become substantial in many LDCs in the 1920s and 1930s.

Of course, industrialists might lobby for controls, which are more securely protective than tariffs, but then many developing countries had no influential industrial lobby when they instituted controls. The fact that controls put on for other reasons created protection is the main reason why protection turned out to be, as we shall see later, haphazard, unrelated to any economic rationale for protection, and certainly excessive.

By "import restrictions" Myrdal meant any restriction, including mere tariffs. This would seem to be a mistake. Increased investment, if not matched by savings, causes excess demand for imports even in the face of a high-tariff structure (for manufactures). This is what happened. Excess demand does indeed necessitate controls. If increased tariffs did the trick, they would do it by eliminating the excess demand. The issue is thus whether excess demand, made possible by trade and other controls, is favorable for development. We have already addressed this issue. But Myrdal does not seem to have seen it clearly as the issue. He went on in the same chapter to say that controls have many serious disadvantages:

> The system tends easily to create cancerous tumours of partiality and corruption in the very center of the administration, where the sickness is continuously nurtured by the favors distributed and the grafts realized and from which it tends to spread out to every limb of society. Industrialists and businessmen are tempted to go in for shady deals instead of steady regular business. Individuals who might have performed useful tasks in the economic development of their country become idle hangers-on, watching for loopholes in the decrees and dishonesty in their implementation. This is all the more dangerous as a general weakness in underdeveloped countries, inherited from a long history of stagnation, is that their business classes are too much inclined to look for easy profits in place of sustained enterprise.[16]

He then commended restricting imports by such price mechanism methods as tariffs and multiple exchange rates. Finally, however, he came to the conclusion that fluctuating export proceeds necessitate controls. Since this is a reason that can apply strongly only to a small number of countries, Myrdal clearly had an exaggerated impression of the trade-dependence of LDCs and of the instability of that trade.[17] (See also chapter 13.)

There were rebels. G. Haberler in a notable article formalized what may be called the "deindustrialization" argument, one that has played a large role in radical attacks on free trade.[18] It is a special case of malfunctioning of the price mechanism, whereby handicraftsmen in a no-trade situation can earn more than their marginal product in farming. In the extreme case, the marginal product in farming may be zero. When trade opens, the farmers buy cloth from abroad on better terms than they got from the weavers. At these new terms of trade, the weavers starve, and total output falls. Haberler showed that he did not think much of this as a general rule[19] and pointed out that even List had said that if any industry requires more than 20–30 percent protection then it deserves no support. There was a vituperative exchange with Balogh, who stressed the potentially bad income distribution effects of trade without showing why they should in fact be both bad and uncompensatable.[20] As there was no free trade for any LDC in our period, except Hong Kong, the deindustrialization argument relates better to what is supposed to have happened in some parts of the Third World in the nineteenth century.[21] Nevertheless, it has probably played a role in prejudicing developing countries against anything but controlled trade, especially after its dramatic use by P. A. Baran in his *Political Economy of Growth*, first published in 1957 and continuously reprinted.[22]

In 1950, Jacob Viner attacked the Singer-Prebisch doctrine in six lectures delivered in Rio de Janeiro.[23] He denied that there was any case for the "artificial" stimulation of industry. While accepting the "infant industry" argument in theory, he claimed that in practice there was no case. Protection tended to be arbitrary or irrational (that is, unrelated to any theoretical reasons supporting it); it spread contagiously, and by sheltering producers did more to perpetuate high costs than reduce them. He pointed out that an eventual fall in costs was not a sufficient reason to support an industry initially and that even if a good case could be made, then subsidy rather than protection would be a better method of initial support.[24] He dismissed the declining terms of trade argument as both false and irrelevant, saying: "These natural laws seem to me for the most part mischievous fantasies, or conjectural or distorted history, or, at the best, mere hypotheses relating to specific periods and calling for sober or objective testing."[25]

He suggested that protection, supported as providing better employment opportunities for the agricultural population, may itself be a major instrument for depressing real agricultural incomes, adding that the situation was already often one of urban exploitation of the rural population—"urban bias," as it has since been called.[26] He suggested that development should be measured by the levels of living of the poor. Finally, he clearly distinguished protection by controls from protection by tariffs. Direct controls over foreign trade had been the first stage of planning.

They were contagious and inevitably spread from there to internal markets. They were the major cause of distortion of the price mechanism; but once it was so distorted, then this provided justification for trade controls. "Once a man has determined to use stilts, he had better use a pair than a single one."[27] On a more positive note, Viner stressed the importance of training and education (especially rural education and agricultural training), of health and family planning, savings promotion, an open economy, and improving the operation of the price mechanism. This radical book was ignored by both LDC elites and orthodox development economists.

I have called Haberler and Viner rebels.[28] Their opponents would have referred to them as orthodox neoclassicists. Neoclassical certainly, but orthodox is another matter. If one judges orthodoxy by the criterion that those are orthodox whose views largely coincide with those of the policy-makers, or with the spirit of the times, there is no doubt about their unorthodoxy. I think that few academics among those who wrote mainly about development (which excludes Viner and Haberler) would have accepted, in the 1950s, that developing countries should avoid direct trade controls and have at most a modest tariff. They would not have accepted either that LDCs should have agreed to the United States draft of the Havana Charter, or that they should be neutral between manufacturing industry and agriculture and so on. (Or perhaps favor agriculture, since there are more things that farmers cannot provide for themselves than is the case for industry.) Certainly, United Nations officials were not in this camp, and almost no LDC policy-makers would have endorsed such views. It therefore seems fair to say that the development establishment was in favor of planning trade, and much else, by direct controls, and also in favor of direct governmental initiatives in manufacturing investment.

The reader may rightly wonder to what extent the discussion of trade regimes in this chapter relates to planning in LDCs. On the one hand, trade controls and conscious efforts to influence the pattern of imports certainly amount to a degree of trade planning. On the other hand, there was little relationship between attempts at comprehensive central planning and the pursuit of import substitution policies through controls. The degree of the former varied widely, while the latter was almost universal. There is also much variation in the extent to which trade and other controls have a discernible rationale in the light of supposed governmental aims. In the latter sense of "planning," a highly controlled economy may scarcely be planned.

Chapter 5

Structuralism and Monetarism: The Latin American Debate

There was evidence of inflation in certain Latin American countries before World War II, especially in Chile, where inflation was already chronic and reached about 10 percent per annum in the 1930s.[1] But it became fast as well as chronic, especially for Chile, Argentina, Uruguay, and Brazil, only in the 1940s, when it reached about 20 percent. From the middle 1950s to the early 1960s, it was almost explosive. At varying dates, depending on the timing of governmental attempts to reduce the rate, it rose to 80 percent or more in Chile and Brazil and 100 percent in Argentina. The trend was clearly accelerating.

Elsewhere in the world, there have been explosive inflations from time to time, usually, if not invariably, associated with war. But chronic double-digit inflation, tending to run away but then contained without exploding, was, in the 1940s and 1950s, unique to a handful of Latin American countries. Since then, it has become a more general phenomenon.

As a result of accelerating inflation, and its associated balance-of-payments problems, foreign advice was sought. The Klein Saks mission went to Chile in 1955, and the International Monetary Fund (IMF) was called in to advise several countries. Their deflationary advice sparked off the structuralist-monetarist debate. The structuralist school, originating in Chile and the Economic Commission for Latin America,[2] held that the basic cause of inflation lay in structural rigidity of one sort or another and that deflationary policies were attacking only the symptoms. It was this debate that created the label "structuralism." However, the central idea was not new, namely that rigidity makes the price mechanism work relatively badly, and that unwanted side effects may occur as a result of relying, in such circumstances, too much on prices to cause needed change and readjustment. We have seen that this idea was to the fore in the post-World War II planning debates in Europe, and also that supposed price inelasticities (of both domestic supply and foreign demand) were part of the rationalization of, if not the reason for, the shape of the Indian Five Year Plans. What was new was the special association of inelasticity with inflation.

The deflationary measures failed to have any lasting effect on the rate of inflation in the chronically inflationary Latin American countries. Before discussing the reasons for this, some analysis of the structuralist position is required. There were many members of the structuralist club, and views diverged, so we can give only a sketch of what seem to be the essential features of their theory.

A key postulate was that of inelasticity of both supply and demand for agricultural and livestock products. The supply inelasticity was generally attributed to the latifundia, while demand elasticity was inevitable. Furthermore, investment and technological improvements did not result in food output increasing fast enough to satisfy an increasing demand. An inflexible infrastructure was supposed to exacerbate the situation. There was thus a mismatch between the pattern of supply and demand, which could be eliminated only by a large relative price change.

In these circumstances, food prices rise sharply. If we further assume that nonfarm money incomes are inflexible downward, this rise is not offset by price falls for industrial products or services—and so there is substantial inflation. Thus far, these structural elements explain only a once-and-for-all rise in prices, which is required to effect a relative price change when nonfood prices are inflexible downwards. It is assumed that money does not impede the inflation, either because its quantity or its velocity of circulation rises.

If the inflation is to continue, something more is required. This is the familiar cost-push story according to which powerful elements in the economy fight to get parts of the cake that exceed the whole. Thus, when food prices rise, large segments of the urban population are strong enough, via industrial action or political influence, at least to prevent their share from being reduced by as much as is required for the share of agriculture to rise enough to cure the imbalance of supply and demand. The result is a rise in urban money incomes, which further increases the monetary demand for food, and so the spiral develops. As we have already noted, there is a further tendency for the inflation to accelerate as people come to realize that they have to demand increases greater than the current rate of inflation if their real incomes are to rise.[3]

This cost-push part of the story can, of course, be called structuralist. It involves the political and power structure of society, or the oligopolistic structure of markets, which are essential elements of a cost-push theory. As before, money supply is endogenous to the model: the authorities are forced to accommodate the inflation as a result of the assumed imperatives of development or a reasonably high level of employment and output. The cost-push phenomenon was not, however, usually stressed by the structuralist school—perhaps because it was not novel. They stressed the supposed inelasticities. The inelasticities are an exacerbating element; they imply that the shift in the distribution of income, required to alleviate the imbalance, is greater than otherwise. It is the ensuing social struggle, however, that accounts for the continuation and probable acceleration of inflation.[4]

We have thus far told the structuralist story for a closed economy, without even mentioning the balance of payments. In a closed economy, as long as food production is growing at a given pace, and the demand for food has zero price elasticity, the maximum rate of growth of the whole economy is strictly determined. The inflation described therefore comes from increasing industrial output by more than the income elasticities of demand warrant. The inflation thus caused can have a beneficial outcome only if it results in a slower growth of industrial output and a more rapid growth of agricultural output—as a result of a shift of investment and other resources to agriculture. It would clearly be better if more resources had been devoted to agriculture in the first place. This is doubly true if in fact the inflation fails to shift resources sufficiently. Indeed, in the absence of aggregate excess demand, the inflation continues only because it fails to effect the required shift. Such an inflation can do no good, even if it does not accelerate, an essential point that the structuralists did not seem to recognize.

Opening the economy clearly gives an added element of flexibility. If agriculture and husbandry are stagnant, rapid growth can still occur without excess demand for food, provided exports are buoyant enough; food can then be imported, as well as the machinery and materials required for growth. Indeed, if agriculture is price irresponsive as well as stagnant, it can, in an open economy, be squeezed for the benefit of industrialization. It is therefore not surprising that an inelastic supply of exports, or inelastic world demand, or both, was an essential part of the structuralist story. An inelastic supply of agriculture-based exports followed from the presumption that agricultural output was inelastic, while the possibility of a rapid growth of manufactured exports was implicitly denied. Import substitution was still the rage.

The monetarists had three central tenets. First, they insisted that stability could not be achieved without a reduction in the rate of increase of the money supply. Second, they held that stability would be good for long-run growth, for only with reasonable stability could free operation of the price mechanism achieve the efficiency required. Third, many of the inelasticities that the structuralists pointed to were the result of inflation itself or of misguided policies that needed to be corrected. The monetarist remedies went far beyond a simple reliance on reducing the rate of increase of the money supply. Measures intended to make the price mechanism work, and work better, were always included—notably, unification of exchange rates, devaluation, and liberalization of imports. Direct attempts to control the wage increases seem always to have been part of the stabilization package, and thus full reliance on the price mechanisms was not apparently advocated, and certainly not implemented.

Much of the debate seemed scholastic, centering on the meaningless question as to what is the fundamental cause of inflation. Is it the electrical system or the carburation that is the fundamental cause of the revolution of the engine? The argument was really about which variables should be treated as endogenous, and which exogenous and therefore subject to policy intervention. Perhaps this is always the meaning of causation.

An extreme structuralist position would be that money supply was endogenous and that only plans to change the structure of the economy—land reform, more import substitution to make the economy less dependent on foreign trade, educational advancement, and improved fiscal systems[5]—would be of any avail in the long run. While monetary repression would admittedly bring down the rate of inflation, it would be too costly in real terms. When inflation was accelerating toward 100 percent per annum, when the currency was hopelessly overvalued, when there was an insupportable balance-of-payments deficit, and when repudiation of foreign debts was threatened, such a position seemed nihilistic. The endogeneity of the actions of fiscal and monetary authorities was also exaggerated. It is clear that public deficits were not always forced, and that they were often the initiating or exacerbating factor.[6]

Most structuralists were shy of making policy pronouncements.[7] This was a basic weakness, for once inflation was initiated and had become serious, the issue was how to cure it. Another weakness was the failure to understand and admit that many of the inelasticities were caused by policy and by inflation itself. A Latin American critic of structuralism, Roberto Campos, thus rightly pointed out that infrastructural bottlenecks, and the slow growth of food supply, savings, and import capacity, were all exacerbated by misguided policies that were partly induced by inflation itself.[8]

It is notable that Dudley Seers was still insisting on import substitution, supposing that this would reduce the vulnerability of these economies to external trade (see note 5). Yet forced import substitution, via overvalued currencies, import controls, and creation of inefficient industry, contributes powerfully to discouraging exports. This in turn results in import starvation, so that such imports as remain—food and raw materials—are in highly inelastic demand. Indeed, at times, some of these economies have been in the position where enough materials and components for the industrial capacity already created could not be imported. The vulnerability to any trade fluctuation was thus increased. However, some more or less structuralist writers, notably David Felix, understood well that a breakthrough into exporting manufactures was important.[9] More important perhaps are the incentives to export. A lagging home demand is no hindrance to export, and resources would probably not be lacking if exporting manufactures were profitable. An "equilibrium" exchange rate, and liberalization of controls, is not enough if this equilibrium exchange rate is supported by heavy tariff protection, and if the prices of industrial inputs are above world levels. In this respect, IMF perspectives may well have been too narrow. But no one in the 1950s or early 1960s seems to have understood that protection may virtually prohibit many potential industrial exports.

Another important reason for the failure of stabilization policies in Latin America is that they were not expected to succeed. For instance, a large devaluation may make, say, investing in agriculture or exporting shoes profitable at the prices prevailing immediately after the devaluation. But if it is expected that inflation will continue and quickly result in a restoration of the pre-devaluation relative prices, then such investments will not be made. This history of rapid inflation, punctuated by large devaluations, must have influenced expectations in a way that made any cure extremely difficult.

One interpretation of the debate, albeit one that is unduly kind to the structuralists, would be that they were advocating gradualism in contrast to the monetarists' shock treatment. It is possible in principle, by widespread indexing, to prevent inflation from so distorting prices as to cause the inelasticities that exacerbate it. But if a distorted set of prices is inherited, the indexing cannot be automatic but must guide relative prices gradually in the right direction. This might also be combined with a sharp change in some prices, followed by indexation (for example, a devaluation followed by a trotting peg*).[10] This line of policy was roughly that adopted by Brazil, with some success, in the mid-1960s. The essential idea is that improvements in efficiency, and the elimination of bottlenecks, can proceed, while quite a rapid, but declining, rate of inflation is permitted to continue for some years. The IMF was presumably inhibited from attempting such gradualism because of the philosophy of Bretton Woods. If a fixed exchange rate, which would be only rarely changed, was to adhere, then stabilization had to be achieved very quickly.[11] This is not to say that shock treatment may not be best for some economies. For example, both India and Taiwan, in the 1970s, brought quite high rates of inflation down to almost nothing in a matter of months. But it is much more likely to work where there is no long history of inflation and where product and factor markets are competitive.

Some monetarists may also be accused of insensitivity to the possibility of social and political backlash.[12] For this reason, a successful policy might have to soften the income redistribution effects of the real wage and price changes (though this is not easy to do without undermining the efficacy of the changes). It has also been argued that more direct measures might have been used to back up the price changes.[13] But any blame, which subsequent analysis and experience may suggest, cannot necessarily be laid at the door of the IMF. Thus, Diaz Alejandro reports that President Frondisi of Argentina may, in 1958, have chosen the harshest of alternative plans suggested by the IMF.[14] It is also worth noting that Prebisch's stabilization plan of 1955–56 for Argentina was not dramatically different from the IMF type. It included devaluation, rationalization of exchange rates (though not

---

* A trotting peg is a series of frequent mini-devaluations.

complete unification), and liberalization of import controls. It may, however, have been rather more gradualist than the IMF as far as the elimination of price and quantity controls was concerned (though this is impossible to say for sure, since only the measures taken, and not IMF advice, are known).

The achievement of stabilization and a tolerably efficient economic system is an exceedingly difficult operation—after decades of inflation and policies that serve to make matters worse. However well such an operation is tuned to the social, political, and economic circumstances of a country, it may fail, unless it is imposed by an unshakable dictatorship. During the two decades after the structuralists were writing, matters got much worse in Argentina and Chile. Brazil did better but was still very far from a satisfactory solution. With this hindsight, it would be invidious to blame the authors of efforts in the 1950s who were operating more in the dark than their still unsuccessful successors.

Instead one may ask what was, or should have been, learned from the debate. Certainly, the structuralists made the point that supply and demand inelasticities make growth without inflation more difficult. But the more extreme claims that this rigidity was at the heart of inflation cannot be sustained. The intractability of inflation, once it is allowed to take hold, is now evident from the experience of countries where the inelasticities claimed for Latin America are implausible. Even at the time, it could be strongly argued that there was no observable relation between inflation and "natural" (that is, not policy induced) inflexibility.[15] Nor was the idea made plausible that inflation was desirable for growth in circumstances of such structural rigidity. It has become still less plausible in the light of further experience.

That inflation is as much a political problem as economic is now obvious to all. But the structuralists seem to have stressed economic structure more than political structure. In so doing, they were as much at fault as the monetarists. Moreover, they stressed the wrong kind of economic inflexibility. The inflexibility that is most important in the context of reducing inflation is a downward rigidity in wages and prices, where downward rigidity means that it is difficult to reduce the rate of increase of wages and prices below the *expected* rate of inflation. The less flexibility there is, the more serious the unemployment and loss of real output caused by deflationary policies. Wage inflexibility stems from the economic or political power of organized labor, and price inflexibility from a monopolistic or oligopolistic industrial structure.

In such circumstances, it is tempting to argue, in the case of a highly industrialized economy, that all-out expansion, which inevitably implies some excess demand, may be better, since rising productivity could reduce the rate of increase of prices if these are cost determined. This solution, however, assumes that prices are inflexible upward when demand is strong—a much more dubious proposition than that they are inflexible downward.[16] I am not aware that such a policy has ever worked for long. Finally, demand restraint may be combined with temporary wage and price controls in order to limit any real damage during a period in which inflationary expectations are scaled down. Such policies have not been very successful in more developed countries, and would not be feasible in economies that lack a strong administrative structure.

Chapter 6

The Dual Economy: Surplus Labor and Resources for Industrialization

Introduction

The concepts that form the title for this chapter are closely related. Historically, the dual economy comes first, and is attributable to J. Boeke.[1] He saw duality as essentially a conflict between cultures. Capitalism is largely imported, but the essence of the conflict is between capitalism and the traditional society rather than between the foreigner and the native. Some natives become Westernized. Boeke clearly grasped the notion of a "collaborating elite."

The distinction between capitalism and the "subsistence economy" (to use a later phrase) is virtually the same as that stressed by W. A. Lewis a decade later in his fecund article "Economic Development with Unlimited Supply of Labour."[2] But Boeke was far from tracing the potential path of development that might result from the interaction of these two sectors in the manner of Nurkse, Lewis, and many of their followers. In particular, he had no concept of surplus labor and subscribed to the "colonial" view of a backward-rising labor supply curve.

The notion of "unlimited supplies" of labor (to use Lewis's phrase) can be traced to the classical economists, especially Ricardo and Malthus, who introduced the idea that labor, in the long run, might be in perfectly elastic supply at a "subsistence" wage (which might, however, depend to some extent on conventional standards, and not solely on the minimum that would keep labor working fit). Unlimited supply in this sense does not, however, imply surplus labor in the sense that increased employment in one sector would have no repercussions on output in other parts of the economy; this seemed to be true only when the working population caught up with the increased demand, which would take about fifteen years.

In our period, there are two entwined but distinct strands of thought: (1) analysis of the development potential of surplus labor, and (2) analysis of the growth path of a dual economy, in which people move from a traditional to a modern sector.

The Development Potential of Surplus Labor

In the postwar literature, "surplus labor" must be taken to mean that, at the prevailing wage, more labor can be taken on in modern sectors of the economy without raising the wage, and without loss of output in the traditional sectors.

Labor can always be withdrawn from any sector without affecting output if sufficient capital is introduced. But this would defeat the purpose of the idea, which was intended to show that this surplus labor was a free, or almost free, resource. It would therefore seem that ceteris paribus has to be introduced. But it can be allowed that some consequential changes would occur as the result of the withdrawal of labor, provided these did not amount to more than a negligible introduction of any costly substitution for the withdrawn labor. This weaker version of ceteris paribus has been dubbed mutatis mutandis.

The existence of very large amounts of "surplus" agricultural labor in many developing countries was widely accepted almost without challenge until the mid-1950s. Surplus labor implies that labor could leave agriculture without any loss of output.[3] The empirical basis for this presumption was a set of studies of labor use and availability in agriculture, in southern Europe, Egypt, and some Asian countries, beginning in the 1930s with J. L. Buck[4] and Doreen Warriner.[5] These studies are now recognized to be defective for various reasons, including the neglect in some of them of the seasonality of agricultural work and of off-farm employment.[6] They also assumed that other family members would take up all the work of the defecting member, if they had the time. They did not establish the existence of a large amount of surplus labor in the required sense.

M. Dobb[7] and R. Nurkse[8] argued that surplus labor, even if some of it were only seasonal, could be used to create capital. The problem was to induce the corresponding savings. In a sense, however, the savings were already there (but disguised, like the unemployment) because the nonredundant workers were consuming less than they produced. Their savings supported the redundant workers. If only the nonredundant agricultural workers could be induced to continue to support the erstwhile redundant when the latter were put to work on construction projects, there would be no problem. Nurkse, of course, recognized the obvious difficulties.[9]

Unfortunately, however, there are also difficulties with the basic analysis. Suppose there were three working members of a family and one left; then the two that remained would have to work half as hard again if output were not to fall. This is true whether or not the marginal product of a man-hour of labor had previously been zero.[10] Nurkse thus implicitly assumed that the remaining members could and would work harder, which is hardly likely to be true in tropical climates, even apart from the fact that extra energy output requires more calorie intake. Alternatively, output could be maintained by more effective work, without extra effort, but this too seems implausible.

The above relationship between consumption and the desire and ability to work harder was introduced into the literature by

Leibenstein.[11] His scenario was that of landowners employing landless labor, not small farms worked by their peasant owners. He showed that if higher wages resulted in more work output per man, then it would pay landowners to set a higher wage than the market-clearing wage, leaving some unemployment. However, if there were nowhere for the unemployed to go, and if either society required the landowners to employ everyone— or the presence of unemployment forced the wage down—then it would still pay the landowners as a group to employ the whole labor force at a wage higher than the market-clearing wage and higher than the marginal product.

If casual employment rather than annual employment is the norm,[12] then there is no incentive for the individual employer to try to improve the quality of the labor force by paying more than a market-determined casual wage, even supposing that a positive relationship exists between earnings per period and the amount of work units supplied per period. D. Mazumdar explored the nature of the equilibrium in these circumstances.[13] The wage cannot fall to zero. It settles at the point where the supply of work units equals the demand. Each laborer may work little, but given the low equilibrium earnings determined by the daily wage and the number of days he gets employed, he is unwilling or unable to offer more work units than are demanded. The marginal product equals the wage, and "underemployment" has become identical to malnutrition.

What happens in the above circumstances if labor is withdrawn? The daily wage rises, and the remaining work force offers more work units per man. It is then possible that there would be no change in output. This possibility would be realized if the proportionate rise in work units offered was equal to the proportionate rise in the wage. The cost of a work unit, the wage bill, and the output would all remain the same. Surplus labor thus exists. The smaller labor force *does* take up the work of those who depart. But it does so only because it consumes as much as the previous larger work force. It follows that there are no hidden savings (equivalent to a reduction in the peasants' demands for food) to finance the use of the released labor for investment.[14]

Before turning to Lewis's contribution we may note that there were strong attacks on the notion of surplus labor almost as soon as it was formulated. Some of these misfired in that they (convincingly) attacked the proposition that the marginal productivity of a *man-hour of labor* was zero. But, as we have seen, this was not the point. Others attacked the idea that significant quantities of labor could not be withdrawn from any sector, notably agriculture, without affecting output (that is, the marginal product of *the labor force* was zero). A little later (1964) C. H. C. Kao, K. R. Anschel, and C. K. Eicher summed up their above-mentioned survey as follows:

> ... it is an understatement to say that the development literature in this period was optimistic about development through the transfer of redundant agricultural labor to other occupations. We have shown that the empirical studies supporting this optimism were often poorly conceived. In addition, we have noted that by considering temporary rather than permanent labor transfers and by allowing some reorganization of production, various writers have arrived at a high percentage of disguised unemployment. To date, there is little reliable empirical evidence to support the existence of more than token—5 percent—disguised unemployment in undeveloped countries as defined by a zero marginal product of labor and the condition of *ceteris paribus*.[15]

This continued to be a valid observation in 1981. But it should be noted that it does not imply that the social cost of labor is not overstated by its supply price to nonagricultural activities (see also chapter 9).

Development with Unlimited Supplies of Labor

Lewis used the notions of duality and surplus labor to tell a development story.[16] Some discussion of his work, which has spawned a whole literature, is unavoidable.

Before examining the mechanics of the "model" (the story is so flexibly told it is not clear that there is a single model), some preliminary observations are in order.

1. The essential duality is between the capitalist sectors and the subsistence sectors.
2. Capitalists are profit maximizers, and they are also the savers: they automatically invest what they save. They save and invest as long as profits are positive. The marginal product equals the wage. Capitalism is not necessarily confined to industry (for example, plantations are capitalistic).
3. The "subsistence" sector is everything else: it includes not only peasant agriculture but also traditional services, and perhaps even government. The essence of these sectors is that the wage exceeds the marginal productivity of a man (which was thought to be negligible, although this is inessential to the argument). These sectors are supposed to operate virtually without reproducible capital. The wage is conventional, determined partly by subsistence and partly by custom and even by morality. But it has to be greater than the marginal product, as people would not otherwise survive. In purely peasant family agriculture, with no hired workers, the "wage" is the average product (it equals average consumption). The traditional sector scarcely saves.
4. Although Lewis included nonagriculture in the subsistence sectors, he thought his theory applied mainly to Asia (and Egypt). He clearly had in mind, therefore, countries where land was scarce. If land was not scarce, it can be presumed (one supposes) that surplus labor would not exist in any sector.[17] It would seem that we can therefore tell the story in terms of the capitalist sectors versus agriculture (as most commentators have done) while bearing in mind that agriculture is not the only source of labor for the capitalist sector.

We can now set things in motion, supposing first that we are dealing with a closed economy. The central theme of the story is that the capitalist sector can develop with a low fixed real wage. This wage was thought to be some 30 percent above the conventional wage in the subsistence sector. This in turn is tied to the standard of living in the subsistence sector and to average productivity in agriculture.

Given a closed economy, the industrial sector must, in part, produce consumer goods for sale to the agricultural sector in order, in effect, to pay for the food its workers consume (for the rest it can make "luxury" goods for capitalist and workers' consumption and the capital goods corresponding to its own savings). Thus, the terms of trade between industry and agriculture enter in, unless we assume that the capitalist sector produces its own food and is thus self-contained (Lewis toys with this idea, but it is obviously unrealistic in a closed economy).

As long as this fixed real wage holds, and the terms of trade remain constant, industrial growth rockets. Under plausible assumptions, the rate of profit should be high, and most is saved. Moreover, the fruits of technical progress accrue entirely to the capitalists, so that the growth rate is not merely high but accelerating. Investment rises continuously as a proportion of national income. However high population growth, which feeds into surplus labor, might be, it could not keep up with this dynamism.

The end of the story is, therefore, that surplus labor is all absorbed. The marginal productivity of labor in agriculture rises to equality with the wage. Both then rise together, raising the industrial wage and thus slowing down industrialization as profits and savings are squeezed—eventually to zero in the absence of technical progress.

But Lewis concedes that development may peter out before any such happy (or, anyway, wholly capitalist) ending. Two of his reasons for this failure are essentially endogenous to the model. First, as surplus labor is reduced, average earnings per head in agriculture rise. If we assume a constant population, this force must operate from the very beginning of capitalist development, and this belies the constant real industrial wage. If we assume a rising population, the same will happen as soon as the industrial demand for labor begins to make any inroads on the volume of surplus labor. This does not imply that industrial growth cannot eliminate surplus labor, but it may do so at a decreasing rate (depending on the speed and nature of technical progress in the capitalist sector). The essential point here is that the existence of surplus labor is not a sufficient condition for unlimited supplies of labor, that is, a constant real wage.[18] A theory of population growth, such as the classical authors provided, is needed to keep living standards in agriculture at a constant level (in the long run).

Second, if the terms of trade are to remain constant for any long period, we need an agricultural scenario that permits greater sales of food and greater absorption of industrial products. But at the same time, the average earnings of peasant farmers, and the conventional wage of employed laborers, must not rise if the real wage is to stay constant. It would seem that this could occur only if all peasant farmers are tenants and the increased agricultural earnings accrue only to landlords.

Lewis did not bother about the workings of markets and institutions in the traditional sector. He believed that real industrial wages remained constant in England from the Industrial Revolution until around 1840 and that an enlightening story could be told of how industry, and industrial investment and employment, might in these conditions grow at an accelerating pace, generating its own savings, until such time as real wages began to rise.[19] It is, indeed, an enlightening story. The problem in a closed economy is to see why, except by purely coincidental technical change, the real wage should remain constant for a long enough period for the industrial explosion to continue and to eliminate surplus labor.

In an open economy, the terms-of-trade problem vanishes. The capitalist sectors can trade with the rest of the world and can thus import food; the terms of trade will not be significantly affected and can thus be treated as exogenous. Labor can also be imported, and any effect on the standard of living of the supplying countries, with massive populations, will be negligible. This happened historically, with the import into many countries of Chinese and Indian labor for plantations and construction. In the postwar period, it is notable that, during the period of massive influx of refugees from the mainland, Hong Kong provides the clearest example of the Lewis model in operation. Labor imports reduce or eliminate the benefits to local labor that arise from internal migration to the capitalist sector where earnings are higher. But the immigrants benefit. South Korea and Taiwan in the 1960s may also be regarded as examples of the Lewis model, although the real wage rose slowly (until around 1968, when it accelerated).

93

The openness of an economy may help industrialization in yet another way. In a closed economy with, therefore, a small initial market for manufactures, any modern industry is inevitably monopolistic or oligopolistic. In such noncompetitive circumstances, it is more likely that real wages will rise and, whether they do or not, the profits will be devoted to increased capital intensity, thus limiting the demand for labor.[20]

Classical Economics and Dualism

Lewis derived much of his inspiration from the classical economists.[21] What is the essential distinction between classical and neoclassical economics? Lewis puts it as follows: "The fact that there is not enough capital to provide employment for everybody is a vital distinction between the (classical) model and neoclassical analysis," and again, "In the early stages of economic development there is not enough capital to provide employment for everyone in the capitalist sector."[22] In a competitive capitalist system, a worker would earn his marginal product. But if there is very little capital, such earnings may be too low to sustain the working force. Therefore, the whole economy cannot operate on capitalist lines. There has to be a noncapitalist sector, in which people earn or consume more than their marginal product. Income is shared rather than distributed according to any contribution to output. The self-employed family, whether peasant or urban, is the archetype. But self-governing collectives, such as kibbutzim, also rank.

Such sharing arrangements may be made because people prefer them. When necessity does not drive, this is rare. Kibbutzim are rare, even in Israel. But, in an exceedingly poor economy, there must be a large part of the economy operating through such income-sharing arrangements. They may even apply when there is, on the face of it, normal wage employment—if the employer is guided in a feudal manner by the need or desire to sustain a certain number of employees rather than maximize profit. N. Georgescu-Roegen thus argued that feudalism (regarding the paterfamilias as a feudal entrepreneur) is the appropriate system for overpopulated economies and that capitalism came too fast in Eastern Europe.[23] Recent enthusiasm for the "informal sector" might be regarded as an implicit recognition of the validity of Georgescu-Roegen's argument.

The above discussion presupposed an economy in which income sharing would be a necessity however capital was distributed. But if capital is needlessly concentrated in sectors with a high capital-labor ratio, or if the capital-labor ratio is needlessly high in such sectors, or both, then large income-sharing parts of the economy may needlessly continue to exist.

Duality can be defined in many ways. But a useful analytic institutional definition would seem to be that an economy is dualistic when a significant part of it operates under such a paternalist or quasi-feudalist regime, while another significant part operates under a system of wage employment—which may be capitalist or socialist (if state capitalism is regarded as a variety of socialism).[24] Surplus labor may exist in such a situation, but not necessarily so.

It is arguable how much dualism there is in less developed countries. Even in the poorest LDCs, there is more wage employment than writers of the 1950s imagined. Very small enterprises and farms often offer some wage employment, especially during peak seasons in agriculture. A small farm may be feudal most of the year, and capitalist at harvest time. The same small farmer himself vacillates from one regime to the other. He may do off-farm work off-season or hire himself out when a neighbor's peak does not coincide with his own. This untidiness may bother political and social theorists, but not economists.

The Agricultural Surplus

The need for a sufficient agricultural surplus—meaning that agriculture consumes less of its own products than it produces, especially food—was rather overshadowed in the 1950s by the debates on labor surplus.[25] This was surprising in view of the great Soviet debates on the problems of supplying the towns with food. Even Nurkse's worry about the need for savings to employ surplus labor without inflation addressed the problem only obliquely.

Lewis has stressed in many places the need for a buoyant agriculture and rising productivity, especially in food production.[26] Nevertheless, his 1954 article seemed to emphasize a labor surplus rather than an agricultural surplus. I say "seemed to stress" because inadequacy of food supplies is implicit in the discussion of declining terms of trade for the capitalist sector. It was not until the 1960s that the need for agricultural growth was strongly emphasized in many articles. An exception is a paper by Nicholas Kaldor read to the International Conference on Underdeveloped Areas in Milan in 1954. It is worth quoting:

> The key to an accelerated growth of the underdeveloped areas of the world has been in bringing about fundamental changes in both the mental outlook and the technical knowledge and skill of their peasant populations. Economic development will, of course, invariably involve industrialization—but this can be expected to follow, almost automatically, upon the growth of the food surpluses of the agricultural sector. Once this is recognized, the efforts of underdeveloped countries could be concentrated—far more than they are at present—in tackling the problem of how to raise productivity on the land, as a prior condition of economic development. The most promising line of approach (even though it is not one that yields immediate fruits) seems to be in a vast effort at raising the general level of education in rural areas.[27]

The similarity of this view to that of Viner is notable (see above). In contrast one may quote Nurkse: "And yet it seems plausible to maintain that drastic improvements in farming methods are not the first crucial pre-requisite in the initial stages of economic progress in a society endowed with large reserves of surplus labor on the land."[28] Or the United Nations: "In a country where there is no surplus labor, industrialization waits upon the improvements of agriculture. The way to industrialization is through the improvement of agriculture.... The reverse is the case for a country where population is so large in relation to cultivable land, that the land is carrying more people than can be fully employed in agriculture. Substantial technical progress in agriculture is not possible without reducing the numbers engaged in agriculture."[29]

Apart from the mistaken emphasis on surplus labor, this latter quotation shows that the authors did not realize how fast population was growing[30] and how relatively small industry was. Amazingly enough, it was not until 1959 that it was pointed out in the economic literature, and then in a relatively obscure publication, that one was forced to assume that the agricultural population in most LDCs would grow for many years.[31] However, it was realized somewhat earlier by some planners at least.

The need for an agricultural surplus strictly applies only in the case of a closed economy that wants to industrialize. In an open economy, agriculture can be neglected, provided that industry exports enough. This does not imply that it should be neglected. Considerations of welfare and equality suggest the opposite.

Chapter 7

Other Elements and Areas of Neglect

Hares that Hardly Ran

EXPLANATIONS OF STAGNATION OR POVERTY

The main, and prima facie influential, themes in the economic development literature that we have so far examined were forward looking and operational—and very much policy oriented. It is natural to ask to what extent they were based on any analysis of underdevelopment. Descriptions of the characteristics of poor countries abounded, and description alone often led to prescription. Thus, poor countries usually have, relative to rich ones, little industry, little education, etc. Therefore, it is assumed they must industrialize, educate, etc. But this is not profound and has provided inadequate and often misleading guidance. Clearly, description of a state of affairs does not amount to explanation.

Aside from neo-Marxist explanations in terms of exploitation, which we examine elsewhere, the main explanation of poverty in the literature, due to Leibenstein, was that of a low-level equilibrium.[1] In its most general form, this says that a growth of income per head, from a low level, due to some chance—say, a succession of good harvests—brings into play two sets of forces, one promoting growth and the other decline, with the latter winning. The obvious example is that savings and investment may rise with a rise in income, but so also may the rate of population growth. After a lag the latter dominates, and returns income per head to its previous low-level equilibrium. Leibenstein thus essentially generalized Malthus but suggested that, while the above might be true of a small change in income per head, the reverse might be true for a larger change. This seemed to be a powerful argument for a big push, or "critical minimum effort."

This is not the same argument for a big push as that of Rosenstein Rodan, which was more of an explanation of why a country cannot get off the ground than of why it might flop back. Investment was, in effect, limited to a very low level by the size of the market. The size of the market also limited investment in poor-land and labor-surplus economies, according to Hla Myint's (and Adam Smith's) theory of the vent for surplus. Essentially, with a very limited knowledge of techniques, there was no productive investment worth making until trade enlarged the size of the market for what the people knew how to produce. There were other poverty-trap explanations of stagnation, which explain too much. The most obvious was that poor countries cannot save and hence cannot grow.[2]

Low-level equilibrium theories may embrace noneconomic variables. Admittedly, population itself was and is often treated as exogenous to economic models. But it is a mistake to think that economists paid no attention to cultural, social, and institutional variables. Most textbooks of the period stressed them,[3] and earlier writers such as J. S. Furnivall held them to be dominant. We have already seen that one element in structural theories was the view of the peasant as an ultraconservative being, dominated by tradition-bound authoritarian cultures. The extended family, caste systems, property laws and conventions, the Catholic and Hindu religions, and modes of early education that inhibited ambition—all received emphasis. So also did those social values that channeled the energies of such people as were motivated to achieve wealth or prestige into martial or other zero-sum activi-

99

ties. One economist, E. E. Hagen, made changes in human personality the dominant explanation of economic progress, implying that such changes are not themselves the result of otherwise induced changes in the mode of production.[4]

One must distinguish between a static treatment of noneconomic factors as favorable or unfavorable, and consideration of the manner in which they themselves will change in response to increases in national income per head. If they are static obstacles, they play no part in the theory of low-level equilibrium, which requires that economic growth sets in motion *changes* that resist it. Static obstacles slow down but do not reverse an initial impulse.

There is disagreement as to the importance of particular cultural and institutional factors. It is easy to agree, in general, that they must be of great importance. But as soon as one begins to particularize, consensus breaks down. For instance, are all other religions than Protestantism relatively inimical to economic motivation? How do others rank? Admittedly, the question of whether a particular feature of a culture or society is favorable or unfavorable for growth often leaves little room for doubt. A low prestige for bankers, traders, and manufacturers can hardly be favorable; nor can communal ownership of scarce land (unless access and use is managed), or a caste system, or bans on cattle slaughter. But, at the same time, they may not be very important obstacles. When people ask me whether Hinduism is a very important obstacle to Indian development, I say that I do not think so. I may be wrong, but no one can prove that I am.

The equally important problem of whether cultural and institutional factors change in a favorable or unfavorable manner in response to economic growth seems to have been less debated, though not unnoticed. Thus, Arthur Lewis argued that "the most important characteristic of institutions, from the angle of economic growth, is the amount of freedom to manoeuvre which they permit... given the chance to seize opportunities, men will in due course alter all their institutions accordingly... it follows that change reinforces itself cumulatively. Once economic growth has begun, institutions change more and more in directions favourable to growth, and so strengthen the forces making for growth."[5] Lewis argued that the growth-promoting force, resulting in a cumulative process, could arise either from economic advance or from institutional change, making it in practice impossible to decide which was the cause. It may have been economic forces that promoted the Reformation, or vice versa. "All such questions are unanswerable."[6]

Lewis also envisaged a process of cumulative (relative?) decline, whereby success bred defensive institutions—monopoly, trade unionism, and, in general, protection. These limited the possibilities of individuals to seize opportunities and reinforced the process of institutional arteriosclerosis. This anticipated the work of Mancur Olson,[7] who has elaborated on this theme. He seems to have envisaged this process of decline as being relevant to mature societies—particularly, perhaps, the United Kingdom.

Historically, as land became scarce, private property was instituted and extended. This continues to the present day. Monetary institutions also evolve in response to needs. Even so deep-seated a phenomenon as caste in India may be (very slowly) eroded by the personal contacts appropriate to the industrial sector, and so on.

In general, the economic literature of the 1950s, after surveying such matters, tended to assume that they were either not such important obstacles as to nullify the effects of capital accumulation on output per head, or that they would change in response to increasing capital and output per head, or both. They would, in short, not be retarding factors of such importance as to determine a low-level equilibrium. As we shall see, the performance of developing countries suggests that this was, in general, a sensible assumption; although events in Iran in the 1970s also suggest that, in rather extreme circumstances, a cultural backlash can occur, which makes a mockery of capital accumulation.

The assumption referred to above did not preclude suggestions that so-called noneconomic obstacles to development should be directly assaulted. Thus, governments were called upon to influence people's attitudes in growth-promoting ways—in favor of thrift, punctuality, hard work, honesty, cooperation, acquiring a scientific outlook, and, above all, family planning. Governments were also expected to promote appropriate economic institutions, or at least see that the law was favorable to the private development of such institutions, in banking, insurance, cooperatives, etc., and to prevent counterproductive backlash by seeing that benefits were widely spread—for example, by land reform, which few writers of comprehensive treatises failed to stress.

STAGES OF GROWTH

Historians and economists concerned with the broad sweep of events over the centuries have often been tempted to produce a theory of stages of development, whether in terms of the modes or structure of production or, on the political plane, of economic and power relations. Such patterns can clearly be discerned in broad outline, but the resulting schema may easily become too Procrustean and lead to distortion of facts to suit the theory. And it may also lead to (or result from) a belief in historical determinism, as in the case of Marx.

In our period, W. W. Rostow caused much discussion by advancing such a theory.[8] The reaction of economic historians seems to have been very unfavorable. Highly critical comment came from a phalanx of pundits[9]—Kuznets, Fishlow, Ohlin, Cairncross, Habbakuk, Gerschenkron, and probably others. But, despite criticism, the book was certainly popular. This was, no doubt, largely because of its optimism. The "preconditions" for a "take-off" did not, perhaps, look too difficult to achieve. These may be summarized as: (1) a change in effective attitudes; (2) a rise in the rate of investment toward the 10–12 percent supposed to be required for "take-off"; (3) an improvement in agricultural productivity; (4) the provision of social overhead capital; and (5) the emergence of a new elite, associated often with a "reactive" nationalism. Of these, there was a new elite and certainly a reactive nationalism in most newly independent countries. The provision of overhead capital was proceeding apace, and there was a lot of foreign aid for this purpose. Most less developed countries were already approaching the required levels of investment in the 1950s, and many had exceeded it. Admittedly, a rise in agricultural productivity was less in evidence, and a change in attitudes arguable.

The second optimistic feature was that the "take-off" period was short. It usually took about twenty years for "rotation" to occur.[10] Thereafter—well, aircraft seldom crash, and Rostow's further stages need not concern us. Apart from achieving the required rate of investment, there were two further requirements for "take-off": (1) "the development of one or more substantial manufacturing sectors, with a high rate of growth," and (2) "the existence or quick emergence of a political, social and institutional framework which exploits the impulses to expansion in the modern sector and the potential external economy effects of the take-off and gives its growth an on-going character."

The second of the above conditions is so nebulous as to render the theory unfalsifiable. If an economy appears to have satisfied everything else, and then fails to grow, Rostow could always argue that (2) must have been inadequately fulfilled. The first condition is more interesting, although also rather vague. This condition is shorthand for the leading-sector approach.[11] Spelled out in more detail in *The Economics of Sustained Growth*, with emphasis on forward, backward, and lateral linkages, one can say that "Rostow's linkages now become virtually the historical analogue of Hirschman's strategy for contemporary unbalanced growth."[12] This means that a sector should not be considered to be a leading sector merely because it grows very fast and is highly profitable and hence gives a powerful impetus to growth. Thus, by this criterion, neither the clothing nor the electronics industry, which together revolutionized the "baby tigers" in the 1960s and 1970s, should be called a leading sector. ("Baby tigers" is a Mainland Chinese sobriquet for South Korea, Taiwan, Hong Kong, and Singapore. They have also been dubbed the "gang of four" by some irreverent economist.) It is necessary that a leading sector should induce output decisions (linkages) or raise productivity elsewhere as a result of some externality. Rostow's favorite leading sector for the more developed countries was railroads. (That railroads failed to lead in LDCs was for lack of other preconditions, but the essence of Hirschman's unbalanced growth argument is that lack of other preconditions is overcome by the stimulus of disequilibrium.) Fishlow denies the impetus given by the railroads to machinery, and iron and coal production, in the United States.[13] Rostow is reluctant to admit cotton textiles as a leading sector, but does so for the United Kingdom, on the grounds of its large size.[14]

For other countries he admits anything that apparently grows fast at about the right time: timber in Sweden, meat and dairy products in Denmark, silk in Japan. Perhaps the importance of a leading sector, in the unrefined sense of a sector that leads, is that it grows fast to a considerable size and is (socially) profitable—and damn the linkages!

Success in some lines of activity will always lead to developments elsewhere, quite apart from inventions. It is equally clear that inventions may, and often have, opened up profitable opportunities, and have stimulated and influenced the pattern of applied research. It is interesting historically to trace the resultant lines of cause and effect; the upshot has been that some sectors and subsectors grew faster than others, and, in this limited sense, there have been leading sectors and unbalanced growth. Such historical links are often described as if they were examples of linkages in the sense of Hirschman or Scitovsky. But they may involve no significant externalities, and simply be explicable in terms of the profit motive and the price mechanism. Nor, of course, is historical imbalance a reason for deliberately induced imbalance.

Areas of Neglect

AGRICULTURAL AND RURAL DEVELOPMENT

There was little published about LDC agriculture from 1945 to 1960. In C. Eicher and L. Witt's collection of articles published in 1964,[15] only seven out of twenty-five date from the 1950s. Of these seven, only five are concerned at all with developing countries. Of these five, only two are about agriculture (or rural development),[16] and even these are about land reform rather than the development of agriculture in given conditions of land ownership and tenure. Glancing through other bibliographies leaves the same impression.

Ignoring land reform and new settlements, economic work on agriculture and rural development must include description and understanding of the workings of rural markets for labor, credit, and land; and the upshot in terms of loans, labor, and land contracts, and the resulting levels of wages, earnings, rents, and interest rates, as well as the transformation of inputs into outputs, product markets, and investment. Almost nothing of this seems to have found its way into Western journals or books.[17] This does not imply that nothing was going on. In India, for instance, there were official Agricultural Labour and Credit surveys and Farm Management studies. But there was little academic or analytic work in this area in the 1950s.[18]

The role of agriculture in development was discussed in this period independently of the determinants of agricultural performance or policy. It was treated more as a black box from which people, and food to feed them, and perhaps capital, would be released. Discussion of these three "surpluses," focused on surplus labor, we have already reviewed. Most of the discussion was a priori. There was evidently so little knowledge of the actual conditions and possibilities in developing countries that most references were made to the historical experience of MDCs, the USSR, and Japan. As early as 1951 the Japanese agricultural experience was reviewed by Bruce Johnston as being more relevant to other Asian countries than that of the USSR.[19] Japanese agricultural food productivity had grown, since the 1880s, significantly faster than population and fast enough to release both labor and rice. Moreover, this growth was achieved mainly by improved techniques, including new seeds, and a rapid increase in chemical fertilizers. Thus, little new capital was needed, and agricultural savings were diverted to the industrial sector through heavy land taxes. A somewhat similar experience, although the system of agricultural taxation was quite different, was developing in Taiwan, influenced by colonial experience under the Japanese and led by the now famous Joint Commission on Rural Reconstruction (JCRR)—a joint Chinese-American body originally formed in Mainland China in 1948. (But this success story was not yet written up.)

We have treated agriculture as a neglected area in the 1950s. It is, however, true that many, though not all, textbooks argued that industry and agriculture must march together. A lagging agriculture would impede industrialization, in that the price of food and the cost of labor would rise, or food imports would strain the balance of payments. So agriculture must not be neglected. But such rather obvious benign statements were not backed by a knowledge of how agriculture might best be promoted. It is fairly obvious from reading their works that the leading development economists of the 1950s knew nothing about tropical agriculture or rural life.[20] One cannot perhaps blame them: they had no time for rural rides, and there was no considerable body of empirical grass-roots literature on which they could draw. The planning enthusiasts also gave no clues as to how agriculture could best be planned and administered, and yet it is clear that government should play a greater role in the agricultural sector than in almost any other.

Was agriculture, and in general rural development, neglected on the ground? The consensus of the 1970s would surely say that it was. It is implied that growth or equity, or both, would have been improved if the terms of trade for agriculture had been better (and in many countries they were turned against agriculture by the policies pursued), or if more public expenditure and attention had been diverted to agriculture and less to industry. Some would argue that this would have been true only in the context of agrarian reform, but most observers would probably argue that in many countries there were great possibilities without far-reaching reforms of land ownership or tenure.

While it became clear later that much industrial investment had very low returns, or even served to reduce growth, it also has to be remembered that there were many failures of agricultural investment. Many large irrigation projects and attempts at large-scale mechanized farming, especially in Africa, were failures. Ghana, for instance, managed to spend a lot on agriculture, while neglecting and even discouraging the farmers.[21] It could be argued, and was argued, that there was insufficient knowledge to be able to spend much money on agricultural development. If one thought in terms of great schemes, this was perhaps true. But it is very difficult to believe that more investment in improving such elements as agricultural departments; agricultural education and research; seed farms; greatly increased extension services as trained people became available; the availability of fertilizers and improved seeds; or minor irrigation schemes, would not have been a socially profitable use of resources even in the Tropics. Twenty years later, in reviewing rural development projects in Africa, Uma Lele found that the greatest difficulty encountered was still the lack of trained people.[22]

We cannot explore this large question further until the experience of the 1960s and 1970s has been examined. But if the consensus is right, the neglect of agriculture in the development literature was a contributory cause, even if a minor one. Or, to put it another way, those agricultural economists and agronomists who were convinced of the need for giving more attention to agriculture had an uphill fight and were often regarded as reactionary. It was not until the bad harvests and food scares of the mid-1960s, and the temporary glamour of the green revolution, that there was a shift of emphasis.

POPULATION THEORY

Almost all economists seem to have believed that the rate of population growth reduced the rate of income growth per head, and that it was a threat to there being any growth at all, at least in the most densely populated countries. That it was supposed to be such a threat is a little surprising in view of the fact that it was wrongly thought that the average rate of growth in the densely populated countries was quite low. To quote:

> The growth of population in the developing world has been even more flagrantly under-anticipated [than that of Europe and North America], in spite of the fact that a decline in mortality was expected. In 1949, Colin Clark projected the growth of world population at 1 percent a year, yielding 3.5 billion by 1990, and in 1950 one of the world's leading demographers presented a world total for 2000 A.D. of 3.3 billion, which is about the number of people thought to be alive today [1967]. A United Nations Study of 1951 expected the rate of growth for Africa and Asia (without Japan) to fall between 0.7 and 1.3 percent per annum between 1950 and 1980, and its projections for world population in 1980 fell between 3.0 and 3.6 billion. The lowest of the figures was

reached in 1960, and the highest will almost certainly be so before 1970.[23]

This low expectation was, however, balanced by a low expectation of the possibility of income growth. Sir Arthur Lewis wrote: "The hardest task of all is to raise the standard of living. If population is growing at 1½ percent per annum, the minimum target we can set is to increase total output by 2 percent per annum. . . . But raising total output by 2 percent per annum is no mean feat."[24] This pessimism was quite general. I have not read any economist of the 1950s who claimed, implicitly or explicitly, that the growth rate of output in LDCs would achieve the 5 percent actually achieved in the 1960s. If the population growth rate was unanticipated, so too (and perhaps more so) was the performance of the world economy. This is worth underlining in view of the frequent assertion, made in the 1970s, that the development establishment of earlier years was absurdly optimistic concerning the prospects of development.[25] This was perhaps true of some Western technocrats, some nationalist politicians, and a handful of developing country economists who exaggerated the benefits of decolonization, but certainly not of the great body of practitioners of the dismal science.

We have seen that Leibenstein explored the dynamics of population growth in connection with his theory of a low-level equilibrium. But population and income growth were related to income levels in a rather crude way that lacked adequate empirical backing. A later and major contribution was made by A. Coale and E. Hoover in 1958.[26] While few had denied that population growth would reduce the rate of growth of income per head,[27] their work suggested that population growth would reduce the growth rate of income itself, for two reasons. First, the faster the population grows the higher is the dependency ratio, which, it was argued, would reduce savings. Second, growing numbers imply a diversion of investment to education, housing, and urban construction, and these forms of investment are supposedly less productive than investment in land improvements and factories. These negative effects could well outweigh any direct contribution made by the increase in labor supply, especially in densely populated countries where the marginal product of labor was low. The truth—and, if true, the importance—of these factors, especially the former, has since been challenged, and the debate is still alive.

These contributions shifted discussion away from the concept of optimum population.[28] Despite the nebulous and morally dubious character of this concept, most people would probably agree that much of Asia is certainly overpopulated, and much of Africa and Latin America probably underpopulated. But even if a country is seriously underpopulated, it is unlikely that welfare would be maximized by a maximum rate of growth of the population. By now this proposition would be accepted by most governments, but this was surely not so in the 1950s, when only India and Taiwan had official though tiny birth control programs.

Empirical work on the determinants of population growth in LDCs was notably lacking. The arguments were based on the experience of the demographic transition in Europe and North America. It was realized that the cause of accelerated growth was a fall in mortality, which probably had very little to do with any increase in income per head but resulted from public health improvements; strong empirical support for this belief was, however, forthcoming only in the 1960s.[29] Writers speculated about the determinants of fertility in LDCs, but there was no hard quantitative evidence—not surprising, given the subject was almost taboo.[30] Thus, there was no very sound basis for models of interaction between income and income growth on the one side and population growth on the other. Moreover, active population policies would be designed to change the parameters of any such model.

CAPITAL MARKETS

The malfunctioning of factor markets in LDCs later became a very prominent theme. We have already considered work on labor markets in chapter 6. It remains only to note that there was very little study of domestic capital markets. Development was overwhelmingly thought of in real terms.

There were some descriptions of central and commercial banking in a few LDCs. Commercial banks were attacked for their developmental inadequacy: they did not give long-term loans and neglected small producers, especially farmers. The attacks were, of course, popular, since foreign banks were prominent in many LDCs, and quite often dominant. New institutions, such as development banks and cooperative credit societies, were called for. There was, however, very little study of the actual working of capital markets. There was the All India Rural Credit Survey in 1954, and in 1957 U. Tun Wai described the structure of interest rates in two celebrated articles, which also refer to the available sources.[31] George Rosen was studying industrial finance in India in 1958-59,[32] and work on flow of funds was initiated at the Central Statistical Office. But plans, in India and elsewhere, simply assumed that funds would flow in the directions indicated by the planned patterns of investment.[33] There was no financial plan, although selective credit controls and preferential interest rates were widely used by governments.[34] Wider aspects of the role of financial development in economic development, and the part that might be played by improving capital markets, were scarcely mentioned.[35]

HUMAN CAPITAL

The concept of human capital is almost as old as economics.[36] It was recognized that human beings were valuable even if they could not be bought and sold. More relevantly, it had long been recognized that investment in improving human beings by education and medical services was closely analogous to buying a machine. But, for some unexplained reasons, these insights did not lead to any analysis of the economics of education and health care until the 1950s.[37] It is not surprising that these new branches of economics did not begin to be applied to developing countries until the 1960s. It is true that there had been many references to the importance of skills and their lack in LDCs. This lack was indeed one of the reasons for an early enthusiasm for technical assistance, as exemplified by "Point Four" of Truman's Inaugural Address of 1948. But there is a lag between recognition of importance and economic analysis.

Entrepreneurship may not best be included under the title of "human capital," but for convenience we do so. There seems to have been little LDC research on the subject before 1960, although the work of D. C. McClelland[38] and E. E. Hagen[39] was in progress. Lack of entrepreneurship was, however, frequently mentioned in textbooks as a major obstacle to growth.

Continuing Themes of Practical Importance but of Minor Theoretical Interest

AID

Aid literature in the 1950s, and indeed since, has contributed little, if anything, to ideas about development. It is natural that influence should run the other way, from development theory and general economic principles to discussion of terms, modes, and administration of aid—that is, the flow of concessionary public funds to developing countries. One could stop there: however, this book is also about international economic relationships, of which the aid relation, as it has come to be called, is an important component.

Although a number of noncolonial powers, including the USSR and Japan, started small programs in the 1950s, the great bulk of aid was from the United States to foreign countries and from colonial powers to their colonies. The latter was an ongoing activity that excited little comment. It is therefore not surprising that almost all theorizing about aid in the 1950s came from the United States. The United Nations, however, did much to promote the idea that aid should be given to poor countries, and that the machinery of the organization should be used for this purpose.

Since it was novel that a rich country should assist poor independent countries in the name of development, it is also not very surprising that most consideration was given in the United States to the question of why it was doing it. The reasons adduced were not wholly convincing to Congress, for United States aid fell rapidly in real terms after 1962.

People support aid for both humanitarian and self-interest reasons. Humanitarian reasons include both a simple desire to help the poor and political idealism. Thus, some believed that aid would promote liberal democracy and that this was desirable, whether or not it contributed to the security of the United States.[40]

Self-interest includes economic and strategic motives. That the donor country should benefit economically from giving aid is paradoxical and unsustainable, and few serious analysts have suggested that it does. Many aid advocates nevertheless used and continue to use the argument, which can be made to sound plausible.[41] Particular interests in donor countries will, however, benefit, and aid advocates may want to appeal to them.

The most influential contribution by economists was that of M. F. Millikan and W. Rostow,[42] which stressed the long-run strategic interest of the United States in the independent and politically stable development of LDCs. Although the suggested reasons for aid were thus ultimately political, they also argued that aid must be for economic development and should not be used as a lever to influence nondevelopmental negotiations, for example, for an air base.

It was implied that aid would promote a broad-based development. There was thought to be little problem concerning the international distribution of aid because the hoped-for amounts would suffice to meet all demands for capital that could be used with reasonable efficiency. In other words, "absorptive capacity" was limited enough to make the problem of aid distribution a minor one; but if choices had to be made, then more should go to countries that helped themselves (some stress was in particular laid on the criterion of a high marginal savings rate). The influence of Rostow's theory of the "take-off" can probably be seen here. If only countries could be led on to a path of self-sustained growth, then the need to give aid could be seen to be limited in time. This was an attractive argument for the liberal proponents of aid to use against those who disliked the idea of an unending commitment to help poor countries.

Thus, political self-interest was stressed in official pronouncements on aid, and it is clear that the cold war was a large part of the explanation of why United States aid rose rapidly in the 1950s. By 1960, United States official development assistance (ODA) was $2.7 billion per annum, accounting for 58 percent of total aid provided by the Development Assistance Committee (DAC) of the Organization for Economic Cooperation and Development (OECD). The United States made considerable efforts in the DAC to get other countries to do more. In this, she was successful, and her share of DAC aid afterward fell steadily to less than 30 percent in the late 1970s. Humanitarian motives seem to have been more important for the smaller European countries, and Canada and Australia, which all greatly increased their programs.[43] Total ODA from DAC members continued to rise very slowly in real terms, but fell as a proportion of gross national product from about one half of 1 percent in the early 1960s to about one third of 1 percent in the 1970s.

The United Nations line was, from the beginning, very different from that of the United States. The principle invoked was that of equity and human solidarity. Aid should be given without political strings, or even surveillance, which might usurp the recipient's sovereignty. Multilateral aid was to be preferred, and throughout the 1950s the developing countries canvassed the idea of a United Nations development fund, the Special United Nations Fund for Economic Development (SUNFED), that would replace much bilateral aid. It was proposed that unlike the International Bank for Reconstruction and Development, developing countries would exercise voting control over SUNFED via the Economic and Social Council of the United Nations (ECOSOC) and the General Assembly.[44]

A conflict was clearly in the making. The donors would insist on a considerable surveillance to try to see that aid was well used, with an emphasis on investment, not consumption. At least they had to see that aided projects were not white elephants or, if aid was not for projects, that the countries' economic policies were conducive to growth and did not benefit only the relatively rich. They were responsible to their own taxpayers. The large donors at least wanted a partnership. The developing countries, in contrast, wanted no surveillance and to control the direction of aid themselves. This was not, however, universally true

113

of the citizens of developing countries. In some such countries people were conscious that aid was often ill-used and encouraged corruption, and that their own governments' policies did not favor the poor.

It was only in the early 1960s that aid statistics came to be published, the DAC was created, and many noncolonial powers other than the United States came to have significant programs. At that time, aid-studying and aid-promoting bodies such as the British Overseas Development Institute (ODI) were formed. Thereafter, there was a flood of literature that discussed technical assistance, capital aid terms, aid for plans or projects, surveillance, leverage, aid tying, aid administration, and so on. Empirical evidence of some of the failings of aid also mounted, and criticism grew.

LAND REFORM

Land reform and land settlement received greater attention than agricultural development within a given land distribution and tenancy framework.[45] There was the United Nations Report of 1951,[46] and Doreen Warriner's Cairo lectures of 1955.[47] These relied mainly on prewar experience in Europe and Mexico. Very important land reforms were taking place in LDCs in the late 1940s and 1950s. The most radical, successful, and comprehensive were in Japan, Taiwan, and South Korea. These were little noticed in the 1950s.[48] R. P. Dore's book on the Japanese reform appeared in 1959.[49] Wolf Ladejinsky, one of the architects of this reform, which was promoted by General MacArthur, never seems to have written a full public account. Ladejinsky also advised on the Taiwan reform. He wrote an early account of the JCRR, which impressed him greatly, and of the beginning of the land reform, in *Foreign Agriculture* in 1950.[50]

Other new but less comprehensive and radical reforms were proceeding in the 1950s in Vietnam, India, Egypt, Iraq, and Bolivia. Except for India, there seems to have been little evaluation during the 1950s. In India there were a number of evaluations, though far fewer than in the 1960s and later. These, and more general work on the agricultural structure in India, have been comprehensively reviewed by P. C. Joshi.[51]

Land settlement was taking place in most parts of the world. In a 1954 article, Lewis wrote that he had read a great deal about experience with settlements in Africa and Asia.[52] But this article seems to be one of the rare attempts to pull the experience together. Arthur Gaitskell's account of the vast and economically successful Gezira scheme, begun in the 1920s, was published in 1959.[53] Israel's remarkable success in this area was not written up until the 1960s, when her agricultural planners came to be in great international demand.

TAXATION

There was a wide consensus that governments must play a major role in mobilizing resources, whether for developmental spending that was not conventionally counted as investment, or for public or private investment. There thus seemed to be a crying need for raising tax revenues. Many tax missions went to developing countries from the United Nations and other technical assistance agencies.[54] Most textbooks of the period devoted many pages to the subject of mobilizing resources via taxation.

While raising revenue to cover real public expenditures can perhaps be said to be the primary purpose of taxation, there are other general objectives that the tax-subsidy system may serve or conflict with. These are: (a) income redistribution, (b) correcting distortions, and (c) stabilization both of general levels of activity and in particular markets. An objective that applied particularly to LDCs was that taxation should not discourage savings and investment and might even raise them. In reaching for those objectives, many other considerations have to be kept in mind: these include administrative feasibility and economy, problems of evasion and corruption, horizontal equity, and avoiding distortions. Finally, political acceptability by both government and public is important, although tax advisers may take the view that that is the responsibility of politicians.

With all this, it is not surprising that public finance is, even to a greater extent than other branches of economics, more of an art than a science. Although it is closely related to conventional welfare economics as far as the problem of distortions is concerned, and to macroeconomic management as far as stabilization is concerned, these disciplines provide clues rather than very firm guidelines.

While increasing revenue was the dominant theme of the 1950s, equity considerations are inescapable when designing a tax system, and they were not neglected. Indeed, strong positive suggestions were made to the effect that tax systems in LDCs should be much more progressive. In this connection, increased reliance on direct taxation was often advocated, although the administrative and political difficulties involved were well recognized.

The effects of taxation on resource allocation were, however, relatively neglected. The pursuit of revenue, whether to increase development spending or for reasons of redistribution, or both, inevitably results in some production or consumption inefficiencies; so also does the use of taxation to promote narrower aims such as industrialization. The minimization of such inefficiencies should have been an important aim, but it was little analyzed. In particular, an understanding of the gross inefficiency that arose from many LDCs' taxation of foreign trade went largely unrecognized until the 1960s (see chapter 9).

Most development economists in the 1950s would have subscribed to the quotation: "The uses of fiscal policy for promoting capital formation and restraining inflation are, however, far more important than those of affecting resource allocation and income distribution. For, as has been stressed previously, the problem of development is much more that of insufficient resources, especially capital deficiency, than it is that of inefficient use of resources."[55] I would not have raised my eyebrows if I had read this around 1960. It later became clear that it was at least as important, perhaps more important, to stress the efficiency with which savings were used as it was to stress the level of savings.

The use of fiscal policy for year-to-year demand management was hardly mentioned.[56] Some attention was paid to stabilizing producers' incomes in the face of fluctuating commodity production or export prices, via progressive export taxes or the operations of commodity boards,[57] but there was no deep analysis of the possibilities. There was some work in the 1940s and 1950s on the related but different problem of stabilizing export prices or country export incomes, but this is more conveniently dealt with in chapters 15 and 17.

Even the briefest account of the 1950s literature on taxation is incomplete without mention of Kaldor, whose tax reform efforts in this period were famous. His advocacy in the 1950s of changes in the bases and forms of direct taxation (originally with the United Kingdom in mind) was the most original contribution to taxation theory of the 1950s. He advised the governments of India, Ceylon, Turkey, Ghana, Mexico, and Guyana.[58] His "Report on Indian Tax Reform"[59] included proposals for an annual wealth tax, capital gains tax, expenditure tax, and gifts tax. This was all legislated, but with more loopholes and exemptions than Kaldor envisaged.[60] Nevertheless, this was probably a transfer of inappropriate technology. The Kaldor taxes had a negligible yield. In 1959, when I tried to design a large increase in revenue for the Indian Third Five Year Plan, it seemed that the great bulk must come from indirect taxation.[61]

Chapter 8

Interim Summary and Forward Linkage

The mainstream development economics of the 1940s and 1950s was structural. It was based on a stereotype of less developed countries, of which the main feature was inflexibility; and this arthritic creature had to operate in an unhelpful world that would impose no invigorating demands. Trade pessimism was dominant. The great hope, and the only hope, according to some, was for newly independent governments to plan change. They had to think big and operate in a big way. Planned investment in new physical capital was the main method. Large reserves of surplus labor would make increased investment easier, but mobilizing savings by increased taxation was a necessary complement, and so was foreign aid. As much new investment as possible must flow into industry, which, in view of export pessimism, would be mainly import substituting. This investment, since it would be centrally planned to take account of interindustrial relations and trade inelasticities, would be more productive than market-directed investment. In view of the lack of private entrepreneurship, and the poor development of markets in LDCs, the role of government was very great. Few doubted that the primary aim of LDC governments was to improve the standard of living of the mass of the people.

These were the main features of the dominant school, and they are only slightly caricatured. The leading thinkers of the period displayed great originality. But they were being original in theorizing about the behavior of a creature concerning which extremely little was known. Some had little experience of LDCs. Others who did, still could not know a great deal (even about their own country), because figures and facts were lacking, and research into behavioral relationships was virtually nonexistent. A priori postulation and premature stereotyping ran far ahead of empirical research. Hypotheses were accepted as facts, and it has taken years of patient work to undermine the myths thus created.

One wonders why anyone thought that the pattern of LDC output was inflexible. A priori and historical considerations should have suggested the opposite. Agriculture was much more important in LDCs than in MDCs, and farm output is more flexible than factory output. History, moreover, showed that LDC farmers would switch crops if incentives were offered—there is almost no such thing as an original indigenous crop; crops, like people, always come from somewhere else. Poor people are more mobile than richer ones, since they have fewer possessions and their children are often not in school. The facts about large migrations both within and between LDCs were surely known. There were also fewer immobility-creating institutions in LDCs. Only financial capital was less mobile, because of inadequate financial institutions. But even this could be exaggerated. For instance, interest rates were not very different in different parts of India, and indigenous banking was quite well developed. In general, the poorer and less capital intensive an economy, the more flexible its output structure was likely to be. The exception was, and is, in areas where there was specialization on tree crops and mining. But this was not a vast part of the LDC world.

Subsequent research and events have shown that most of the presumptions outlined above were wrong. Neither large nor small farmers proved to be stuck in the mud. In general, entrepreneurs were not lacking, and investment opportunities were often quickly seized. Trade proved to be a great engine of growth where LDC policies permitted it to be so. For only a few countries have external conditions been consistently unfavorable. Planning was, by and large, a failure, and sometimes a disaster. Big pushes, where they occurred, resulted in much wasted investment and a piling up of debt and inflation.[1] Large reserves of surplus labor did not exist. LDC governments were not always benevolent and almost nowhere showed much concern for the welfare of the poorest sections of society.

However, not all the accusations leveled at the economists of the 1950s are accurate, and exceptions can always be found. The now frequent accusation of excessive optimism, and that development was considered an easy matter, does not stick. Growth of per caput income turned out to be faster than almost any economist predicted, and many adumbrated obstacles turned out to be phantasms. Economists did not claim, even by default, that physical capital was all that was needed. They did warn that the LDCs' obsession with industrialization might be overdone. That there was an overemphasis on growth is perhaps more justified, though it is hard to find anyone preaching growth at any cost; and that there was an optimum rate of investment, less than the maximum, was part of the literature. Lack of attention to poverty and distribution was, however, evident.

Although the "trickle-down" theory in development economics is merely a stick invented to belabor the past, very few economists warned that the style of development adopted by most LDCs was likely to defer benefits for the mass of the people almost indefinitely. One of these very few was Jacob Viner. He wrote in 1951:

> In all the literature on economic development I have seen, I have not found a single instance where statistical data in terms of aggregates and averages have not been treated as providing adequate tests of the degree of achievement of economic development. I know, moreover, of no country which regards itself as underdeveloped which provides itself with the statistical data

necessary for the discovery of whether or not growth in aggregate national wealth and in per caput income are associated with decrease in the absolute or even relative extent to which crushing poverty prevails.[2]

With only a handful of exceptions, this was still true twenty years later.

PART III

A Resurgence of Neoclassical Economics After 1960

Chapter 9

Planning, Trade, and Labor Markets After 1960

Planning

From the mid-1960s on, the planning literature concerning less developed countries falls into three distinct parts. First, there are descriptions and critiques of actual planning, which are almost invariably critical.[1] These are most often written by political theorists, or organization men, although there are some by critical economists.[2] Second, there are cookbooks, written by applied economists.[3] Third, there are those fighting on the theoretical fringes of economics and mathematics. The latter two categories overlap and may even communicate. But most theoretical modelers seem to live in a different world from those who worry about planning as it is.

By the late 1960s, there was an armful of books and articles with variations on the title "Crisis in Planning,"[4] which shows just what great and unjustified expectations had been entertained. Planning was evidently a failure, and it did not recover in the 1970s either. But what sort of planning was it that failed, and in what sense was it a failure?

We have seen that planning and plans have various purposes and that one was to attract aid. For this purpose, a plan had to claim to be about the whole economy, that is, to be comprehensive. Thus, donors would not usually regard a budget deficit as a reason for aid. It had to throw up a balance-of-payments deficit while also plausibly claiming consistency or viability in other respects. Backing such claims required at least some elements of sectoral disaggregation, with target figures. The targets in some sectors might be simply projections (that is, the government need not be claiming to exercise control over everything). A second reason for producing a plan is that it is a political symbol. We shall not be concerned with these purposes of planning and need only remark that, if plans repeatedly fail in the sense of bearing no relation to subsequent events, they will surely lose their political value. This has clearly happened in India and elsewhere. Aid donors may be more gullible, but they, too, have come to rely less on a country's plan. What we shall be concerned with is planning as a means of steering the economy toward the fulfillment of national objectives in the middle run to long run (say, five to fifteen years).

The cries of "crisis in planning" in the 1960s preceded the reawakened interest in distribution. The evidence was the failure to achieve targets, both at the macro and micro levels. If not due to unforeseeable exogenous events—harvest failure, a slump in the price of an important export, etc.—the failure tended to be regarded as a failure of implementation. This was, however, not a satisfactory diagnosis for several reasons. First, the plan was often not intended to be implemented. Second, it was often unimplementable because it was, in fact, not consistent. Third, since there were often no levers or instruments in particular sectors, especially private sectors,[5] the "targets" should be regarded as merely projections or exhortations. Fourth, there were often no sectoral plans or projects that could possibly be prepared in time to give reality to the investment allocations of the plan.

The fact that, in most LDCs, there are large areas of the economy over which the government has only the indirect controls of manipulating the price mechanism, selective credit controls, and the negative control of prohibiting some investments or transactions, has led to the claim that the plans are essentially indicative. Usually, this is a far-fetched claim, for the close consultation with industrialists (the hallmark of French indicative planning in the 1950s and 1960s) was, with some exceptions, lacking. More important, if the plans were indicative, they were counterindicative. To the extent that decentralized sectoral investment decisions (public or private) were ever based on the plan, they were at least as likely to have been worsened as improved. Sometimes, they were fortunately not based on the plan.

The most essential feature of a comprehensive development plan is the attempt to allocate investment with a view to altering the structure of the economy. The worst feature is that such sectoral and subsectoral allocations (for example, to branches of industry) were often made not merely without there being investment projects, but without examination of whether any potential investments in that sector would be likely to be adequately socially profitable. It is rather like an architect designing a building with no knowledge of the strength of the materials—the building blocks—that might be used. It could thus be a redeeming feature that so much of so many plans went unimplemented. However, misallocation of investment is not a prerogative of comprehensive central planning. Probably there has been as much inefficient industry created in defiance of comparative advantage, and as many opportunities for good industrial investments (especially for export) missed in Latin American countries, with little emphasis on comprehensive planning, as in India.

One can be more sure that certain sins of omission and wrong emphasis partly resulted from the insistence on central comprehensive planning. We shall discuss this under two headings: level, and range and horizons.

LEVELS OF PLANNING—PROJECTS

The importance of distinguishing planning levels can be most easily illustrated in industry (partly perhaps because the planning literature is anyway dominated by industrial planning). I believe that until recently the worst neglect was project planning. I deal particularly with the neglect of social cost-benefit analysis to help in the design of, and ultimately to accept or reject, particular investment projects.[6]

One can distinguish three reasons for this neglect. The first reason, an argument we have already met,[7] was that comprehensive planning enthusiasts among economists insisted that the costs and benefits of one project depended on others. While it is undoubtedly true, its importance is, in my opinion, often overrated. The further argument that therefore everything must be decided simultaneously (every five years) by a central authority can appeal only to those who live in cloud cuckoo land. Some others argued, in effect, that immeasurable benefits were so important (and measurable ones so uncertain) that the seat of a planner's pants, woven perhaps with threads plucked from history or the structure and coefficients of more developed countries, would prove a better guide than laborious attempts to measure the social value of the effects of the investment. I shall not go into the reasons why I reject these arguments, since I have written so much on the subject elsewhere.*

The second reason was that only in the 1960s did economists begin to learn that many industrial projects in LDCs were apparently producing goods at an enormously higher cost than the cost of importing them. A simple form of cost-benefit analysis, which in effect contemplated a shadow price only for foreign exchange (now known as the "domestic resource cost" method), showed that the domestic resources used in saving foreign exchange by import substitution not only varied widely but were often so great as to imply a value (or shadow price) of foreign exchange that was far too high to be credible.[8]

A third reason (deriving from the second) was that there was no cookbook available for the concoction of a consistent set of shadow prices. In the 1950s, there was wide agreement already that actual prices in developing countries, especially wages, were misleading and therefore that shadow pricing was required (for example, Chenery, Tinbergen). We have already referred to the

---

*For example, I. M. D. Little and J. A. Mirrlees, *Project Appraisal and Planning for Developing Countries*, Hememann Educational, London, and Basic Books, New York, 1974.

"investment criteria" literature, in which the considerations that could have led to a formulation of shadow prices were deployed. A. K. Sen gave an admirable account of these arguments in his *Choice of Techniques*.[9] But he presented the issues as dependent on whether output or growth should be maximized (an issue that dominated the discussions of the 1950s to the exclusion of more important considerations), without showing how a compromise decision in terms of the relative value of investment and consumption would lead to a determination of the shadow price of labor, or could otherwise be incorporated into a logically consistent set of usable shadow prices.[10] This step waited upon the work of S. A. Marglin.[11] The first cookbook available was the Organization for Economic Cooperation and Development *Manual*.[12] It was followed by the United Nations Industrial Development Organization (UNIDO) guidelines,[13] and by a revision of the OECD *Manual*.[14] These volumes are formally very similar, but the work of Little and Mirrlees puts greater stress on the price distortions arising from excessive protection.[15] Shadow pricing based mainly on the Little-Mirrlees methodology has been adopted by most of the main donor agencies, which have derived their own manuals from it.[16] In the 1970s several LDCs incorporated project appraisal departments, using shadow prices, in their planning machinery, notably India and Ceylon,[17] and probably also Korea and maybe others.[18] How effective this innovation will be in the long run remains to be seen.

LEVELS OF PLANNING—INDUSTRIAL PROGRAMMING

Industrial programming is the second level of planning. It becomes desirable when there are good reasons for supposing that one project, say a fertilizer plant, might be far from optimal if designed without considering other fertilizer plants in the future or in other parts of the country (and, perhaps, also mines or plants to produce its inputs). This arises primarily when there are economies of scale. Foreign trade tends to eliminate the difficulties and would do so altogether if there were no transport costs and there were a perfectly competitive market. Thus, in a closed economy with a rising demand for fertilizers, there is a trade-off between building small plants quite frequently (losing economies of scale but not suffering excess capacity) and building large plants less often. With perfectly competitive trade, the problem vanishes. One either builds an optimum-sized plant (taking into account any nontraded input elasticities) and runs it to capacity by exporting, or it is not worth building a plant at all. In this case, single-project evaluation is correct. Thus, we can also say that industrial programming is most likely to be useful in the industrial subsectors that produce nontraded goods (recognizing that if foreign demand is inelastic, it may be necessary also in the case of traded goods with important scale economies), especially as economies of scale are common in these subsectors (transport and power).[19]

It is thus true that some projects, but only some, are best designed and appraised as parts of a whole. Development of the methods required for the optimization of such industrial sector programs began, in the LDC context, with A. Manne's work in India and have been further elaborated in recent years.[20] It is important to note, however, that the planning of industrial sectors, involving several subprojects, often undertaken at different times and places, is essentially complementary to the project analysis work reviewed in the previous section. Shadow prices have and should be used in the same manner; and each subproject, allowing for its effects on foreign trade and on other subprojects, should pass the same tests, as should the entire program.

The highest stage of industrial planning is to plan it all. This is not only impossible to do well, but also unnecessary. Plans are stuffed with commodity balances (production *plus* imports equals domestic use *plus* stock changes *plus* exports). In the event, the equality holds of necessity, but the components usually bear very little relation to the planned figures—nor should they. The amounts of particular commodities that are produced, imported, and exported should be by-products of good planning, not objectives. Furthermore, even India produces commodity balances for only upwards of one hundred commodities, while the total number of distinct commodities is numbered in millions.

LEVELS OF PLANNING—OTHER SECTORS

How far does the distinction of levels of planning apply in other sectors? In agriculture, it applies rather well. There are many agricultural investment projects that do not need to be regarded as part of a system that should itself be optimized. But there are great projects, such as the planning of a whole river basin, that do need to be so regarded and are therefore analogous to industrial programs. Neither should be beyond the reach of cost-benefit analysis. Some agriculturalists seem to be biased against the economic analysis of investments. For example, Wortman and Cummings entitle an eleven-line section "De-emphasizing Benefit-Cost Analysis." Elsewhere they claim that economic analysts will overestimate the benefits of large irrigation schemes because they will assume that all the supporting complementary inputs will be in place. The neglect of these inputs (field channels, drainage, reeducation of farmers, supply of fertilizers and pesticides) has been frequently noted. But it seems to me that a good economic analysis will call attention to the necessity for such inputs if the projected benefit is to be realized, and make it a little more likely that they will be provided. They also argue[21] that the economic analyst will underestimate the benefit of small schemes, assuming that the measurement of benefits will neglect a number of factors that standard methods in fact allow for (for example, multiplier effects) and will neglect income distribution, which can also be allowed for if the country authorities permit it. (And it is, for instance, allowed for in current World Bank methodology.) Many cost-benefit analyses of agricultural and rural investments have been undertaken in the 1970s, a few by private researchers[22] and many more by the World Bank and other agencies. They tend to show high returns. We discuss agricultural planning again in chapter 10, where the subjects of education and family planning are also briefly treated.

THE RANGE AND HORIZONS OF CENTRAL GOVERNMENT PLANNING

The critics rightly attribute part of the failure of planning, as they observe it, to trying to do too much. An obvious conclusion is to argue that planning had better be limited to the public sector. Let us start with this as a preliminary guideline. The most essential role of a planning commission or department is to try to achieve better allocations of the investment and other developmental expenditures approved in annual budgets. These expenditures will normally form part of longer run programs of ministries or agencies (which must surely do their own forward planning). If it is to achieve this, the plan must be an expression of consensus as to the relative importance of these programs, and this consensus should have been achieved with the aid of such expertise as the planning commission has, or can muster, as to the benefits and costs of such programs. If, as will inevitably happen, cuts have to be made (or, more rarely, there is an unexpected increase in resources), the planning commission should be able to advise where least harm is likely to be done by the cuts (or what is the best use of temporarily surplus resources). In many LDCs, this limited role is far from being achieved. It can hardly be achieved if there is no effective budgetary control over departmental expenditures, as is often the case.

A major part of effective planning should lie, however, with the ministries, agencies, and public enterprises. If we ask the question what needs most to be planned, the answer will be programs in the nontraded goods sectors of the economy—in health, education, roads, ports, power supply, etc. (Some of these programs cut across departmental boundaries, in which case special interdepartmental agencies may be needed.)

The idea of reducing the need for central planning by limiting it to the public sector is not, however, very satisfactory. It begs the question of what is, and should be, in the public sector and neglects the distinction between centralized and decentralized price-mechanism planning. Far more satisfactory is the economist's typical answer. Put more faith in the price mechanism. As we saw in chapter 3, this does not alter the fact that all expenditure is planned by someone or some agency. What it implies is that the coordination of different plans is left more to the price mechanism, while the central government seeks to improve this mechanism. Unfortunately, the price mechanism *is* badly distorted in many LDCs, which is bound to throw more burden on central evaluation of investments if good decisions are to be made (because decentralized agencies, as well as the private sector, cannot usually be expected to use shadow prices).[23] The moral is obvious.

Even where the price mechanism is reasonably undistorted, there remain very large areas where investment budgeting or control is indicated: (1) where the price mechanism is no guide because the product cannot be sold on a market; (2) where there are overriding social reasons against it being marketed (for example, education); (3) where uncoordinated investment decisions might go very wrong; and (4) in the case of very large investments, which would make a noticeable dent in the total amount of investment. The first and second points need no comment. The third arises primarily where the investments are lumpy, and have scale economies, and where there is no monopoly. For instance, a large country might have several port authorities, and competition could lead to overcapacity or expansion in the wrong place. Either a monopoly should be created, or there should be central planning. Of course, this is a traditional case for a public monopoly, since a private monopoly would need to be controlled anyway to prevent restriction of facilities and excessive profits.

With their small markets, LDCs have created (by protection) a number of industries where economies of scale suggest the need for a monopoly. With traded goods (for example, automobiles) there should be less need for public ownership, since profits can be controlled by permitting imports and adjusting the amount of protection. Whether or not such a monopoly is in the public or private sector, investment planning can be decentralized, with the exception of very large investments.

Very large investments will generally require finance from a public agency and have to be vetted on this account anyway. An exception could be a foreign-financed investment. Large foreign investments should be, and are, controlled, if only for political reasons.

It is evident that there is a lot for central investment planning to concern itself with, even if only the most urgent requirements for such planning and controls are met.

A Resurgence of Neoclassical Economics After 1960

The critics of planning have sometimes suggested that planners should content themselves with one-year plans. This does not seem to me to be a sensible limitation. The essence of planning is to look ahead. Many investments have a long lead time, and one year's investment expenditure invariably commits future expenditure (if it is not to be wasted). But I do not mean by this that an attempt to target or even predict the state of the whole economy in detail over a five-year stretch or longer is sensible—far from it. It is very difficult to discern what the future will bring, and it should be attempted only where the need is greatest, and successful prediction most likely. Flexibility should be a keynote when addressing the future.

COUNTRY-WIDE PLANNING MODELS

A planning model is often confused with planning. Students who take planning courses are taught to construct planning models, not how to plan. Planners on the spot are also often mainly occupied with models, rather than with planning. However, their models sometimes have a lot of influence on the plan, even if little influence on what actually happens.

Typical planning models assume fixed input coefficients and linear relationships and aim at terminal-year consistency. Some arbitrary assumptions have to be made concerning levels of terminal capital stocks. Optimization, if attempted, is achieved through linear programming. Typically, many constraints have to be introduced to prevent the model producing extreme results. This applies particularly to exports, which are arbitrarily constrained. Many commentators, including the best model builders, have pointed out the rather obvious objections. The basic data are often very weak and out of date. Coefficients are not fixed, and substitution occurs in reality, though not in the model. The model often initially produces absurd results, and there has to be much juggling with the constraints to produce "plausible" results. A reading of the experts[24] suggests to me that none of them would claim that investments should be allocated between sectors on such a basis (though this would appear to have been done in India by the time of the Fifth Plan). If this is so, I would concur. For instance, such planning would have effectively prevented the economic miracles of the Far East. Exports would undoubtedly have been constrained at levels far below those achieved; hence investment would have been prevented in export industries, and the achievements thus themselves prevented.

The solution of a model yields shadow prices. Can we identify these with the shadow prices whose use is advocated in project planning and programming? The reader can be referred to M. Bruno, "Planning Models, Shadow Prices and Project Evaluation."[25] To quote:

> Models often turn out shadow prices that look unrealistic under any kind of test of "reasonableness." Dominance of linear relations, for the sake of computational simplicity, and artificial attempts to prevent the almost inevitable flip-flop behavior often cause jerky or otherwise unreasonable behavior of price solutions. Lack of sufficient factor or commodity substitution possibilities (which would presumably be found in real life but not in the model) and too narrowly defined constraints are also contributing causes.

The planning models have really been designed for direct solutions, and the more sectors and equations the better from this point of view. (Even so, they are inevitably far too aggregated to solve for the amount of investment required for particular commodities.) It may be possible to devise smaller formal models that are helpful in assisting the more judgmental and informal approach to shadow pricing advocated in the project planning manuals. But this is, I think, more hope than firm promise.

There has undoubtedly been a tremendous development in planning models since the early 1960s, and great efforts are in progress to make them mirror reality better. Again, the reader is referred to Blitzer et al. It seems to me, however, that there is still a long way to go and little consensus as to the best route to take. In the meantime, it may be useful to sup with the devil, but one needs a long spoon.

CONCLUSION

The theme has been that the planning emphasis of the 1950s was topsy-turvy. Comprehensive overall planning was most emphasized, then sectoral planning, then projects. The order of importance is the reverse. LDCs suffered from a lack of projects, while many of those that came to fruition had poor, sometimes even negative, social returns. The interdependency between projects was overstated; but where industrial programming was most essential, in the nontraded fields of power and transport, and in the more developed of the LDCs, it was often poor (as witness India's recurrent bottlenecks, despite the overall growth rate always falling below planned levels).[26] The planning of agricultural administration and services to agriculture, and research, was neglected in most countries. In at least one country where it was not neglected (that is, Taiwan) it was, by common accord, extremely successful. Few, nowadays, make high claims for comprehensive planning. Where planning is now admired it is mostly sectoral planning of manufacturing. Japan is often held up as a model, but only in the above respect, for no one could admire the Japanese attempts at *comprehensive* planning, where targets have been as awry as anywhere and the Economic Planning Agency has had little or no effect even on public capital formation.[27]

Trade Regimes

PROTECTION AND EXPORTS

Some of the undesirable results of the import substitution policies of the 1950s had been recognized by Prebisch by the time of the first UNCTAD in 1964.[28] These included capital intensity, low value-added at international prices, loss of scale, lack of competition, and the growth of "inessential" production behind trade barriers. These disadvantages were placed in the context of a plea for reducing barriers in the industrial centers. There was, however, no clear recognition that protection inhibits exports, or that the LDCs' failing share of world trade was due either to this or to lagging agricultural production. The idea of the long-term decline in the terms of trade was still in place, and policies of import substitution continued. No distinction was drawn between protection by tariffs and by controls. The philosophy was still one of controlled trade.

Destruction of the UNCTAD doctrine began at about the same time as it was established. It was assisted by the development of two useful weapons, the "effective rate of protection" (ERP) and the "domestic resource cost" method of investment analysis (DRC); and also by an important theoretical contribution. First to come was the ERP. W. M. Corden's book on the subject contains a history of the concept.[29] Although there were isolated earlier instances of its use, it did not become part of the furniture of economists' minds until the 1960s. The ERP is an attempt to measure the general equilibrium effects of a country's whole system of trade restrictions on value added in particular activities. There are grave problems arising from so ambitious an undertaking. One is that it is rather hard to estimate the effects on the prices of nontraded inputs;[30] and another, possibly more serious problem, is that the system of protection will cause changes in techniques as well as prices. There are several rival measures of ERP. With none of them can one say for sure that, for any pair of activities, resources will have been drawn into the one with the highest ERP. So ERP is not a wholly satisfactory measure of the degree of distortion. V. K. Ramaswami and T. N. Srinivasan attacked the concept as useless for the above reason, and also for its redundancy.[31] Their argument was that if there were no revenue reasons for trade taxes (in a "small" country), then there should be no protection. So why measure it? If there were revenue reasons, then one had to design an optimal tax system. This would take account of elasticities of supply, demand, and substitution. The ERP would be a mere by-product. As so often happens with planners and bureaucrats, in this case applied economists were fastening their attention on an irrelevant magnitude. This is all true. Nevertheless, ERP *is* a measure of distortion, even though a flawed one.[32] In LDCs it first came to be used in Pakistan.[33] Researchers were hard at work in the late 1960s, under the umbrellas of either the OECD or the World Bank project or both.[34] Despite the flaws, these inquiries effectively showed that (a) the average effective protection of manufacturing was very high indeed in some LDCs in the 1960s, notably in Chile, Brazil, Pakistan, and India; high in the Philippines, moderate in Mexico and Taiwan, and about zero in Malaya. Perhaps more important, it showed that (b) it varied from negative to astronomical heights in different industries for no obvious reason; (c) there was a systematic bias against exports; and (d) there was a tendency to protect capital goods less than intermediates, and intermediates less than final consumption goods.

The ERP should not, however, be taken to be even a rudimentary measure of where comparative advantage lies.[35] The DRC measure, can, however, be so taken.[36] It was used in the 1960s, to draw attention to the apparent maldistribution of investment in Turkey.[37] With modifications from the original formulation, to take account of imperfections in labor markets, it has been extensively used in the 1970s where full cost-benefit analysis could not be applied.[38] With the appropriate modifications it differs from project analysis only in that it uses conventional depreciation allowances rather than discounted flows and present values. Full Little/Mirrlees style cost-benefit analysis of existing investments and projects also began to get under way in the late 1960s under the auspices of the OECD Development Centre, and partly in preparation for Little, Scitovsky, and Scott (in which some results are reported), and also for the OECD Manual. They, too, showed very mixed results, with some accepted projects showing negative rates of return.[39]

It should by now be evident that investment planning criteria and the analysis of comparative advantage, originally two separate specializations in economics, have come together.[40] This is as it should be, since, in an open economy, they must be the same thing. A planner cannot rationally ignore comparative advantage, although he, or his political masters, may believe some outputs to be advantageous, even when they show up very badly in the typical economists' calculus, which regards personal utilities as the only objective.

Apart from empirical work that suggested there was a good deal wrong with import-substitution projects, other work undermined further aspects of the 1950s consensus. Diaz Alejandro rightly refers to the "rout of export pessimism."[41] In 1964, Manmohan Singh's work showed that supply factors, including controls and mismanagement, accounted for a large part of India's poor export performance in the 1960s.[42] Other works of the 1960s that cast some doubts on export pessimism were those of De Vries[43] and Lary.[44] By 1970, Little, Scitovsky, and Scott could conclude that export incentives (and disincentives) do work.[45] This applied not only to manufactures, but also to primary products, in many of which the LDC share of world trade was declining. That incentives work is shorthand for saying that export demand and domestic supply are both elastic. Export pessimism had been based largely on gloomy views about the growth and elasticity of world demand. Not only did the purchasing power of exports from the LDCs in fact grow much faster in the 1960s than in the 1950s (three times as fast), but the 1960s also saw the undermining of the suppositions that peasant producers did not respond to incentives,[46] and that a lack of local entrepreneurship and good management would prevent any elastic response in manufactures. The fantastic response of Korea and Taiwan in manufactures was already apparent; but it was at first often wrongly and without evidence attributed mainly to the multinationals, as if exports by multinationals did not count at all!

The Singer/Prebisch argument of a declining trend in the terms of trade of primary goods had suffered in the 1950s the attacks of many critics, who could at least claim that no good case had been made out. It suffered a further rebuff in 1963 from Robert E. Lipsey, but it remained UNCTAD doctrine at least into the 1970s.[47] Let us jump straight to the latest meticulous assessment. John Spraos finds that from the 1870s to 1938 there was a trend deterioration of about ¼–⅓ percent per annum but that Prebisch had exaggerated the trend "at worst by a factor of more than three." From 1900 to 1970 there is no evidence of a trend.[48] Clearly after 1970, oil would have produced a positive trend. Spraos disclaims having had the last word. I would hope he has—at least for twenty-five years. Apart from the trend debate, it should be noted that the LDC terms of trade worsened during the 1950s, starting from the very favorable levels caused by the Korean War, and improved from the early 1960s to the early 1970s.

The ERP had served mainly to highlight apparent price distortions, and especially that LDC regimes were biased against exports. But a more purely theoretical advance underpinned both the various forms of social cost-benefit analysis mentioned above and the recommendations for reform of the price mechanism and trading regimes that have been abundant in the 1970s. It came to be recognized that domestic distortions, which had for long been regarded as arguments for protection, were best dealt with by internal measures, mainly taxes and subsidies but also perhaps by institutional improvements. Protection was invariably inferior (or second best) and might often make things worse. There had been some earlier scattered recognition of the proposition that subsidies were better than tariffs, but the more general proposition that the way to deal with a distortion is to attack it at its source did not become part of the standard mental equipment of economists until the mid-1960s.[49]

Only two arguments remain for protection by taxation (and none for protection by quota and other nontariff barriers). The first is the traditional optimum tariff (or export tax) argument, by means of which a country may take advantage of imperfect elasticities in world markets. In the case of a large LDC, this could be an argument for a low tariff across the board. Even small LDCs could advantageously impose a tariff where there is a monopoly supplier. A few other LDCs may be able to impose beneficial export taxes on a few commodities but, for obvious reasons, only if they can concert such taxes with other actual and potential producers. The second argument is that traded goods are relatively easy to tax at the point of exit or entry. The word "relatively" is important. If it is desirable to tax a particular commodity, and it can be as easily taxed at the domestic point of production, then there is no case for protection, for the import duty can be matched by an equal excise tax. For some countries, and some goods, massive smuggling suggests that it may actually be easier to tax domestic production.[50]

The upshot is that industrialization could be adequately and efficiently encouraged without the bias against exports, and without the inappropriate choice of import substitution projects, which was so rife. A sketch of appropriate policies was made in

Little, Scitovsky, and Scott, chapters 4 and 9. It was, however, recognized that transition from an overprotected system to a more open one was not likely to be easy, and a chapter on "Problems of Transition" was included.

Both contemporaneously with Little, Scitovsky, and Scott and its companion volumes, and in the 1970s, there has been a great deal of further work on LDC trade regimes and on the general problem of using trading opportunities to maximum advantage in the process of development. There is indeed so much that only a very sketchy review is here possible.[51]

We divide the work into three (overlapping) categories. First, there is a description of trade regimes and their results. Where this has been of the more closed economies, the inefficiency of import substitution and the bias against exports of both primary products and manufactures fully confirm the findings of Little, Scitovsky, and Scott. But there has been a lot more work on the open economies, especially on Korea and Taiwan. Starting in the years around 1960, these countries made policy changes that by the middle 1960s combined selective protection for certain import competing sectors with a virtual free-trade regime for exporters—by which we mean that exporters could obtain inputs (including tradable domestic inputs) at world market prices, while the effective exchange rate for exporters was close to that which would have ruled under free trade. Overall effective protection for industry was zero for Korea, and, of course, Hong Kong, and low for Taiwan and Singapore. The consequential growth of exports was phenomenal, far exceeding what anyone could have predicted or did predict.

While the export boom can certainly be attributed to the policy reforms resulting in such trade regimes, it would be wrong to attribute the whole success of these countries, in terms of employment, growth, and income distribution, to such trade policies. Nevertheless, it is impossible to doubt that they played a very large role.[52] Many countries in the 1960s and 1970s started to "promote" exports. But generally speaking, this "promotion" was only a partial offset to their overvalued exchange rates and the fact that the prices of domestic tradable inputs into exports were above world prices.[53] Export subsidization was also usually selective (unlike Korea and Taiwan, where most exporters got similar treatment). While on average a bias against exports remained, such selective subsidization could sometimes lead to an export being more profitable than under free trade. Such export protection could be excessive. However, excesses of this kind are certainly much rarer than in the case of protection of the home market, although a few cases have been unearthed.[54]

That exports have responded strongly to policy changes that improve the incentives can hardly be doubted. In the case of Korea, Taiwan, and Singapore, this is obvious indeed. But there is other evidence also.[55] Of course, no one should advocate exports for their own sake. The bottom line is whether a country's performance (in various dimensions) improves as a result, as all the a priori arguments suggest it should. There is strong evidence that output and growth improve as a higher proportion of domestic production is exported.[56] Among the reasons given for this by Bhagwati[57] were that consequentially increased imports reduced the chaos in the pattern of import substitution incentives and ensured a freer flow of inputs with benefits for capacity utilization and the size of stocks held. The growth of exports made it easier to borrow, and more direct foreign investment was attracted, some of it to the relatively labor-intensive export sector. It seems to me that another more dynamic reason, valid at least for the Far Eastern countries, was that exports were very profitable at both actual and shadow prices and that this led to a rise in savings and investment.

Little, Scitovsky, and Scott claimed also that a more open economy would increase the demand for unskilled labor, and this would tend to lead to greater equality. Since this claim was made, firmer evidence that marginal exports are much more labor intensive than marginal import substitutes is available for several countries.[58] This is, of course, what is to be expected from a simple Hecksher-Ohlin view of comparative advantage. If exports are promoted in a very selective manner, it is possible to have rapidly growing capital-intensive exports. It is also possible to turn an export that has a low direct and indirect domestic capital-labor ratio into one with a high ratio by promoting the domestic production of capital-intensive intermediates. This happened with textiles in Taiwan between 1966 and 1971.[59] However, despite these practical attempts to overthrow Hecksher-Ohlin, the proposition remains valid.

Turning to equality, it was sometimes argued in the 1950s that openness caused inequality. The idea was that exports of primary goods benefited mainly large landowners, or mine-owners. This was true for some countries, especially in Latin America. But it does not apply to countries with more equal land ownership and those in which mineral exports come from nationalized (or, indeed, foreign-owned) undertakings. But, most important, where the greatest effect of removal of the bias against exports is likely to be an increase in the export of labor-intensive manufactures, there openness will be an equalizing force. All observers agree that this was the case in Korea and Taiwan.[60]

Our second category is the design of optimum trading policies. This is not easy, especially as it now forms part of the broader subject of optimal taxation. Or, to put the point more starkly, optimum trading policies are a mere fall-out from optimum tax and subsidy policies.[61] Little, Scitovsky, and Scott put some stress on labor and training subsidies (and possibly production subsidies in special cases where an externality justifying the subsidy sprang from the production itself). So far as I am aware, only the United Kingdom has used labor subsidies to encourage manufacturing employment, though training subsidies are in use in some LDCs. Production subsidies are common everywhere—but these are more often given to sick industries than to those with any supposed developmental role. The most active adviser on how to reform manufacturing incentives tends to stress the use of tariffs-cum-export subsidies.[62] If the export subsidy (together with rebates for indirect taxes on inputs) is designed to see that exports are just about as profitable as production for the home market, then there is, in effect, a system of production subsidies paid for partly by the domestic consumer in the form of higher prices and partly via government subsidies. If domestic sales predominate, then of course the government subsidy is a relatively small burden on the revenue. This system of effective production subsidies, on all output including exports, is a great improvement on mere protection. But it does not go to the heart of the matter, if one believes that the latter may be inadequate employment due to the relatively high wages paid in manufacturing. I have shown elsewhere that the production subsidy given by a tariff can always be transmuted into an input subsidy, provided that domestic production can be taxed as easily as imports.[63] This does not, however, cover cases where it would be desirable to remove the existing tariffs and taxes, as in the case of intermediates. In many LDCs, high-cost production of such intermediates hampers more appropriate downstream activities: high-cost steel handicaps engineering, and high-cost petrochemicals handicap textiles and clothing.[64] There seems to be a strong case for subsidizing (or closing down) these high-cost intermediate plants. In other words, this is a high priority for use of government revenues. However, a realistic general equilibrium analysis (tailor-made to the country in question since taxability and distortions vary greatly) is needed to produce the set of taxes and subsidies that seem best in the circumstances.

The third category of trade regime work has been on problems of the transition. Although not exclusively concerned with this, it is one of the main thrusts of the massive study by the National Bureau of Economic Research (NBER) and is extensively discussed by A. O. Krueger.[65] Twenty-two "liberalization" attempts were recorded for ten countries[66] between 1950 and 1972. Liberalization meant the reduction of trade controls and a more realistic exchange rate. All the attempts involved packages. Devaluation was combined with import liberalization, reduction of tariffs and export subsidies, and deflation, in varying degrees. In some cases, after allowance was made for the changes in tariffs and subsidies, the effective exchange rate change was very small. Most efforts were made in periods of crisis and from a position of government commitment to an overvalued exchange rate. The crisis usually involved loss of reserves or debt rescheduling, but sometimes arose less critically from the fact that the country was plainly import starved, although there was no immediate payments problem. Many efforts were combined with attempts at stabilization.

If a simple devaluation was to be effective, inflation had to be stopped. It was the consequent deflationary measures and the foreign (or International Monetary Fund or World Bank) involvement that often made these attempts unpopular and resulted in a reversal. It must be remembered that the IMF norm was then a fixed rate. But a floating rate or a sliding (trotting) peg was used in several countries. Except for Chile, where the sliding peg rate always remained overvalued, greater success was achieved where stopping inflation was not thought a necessary condition for maintaining liberalization. Brazil, Korea, Israel, and Colombia all used either floating rates or sliding pegs or other means of maintaining a reasonable rate for exports, and all had liberalized substantially by the middle or late 1960s and maintained this position—although of the ten only Israel achieved single-figure inflation in the decade. Of the ten, however, only Korea eliminated the bias against exports.[67]

There are several reasons for failure. The effective devaluation was inadequate, or the bias against exports was not removed or much reduced (for example, India, the Philippines), so that exports did not respond sufficiently. Inflation and a fixed rate continued or were reimposed, for example in Chile under Allende. There was insufficient political and intellectual commitment (India, Chile); an actual reversal for political reasons (Ghana); or bad luck (India again). Needless to say, manufacturers require some expectation of continuing profitability for exports if they are to invest for export production, make products designed for export, and spend money on a marketing organization. In only a few countries was the government commitment to the change of policy sufficient for this expectation.

But although failure was frequent, there was progress among the ten. The Bhagwati-Krueger analysis suggests an increasing degree of liberalization after the mid-1960s. But this should not be exaggerated. Only the "baby tigers" had achieved a high degree of liberalization and rationalization of incentives.

It is clear that crisis, combined with the manifest inefficiencies of ever more complex controls, was the driving force. The countries did not have a well worked out system of incentives that they were striving to achieve, and a fortiori, they did not have a plan for achieving it by stages that would minimize the inevitable transitional costs—nor did the IMF or the IBRD. The Little,

Scitovsky, and Scott volume of 1970 was the first to give a sketch both of a rational system of incentives and of the transitional problems involved in achieving it. Only when a country itself has a strong and determined government that sees the need for reform is reform likely to succeed. In most cases, however, an immediate need for foreign credits resulted in the foreign devil driving. The corollary, however, is that the IMF has been, and will be, called on for credits that will not be of any long-run value, because the government either has no heart for reform or lacks the power to achieve it.

A final word on trade regimes is needed. The economic literature tends to assume that the government creates a price system and that the consequential incentive structure governs decisions as to what to import, or to make, or to make and export. This is only partly true. Almost all LDC governments promote industries directly. The chain of causation is thus reversed. The government first decides on the industry and then twists the price mechanism, most often by applying import controls but also by high tariffs, to limit the degree of subsidy required. This still goes on apace, and the favorites for such promotion are, apart from motorcars, invariably the capital-intensive intermediates with marked economies of scale. Such industries may be appropriate for those few LDCs that are swimming in capital and have to import workers. For other LDCs they not merely waste capital, which could employ people, but also discourage the more labor-intensive activities in which they might be employed.

INSTABILITY

It was widely believed in the 1950s that instability of export receipts was a special problem for LDCs, that it inhibited their development, and that it arose from the volatility of demand in the industrialized countries. This was a natural preconception for those whose thinking was still influenced by the 1930s. But after 1960 the doctrine was mauled by empirical research.

A. I. MacBean found that although from 1946 to 1958 LDC export proceeds were more unstable than those of more developed countries, the difference was not very great.[68] Other findings were that aggregate primary product export proceeds did not fluctuate more than those of manufactures, that fluctuations were due more to domestic disturbances than to export demand variations, and that, if anything, instability favored investment and growth. Much subsequent research, all based on cross-country correlations but employing different measures of instability, country sets, and time periods, has tended to confirm most of these findings. One study, however, found a negative correlation between instability and investment in the 1960s.[69] Other research has suggested that, if anything, the higher the ratio of exports to gross national product the less do export proceeds fluctuate. Summaries of the research can be found in Diaz Alejandro[70] and in P. A. Yotopoulos and J. B. Nugent.[71]

It is worth noting that for both LDCs and MDCs exports were much more stable in the 1960s than in the 1950s. Interest in stabilization schemes therefore flagged. There was a resurgence of instability in the early 1970s and a revival of interest, but most of the analysis of the problems that had been done in the 1950s was buried and only slowly resurrected.

This kind of cross-country analysis, even if it produced firm conclusions, would have little operational significance. Whatever the findings, instability deriving from variations in export demand is a major problem for a few countries. But the inhabitants of such countries, which are small, account for a very small percentage of the population of the LDCs. The problem of instability is not, in this sense, a Third World problem.

THE TWO-GAP MODEL

We have seen that the structuralist preconceptions of the 1950s were undermined in the 1960s and 1970s, partly as a result of empirical research and partly because exports of LDCs grew rapidly despite the bias against them. It is therefore paradoxical that the structuralist two-gap model was born in 1960 and became part of the thinking of the United Nations and aid agencies. This survived into the 1970s, when I can recall a very high United Nations official saying that there had been just two very important ideas in development economics. One was the "two-gap" idea. I forget which the other was—probably "surplus labor."

The idea was common in India in the late 1950s. After a brief

A Resurgence of Neoclassical Economics After 1960

review of India's plans and patterns of trade, I wrote in 1960: "One can conclude that domestic saving is no substitute for aid, so far as financing industrial expansion is concerned. India cannot herself produce the plant and equipment needed, and further austerity would not permit her to buy significantly more capital goods without foreign finance."[72] Later, in 1956, I reviewed the idea more circumspectly while stating the rather strong conditions required for its validity.[73] The treatment, however, was still too much influenced by export pessimism, and it was thought that the theory could still apply to India. However, in the meantime, it had been independently promoted by Chenery and Bruno,[74] and R. I. McKinnon,[75] who incorporated it into growth models. It therefore took off and supported many projections of aid requirements by the UNCTAD and other agencies. I believe two-gap models are still used by the World Bank.

It has long been accepted theory that unless there is very general excess demand, more savings alone will not cure a balance-of-payments deficit without reducing domestic activity. If the latter is to be avoided, "switching" policies in favor of domestic production are also required. That foreign exchange should be regarded as a special bottleneck, over and above savings, therefore requires either the political contention that such switching policies are impossible to implement, or the economic contention that no such policies could be effective. We will here confine ourselves to elaborating the latter.

There are four requirements:

1. It must be impossible to increase export receipts because foreign demand has unit elasticity (or there is a kink in the demand curve).
2. The import bill cannot include any payment for final consumption goods.
3. The import content of current domestic production cannot be reduced.
4. Investment cannot be made more labor intensive (and hence less import intensive) without reducing its social yield.

Given time to make adjustments, I doubt whether any country has ever been in such a position as the above. In the very short run, however, *all* countries are in such a position, for import saving or export expansion always takes time.[76]

Giving aid on the basis of projected foreign exchange deficits is not a good idea, because it inhibits policy and adjustments in favor of increasing exports and increasing labor intensity. Giving aid during a period of adjustment is a different matter, but that is not really encompassed by the notion of a foreign exchange gap, which was always envisaged as at least a medium—if not a long-run—problem of development. Giving aid to supplement domestic savings (and domestic consumption, at least in times of crisis) was the old idea, and the better idea.[77]

Surplus Labor and Labor Markets

THE RURAL SCENE

Twenty-five years and more after the idea of surplus labor was widely accepted, the question of whether it exists anywhere is still asked. But it does not have quite the same meaning. No one thinks that the opportunity cost of labor to the modern sectors of the economy is zero, and this after a doubling in many countries of the number of people in the so-called traditional sectors.

The old view of rural life—a subsistence peasant family agriculture with near zero marginal productivity, some larger landowners employing labor at a conventional wage, and few if any employers outside agriculture—has changed rather dramatically in the past fifteen years. The stylized facts now run somewhat as follows.[78] At peak periods of the agricultural year, all are working from dawn till dusk except those who would not soil their hands for cultural reasons. There is an active labor market, and all but the smallest operators demand outside labor at times. Most peasant families also offer labor for both agricultural and other purposes. There is no sign of the real wage being conventional; it varies from year to year and month to month. The "nutritional" or efficiency wage has yet to be discovered. To all ap-

A Resurgence of Neoclassical Economics After 1960

pearances, in short, the wage is determined by supply and demand. Peasant farmers are active in other markets, for rented land and credit, for inputs and outputs. The interactions of these markets (for example, a sharecropping contract may include not only land but all the others mentioned) are highly complex, quite possibly highly rational, and certainly defy brief description.

UNEMPLOYMENT

It was paradoxical that, as people began to be convinced that there was little surplus labor, concern with unemployment grew. The first work program to analyze the nature and causes of unemployment and underemployment in LDCs was that of the OECD Development Centre in the late 1960s. The first major worldwide survey and interpretation of the facts was that of D. Turnham and I. Jaeger.[79]

We cannot proceed without some discussion of the meanings of terms. First, "open unemployment" refers to those not working at all during the survey period while actively looking for employment. It excludes those who do not look for employment, because they reckon the chances of finding work are small.

"Underemployment" has been given many meanings, some of which were examined in chapter 6. One is the difference between requirements as measured by some production function and availability as measured by normal hours for normal labor force participants. This measure has largely dropped out of use after much criticism of its validity. The second obvious meaning is to count hours actually worked by actual (or potential) participants, and subtract from some norm. The two main difficulties are: (a) that this includes those who do not want to work more, and (b) that the underutilized hours may be available only at certain places and certain times. Thus, underemployment in this sense does not guarantee that there is any willing and available labor, and would in general greatly overestimate the latter. A volitional measure that asks the question whether more work is wanted, at least eliminates those who do not want more work, although it includes some who are already working long hours. A difficulty with many surveys along the latter lines is that it remains unclear what further work would be acceptable, at what wages, and where. Also, the amount of extra work wanted is undetermined.

Finally, there is the so-called poverty definition. The Turnham and Jaeger survey made it clear that very often the major problem was very low earnings rather than unemployment. With the grave difficulties involved in measuring underemployment, together with the facts (see below) that many who worked less than normal hours were not poor and that more who worked long hours were exceedingly poor, it seemed clear that measuring earnings might be a better approach. But this unfortunately led to some inquiries, especially those of the International Labor Organization (ILO), propagating the misuse of language by which all those with earnings below some arbitrary level are termed underemployed, even if they are working a seventy-hour week. Presumably this was done to bring poverty within the terms of reference of the ILO, but it gives rise to analytic confusion, and sometimes the dissemination of meaningless numbers. Low earnings are a matter for concern. But they may or may not be part of an employment problem (see below).

We now turn to a few orders of magnitude, mostly for some year in the first half of the 1970s. Urban open unemployment rates are estimated by the ILO as 6–7 percent for Asia and Latin America, and 11 percent for Africa. The figures for particular countries range from negligible to over 15 percent (Sri Lanka). Rural open unemployment is much lower—it has to be since a much higher proportion of the population is mainly self-employed on the land, where there is always some work, however unproductive.[80] For most countries for which there are any figures it is below 5 percent. Despite much assertion to the contrary, there seems to be no evidence that unemployment rates, either urban or rural, have generally become worse in the postwar period,[81] although the absolute numbers have (absolute numbers, especially in the towns, are an important concern for politicians). Unemployment seems to vary considerably as between countries, but there is no trend in the figures for most individual countries—with a few exceptions that show a decline: Taiwan, Korea, and Syria.[82] Figures for underemployment mean

A Resurgence of Neoclassical Economics After 1960

too many different things to be worth quoting. But there can be no doubt that for many months of the year the rural population in most LDCs is underemployed in the simple sense that many do little work; this does not necessarily mean, however, that very many would be willing to work more at the low seasonal rate for casual labor that prevails, or work far from home in the slack periods.[83]

THE EMPLOYMENT PROBLEM—THE CONCEPT

As we shall define it here, there is an employment problem if there is a suboptimal use of voluntarily available labor. We mean by "suboptimal" that welfare could, other things being equal, be increased by a redeployment of such labor or potential labor. In other words, actual wages are not equal to the shadow wage.[84]

Surplus labor was an extreme form of the employment problem. If there were no loss of output in agriculture, and the marginal product in industry was positive (equal to the wage), then redeployment would clearly raise national income (apart from movement costs). The shadow wage is then zero (neglecting dynamics and distribution). But there is also an employment problem if the shadow wage is positive but below the actual wage. This situation can be called one of "surplus labor" in a weak sense. But the old strong sense is so entrenched in the literature that it is now better to avoid using it in a different sense, and rather to talk of labor market "distortions," or divergencies of shadow and market wages.

Differences in marginal products in different activities do not necessarily constitute an employment problem. The example of small farms that use (at times) only family labor, and large farms that use only hired labor (discussed in chapter 10) can be used to make the point. The marginal product on the family farm may (at times) be below the agricultural wage, for the reasons discussed in chapter 10, and therefore below the marginal product on the large farm. But there is no distortion of the labor market implied, since, given the distribution of land holdings, the difference in productivities arises from the free choice of family members. There is a distortion, but it is in the land market. If there were a perfect market in land tenancies, the large-farm operator could profitably rent out more land to peasant families.

Open unemployment is not necessarily a distortion. Some searching around is required if round pegs are to find round holes, so that some unemployment can be productive. This is the traditional "frictional" unemployment, which could be quite high when there are rapid changes in both employment opportunities and the size, age, and educational structure, of the labor force.

It has been argued that there can be a conflict between employment and output, implying that output might be maximized by leaving some unemployed. We have defined the employment problem in terms of distortions in the labor market that result in a failure to maximize welfare, not output. If defined in the latter manner, which is more usual but less correct, it has been suggested that there may be a conflict between employment and output. This dates back to the structuralist idea of fixed-factor proportions, implying that maximum output may leave some labor redundant. It could be fully employed only by using inferior techniques—those that use both more labor and more capital per unit of output. I believe that, in reality, substitution possibilities are such that the entire labor force could everywhere be employed at a positive marginal product. Even if this were not true, there could be no *technical* reason for the use of inferior techniques: one can always employ redundant labor—quite a common practice.

Despite the above, conflict can arise, but only as a result of price and wage distortions, which, for some reason or another, cannot be corrected. Thus, it is easy to imagine the actual price system in a country resulting in a low demand for labor, such that the government feels that it must take some action to remedy the consequences. It might do this by a public works scheme that uses some capital, even if only a little, to produce a valueless output, clearly an inferior technique. Output would be greater if the government subsidized industry to give the same employment and then used the capital thereby saved in a productive manner.

Finally, on our definition, the employment problem vanishes if labor is deployed to maximize welfare, *not* output. What difference does this make? Suppose we have two regions in a country, A and B, with a high cost of movement (in terms of welfare) between them. B is infertile and the people underemployed. Investment in A, where there is full employment, would yield more output. But although investing in B is technically inferior, it could produce more welfare. However, we must ask the further question, "Why worry about employment?" Is not welfare increased still further by not investing in B, but instead transferring income to the people there? The answer is "Yes," unless employment is deemed to be valuable in itself, over and above its income-creating aspect.[85] Thus, we have here an employment problem (rather than a poverty or distributional problem), only if employment is regarded as valuable in itself—or if transfers are administratively difficult or themselves regarded as demeaning. Such considerations can be important.

IS THERE AN EMPLOYMENT PROBLEM IN PRACTICE?

Another way of putting the question is to ask whether labor markets function well. To avoid misunderstanding, let us emphasize that a well-functioning labor market may still leave a great deal to be desired. First, it does not imply that most people work "normal" hours. In a poor country with a highly seasonal agriculture, people will work for few hours in the year; further work work has such low productivity that it is better to sit and talk. Second, it does not imply that there is an optimum level of employment. The aggregate demand for labor may be much less than would maximize welfare, but this can arise from distortions in the product and capital markets.

Consider rural labor markets first. There is no doubt that empirical work in many countries in the past fifteen to twenty years has shown that they work a lot better than had previously been supposed.[86] By and large, people can get agricultural and off-farm work at the going wage, and supply and demand are equated without many nonprice restraints. There are doubtless areas of monopsony, where a few large employers dominate, but this seems to be exceptional. There is certainly widespread discrimination by caste, race, and sex. Such discrimination may not be very important from an efficiency point of view (in the Paretian sense), but many would agree that it is serious when a broader welfare point of view is taken. In all these respects, there are differences between countries. The clearest evidence of well-working markets seems to come from Thailand, Malaysia, and the "baby tigers." It is somewhat absurd, and unscholarly, to sum up the world in these few lines, but I believe that they express a growing consensus.

Attention shifted in the 1970s to urban labor markets, and to rural-urban migration, as a consequence of growing awareness of high urban unemployment. It is here that major distortions have been asserted in recent years. The Harris-Todaro model has become famous.[87] In its simplest form, it posits a high-wage modern sector, relative to rural earnings. There is thus excess supply to that sector. But people have no chance of getting a modern sector job if they do not go to town. So they go, and join an unemployed pool. The size of this pool equates rural earnings with expected urban earnings. Thus, if earnings in a modern sector job are double rural earnings, the expectation of a job must be 50 percent, and urban unemployment is 50 percent also.[88] This is far too simple to be true. It neglects the low-wage traditional urban sector, assumes one must be fully unemployed to have a chance of employment, assumes that firms do not recruit directly from the country, and assumes that an unemployed person has the same chance of employment as one already employed. However, the model can be and has been embellished to take account of many criticisms. The essential point remains. The rate of unemployment is an increasing function of the wage gap whether it is an urban-rural or a formal-informal urban gap. The wage gap causes urban unemployment. The unemployed have zero productivity compared to positive productivity in the country. So there is a distortion, and loss of output—and, ceteris paribus, a loss of welfare. The nature of urban unemployment lends credence to the model. Unemployment is predominantly among the young, especially women, who are not heads of families. The average educational level of the unemployed is higher than for the employed. They, or their supporting family, can (in the absence of any dole, which exists in very few LDCs) afford to keep them unemployed in the hope of a good job rather than continue on the farm or take a low-wage "informal" sector job. The wage-gap theory explains also some of the differences between countries.

The above model was developed in and for East Africa. There is little doubt that it incorporates some truth, both there and in many other, but not all, LDCs.[89] Given its reality, attention then centers on the cause of the wage gap; on whether the loss of output is very significant; on the migration function, and the related question of whether, given the wage gap, extra urban jobs reduce or increase unemployment;[90] on whether the unemployment is a serious welfare or political problem; on the effects of education; and on what remedies, if any, are called for.

Some authors stress the institutional factors, unions and government wage policy, as prime causes of the wage gap. In many LDCs, the government is the dominant modern sector employer. Others stress that there seem to be gaps where the institutional factors are weak or nonexistent, and give reasons why it pays modern firms to offer wages that create excess supply. The primary reason suggested is that high wages reduce turnover and lower training costs. A more Marxist suggestion is that firms want to reconcile their workers to capitalism. Foreign firms often pay more than local firms (but not always, and often not much more),[91] and this may be for political reasons. It is likely that profit-maximizing reasons also operate, but they might account for only a small part of the gap. It is notable that the gap is low where the institutional factors are clearly nonexistent. For instance, in Taiwan the average unskilled factory wage was about 20 percent above the farm laborer's average wage in the 1960s (and the gap has since been eliminated). In East Africa, Sabot put the gap at 40–80 percent.[92] In some countries, it seems to be even higher.

On the seriousness of urban unemployment, the recent tendency is to downplay it, both because the loss of output may be quite small (the urban unemployment rate may be high but contributes little to the overall rate) and because the unemployed are not among the poorest.[93]

On remedies, it is easy to recommend that institutional encouragement of a wage gap be removed or even reversed. This has sometimes been opposed on distributional grounds. If labor demand in the modern sector is inelastic, the wage bill is reduced by a fall in wages. This is clearly a good argument only on the assumption that profits take all the gain, which certainly would not be the case in any competitive situation. One must also take account of the fact that regular modern sector employees usually have incomes that are well above the median.

The idea of subsidizing employment (by a tax on production, sales, or profits) has come in for strong criticism.[94] The argument is that workers would get some of the subsidy, thus increasing the wage gap and the rate of unemployment. It is not obvious, however, that a subsidy must raise wages; moreover, any such tendency might be counteracted by a maximum wage beyond which no employment subsidy was allowable. There would certainly be no case for a wage subsidy if the simple Harris-Todaro model were valid, for then the actual wage equals the opportunity cost (see note 88). If it is not valid, a case can perhaps still be made. Finally, to the extent that high wages are paid because of training costs, a training subsidy is indicated and has long been advocated.

Some recent theorizing about wage determination in the face of uncertainty and ignorance of a person's productivity and qualifications, and the role of internal labor markets, is beginning to be applied in the development field. This recognizes that many markets cannot be other than imperfect, and examines the rationale of institutions and contracts in achieving second best solutions.[95] It is similar in this respect to new theories of land tenure, where contracts and informal understandings encompass a composite "solution" to market imperfections in land, labor, credit, and product markets. Perhaps the main lesson of this kind of work is that it may be very hard to improve upon the workings of imperfect markets and that simple solutions—such as abolishing land leasing—may do more harm than good.

My own feeling is that the seriousness of labor market distortions are not adequately measured by speculating about current loss of output. It seems very likely that they also contribute to inequality. Perhaps even more seriously, they contribute to the choice of capital-intensive techniques and therefore to a growth path that is inadequately labor demanding. But they are only one among many causes of this. I tend to agree, cautiously, with one of Lyn Squire's conclusions: "If poverty-alleviation is a primary goal of economic policy, concern should be focussed mainly on the factors influencing labor demand and supply, and not on the operation of the labor market per se."[96] The interactions between education, earnings, and "educated unemployment" are further discussed in chapter 10.

Chapter 10

New Topics

Agriculture

THE ROLE OF AGRICULTURE

To caricature the 1950s,[1] agriculture was to be bullied into providing the means for industrialization. It could shed labor without affecting production. It must be taxed or otherwise forced to yield up enough food to feed the departing surplus labor. Preferably, it should not demand much in return, whether in the form of inputs or consumption, so that as much as possible could be devoted to development, meaning industrialization.

Beginning around 1960, agriculture began to be seen in a more positive light. It still was thought of as having a "role" in development, rather than being a large part of what needed to be developed for its own sake. But many economists now began to realize that agriculture was unlikely to produce enough food to support a growing population with a rising average real income, if it were so squeezed as to leave little for investment, and if the more talented scientists, administrators, and planners looked in other directions. Thus, the numerous articles in the first half of the 1960s that discussed agriculture's role, while still mostly thinking in terms of its "contribution," now stressed that, without a sufficiently balanced approach, industrialization itself could be impeded by inadequate food and agricultural raw material supplies. A macroeconomic structural approach clearly suggested this in the case of a closed economy. In open economies concerned with industrializing, agriculture could be ignored, provided that enough manufactures could be exported and provided food and materials could be easily bought on world markets.

The argument that even relatively closed economies should devote more attention to agriculture seemed to require for its support two propositions: first, that agricultural output, and the marketed surplus, would respond to changes in incentives and to further investment; and second, that the performance without such changes was unlikely to be good enough.

During the 1960s, the idea that peasants would not respond to economic incentives was laid to rest. Where innovations were not adopted, it was increasingly found that they would either have been unprofitable or would have increased the operator's risk. T. W. Schultz's *Transforming Traditional Agriculture* published by Yale University Press in 1964 was a landmark work. He argued that peasants skillfully maximized (risk-discounted) profits, and that within the confines of a traditional production function there was therefore little to be done. New possibilities had to be opened up, and this required public action in research and education. However, with some instruction, the peasant could be relied on to choose intelligently between new alternatives, and to accept innovations that would increase his income, provided they were not too risky. By the time Schultz wrote, there was some supporting evidence for the last proposition.[2] By the end of the 1960s, the evidence was overwhelming. There also, of course, had to be new and profitable opportunities, hence the strong emphasis on research. Evidence was mounting that the performance of agriculture had been sluggish. Not only was food output barely sufficient for domestic demand, but export opportunities were being lost. Although proof is usually beyond the powers of economic science, the accusing finger could be pointed at the widespread squeeze on agriculture in the 1950s. In many less developed countries, the internal terms of trade were turned against agriculture, and agricultural exports were discouraged, by protectionist policies and by taxation of agricultural exports.[3] As a consequence, there was some debate as to whether an improvement in the terms of trade of agriculture would result in (a) more output and (b) more marketed "surplus." That poor peasants might prefer more leisure, and might eat more if they got better prices (the income effect outweighing the price effect), is a bogeyman that continues to haunt those who see the peasant as a reluctant industrial prop.[4] While empirical research has made it clear that farmers would switch crops in response to price incentives, it was hard to produce an answer for *aggregate* farm output, or marketed surplus, though such efforts as there were suggested that both would be positive.[5]

Where a defined area with homogenous land produces a single crop, however, responses can be more easily measured. This has been done most recently for the exclusively paddy-growing Muda River area in Malaysia, using a model of household behavior incorporating both production and consumption elements, and data from a large intensively researched sample.[6] If the change in the paddy price were consistent with a constant wage, then the elasticities of both output and marketed surplus were positive and between 0.6 and 0.7. Since labor demand increased with the paddy price (and the supply of family labor fell with the rise in income), a constant wage presupposes a perfectly elastic supply of hired labor. In reality, it was thought that the labor supply had virtually zero elasticity. This being so, the results were quite different. Output and marketed surplus were virtually unchanged; the rise in wages exceeded the rise in the paddy price. Both the farming families and hired labor benefited. The Malaysian government (unusually) maintained paddy prices above world market levels, hoping thereby to promote self-sufficiency. The model suggests that the higher price did nothing for self-sufficiency, since demand rose as much as supply. But the rural poor benefited considerably.

The above results ignored possible longer term effects, such as migration into the area, rent increases, or increases in savings and investment. The longer run effects are likely to raise output and sales. An improvement in profitability combined with more cash to invest, especially in working capital (seeds, fertilizers, pesticides), will have its effect on output. Microstudies suggest that the effect can be dramatic when modern inputs are available. The fear that output would suffer because farmers would work less has little plausibility where labor can be hired and modern inputs applied.

With increased output, the rural demand for food will rise, on the part of landless laborers as well as poor peasants. The urban demand for food might fall a little, even if real wages were maintained, especially as migration might be slowed down. A fall in the "marketed surplus" (or more accurately, urban food supplies) implies a fear that higher farm prices cause the demand for agricultural output to rise more than the supply, so that prices would rise again until the towns starved. I am not aware that this has ever happened historically, as a result of improving agricultural prices. It can, of course, happen as a result of agricultural *failure*, with consequential price rises. I suggest that discouraging agriculture is enormously more likely to result in urban food deficiencies than encouraging it.

Discouraging or encouraging agriculture is much more than a matter of price incentives. Taiwan achieved great success in agriculture, squeezing with one hand (the price incentives for rice output and fertilizer use were considerably less favorable than under laisser faire) but encouraging with the other by supplying a level of services for agriculture, in research and extension, and infrastructure that is far beyond anything achieved by any other LDCs.[7] She also led the world in the speed of her industrialization.

FOOD ALARMS AND THE CHANGE OF EMPHASIS

It became evident in the 1960s that with a few exceptions, such as Mexico and Taiwan, food output in LDCs was barely keeping pace with population growth. Imports were increasing, but even so the increase in apparent consumption was lower than might have been expected given the rise in income per head. Moreover, as 1960 census results became available, population projections had to be raised. Not only would there be more people to feed, but more people than expected would have to find a living in agriculture (and other rural pursuits largely dependent on agriculture). The result was an outbreak of works on the "World Food Problem,"[8] largely from the United States, but also from the Organization for Economic Cooperation and Development and the Food and Agricultural Organization (FAO). The latter instituted a "Freedom from Hunger" campaign in 1963, and in 1970 published its pretentiously titled *Provisional Indicative World Plan for Agricultural Development*. According to S. Wortman and R. W. Cummings, "The Indicative World Plan (IWP) not only improved understanding of the world food situation but led to the widespread conviction in the late 1960s that massive investment in improvement of conventional agriculture was urgently needed."[9]

There is room for argument as to how far this global approach was likely to influence, has influenced, or should influence LDC government policies. Economists are as rightly suspicious of food fundamentalism as most of them are of heavy-industry fundamentalism. For instance, the paper of W. H. Nicholls cited in note 1 of this chapter was attacked at the time as "physiocratic." In the last analysis, investment should be applied where it will be most socially profitable. Food is just another "commodity," and a highly tradable commodity at that. Many countries have to rely on trade in food to an extent that implies a major catastrophe if it were cut off.[10] A. T. Mosher, an agricultural economist, put the point admirably:

> Even with respect to food production—and agriculture can and does produce much more than that—a productive agriculture is desirable not so much because it produces food as because it can produce *income* for individual farmers and for the nation. Families and nations can have enough to eat if they have sufficient income, no matter how that income is earned. Food can be purchased, and it can be imported if it is not produced in sufficient quantities and variety domestically.
> Consequently, the basic reason why agricultural growth is so important in many countries is not because people need more food. Instead, it is because so many and such a high percentage of people are dependent on farming for their income and because alternative employment opportunities are so limited.[11]

However, it was the bad monsoons of 1964–65 and 1965–66

that turned Indian policy more in favor of agriculture. India is a huge country, and two successive bad monsoons could, and did, make it impossible to import and distribute enough food to prevent hardship. Not only that, but it was felt that the United States, food supplier of last resort, used its position to influence Indian policies—a kind of dependency that any government would want to avoid. Of course, in the face of fluctuations rather than a trend, reserves are the answer. But this bad experience also resulted in worries about the nature of the trend.

The investment-and-incomes approach and the global food scare approach come together insofar as unfavorable world predictions of the balance of supply and demand for food (and, more generally, agricultural output) suggest rising relative prices for food on international markets. This should make agricultural investments appear more attractive. To this extent the global approach has an "indicative" value. Only India, China, and the USSR should worry about their own impact on world markets or the prices they may have to pay. But all may worry a little about the danger of supplying countries, especially the United States, restricting exports or making exports conditional, and about large importers preempting supplies in an imperfect, politically controlled market.

PUBLIC INVESTMENT IN AGRICULTURE AND PLANNING

In the early days of planning, the central concept of agricultural planning was little different from industrial planning. Attempts were made to estimate demand, some usually rather arbitrary allowance was made for imports and exports, and hence production targets were arrived at. But there was no direction of output, and means of achieving the targets through pricing policy, new investment, etc., were usually discussed in the vaguest terms. In short, this was no more than paper planning.

Public investment in agriculture tended toward large schemes. In Africa in the 1950s and early 1960s, there were state farms and large-scale attempts at mechanized production of particular commodities. These were all failures. There were some countervailing successes, notably with supervised small-farmer production of such crops as sugar, cotton, tea, and palm oil. Everywhere there were large irrigation schemes, which were often very disappointing. This does not, of course, imply that the water was not potentially valuable. The trouble usually lay, as countless documents testify, with a failure to plan downstream activities properly or in time. Feeder canals and ditches are needed, farmers must be educated in new farming systems and good water control, and drainage must be arranged. There were also many settlement schemes. Almost invariably the cost per settler was too high for replication on a sufficient scale to make any impact. The targeted income for settlers was also usually too high, unless the aim was to form a rural "elite."

In India there was an effort in principle to modernize village life. This Community Development Programme—today it would be called "integrated rural development"—was much emphasized in the First and Second plans. But with sparse resources, it was spread so thin as to be futile. The poor village-level worker, at the bottom of an overextended pyramid, was supposed to concern himself with everything; as an agricultural extension worker, he had insufficient training, and there was no assurance that even the best among them had anything to teach the villagers. There was also in theory an effort at grass-roots participatory planning. Democratic village plans, with output targets as well as community investment projects, were supposed to be integrated into "block" plans, and so on up the planning chain to New Delhi—and down again, since total resources demanded would always be too great. In theory this is a nice idea. In practice, the poor education of villagers, the local power structure, the wholly insufficient time for such iteration, and the burden placed on the administration made the idea farcical. The reach of these Indian efforts far exceeded their grasp, nor is it clear that the reach was well conceived.

There has been a shift of emphasis since the middle 1960s, partly because of disillusionment with central planning, but largely because of the importance of new techniques with an increased need for imports in the past fifteen to twenty years.[12] The planning of agriculture has thus come to be regarded largely as the planning of supportive institutions. Even large farmers cannot be very progresssive unless new and profitable technologies are developed by research and transmitted by agricultural colleges and extension workers, as well as through normal marketing of inputs. In addition, small farmers are likely to lack access to modern inputs and credit unless institutions are developed to reduce the cost, and overcome (so far as they can be overcome) the problems of small deliveries.

Some supervision of production, and special marketing institutions, combined with credit, may also be required for certain crops. Some of these supportive agencies are provided by private enterprise. But enough support of large-scale genetic research is unlikely to be so provided. Other services, such as credit, it is commonly thought, are provided only on monopolistic terms, though any positive evidence of such exploitation is scanty.[13] The degree of public investment justified must depend on local circumstances and markets and take into account the need to economize in public planning and administration.

Cooperative institutions seem to be an obvious answer to many of the small farmer's problems, for example, in buying seeds, fertilizers, and pesticides, in the supply of credit for working capital, in processing where relevant, and in marketing.

Apart from such institutions, there is investment in rural infrastructure, local roads, and perhaps electrification. Finally, some quite minor investments in land improvement, irrigation, tree planting, etc., may be beyond the reach of small farmers and require public organization at some level. A simultaneous combination of appropriate policies, necessarily involving several ministries and therefore raising difficult problems of coordination, is clearly needed if efficiency in the design and implementation of programs is to be achieved.

All elements of such planning and provision of services have been tried. There have been notable successes, but also much failure. Although the lessons have begun to be studied on an adequate scale only in the past decade, there seems to be a good deal of consensus on some of them:

1. Adaptive research is still insufficient in most countries, especially in Africa, but even in India where it has been greatly developed in the past fifteen years. The new international research institutions, modeled on the International Rice Re-

search Institute (IRRI) in the Philippines and the International Wheat and Maize Center in Mexico (CIMMYT), cannot do everything and cannot produce appropriate seeds and systems for every soil and climate. It is also essential that there should be good levels of communication between research and extension.

2. Extension work has suffered in the past from both insufficient training of extension workers and from their all too often having nothing to offer that would significantly increase profitability. This gap could arise either because inadequately researched systems were promoted or because prices were distorted. Where the extension workers were competent and had something to offer, then they were always too thin on the ground.

3. There is insufficient provision for the training of administrators, and administrative systems are often ill-adapted for development work.

4. Subsidies, whether to promote acceptance of new systems and so encourage production, or to raise the income of the poorest classes, are to be avoided and indeed are all too likely to be counterproductive. Supplies, whether of credit or physical inputs, are nearly always rationed or in short supply when a subsidy is operative. The result is that the larger influential farmers get a disproportionately large part of the benefit (not merely an absolutely large part, which is unavoidable even if supplies are unlimited). Furthermore, the new systems, such as tractors, that are subsidized are often labor displacing.

5. There is probably less consensus concerning cooperatives. There have been notable successes, obvious examples being the moshavim in Israel and farmers' cooperatives in Japan and Taiwan. Many of the special commercial crop schemes have also been successful. None of these is a production cooperative, although there may be considerable supervision in the latter cases. Production cooperatives (and small collectives) outside Communist countries are mostly failures or frauds[14]— except for kibbutzim in Israel. Even service cooperatives have often failed. The management of cooperatives is difficult, and strong elements of public support and training are likely to be required, especially as the spirit of cooperation is often notably absent. It is far more likely to be present, or to be capable of being aroused, if there is a high degree of equality among the farmers; if not, the stronger elements are likely to be able to capture most or even all of the benefits. The condition of a fair degree of equality seems to be present in all the success

167

stories. Finally, a multipurpose is more likely to succeed than a single-purpose cooperative, especially a credit-only cooperative; there is, for instance, a very obvious advantage in a credit institution also handling an important part of sales.[15] In general, cooperatives are more likely to succeed when the farmers are literate and significantly involved in buying and selling, that is, are already well removed from purely subsistence operations.

The conception of agricultural planning sketched above presumes that the choice of crops and farming systems, and production decisions, rests with the operator (collaborating, perhaps, with the landlord if he is a sharecropper). Some influence and surveillance may be exercised for high-value commercial crops where the operator is in reality or effect a tenant of the scheme, but this is far too expensive in terms of management to be widely applicable. This implies that the price mechanism is the determinant of what is produced. It could hardly be otherwise given that prices are the only way of communicating continuously with millions of farmers. Most of them never see an extension worker or other official, and even those who do will hardly take unprofitable advice or instructions. The pure subsistence farmer hardly exists, so that prices not only determine what is produced but also determine to a considerable degree the farmers' income. To quote A. T. Mosher again:

> It is because of the predominant importance of this income aspect of agriculture that it is better to plan and conduct public agricultural activities so as to surround farmers by more profitable opportunities to engage in the biological processes of farming, regardless of what they produce, than it is to plan primarily to increase the production of specific farm commodities.[16]

In almost all the LCDs the government has exercised a great deal of influence on agricultural prices, directly and indirectly. As we have seen, agriculture was, and still is, squeezed in most countries; more precisely, there is widespread antiprotection, so that agriculture is less profitable than it would be under a free-trade system. Moreover, some agricultural operations are more antiprotected than others for no good reason. Almost all economists would agree that if agriculture is to be squeezed, it is better done by progressive land taxes or agricultural income taxes. But governments find this more difficult for administrative, political, or even constitutional reasons (in India). On the equity side, it is true that squeezing by commodity price distortions is progressive in that it affects larger farmers proportionately more than smaller farmers; but then so too would any good direct tax system, which would not or should not impinge on the smallest. Some of the most unfortunate price distortions are those that encourage labor-saving innovations and discourage land-stretching ones. For instance, some of the bias against agriculture has been partly offset by cheap credit (for large farmers), while fertilizers are more expensive than on world markets. We cannot go further into this large subject, which remains less studied than the industrial distortions produced by excessive protection.

INTEGRATED RURAL DEVELOPMENT

Agricultural planning and development cannot, in all their aspects, be clearly dissociated from rural development and planning. The provision of rural power, transport, education, and health services presupposes some spatial planning, and affects rural activities in general and not merely agriculture. The concept of integrated rural development became popular in the late 1960s. Its meaning, however, is not altogether clear. It may simply be an expression calling attention to the desirability of some coordination of public rural activities that are normally the provision of different ministries. Or it may refer to special area-defined projects with a project authority that overrides normal administration and plans and implements the provision of a package, which on the productive side may extend beyond agricultural services to local industries and also include various welfare services. There are obvious dangers in such an approach. Resources and administration may be excessive, in that the project may weaken efforts elsewhere and could not be widely replicated. There is also a danger of excessive bureaucratization imposing an antipathetic formula from above, and precluding a more natural, even if piecemeal and untidy, evolution.[17] Integrated rural development seems to lack any good theory as yet that

A Resurgence of Neoclassical Economics After 1960

can point to those essential interactions that make an "integrated" approach necessary—unlike, for instance, the seed, water, and fertilizer interactions, which are well known.

In line with Robert MacNamara's 1972 Nairobi speech, which put special emphasis on the problem of rural poverty, the World Bank has been active in designing a new style of rural development project, embodying new technologies but specifically intended to channel benefits to the small farmer and the landless, thus trying to make operational the concept of redistribution with growth. Many bilateral aid donors followed with poverty-oriented programs. It is, however, still too early (for an outsider, anyway) to assess the success of these important endeavors.[18] It is not easy to prevent benefits from trickling up.

LABOR DEMAND, EQUALITY, AND THE GREEN REVOLUTION

The need for agriculture to absorb ever-increasing numbers of workers, and the effect on labor demand of new techniques, received little attention until the 1970s.[19] The technology of the green revolution needed analysis. It became clear that it was technically neutral as to scale (the new inputs are as close to being infinitely divisible as can be). Moreover, it was land stretching rather than labor saving, per unit of output—since, provided there is no mechanization, the labor input is very closely related to the size of the crop.

But very soon after the green revolution was well under way, especially in the wheat areas of India, Pakistan, and Turkey, it came under attack for creating inequality. In practice, it was not scale neutral, because of imperfections in the supply of credit, water, and fertilizers. It is also possible that the better educated larger farmers are quicker to seize opportunities than those who are less educated. More recent analysis suggests that one can be too quick to find fault on distributional grounds. To quote I. Singh:

> There is considerable evidence that small farmers have adopted the "green-revolution" technologies—high yielding varieties (HYVs) and nutrient use—extensively and have benefitted considerably as a result. Although HYVs have been limited mainly to irrigated areas, the HYV wheat has been adopted much more ex-

tensively than HYV rice (which has required more location-specific adaptation), small farmers in recent years have matched the performance of large farmers, in terms of i) percentage of farmers using HYVs, ii) percentage of sown area under HYVs, and iii) intensity of nutrient use per hectare, at least in India and Bangladesh. In Pakistan they have generally lagged behind larger farmers but more recently—since 1974—they have started to adopt these technologies more rapidly.[20]

MECHANIZATION

Mechanization is an important component of the agricultural plans of many LDCs. In the form of large tractors and harvesters, it is generally labor saving. The exception is when better and quicker plowing can increase yields (sometimes by permitting double or treble cropping), and hence the labor required for weeding and harvesting, to a degree sufficient to offset the labor saved in land preparation. Farmers in some areas complain, however, of a shortage of labor for planting or harvesting or both. Where this is the case, there may be other possibilities, such as increasing labor supply at peak periods (for example, by encouraging release of labor from other activities, and by spreading the peak by using seeds that mature at different times). Ultimately there is no way of sorting out these arguments and possibilities other than by trying to see that the prices of inputs reflect social costs. But, if there is to be a bias, it should be in favor of the biological inputs and against tractors and harvesters—in view of the fact that farmers (as well as industrialists) are probably biased in the degree to which they find labor more troublesome than machines. Prices have been biased the other way in most LDCs, reflecting policymakers' concerns with the "marketable surplus," and hence the concerns of large farmers, rather than with the level of incomes of the mass of small farmers, or sufficient demand for landless labor.[21]

BIMODALITY AND LAND REFORM

The debate on land reform continues. The main thrust derives from considerations of equity.[22] But an important question is whether output would be greater and grow faster with an appropriate land reform. The land reforms of Mexico and Taiwan

171

(and also Japan) have been compared.[23] The former is designated "bimodal" in that a dual structure of large commercial farms exists alongside small operational holdings in the *ejido* sector. The former have provided an impressive increase in output associated with both increased fertilizer and water use and extensive mechanization. The latter have contributed little in terms of yield or labor productivity. In Taiwan, where all farms are small (maximum four hectares) but highly serviced, unlike the Mexican *ejidos*, increases in output have been as impressive as in Mexico, and increases in both yield and labor productivity much higher. Political considerations apart, there is little doubt that the unimodal model (which applies also to Japan and Korea) is preferable.

There is widespread evidence for many countries that aggregate output per hectare of farmland is higher on small farms, although it is not so generally true that yields per hectare cropped are higher.[24]

The higher output per hectare is strongly associated with high labor input. Why should this be? One rather convincing answer, frequently advanced in the literature, is that the real cost of family labor is lower than that of hired labor, whether casual or longer term. There are several possible reasons for this. People may simply prefer to work on their own land or even on rented land. There are sometimes inhibitions, especially in the case of women, about working outside the family. It has also been argued that family labor can be more efficiently organized (and perhaps more easily exploited!) than hired labor. The costs of getting to work may be lower, and even in a near perfect casual labor market there is some risk of not getting work. Apart from the last mentioned reason, none of this implies any labor market failure.[25] It points rather to the efficiency of people having multiple options—owning land, renting land, working for wages, or any combination of these.

There is, however, another explanation of differential land-labor ratios and yields in terms of price distortions and differential availability of inputs. It is thus widely attested that cheaper credit is more readily available to large farmers[26] and also access to other inputs when these are in short supply. Finally, very large operators, who are rich, may indulge their preference for machines over labor at the expense of profits.

Provided that adequate arrangements can be made for servicing small farms and that the land reform can be smoothly conducted, without a prolonged breakdown of law and order, it would appear that the "economic" reasons in terms of higher output and greater labor absorption are valid at least in certain areas and countries. At the same time, much improvement in raising yields on small farms and increasing labor use on larger farms can be achieved without land reform.

When a major land reform is planned, the question of the maximum size of holdings has been much debated. This clearly depends on the overall man-land ratios and political considerations and cannot be usefully discussed except in a specific context. It has also been argued that there is a minimum "viable" size of holding, usually put at about one hectare of irrigated land. Less would not be enough to provide a family of, say, five, with "basic needs." (The minimum area has also been sought in terms of the indivisibility of a buffalo; but buffaloes can probably be rented, and small cultivators are more divisible and often can also be rented.) Yet if this were true, more than half of the holdings in Taiwan would be unviable. The argument misses the importance of off-farm rural earnings. It was indeed only in the past few years that any work has been done on this subject.[27] In Taiwan in 1972, for instance, almost half of the earnings of those with holdings of half a hectare or less were from nonagriculture.[28] Similarly, almost half of the earnings of those with less than one hectare in Malaysia were off-farm.[29] The opportunities for off-farm rural earnings are closely dependent on agricultural activity and incomes. At the same time, to the extent possible, opportunities for off-farm earnings (including public works) need to be made complementary with the seasonality of the agricultural demand for labor, so that a peak season labor shortage is not exacerbated. In general, very labor-intensive activities are of this nature, since little is lost as a result of unused capacity when agricultural demand is strong.

LAND TENURE

Tenure reform is sometimes counted as part of land reform. Control over the conditions of tenancy has often been attempted, since the stereotype is one of exploitation by exorbitant rents of small tenants by large landowners. Leasing has even been made illegal, and "land to the tiller" is a slogan that suggests that all tenancy is undesirable.

Such views are very simple-minded and static. In any system of private ownership (or of long leases from the state), however equal, the leasing in and out of land is required in order to adapt operational holdings to the changing structure of the family. Moreover, recent empirical research has shown that the stereotype may be far from typical.[30]

S. N-S Cheung sparked off illuminating new work on tenancy when he claimed that crop-sharing, long supposed by economists to be an output-inhibiting form of contract, was in fact efficient.[31] We cannot here explore the intricacies of the subsequent debates.[32] A sharecropping contract is as much a labor-leasing as it is a land-leasing contract. Wherever labor is involved, one is dealing with nonhomogenous units; and such factors as moral hazard and ignorance of the attributes of the parties concerned, which are relevant to the outcome, become important factors in determining the form of contract. So also do the natural uncertainties which are so important in agriculture. In these circumstances, perfect competition is not a relevant model. The persistence and popularity of both sharecropping and tenant rents (as well as farming with hired labor) implies that they both provide acceptable outcomes to rather complex problems involving ignorance and uncertainty. To quote:

> The presumption that the market allocation is efficient seems, at best, weak. On the other hand, there is no presumption that any simple reforms, e.g., the abolition of share-cropping, would improve resource allocation. For share-cropping is serving a real economic function; if share-cropping is abolished, those functions may be served in some other not necessarily preferable way. Any such land reform is then a delicate exercise in the economics of the second best.[33]

Can it be that economists are becoming more humble?

MACROECONOMIC EFFECTS—AGRICULTURAL OUPUT AND DISTRIBUTION

We have suggested the desirability of an increased agricultural output combined with increased demand for labor. However this comes about, there is a gain for farmers and landless labor provided agricultural prices do not fall. If prices do fall as a result of the supply curve moving to the right more than the demand curve, landless laborers still gain from the increased demand for their labor (presumed to be dependent on the quantity of output). But farmers (and many small farmers are among the poor) may then lose, since competition in the face of an inelastic demand can reduce their receipts more than their costs. Another way of putting this is that the rental value of their land falls with land-stretching innovations. The urban poor gain as food prices fall. But urban poverty is less extensive and less severe than rural poverty. If some of the increased output came as a result of a land reform, equalizing effects are more likely in that the reduced rents from land are now more evenly spread; on the other hand, it is possible that the increased demand for labor would be satisfied by an increased use of family labor, and the landless could suffer.

The effects on equality are thus very complex if a fall in agricultural prices as a result of technical progress and institutional change has to be allowed for.[34] Relying on increased attention to agriculture to bring about favorable results thus depends a good deal on demand. There are demand-increasing policies. First, exports of agricultural products have been discriminated against, and export markets have been lost. Second, many LDCs are becoming increasingly and heavily dependent on food imports (see chapter 13). Third, any success with increasing the demand for labor in nonagriculture will tend to increase food demand, as also will any other measures tending to greater equality. Fourth, part of any set of measures for alleviating poverty can consist of selective subsidization of food consumption. Last, of course, there is the possibility that agricultural prices will rise unless there is a

175

further concentration of effort and measures in favor of agricultural production.

Technology and Production Functions— Capital-Labor Substitutability

There was a tendency, prior to 1960, to assume fixed production coefficients (see chapters 2 and 4). Even the "choice of technique" and "investment criteria" literature did not necessarily deny this structuralist assumption. It was mainly concerned with the choice between output and growth, or present employment versus future employment, and this was as much related to industry choice as to choice of technique within an industry. G. Ranis's work on Japan was a notable exception. He showed how the Japanese "stretched" imported technology to reduce the capital output ratios.[35] Ever since, in many articles and reports, Ranis has continued to stress the flexibility of capital-labor ratios both within most industries and a fortiori for the whole economy, where policies can influence the pattern of final demand. A. K. Sen's *Choice of Techniques* included an empirical illustration of the enormous range of possibilities in cotton textile production.[36] But empirical work was rare indeed. It remained rare in the 1960s, despite E. F. Schumacher's entrepreneurial activities in favor of intermediate technology.[37]

One would think that no one who had observed production in both industrialized countries and LDCs, or who had any historical sense, could imagine that capital-labor ratios were fixed—or indeed that there was anything but a huge range for the great majority of products. But, as the fixed technique school would correctly argue, the range is irrelevant if some highly capital-intensive mode dominates all others in the sense that the latter use more capital as well as more labor per unit of output. Even if labor had zero social cost, the capital-intensive technique is then the socially efficient technique. The argument that this was so was still widely held at least until the 1970s.[38]

It might be thought that, since relatively labor-intensive techniques were widely used in most industries in most LDCs, this argument was also implausible. The fixed-technique school could, however, still claim that if wages were as low in the capital-intensive as in the labor-intensive units (where the wage level is likely to be closer to the opportunity cost of labor), then the latter would be unprofitable. This, again, was implausible, since the wage bill is small in the former; moreover, it was already known that large capital-intensive units often obtained capital very cheaply indeed, and certainly much more cheaply than most labor-intensive units. It is hard to escape the conclusion that structuralists wanted to believe in inflexibility, however implausible their position.

It was not until the late 1960s that any considerable empirical work was undertaken. The inspiration to challenge the structuralist view undoubtedly came from the concern for employment stressed by the research of the OECD Development Centre, and a little later of the ILO.[39] This work can be divided into three types following White (see note 38).

First, there is econometric work that seeks to measure the elasticity of substitution of labor for capital, using constant elasticity of substitution (CES) production functions applied to industrial census data. This has been skeptically reviewed by several authors,[40] including White, who concludes, "The econometric evidence probably does give some support for the position that efficient labor-intensive alternatives for manufacturing exist. But this is probably more an act of faith than a hard conclusion from incontrovertible evidence."

The second kind of evidence comes from assembling production functions from engineering data or actual observations of processes at work, or both. This is a laborious business, and has still been done only for a dozen or so manufactured products and processes. These consistently show that factor substitution is possible, and often substantial. White concludes his review of these studies as follows: "In all, the engineering and process-analysis studies do provide powerful demonstrations of the feasibility of labor-intensive methods and are probably more convincing than the econometric studies."[41]

The most thorough analysis yet made of choice of manufacturing techniques, based on machines (looms), is concerned with cotton textile weaving in Korea.[42] It is not included in White's survey but amply confirms his conclusion. The semi-automatic indigenous loom was the best technique from a social point of view. As compared with automatic imported looms, the same amount of investment would have given ten times the employment and twice the output. There was no problem of quality (except that fabrics of more than sixty inches in width could not be produced) or of skills. Nor, it seems, would the scale of operation have affected the choice. The imported looms were, however, usually favored because trade and monetary policies discriminated against domestic looms. When this discrimination was removed, domestic-loom purchases dominated, suggesting a high elasticity of substitution with respect to factor prices.

Another study, not included in White's review, is concerned with the operation of foreign companies in Brazil.[43] In the metalworking industries, it was found that United States companies made very large adaptations and used one third to one quarter as much capital as in the United States. However, hypothetical questions addressed to foreign companies (both American and other) suggested that the dominant reason for labor intensity was smaller scale not relative factor prices, although small adaptations to factor prices would occur even at the largest scale. This runs counter to other work suggesting that a positive relationship between scale and capital intensity was not to be expected in this class of industries (unlike industries in which containers—boilers, tanks, and pipes—are very important).

Last, White refers to anecdotal (that is, unquantified) evidence, and gives many references to prominent authors, including G. Ranis, H. Pack, and W. Strassman. He concludes: "The anecdotal evidence thus points in the same direction as the earlier evidence: greater labor intensity is not only feasible but is in fact occurring in some LDCs. It does, however, seem to be closely tied to good management." I could add some anecdotal testimony of my own, having visited factories in India, Korea, and Taiwan. One sees in use many instances of much more labor-intensive operations than in MDCs, even for competitive export markets, especially in the Far Eastern countries. Lastly, it should be noted that the anecdotal evidence is rich in explaining how capital-labor ratios are reduced (in some LDCs, but not others). Machinery is used that is often obsolete in MDCs. Less specialized, less automatic machinery is used, and it is bought second-hand. There is multishift working. Machines are run faster. Transfer machinery is left out of the package, work in progress being moved manually from process to process. Ancillary operations, materials handling, packaging, labeling are left unmechanized. None of these things depends on the existence of more appropriate domestic technology, though that too can help (as in the case of the Korean looms cited above).

Outside of manufacturing, studies of efficient substitution possibilities seem to be rarer and to have concentrated on road building. Here the results are contradictory for different countries, some researchers finding labor-intensive methods to be socially efficient, others not.[44] This is not surprising, in view of differences in soils and terrain, and labor productivity.

In agriculture, attention has concentrated on mechanization, especially tractorization (see above). Here no one has doubted that alternatives exist, and that mechanization is responsive to the cost of tractors and conditions in the labor market. The worry is rather that governments unduly encourage mechanization either deliberately or as a by-product of their foreign trade and monetary regimes, which results in tractors being supplied at less than their opportunity cost.

The upshot is that empirical work in the past fifteen years has shown that there is substantial room for the adoption of more labor-intensive and more socially efficient methods of production in LDCs. There is also a mass of evidence, accumulated in countless articles and reports beginning in the 1960s and cascading in the 1970s, that government policies vis-à-vis foreign exchange, credit, and wages have seriously distorted prices in favor of capital intensity in the great majority of LDCs.[45] Finally, the question has to be asked whether producers would respond adequately to changes in prices.

The great bulk of empirical work in both industry and agriculture suggests that most producers maximize the present expected

179

A Resurgence of Neoclassical Economics After 1960

value of profits, or earnings (net, of course, of the cost of the personal effort required), and therefore choose the most cost-effective techniques known to them.[46] The main exceptions lie with public enterprises, with monopolies, and possibly with very large farms. Here there is more room for preferences in favor of prestige, including the use of modern but inappropriate engineering. But, even in such cases, a change in prices that favors a labor-intensive choice would increase the monetary loss from choosing prestigious methods, and would therefore still tend to have the desired effect.

We have shown that there is a lot of room for selecting more labor-intensive techniques of production while taking the shelf of known and available techniques as given. For most LDCs, and except for "traditional" methods of making simple consumer goods, the available techniques are nearly all of foreign origin. India and a few other countries have made quite extensive use of Eastern European and Soviet plant and machinery, but the Western countries and Japan have been the dominant suppliers. Only very recently have a few LDCs begun to supply capital goods on a significant scale.

Since wages are relatively very high in the MDCs, and even in the USSR, it is clear that the machinery being produced is often designed to be more expensive and more labor-saving than it would be if designed for low-wage markets. Until the mid-1960s this presumptive gap in the technology shelf seemed to worry few people, either economists or planners, in LDCs.[47] It was only when the low rates of labor absorption by the modern sectors in many LDCs were highlighted[48] that the supposed "inappropriateness" of techniques became a development household word.

Let us look more closely at the meaning of a gap in the technology shelf. It is a metaphorical way of saying that more socially profitable plant and machinery could be produced but is not. Now economics abhors a vacuum. It is usually quite hard to dream up a new or modified object whose production would be profitable. This suggests that if there were any *large* demand for prima facie more appropriate capital equipment, it would get produced—no new breakthroughs would be required. Often it would be simply a matter of leaving out expensive automatic devices. Proprietary knowledge is not a problem with simple and therefore presumably appropriate capital goods. If there is some blindness on the part of MDC producers that keeps them from making such machinery, a dozen or so LDCs are capable of doing the job.

This suggests either that there never was a gap or that it has by now been filled or, most probably, that the policies of LDCs have steered producers away from appropriate techniques. As already stated, there is a mass of evidence for this latter proposition. In many countries, high industrial wages have been encouraged, and protective labor legislation has also raised the cost of employing labor. In almost all countries, very low and often negative interest rates have prevailed for the organized sector. A combination of overvalued exchange rates and remission of tariffs on imported machinery has also made imported equipment unduly cheap. These latter policies have indeed encouraged industrialization but discouraged appropriate methods. They have also discouraged the development of local machinery, as has high-cost local metal production. There is something to be said for the recent idea that mechanical engineering is a sector that particularly deserves encouragement, for proximity permits easier collaboration between makers and users of equipment and contributes to the possibilities of indigenous adaptation and development. But the first step is to stop discouraging it. In some countries at least, as the Korean example given above indicated, little more may be needed.

Despite the above, recent stress on the inappropriateness of existing technology has been overdone. The earlier vision, that one of the great advantages of backwardness is that more modern techniques can be acquired from abroad far more cheaply than they can be developed and invented, is still valid. Indeed, most of the modern methods for making what ordinary people want and need are available for free, and are incorporated in readily available machinery. Korea, Taiwan, and Hong Kong have shown that a sufficiently labor-intensive development, despite the fact that the rate of growth of their labor force was as rapid as almost anywhere, was possible without any need to develop *new* labor-intensive methods.

A Resurgence of Neoclassical Economics After 1960

The Transnational Corporations

THE ECONOMICS OF INTERNATIONAL DIRECT INVESTMENT

If written a dozen years ago this section would, without change of subject, have been entitled "Private Foreign Investment" (PFI) or "Private Overseas Investment" (POI). Titles were changed in the late 1960s, as authors wanted to emphasize the size and widespread activities of the some 2,000 large corporations that accounted for the bulk of overseas investment, as well as the fact that they might in some measure escape the surveillance of any one nation, and especially the host country. Since, for various reasons, including low real interest rates and risk reduction, foreign corporations often borrowed locally as much as possible and therefore brought in little capital, the change of title was also associated with increased emphasis on the part they played in the transfer of technology and managerial expertise, and in marketing.

Soon afterward, the United Nations adopted the title "transnational" in order apparently to emphasize further the presumed threat to national sovereignty. Although the basis of the powerful emotional reaction against the transnationals stems largely from their size (as well as the nationality of the parent company), it should be noted that any company with any overseas subsidiary or affiliated company over which it has some control, however small, is included in the definition. There are about 10,000 transnational corporations.[49] It is also worth noting at the outset that the dropping of the word "private" is appropriate. There is a significant number of very large *public* companies with overseas investments.

We are concerned only with LDCs, which account for barely one quarter of the stock of overseas assets.[50] For about the first fifteen years after World War II, governments and economists in MDCs, with a few exceptions, assumed that PFI was beneficial to "host" countries, and LDC well-wishers welcomed any moves by MDCs to encourage the outflow to LDCs. PFI was seen as a complement to aid. The LDCs were capital hungry. Aid could do more to help as far as social and economic overheads were concerned, but private investment was more appropriate in mining and manufacturing, areas in which governments had little or no expertise. LDC attitudes were more ambivalent. India, for instance, adopted quite restrictive policies—and, partly as a result, has received very little foreign investment. Latin America vacillated between a perceived need, both for the finance and the technology, and political suspicion, which, however exaggerated, was deeply rooted in the past.[51]

Research on multinationality exploded in the 1960s beginning with S. Hymer's 1960 study, published in 1976,[52] and was followed by notable contributions from R. Caves, C. Kindleberger, and R. Vernon.[53] This work was in the industrial organization tradition. Its chief aim and result were to show that foreign corporate investment could be understood only in the framework of monopolistic and oligopolistic theory. The essential idea was that some special advantage, of the kind familiar in the barriers-to-entry literature, was required to offset the disadvantages inherent in operating in a strange country, disadvantages that might be expected to give local firms a competitive edge. The special advantage of the foreign firm usually lay with its technological lead. This literature concentrated on the reasons for American investment in Canada and Europe. Much of it is rather irrelevant to LDCs.[54] The chief reasons for foreign investment in the latter have been different, and there is much less need to explain why the foreign firm could do well in the face of local competition. In the natural resources field, the objective has been to reduce risks in material supply and to capture part of the rents inherent in a good find. In manufacturing, the main reason has been to preserve sales in markets that were cut off or threatened to be cut off by the import substituting policies of the host country, or sometimes to invade such a protected market, taking the place of previous foreign suppliers. More recently, in some countries, the reason has been to take advantage of cheap labor in making goods designed largely or wholly for export to MDCs. The "host" country very often prohibited foreign investment where there was any established local industry, and encouraged it when there was little or no comparable local production and none in sight.

There was a remarkable absence of any hard analysis of the

A Resurgence of Neoclassical Economics After 1960

costs and benefits that might accrue to an LDC host. G. D. A. MacDougall made a careful neoclassical analysis for Australia in 1960.[55] It was a macroeconomic analysis in the sense that it estimated the effects of an increment to the foreign capital flow, without specifying into what it flowed. For this reason, it could not easily be applied to LDCs, where, in view of the distorted prices, net benefits must depend greatly on the particular projects associated with the increase in the foreign capital inflow.[56] MacDougall concluded that the main benefit was likely to be the direct tax the foreign company paid. We shall see below how far this needs to be modified in the case of cost-benefit studies of particular investments in LDCs. But in any case, this article was not followed up in an LDC context.

The development establishment was more concerned with the "external" economic and political effects of foreign investment than with the visible measurable effects of the net value of the labor and other inputs, and the outputs—the sort of quantities that appear in company accounts. Externalities centered on two questions: whether the entry of foreign enterprise stimulated or discouraged actual or potential local entrepreneurs, and the extent and depth of the technical knowledge that was transmitted to nationals. The second can only be a benefit, though it may be negligible. The first could go either way. In a famous article, A. O. Hirschman put forward the hypothesis that private direct investment helps to create local initiatives in early stages of development but later discourages them. On the basis of this hypothesis he proposed "An Inter-American Divestment Corporation," a sort of giant Crazy Horse Saloon.[57] Latin American countries have in fact done a lot of divestment in the postwar period, often accompanied by an exacerbation of United States-Latin American relations. The political attraction of an orderly, friendly, and fair process of nationalization is clear, clearest perhaps for the United States. But that Latin America would have gained economically is highly questionable.

By the late 1960s, hostility to private foreign investment had been built up by a mass of scarifying literature that claimed that national sovereignty was threatened (see chapter 12). But the more narrowly economic literature began to concentrate on unearthing and emphasizing possible deleterious effects. Much attention was concentrated on the fear that transnational corporations might worsen countries' balances of payments, and it was pointed out that transnational corporations often raised loans in the local market and transferred relatively little from abroad while repatriating profits. LDC fears in this regard resulted in UNCTAD commissioning a study of the balance-of-payments effects of foreign investment. There are some serious errors involved in this fearful approach. First, it is absurd to try to measure balance-of-payments effects by looking at the associated financial flows, since imports and exports are also affected. Second, there can be no objective balance-of-payments effect attributable to the investment alone, since what happens depends on how much real expenditure changes, in response to the real income changes induced by the investment, and this is a matter of fiscal and other policies. Last, a government should be designing its policies to accommodate beneficial foreign investments, whatever their inestimable balance-of-payments effects. In other words, what matters are costs and benefits.

That the only valid way of dealing with the economics of foreign investments was by cost-benefit analysis of individual investments seems, surprisingly enough, to have been first suggested by the present author,[58] who had already been responsible for the first published ex post cost-benefit analysis of any investment in an LDC, an investment that also happened to be a foreign investment.[59] Since then, there has been a small spate of such studies, using the so-called Little/Mirrlees methodology.[60] Even the UNCTAD study referred to above ended up, after some considerable methodological strife, using this methodology in a very rough form, although the authors were strong believers in the importance of immeasurable factors.[61]

It is easy to state the net benefit (or cost) of a wholly foreign investment. It consists of:

1. The taxes (less subsidies) the host country receives, plus
2. Any excess of the amount the foreigner pays for indigenous inputs over their social cost (or shadow price), less
3. Any excess of the price the local user pays for the output over its social cost (or shadow price).

Ex hypothesi, these shadow prices take full account of any excess demand for foreign exchange. They can also include all *measurable* externalities. Of the above, (1) needs no comment; (2) is normally positive, since wages paid usually exceed the real social cost of employment; but a negative item arises if the enterprise raises local finance at any interest rate less than the "accounting" or socially optimum rate;[62] (3) is usually positive in a protected market (the consumer is subsidizing the enterprise). It is thus not surprising that empirical studies almost invariably show that export investments are socially beneficial (this could be reversed only if exports were heavily subsidized). Import substitution ventures, however, quite often show negative social returns—in a highly protected market the consumer is subsidizing the foreigner.

No mention has been made above of the foreign financing, that is, the capital inflow from and the profits accruing to the foreigners. It is indeed wholly irrelevant to an assessment of the host's benefits, if no domestic alternative is available.[63] But if a local entrepreneur could have carried out the projects with local savings, then the country should prefer this if the rate of return is higher than that to be expected on other average new investments in the economy. In principle, such alternatives should always be investigated. Even when no such domestic alternative is possible, it is useful from the point of view of bargaining to know both the country's own benefits and the return to the foreigner. If the latter is high, it may be possible to bargain harder, and so increase the former.

The above analysis can be directly applied to divestment or nationalization as well as to investment. A fair price for an asset from the foreigners' point of view would be the present value of future expected returns, discounting at the expected rate of return on risk capital in his own country. The host would gain at this price only if his accounting or social rate of interest was lower (assuming the expected returns under his management were the same). Only if an LDC has rather limited investment opportunities relative to its level of savings is such nationalization likely to constitute an economic benefit. But when we add in the political advantages, and the fact that the host country may well be able to nationalize at a lower price than the investor thinks fair, without causing undue political repercussions or preventing other new desired foreign investments, then one should not be surprised to see quite a lot of nationalization in the manufacturing field, as soon as LDCs can operate the enterprises successfully. Nationalization of mining ventures, which has been on a large scale, may be a pointer to the future.

Joint ventures have always been popular with developing countries and have been increasing as United States companies have weakened their resistance to them, and as European and Japanese firms, always less resistant, have increased their share of the transnational corporation market. LDCs have, at the same time, toughened their attitudes, and in many countries, in some or all sectors, local equity participation or even control is mandatory. The reasons for this must be largely political, for the economic arguments rather tend to suggest that providing local finance for such joint ventures may not be a particularly good use of a country's savings (unless local bureaucrats or entrepreneurs are very clever at spotting which are likely to be the most profitable ventures to opt into). The foreign company is less likely to transfer secret processes and know-how to an affiliate over which it has less than full control, and access to foreign markets may be more restricted. Local equity holdings may also give an incentive to transfer pricing. It is notable, perhaps, that joint ventures are much less common in MDCs, where political fears are less pronounced.[64]

We turn, very briefly, to two of the most frequently asserted complaints against transnational corporations. The first is "transfer" pricing as between different units of the transnational corporation in different countries. Although there is often no way of establishing an arm's length price, and so no way of saying what is a "proper" division of the transnational corporation's profits between different centers, there is no doubt that many transnational corporations have some latitude of choice as to where they will declare profits, although revenue and exchange control authorities try to reduce this latitude. In most LDCs, corporate taxes are lower than in MDCs, and so there is an advantage in using transfer pricing in favor of LDCs.[65] The United

A Resurgence of Neoclassical Economics After 1960

States tax authorities seem to believe it works in this direction: but development economists have almost invariably assumed the opposite. There may, however, be reasons for transferring profits, despite a tax disadvantage, if the host limits dividends or exercises price control based on costs or import prices, practices that are quite frequent. Apart from balance-of-payments emergencies, limitation of dividends constitutes an attempt to increase the inflow of foreign investment (by reinvestment of profits). On balance, it seems likely both to have the opposite effect and to decrease the host's benefits from such investment, by reducing the tax take. A number of reports and commentators have made this point. But no doubt the practice will continue, since host governments tend to believe that profits that legally belong to foreigners nevertheless in some sense belong to the host country when they arise from operations in that country.

Firm empirical evidence on transfer pricing is extremely scanty and mostly involves pharmaceuticals. It does not support a presumption that it works on balance against the interests of LDCs.[66] It is also, perhaps, worth noting that local firms have almost as much opportunity, and often a greater incentive, for transfer pricing as have foreign firms, by over and underinvoicing of imports and exports; and there is plenty of anecdotal evidence that this is not uncommon.

Transnational corporations may use tax havens to avoid tax in either home or host country. By establishing a trading subsidiary in such a haven, the TNC can realize profits there by manipulating intrafirm prices. These profits, which by definition are untaxed or very lightly taxed, may then be used for investment elsewhere. Tax on undistributed profits is thus avoided. Home governments, especially that of the United States, have taken steps to prevent or limit the use of tax havens, but with what success one does not know. There seems to be no evidence concerning the amount of profit accruing in tax havens from offshore operations.

The second common ground for attack on TNCs is that they introduce inappropriate technology and products. Insofar as all foreign technology is inappropriate, of course TNCs introduce it. But there is no evidence that, on balance, sector by sector, they introduce more capital-intensive methods, or adapt less than do local firms, public and private, which acquire foreign technology by licensing, consultancy contracts, etc. The anecdotal evidence cuts both ways.[67] Turning to inappropriate products, whatever one may think of Coca-Cola and Nestlé's baby food, it is a little one-sided to forget the very large range of chemicals and other products that no one would claim to be inappropriate, or the fact that local firms also acquire many Western proprietary products that advocates of the simple, hard, indigenous, childbearing life would condemn.

If one can sum up the economic arguments in a single sentence, it would be: "they greatly exaggerate the difference between indigenous and foreign enterprise." Problems of monopoly, technology, and products arise in either case. Both foreign and domestic enterprises may do harm in overprotected markets. The only significant difference is that excessive profits belong to nationals in one case, and foreigners in another. But one can make too much even of that. There is zero national social value to be attached to adding unnecessarily to a foreigner's wealth, but the social value of adding unnecessarily to a local tycoon's wealth may be very close to zero.

Education and Human Capital

THE SOCIAL VALUE OF INVESTMENT IN EDUCATION

We have seen that the economics of education and health scarcely existed in the 1950s. The discovery that conventional production functions in terms of physical capital and labor inputs accounted for only a small part of increases in output led to excitement about the "residual factor" and what it was. It could be many things. Some shrewdly regarded it as no more than a measure of economists' incapacity to explain. It was, however, often identified as "technical progress," but then technical progress required knowledge, and knowledge required education. Thus, education becomes a strong candidate for the "residual"

A Resurgence of Neoclassical Economics After 1960

role. This hypothesis had nothing to do with the tremendous acceleration of education in LDCs that had already occurred in the late 1950s. This was largely in response to popular demand, but also in part because LDC leaders were themselves convinced of its importance, both as a means and as one of the ends of development. Economists, as usual, were one step behind events.

T. W. Schultz led the field in developing the concept of investing in human capital,[68] which is the central notion of the economics of education. At around the same time, the growth accounting school fed proxies for human capital into their equations. For lack of data, growth accountancy has been less applied to LDCs than the calculation of rates of return to education.[69] Manpower planning became popular at about the same time.

There was an explosion of calculations of rates of return to education, first in MDCs, but very soon in LDCs as well. The essential idea is that differentials in earnings over life can be related to differentials in amounts spent on education. Primary education is compared with no education, secondary with primary, and so on. Private and social rates are calculated, the latter by including public expenditure in costs while taking earnings gross of tax (other adjustments may or may not be made). The results are expressed as returns to education.

The objections to this particular application of cost-benefit analysis are many. Some relate even to the private calculation. I shall ignore those that relate to the fact that data are poor, short-cut approximate methods are employed, and allowance is often not made for unemployment, etc. Average earnings, not marginal, are necessarily measured. Falling returns over time in the rare cases where information is available over an extended period, and where education has expanded rapidly, suggest that in some cases the marginal return is lower. But for LDCs there is virtually no evidence on this score. Another objection is that both more education and more earnings are related to ability, and to parental wealth and background. Concerning ability there is no doubt that some of the apparent earnings of additional education should rather be attributed to greater innate ability; but there seems to be no evidence as to how much. There is some evidence that parental background is unimportant, although we can probably all think of a person with high earnings and rich parents, who clearly learned little at school and even may have dropped out with no degree. By and large, no one challenges that there are important private returns to education (we discuss the figures later), though they may be somewhat exaggerated.

The most serious objections that have been pressed in the past decade involve basic attacks on the idea that education actually adds to human capital. Educated people earn more, not because they might have been improved by education but for other reasons. In the extreme case, education becomes socially valueless—which is *not* plausible!

First, there is "screening" theory. The employer will pay more for better education, not because education improves but because only better people survive educational tests. Then there is "credentialism," which causes a degeneration of the screening function in that the connection between credentials and qualification becomes weak. Students have often pushed in the direction of credentials. They want degrees for everything, and all who enter should exit with honor. Examinations, if not abolished, should be easy. Where such movements have the sympathy of a majority of students, it implies that most students believe themselves to be below average. Although credentialism can do harm for a while, it must defeat its own aims in the end. Employers will be forced to use other screens as the value of the educational certificate aproaches zero.

"Bumping" is a term for the process by which jobs get rationed by screening when there are excessive wage differentials. Suppose that government job A pays twice job B. There is excess supply of workers for A. The government rations by some educational qualification. Although it may get better workers for A, their marginal value product remains less than double that of B workers. The A workers thus become overqualified as education expands and "bump" potential A workers, who are sufficiently qualified, into B jobs. This can carry on down the scale until potential dons become dustmen. The demand for education will fall, but probably not sufficiently if aspirants are overoptimistic. Even if it falls enough to eliminate oversupply, an inefficiency (and a source of inequality) remains, since the wage differential does not reflect differences in performance. There is an overproduction of skills that are not properly utilized. In this example, the overproduction arises from excessive wage differentials, but it can also arise from excessive subsidization of secondary and higher education. The bumping hypothesis has arisen from observation—and not only in LDCs. But the question remains of how serious it is, and whether it may not be a temporary phenomenon, for unjustifiably high wages have been adjusted downward in a number of countries.

If screening is all there is to education, it greatly reduces its social value, though not to nothing, for screens are useful. But no one in his right mind believes that education adds *nothing* to productivity.[70] Nevertheless, evidence of this is hard to come by because it involves measuring the effect on output directly. This, however, has been attempted in agriculture. Results are nearly all positive.[71]

Confirmation of the value of education has been sought in cross-country econometric studies relating growth rates of GNP to literacy. On balance, countries with higher levels of literacy have grown faster. Indeed, literacy receives high marks for its positive contribution to output and health, and negative contribution to fertility, in a sophisticated simultaneous equation model.[72] Such studies do not, however, show that investment in education is a high priority compared with other investments and use of government funds, for which purpose cost-benefit analysis is needed.

Having already discussed the caveats, we briefly summarize the main results for LDCs of cost-benefit studies.[73] Private returns are almost without exception higher than social returns, government subsidies outweighing any tax recouped. Social returns are, with few exceptions, highest in primary education. They are very high, averaging 24 percent for a sample of thirty LDCs. But they are also quite high in secondary and higher education (15 percent and 12 percent, respectively).

Given the caveats, what are we to make of such figures? Some critics put almost no trust at all in them.[74] All can agree that there is a lot of room for improvement. Most, including myself, would probably cautiously claim them as evidence that primary education is a high priority. It has been pointed out that the screening hypothesis is less likely to be valid in the case of those with only some primary education, a much higher proportion of whom enter informal sectors.[75] On the other hand, the figures seem to take no account of the very high dropout rates in primary education. Attacking this problem might be the highest priority.

Any suggestion that secondary and higher education remain a high priority has to face the objection of a very high, possibly increasing, unemployment among those with secondary education in many countries, and even among graduates in a few countries. This is not usually allowed for in the cost-benefit figures. If the waiting period is only a few months, it makes little difference. But there is evidence that very high unemployment and long waiting periods have developed in some countries, especially Malaysia.[76] The quality of higher education has also deteriorated very seriously in some countries, especially India, as a result of lack of control of numbers, either by fees or entry qualifications. Mark Blaug argues more strongly than some that overexpansion of secondary and higher education is, and has been for some time, a very serious problem in many LDCs.[77]

MANPOWER PLANNING

Manpower planning in LDCs, especially in India, preceded the development of the economics of education. But the increased recognition of the importance of human capital in the 1960s led to a rapid extension of this activity, as exemplified by the OECD Mediterranean Project.

The approach was that of all quantitative planning. The future structure of the economy was estimated and the skill requirements derived by the skill input coefficients for all the different activities. Education then had to be planned to provide the right number of persons with these various skills. Because of the supposedly long lags involved, the horizon had to be long—say, fifteen years. This was impossibly ambitious, and to a large degree unnecessary. It was overambitious because of inevitably large errors in the scale of different activities and because of the often

193

rapidly changing skill inputs demanded by each activity. It was unnecessary to the extent that people are adaptable and many skills can in fact be quickly acquired, that skills are substitutable, and that skill "needs" can be economized (and imported). There were some spectacular failures, such as the excess supply of engineers in India. A particular problem for LDCs is that a need has often been felt to build a higher level of certain skills rapidly. This required a large expansion of training facilities, too great for long-run needs. If overproduction is to be avoided, some of the facilities have to be closed. But this has proved to be politically difficult, and oversupply has resulted. Enthusiasm for manpower planning has waned, but there is still a demand for skill input coefficients on the part of LDC educational planners. Where skills are genuinely specific, and gestation long, there is a need to try to estimate future demand.

As always with planning, there is a choice between, and often conflicts between, a quantitative and a price mechanism approach. There is room for both. In some countries, the government controls both the supply and demand for doctors. Earnings can then be negotiated over a wide range (possibly constrained by emigration). Touch is lost with market values, but this may be regarded as a good thing in the case of medicine. In most other fields, even if the government has a monopoly of supply, the only sensible approach is to try to match the demand. This has to be predicted, as in any business, but predictions must take account of market trends and are unlikely to be assisted by planning models. This is essentially planning by the price mechanism. If the educational or training activity is heavily subsidized, even to the point of offering a free service, this will affect earnings, but the problem remains one of equating the supply of applicants and the demand for them when trained. Trouble comes when the government controls both the training and the earnings, and the two are incompatible. Then it must either suppress the demand for education, which is politically difficult, or it creates the problem of educated unemployment. To quote Blaug:

> When an economist examines the comprehensive educational reforms that are now under way in a large number of Asian and African countries, the overwhelming impression gained is that

the direct links between the educational system and the labor market are still not adequately appreciated in developing countries. Again and again, he will witness countries overhauling their entire educational system without taking steps to alter the prevailing salary differentials by levels of schooling.[78]

Population

In the 1960s, world population growth was seen to be faster than expected, and possibly still accelerating. There was a spate of alarming projections, designed to show that very soon there would be standing room only or that the world was heading for starvation. There is no doubt that space on earth is finite and that nonpositive population growth must arrive. The question is when and how, and the hope is that it will come to pass without a holocaust.

World problems do not, however, much influence particular countries that look to their own space and other resources in relation to their population. Only India and Taiwan had policies to reduce fertility in the 1950s[79] (and the Indian program was tiny). But most of the more densely populated countries instituted antinatalist policies in the 1960s (for example, China, Indonesia, Pakistan, Egypt, and Korea, and many smaller countries, especially islands). Some other less densely populated countries, such as Brazil and Nigeria, began family planning programs (FPPs) on health grounds.

Economists have shifted attention from population size to its growth rate, although sheer numbers may still be seen as a threat for a limited number of countries (see chapter 7). Work in the past fifteen years has not changed the strong presumption that higher growth rates of population reduce the growth of income per head. Further doubt has been cast on the possibly negative influence on savings. But high growth rates imply a low proportion of working population to the whole, and less investment (including education) goes to increasing the amount of capital per head (including human capital). These are very strong arguments, even though they cannot be incorporated into general equilibrium models based on reliably established, and not merely assumed, relationships. (Such realistic models, endogenizing both demographic and economic variables, are beyond the powers of econometrics, especially given the lack of comparable and accurate data.) The only offsetting argument, and it is a weak one, stems from economies of scale, especially in transport and communications.

Countries are more likely to see and be influenced by particular problems caused by high population growth than by economists' arguments about the growth of income per head. A few very large countries may be concerned with the possibility that food production cannot keep pace; this applies only to very large countries because smaller ones can import food without affecting the terms of trade. The fear of increasing unemployment, together with the problems of very rapid urbanization, may be more widespread. There is no economic necessity for rapid growth to cause unemployment or excessive urbanization; but if markets do not work well, and incomes and educational policies are awry, it will certainly contribute—as indeed it does. Governments are also concerned with the high cost of keeping up, and increasing, the educational attainments and health status of populations that are often growing so fast as to imply that half the population is under seventeen.

The result has been that a number of less densely populated countries, such as Chile and Colombia, have developed quite strong FPPs. Almost all noncommunist countries in South and East Asia and in Latin America, but only a few countries in Africa, have some official program. The strength of FPPs has been rated on a scale from zero to thirty.[80] Out of 94 countries studied, 45 scored *zero*. Of these latter, 25 were African countries; 8 were Middle East countries, some of which were clearly short of labor; and 5 were Communist countries in East Asia. Most African countries want higher populations. They see no shortage of land, claim economies of scale, and associate numbers with strategic and political power. What many fail to understand is what is known as the *momentum* of population growth. Even if fertility rates are reduced to replacement levels,[81] the population will continue to grow for a very long time thereafter because of its youthful age structure. Furthermore, it is unrealistic to suppose that replacement fertility will be achieved in less than 25 years, except in the case of a few LDCs. To give two examples,[82] if India achieved replacement level fertility in 30 years' time, projections show that population would continue to increase for another 130 years, and reach two-and-one-half times the present level (that is, 1.5 billion people). If replacement fertility were achieved in Nigeria only after 60 years, the population would grow for another 95 years, and reach five times its present level, about 425 million.[83]

Some twenty-six countries have strong, or moderately strong, FPPs. Since these include China, India, and Indonesia, a high proportion of total LDC population is thus covered. Before discussing their effectiveness, we turn to the determinants of fertility, a subject where previous ignorance has been significantly dispelled in the past fifteen years. Research has recently had more to bite on because fertility began to fall in a number of LDCs just as the population scare was at its peak. In 1967 Ohlin wrote, "Fertility in the underdeveloped world has not yet shown definite signs of declining."[84] Ten years later one could confidently strike out the words "not yet."

In most countries a fall in the birthrate is reported for the period 1960-78, but for many it is very small and does not definitely establish a fall in fertility. But twenty-two countries show a fall of ten points, and these include two very large countries, China and Indonesia. Sensational falls, probably amounting to a point a year or more in recent years, have occurred in Chile, China, Colombia, Costa Rica, Hong Kong, Korea, Singapore, Taiwan, Trinidad and Tobago, and Tunisia.[85] These rates of fall are greater than ever occurred in the MDCs. A few of these have, like most of the MDCs, reached replacement fertility.

The most obvious correlate of fertility is income per caput. At very low income levels, fertility may, for reasons of health, rise with income. But thereafter it clearly falls, although there are wide variations at the same income level. But income per caput is best regarded as an indicator for many interrelated factors that may affect fertility.[86] As income rises, educational levels and the opportunity cost of children also rise, while mortality and the value of children as an insurance against old-age poverty fall. Some of these a priori probable influences are measurable, others not. Attention has been most directed to mortality and literacy.

It is plausible that people want a certain number of surviving children, and that they will therefore limit births when death rates fall. But there may be a long lag before they realize that their children are more likely to survive. Certainly it seemed around 1970 that this hoped-for effect was very slow to show up. But now the influence seems established, although the strength and lags to be expected remain unclear.[87]

Many statistical studies show a strong negative correlation between education and fertility, after controlling for income.[88] It needs little imagination to think of many possible reasons why education may reduce fertility, and many have been suggested. Particular stress has naturally been put on women's education. But no one seems to have been able to sort out which of the possible links are important. Education of women is linked to participation in modern sector activities, which may in turn raise the age of marriage; without such links it could be that women's education would be of little avail. The same sort of remark applies to many determinants. Little is as yet known about which factors may operate independently and which are effective only if other conditions are met.[89]

The main policy interventions are government-sponsored FPPs. How effective are they? Casual empiricism suggests an answer. Every country with a strong program had large or sensational falls in the birthrate. Of the twenty-two countries with large or sensational falls, only two had weak or zero programs (Turkey and Lebanon).[90] A comparison of Colombia and Mexico is suggestive. The socioeconomic indicators, growth rates, and inequality are all similar, except that Colombia is considerably the poorer. With a strong FPP, the birthrate in Colombia fell by 35 percent from 1960 to 1977, the corresponding figure for Mexico being 16 percent.[91] Sophisticated econometrics confirm the casual glance.[92] Yet doubts may still be raised. Often the birthrate had begun to fall before the program got going. This does not go to show that the program is ineffective. Birthrate falls can cause family planning programs without negating the proposition that the latter cause the former. At the World Population Conference in 1974, it was strongly argued by many LDCs not only that programs would be ineffective without development but that development would suffice. This was a debating position belied by the strenuous, even draconian measures taken by some of the countries that thus argued. It cannot be sustained.

A prevalent idea in the early 1970s was that birthrates would fall only in countries that had attained a moderate level of income per head; this made India, Bangladesh, and Indonesia look like hopeless cases. Triage raised its ugly head. But remarkable success in Indonesia, and fair success in India,[93] has shown that low income per head and a lack of social development do not preclude important falls in fertility even if they load the dice. Is development alone enough? Iran and the Ivory Coast prove that rapid growth and the achievement of middle-income status may have no effect, or very little. Ideally, one would like social cost-benefit analyses of family planning programs. At present too much guesswork is involved for this. Illustrative calculations, based more on assumption than firmly based estimates of either the cost or benefit of a birth saved, are nevertheless of some value—all one can do for most kinds of social investment.[94] It is clear, however, that the informed hunch of many economists and LDC governments implies a belief that full cost-benefit analyses would, if they were possible, show high returns in many countries and circumstances.

A final paragraph is in order on the ethics of FPPs. The tradition of liberal economics is to respect individual demands, and to encourage the dissemination of knowledge so that people can make well-informed choices. This alone takes one a long way, and beyond the attitude of those francophone African countries that still ban the sale of contraceptives. But all governments exercise an element of paternalism in taxing and subsidizing. Is the subsidization of family planning programs very different from the subsidization of medical attention? A would-be "acceptor" can still consult his conscience, and his religious mentor. Singapore has gone further and used the fiscal system to increase the cost of children. This does not seem to amount to coercion, though at some indefinable point a tax can be prohibitive. Even this bland comment on my part will set some teeth on edge. Many people otherwise very keen on the economic calculus react hostilely when it is extended to choosing children.

Capital Markets

Financial institutions—commercial and development banks—were and are seen by LDC governments mainly as instruments for mobilizing savings and lending them to the government or to the organized industrial sector. In nearly all LDCs they have believed firmly in low-controlled interest rates and credit rationing. Informal credit markets were discouraged.

Analysis by economists of the results, and in general of the development role of money, interest rates, and financial institutions, was virtually nonexistent in the 1950s (see chapter 7). Where economists did pronounce on interest rates, they favored low rates, dominated by the idea that LDCs suffered from an insufficient demand for loans for production purposes.

Even in the 1960s, writing on capital markets in LDCs was largely institutional or concerned with the determinants of financial development itself, rather than with any analysis of the role of money in development or even description of the actual working of loan markets in LDCs. In general, economists assumed that finance and financial institutions would follow or develop where the real economy led. That financial development could serve any purpose other than mobilizing savings for modernization was not contemplated,[95] and even this supposed function of the development of banking services was questionable.[96] The contrast of this continuing neglect with the attention paid to trade and industrialization is remarkable.

It was not until the publication in 1973 of two catalytic books,[97] by McKinnon and E. S. Shaw, both combining theoretical analysis and illustration of the malfunctioning of capital markets in

LDCs, that the subject became alive; and even then the follow-up has been slow to develop.

The essential message was that with low real interest rates, people would not want to hold much money or other financial assets. This was called "financial repression," a phrase that has become part of the language of development economists. The financial system could not then adequately fulfill one of its primary roles, that of integrating capital or credit markets so that returns to investment might come closer to equality. A fairly extreme case of segregation of credit markets (which could also be called the total repression of such markets, except for the government) would be one where no person, corporate or individual, saved except to invest in real assets. No one would lend, except the government (the most extreme case would be barter—but a socialist economy could avoid that by paying people in money). All investment would be self-financed, except for borrowing from public authorities. Any tendency to equalization of the returns to investment could come about only by government control of investment. In an economy in which there was no call for investment except by public enterprises, or large private enterprises that could easily be controlled and in which the government or such enterprises could do all the savings necessary, this might seem to some to be a sensible system.

But LDCs do not much resemble the economy we have just sketched. In most, more than half of the savings comes from households and unincorporated enterprises, farms, and small firms. These are also the surplus sectors, saving more than they invest. Governments, with a few exceptions, save little and invest more than they save. Corporations save more, but not as much as they invest.[98] The price mechanism, including interest rates, or nonavailability of credit, governs most investment decisions. In such mixed economies, widely developed and well-functioning capital markets are necessary for the efficient allocation of savings to investment, and perhaps, and more contentiously, to increase savings.

The contention of our authors, and by now many other economists, is that instead of improving capital markets, most LDC

201

governments have, by financial repression and in other ways, discouraged or prevented their desirable development and caused them to function in a manner that is often inimical to both rapid and equitable development. A crude measure of financial development is the ratio of M_2 (currency, plus demand and time deposits) to GNP. The normal expectation is that this rises with GNP. McKinnon pointed to three cases of sensational falls in Chile, Argentina, and Brazil. In some other LDCs (Sri Lanka, Pakistan, Peru) it remained constant at the low level of around 0.25 (in the industrialized countries it is around 0.6). In the others examined, except for Korea, it rose slowly to levels around 0.25.[99] In Korea, after the currency reform in the early 1960s, when interest rates were raised dramatically, it rose from 0.10 in 1964 to 0.35 in 1970. The real return on one-year bank deposits had changed from −15 percent to +13 percent, with inflation falling from 35 percent to 9 percent over the same period. Domestic savings rose from 7.7 percent to 17 percent of GNP from 1965 to 1970, while real GNP was rising at around 10 percent per annum. It was this experience that, no doubt, convinced McKinnon and Shaw of the great importance of relatively high interest rates and of expanding the formal capital markets.[100]

Such figures do not disentangle the direction of cause and effect. The enormous *trading* success of Korea and Taiwan probably caused some of the growth in bank deposits relative to GNP. Nevertheless, the timing and speed of the growth in deposits in Korea leave no doubt that the monetary reform was largely responsible. But that interest rates caused deposits to rise does not prove that they were the cause of the dramatic rise in domestic savings.

The growth-productive effect of higher interest rates, and the resultant higher holdings of financial assets, is supposed to operate in two ways. First, savings may be increased; and second, they should be better directed to productive investments. The first point is the more questionable. The a priori arguments are well balanced, and empirical investigations in MDCs have invariably found interest rates to be insignificant explanations of savings behavior. Matters could be different in LDCs because the levels of income are much lower. Also there are instances of huge changes in real interest rates—from −15 percent to +13 percent in Korea—whereas until very recently, when high inflation began in MDCs, changes in the real interest rates were very small. It could be that savings react only to fairly large changes (a threshold effect), or it could be that econometrics cannot pick up the results of small changes. A more recent study of savings and growth in seven Asian countries (Burma, India, Korea, Malaysia, the Philippines, Singapore, and Taiwan) finds that deposit interest rates have a significant influence on savings, and hence on the real supply of bank credit, and on investment and growth.[101] However, savings figures are (or should be) notoriously unreliable, and it will probably need a lot more positive evidence if most economists' conventional wisdom as to the irrelevance of interest rates for savings is to be undermined.[102] Meanwhile, there is a growing consensus that they should at least be positive, which either implies that zero is a threshold, or is based on an argument from equity. It is the relatively poor who often have no wider choice than saving in the form of accumulating things (which may be stolen), and deposits. Negative real interest rates are surely inequitable and almost amount to swindling small savers.

That high interest rates are conducive to savings has to compete with the "inflation tax" argument. The inflation tax operates by reducing the wealth of those who hold financial assets, insofar as nominal interest rates are not raised so as to maintain real interest rates; this cannot occur for currency, and it is also rare that demand deposits earn interest. It is then assumed that financial asset holders reduce consumption to recoup their losses, and hence savings rise. The financial repression school counters by pointing out that people do not necessarily try to recoup their lost wealth and that they reduce their holdings of "inflation-taxable" assets so far as they can. The inflation-tax argument takes a hard knock when savings rates rise as inflation falls, as has been the case in several countries.

That financial repression, caused by low interest rates, reduces the efficiency of investment can hardly be doubted. Some savers are guided to choose useless investment in stocks or other low-yielding projects. Anyone who notices a large number of incomplete buildings as he drives through a country can infer that the real interest rate on deposits is negative. On the borrowing side, the limited credit is subject to interest ceilings and is often further subject to the government's selective credit controls and imposed interest rate preferences. Selective credit controls are sometimes useful in helping to offset other distortions in the system (for example, cheap and ample credit for exporters may help to offset the discouragement to exports caused by the protective trade regime). In other cases they reinforce such distortions, as when already overprotected import-substitution industries also get cheap credit. The most general effect of financial repression is that the large, both farmers and industrialists, are favored at the expense of the small. With interest rate ceilings this is certain to happen, since any bank will channel its lending to where transactions costs and perceived risk are least, if it cannot charge relatively high interest rates as an offset. Some small-scale investments are frustrated altogether, either because it is not worth saving at negative deposit interest rates in order to accumulate the finance necessary to make the investment, or because no loan is available except at very high informal-sector interest rates.

Informal credit markets, ranging from large "indigenous" bankers in India, through credit cooperatives, to village moneylenders, and friends and relatives, expand in the vacuum, which is partly created by financial repression. But they also have a comparative advantage and would form part of any well-working system, at least until countries are rich enough to sustain with advantage a greatly expanded formal system. This is because their transactions costs are often lower than those of banks and because they can more cheaply and reliably assess the risks. Nevertheless, a large gap remains. Even if banks were not unduly conservative, as they usually are, they could not lend to most small borrowers if precluded from charging over, say, 10 percent. Informal market credit suppliers, who may often have some monopolistic power, may start at, say, 30 percent.

Research into the operation of informal markets, and their function, is still in its infancy. However, a tentative guideline for policy, which would almost certainly be better than attempted suppression of informal markets, can be suggested. The banking system should both try to compete with the informal sector and supply it with credit (reducing its monopoly power and in effect using it as an agent where it has a comparative advantage). This requires that interest rates rise and that the banks be free to discriminate.

V. V. Bhatt has suggested that technical innovations in banking, reducing transactions costs, hold out considerable promise; indeed, the whole of the evolution of financial systems can be seen as a series of innovations that reduce the cost and risk of lender-borrower transactions.[103] The climate of financial repression, and controlled credit markets, may be more conducive to high-cost oligopolistic banking and conservatism than would be a freer regime of competition for deposits and lending outlets. Bhatt and Roe point out that "if we accept the presence of large imperfections in the money and capital markets of LDCs, there is every reason to expect that the financial sector can be an *initiating* influence in the process of development rather than a merely passive one as is often assumed."[104]

PART IV

The New Radicalism

Chapter 11

Equality, Poverty, Labor Demand, and Basic Needs

Equality, Poverty, and Growth

The resurgence of neoclassical development economics that began in the 1960s and blossomed in the 1970s was almost contemporaneous with the growth of the dependency school, which itself grew out of Latin American structuralism (see chapter 5). But it also coincided with the basically much more orthodox movement toward an increased concern for unemployment and, a little later, poverty and "basic needs." In a survey article,[1] D. T. Healey linked the publication of the Organization for Economic Cooperation and Development series on trade and industrialization with work on employment by the OECD Development Centre,[2] and the International Labor Organization,[3] as landmarks in a new realization that all was not well with the pattern of development of the 1950s and 1960s. Naturally, there was a different focus to works on industrialization and trade on the one hand

and employment on the other, but Healey was right to link them, for there was much in common in both diagnosis and proposed treatment. In particular, it seemed that there was much that could be done to assist all three objectives—growth, employment, and equality.

However, any incipient consensus, even among the development establishment of the North and of international organizations, became so overlaid in the 1970s by divisive sentiments that it is now hard to discern. First, there was an increasing radical element whose basic message was that there was no hope for the poor in less developed countries unless their repressive and capitalist-serving governments were overthrown. Second, there was a populist movement that minimized the achievements of the past, often misconstrued the reasons for failure, put great weight on new slogans, and was short on analysis. The distinction is, I think, recognizable. It is with the populists that I am concerned in this chapter.

What was achieved in the 1950s and 1960s? The record in terms of growth of GNP per caput, and the changing structure of employment, production, and trade is examined in chapter 13. Here it need only be said that the 1960s was the best decade in history for virtually all LDCs, and that the rate of growth was almost incredible in some. The 1970s was not much worse, and was indeed the second-best decade for growth in LDCs in history.

The attack on growth as an objective began mainly among Western intellectuals and a few international civil servants from LDCs when they came to realize that inequality was extreme and urban unemployment high in most LDCs (which anyone acquainted with them must have known all along).[4] More starkly, such observation and belief soon led to the assertion that the poor were left out and even that the welfare of the mass of the people was deteriorating. Work began to try to prove this case.

What are the facts about poverty and equality? And how do they relate to growth in average per caput incomes? Unfortunately, nothing can be said briefly about this. In a sense, there are no facts. Even when definitions do not differ, there are only unreliable estimates. In only a very few countries are there comparable surveys of household or personal incomes at two points in time, let alone a series of such estimates, which is required for establishing any trend. India is the country that has been studied the most. The proportion of people below an arbitrarily defined poverty level of expenditure appears to have fluctuated considerably over time (depending on the harvest) without any overall trend. Absolute numbers of the poor very probably increased.[5] These personal expenditure estimates ignore certain collective consumption items and other indicators. Thus: "The ordinary person in today's villages is more likely to go to school, to possess or be able to listen to a radio, to have access to medical services, to have hope of surviving natural disasters, to be close to a paved road and inexpensive transport, and, at least until recently, his life expectancy was rising and more of his children were remaining alive."[6]

During the 1960s (which comprises most of the period over which the consumption estimates referred to above were made), average consumption per head in India rose at only 1.3 percent per annum. It has to be noted that with such a low rate of growth, it takes only a slight increase in inequality to leave the lower percentiles of the distribution no better off, though there is in fact no evidence of an increase in inequality but, rather, the reverse.[7] Bangladesh is perhaps the clearest case for which there are any figures and where the incidence of poverty increased between the 1960s and the first half of the 1970s.[8] But Bangladesh suffered from war and drought, and income per head fell.[9]

There can be no doubt that many millions of people have suffered absolutely in the past twenty years. But equally, there can be no doubt that the vast majority of these have been in countries where growth has been very slow or where there has been warfare and revolution.

Where growth has been rapid, the poorest have benefited. This was true even of Brazil, where there is a consensus that relative inequality increased markedly in the 1960s, but not enough to prevent the absolute incomes of the two poorest quintiles from rising significantly. In Mexico, although distribution is extremely unequal, it has apparently not worsened since 1963, so that real incomes of the poorer households have risen at the average rate of 4 percent per annum.[10] No one can doubt that the poorest people in those other very rapidly growing countries, the "baby tigers," have benefited dramatically, for income distribution had not worsened much, and was even improved in Taiwan[11] and Hong Kong.[12]

Social indicators strongly support the view that the mass of the people are better off. Life expectancy has risen everywhere from 1960 to 1978, from forty-two to fifty years in the World Bank's low-income LDCs, and from fifty-four to sixty-one years in the middle-income LDCs. In the same two groups, primary school enrollment has risen from 54 to 77 percent and from 81 to 97 percent of the relevant age group; adult literacy has risen from 29 to 38 percent and from 54 to 71 percent, respectively.[13]

Many irresponsible statements have been made, and not only by journalists, to the effect that growth of average income per caput has actually resulted in impoverishment of the masses. All of the scanty evidence points the other way. Where growth was very slow, in parts of South Asia and Africa, there may have been some worsening of the position of the poorest 20 to 40 percent of the population, but this is far from proven. Where growth was rapid, all large sections of the population benefited, though some more than others.

We turn to relative equality. The first question to ask is whether one should worry about it. It may be a social and political problem if excessive inequality results in such social tension as to require repressive regimes to maintain it, or it may cause revolution. I shall leave this to other social scientists. Is there a moral problem? I can only record my own view that absolute poverty is so serious in many LDCs that one should worry about relative inequality only to the extent that it causes absolute poverty.[14] But this statement is very imprecise and leaves open further moral problems as well as questions of fact. Let us suppose that as a matter of fact, more equality will cause less growth. Then equalization will reduce absolute poverty now but slow down the reduction of absolute poverty. One answer to this possible dilemma suggests itself. Provided there is positive growth, however slow, the future poor will be a little less poor than the present poor. So why sacrifice the present poor to them? In the limit this argument suggests that the relief of present poverty should have priority up to the point of reducing growth to zero. But here we have implicitly assumed that the present and future poor are different people. Where they are not, they may have their own preferences. A poor person now might prefer, if he is young, to remain very poor for a while if he knew that this would result in more rapid improvement later. Some would sacrifice themselves for their children.

Many people's judgment is likely to be influenced by the depth and extent of poverty now, the level of average incomes, and the cost in terms of growth. That there would be some cost is hardly to be doubted, and it should not be pushed under the carpet, for the aim of redistribution is to increase the consumption of a large section of the people. It is most unlikely that this could be achieved solely by reducing the consumption of the better-off.

There is no answer to these problems. Those who have in recent years tried to "dethrone" growth as an objective are saying that LDC governments have gone too far in sacrificing the possibility of present welfare improvement in favor of future people. At least, this is part of what they are saying. Some of them may also be saying that LDC governments are denying present welfare not so much for future welfare, but for more collective objectives such as prestige, power, independence, or ideology.

Much of the work on equality in the 1970s has been concerned with the question of whether growth causes inequality, rather than with the question of how far greater equality would reduce growth. Kuznets tentatively suggested that there was a historical tendency for inequality first to increase, and then to be reduced, as countries grew from a low level.[15] This has a strong plausibility for countries that start from a very low level of stagnant equality, for growth cannot start everywhere simultaneously, and growth both requires and produces skilled people who will inevitably have above average earnings. The hypothesis has been examined by regressing measures of inequality against incomes per head across countries, based on a compilation of inequality measures produced by the World Bank.[16] The result is at best a very weak confirmation for LDCs, very little of the variance be-

213

ing explained.[17] Bearing in mind the inadequacy and noncomparability of the underlying data, it seems that little follows.[18] Those who have commented that there is no such iron saucer-shaped law of distribution are surely right.

Labor Demand and Basic Needs

After fifty years of assisting the creation of dual labor markets in LDCs by the transfer of Western-style labor legislation, at the end of the 1960s, the ILO began to study unemployment and employment. It soon found, as the OECD Development Centre had also done, that poverty and inequality had little to do with unemployment. It should be added that the case for a pattern of development that is more demanding of unskilled labor does not depend upon evidence of either unemployment or underemployment. Essentially, the case is that a minority of people work with a lot of capital (or land), and a large majority with very little indeed, and thus can earn very little. If new investment called for more participating labor, then either more work would be done or real wages would rise. Either way, the unskilled (or initially unskilled) workers benefit. If increased earnings do not result from increased demand for labor, then increases for some will impoverish others.

Instead of concentrating on an analysis of the essential causes of inadequate labor demand, and remedies, the huge research project of the ILO World Employment Program studied just about everything—population, education, income distribution, appropriate technology, multinationals, etc.—with rather little impact. But the main upshot was the ILO's espousal of the concept of a "basic needs strategy," in its submission to the World Employment Conference of 1976. By the verbal trick of calling poor workers underemployed, even if working a seventy-hour week, the ILO brought poverty and basic needs within the purview of an employment conference.

EQUALITY, POVERTY, LABOR DEMAND, AND BASIC NEEDS

An improved use of labor, implied by the reduction of the many distortions in LDCs that are examined throughout this work, would increase both output and the demand for labor. But not all of the poor would benefit. Most would, even those who cannot work, because private transfers are a feature of LDCs. Even so, it is rightly argued that an earnings approach alone is not enough. Some things may not be available to be bought by the poor—this applies most generally to services that are often or mainly public monopolies or are publicly controlled, such as water, sewage, public health, education, and housing. It is notorious that in many developing countries these systems are designed or operated in a manner that is biased against the poor: perhaps the most notorious case is the bulldozing of shanty settlements. To the extent that the poor can pay, there is no net use of resources.[19]

There remains the question of how far the poor should be subsidized. Direct subsidies are seldom favored. Indirect subsidies almost always include educational and health services. Several LDCs also spend heavily on subsidizing food. Such subsidies often reach the poor only at very high cost. Some are even regressive, as when higher education is more heavily subsidized than primary education. If the poor are to be reached at a cost that most governments are likely to tolerate, some targeting (that is, direct or indirect means-testing) is essential. Similarly, resources should not be used to subsidize the relatively wealthy.

All the considerations, very briefly sketched above, are and always have been part of any discussion of how best to tackle poverty. Moreover, the move toward a greater emphasis on poverty in a few LDCs and in international institutions preceded the "basic needs" approach by several years;[20] in particular, new and overdue work on cheap services appropriate to the poor had begun, especially at the World Bank. What, then, was distinctive about a "basic needs strategy"? Early on, it seems to have been envisaged that basic needs could actually be defined in an appropriate and operational manner; and that governments should then set about, in some direct and dirigiste but essentially unspecified manner, ensuring that every family had so many calories, shelter of an approved standard, all children in primary school, and so on. The suspicion of excessive dirigisme and paternalism (implicit in the word "needs") antagonized some liberals. The governments of LDCs were also very suspicious, but, as we shall see, for different reasons. This element, however, now seems to have vanished. "Basic needs" now occurs in the title of countless articles, but it seems to me that it is indistinguishable from, say, "poverty redressal" or even "redistribution with growth."[21] In particular, "basic needs" are nowhere defined. Governments are being urged to spend more on subsidized services (while finding ways of making the richer pay); on funding and adopting ways of making public services cheaper and more appropriate (preventative against curative medicine, paramedicals, sites and services schemes, etc.). More controversially, subsidization of food is advocated, but in a targeted manner, which limits leakage and the accrual of benefits to the better-off (for example, by food stamps).[22]

As we have seen, the "basic needs strategy" came on stage at the World Employment Conference in 1976. It was formally adopted. But many LDCs were very suspicious, despite the fact that it was proclaimed in the ILO submission that "a rapid rate of economic growth is an essential part of a basic needs strategy"[23] (irresponsibly denying any trade-off with growth). Their main fear was that the value of capital-intensive basic industries was being denied and that attention would be diverted from the New International Economic Order. The policy guidelines were adopted "to the extent that countries consider them to be desirable." Their commitment was largely rhetorical.[24] Later, the Economic and Social Council of the United Nations failed to agree to submit the conference proposals to the General Assembly.

The advocates of policies that would lead to a more equal division of the benefits of increased production (and, perhaps, of some redistribution of assets) have my sympathy, and they require a slogan. "Basic needs" has become just that, and it is now pedantic to argue with it. But has the slogan helped? Have LDC governments become any more committed in terms of actual policies? India and Malaysia, for instance, have shifted emphasis; but this occurred before the international organizations began to campaign. It needs someone closer to very recent policy developments in LDCs to answer the question. But my impression is that the forces that favor capital intensity, with its inevitably skewed distribution of benefits, remain very strong. And many question the right of international organizations and aid donors to preach equality or poverty redressal.[25]

Chapter 12

Dependency and Underdevelopment

Introduction

The development literature of 1945 to 1960 included the work of several writers who believed that trade and private overseas investment did not always benefit, and might even impoverish, poor countries. Singer, Myrdal, and Balogh are the most obvious examples. Examples of a clear Marxist-Leninist interpretation of the backwardness (as it was called in the 1950s) of many countries were fewer until the mid-1960s. Baran is the outstanding example, and his work has clearly influenced the "underdevelopment" and "dependencia" school that has emerged in the past fifteen years. The latter is the Latin American branch of a "neo-Marxist" school that attributes "underdevelopment" in "peripheral" countries to the spread of "capitalism" from "the center." The doctrine, like structuralism, seems to have originated in the Economic Commission for Latin America.[1] It has spread widely in recent years.

All key words in the last few sentences have been placed in

quotation marks because their meanings are unclear, and this chapter is largely a discussion of them. Even "neo-Marxist" is in quotation marks because the doctrines of this school are far removed from, indeed the opposite of, what Marx thought. He saw the imposition of capitalism through imperialism as a necessary jolt to the stagnant economies of the East, a jolt that would eventually lead to industrialization, the emergence of conflicting classes, and hence to socialism. The "underdevelopment" school rather follows Baran, who wrote: "It is in the underdeveloped world that the central, overriding fact of our epoch becomes manifest to the naked eye: the capitalist system, once a mighty engine of economic development, has turned into a no less formidable hurdle to economic advancement."[2] He wrote before a telescope could have discovered that in East Asia capitalism would produce results that make its nineteenth-century performance look like that of a donkey.

Why then is this school often called neo-Marxist or neo-Marxist-Leninist? I suppose because most, perhaps not all, of those I would think of as belonging to it would so describe themselves. Less subjectively, they would all share the view that the center has, over the course of the past four hundred years, exploited the periphery and appropriated its surplus and that it continues to do so through the medium of the capitalist system. It is this that causes underdevelopment. The theory of underdevelopment is the obverse side of the coin of imperialism. Thus, Hobson and Lenin were looking at imperialism from the viewpoint of Western Europe and of its relationship to the economies of Western Europe. The underdevelopment school is concerned with the effects on the periphery. Capitalism in the periphery is "dependent," which makes it a very different and less dynamic animal compared with that of "the center." I do not include in the dependency-underdevelopment school those radicals who, whether regarding themselves as Marxists or not, believe that it is primarily capitalism as such, not dependent capitalism, that is to be held responsible for the poverty and inequality of the Third World.[3] I do include such writers as S. Amin, F. H. Cardoso, A. Emmanuel, A. G. Frank, S. Hymer, C. Leys, R. Sau, O. Sunkel, to mention but a few names from different countries.[4] Although there are quite profound differences among neo-Marxists, including those mentioned, they and many others would, I believe, subscribe to the propositions of this paragraph.

The main doctrines of the dependency school have found little acceptance. Few outside a small magic circle would agree that desirable development is impossible if there is much contact with foreign capitalism. Few leaders of less developed countries could admit to the role in which most of them are cast. Yet the influence of the school has been considerable. Its emphasis is on blaming external forces, either metaphysical, such as the "World Capitalist System," or more concrete structures, such as the International Monetary Fund, for domestic discontents. To this extent, its vocabulary is welcome to many LDC leaders, even right-wing nationalists. Although it has converted only a few erstwhile mainstream economists, its influence on sociologists and political theorists seems to have been significant. Political economy, with the stress on "political," is a new fashion. Political theorists and sociologists see events and relations more in terms of conflict than do economists.

We have briefly described the soft core of the dependency doctrine, and it is clearly enough a Marxist-Leninist derivative. One Marxist feature, common to all or most members of this school, is the manner in which they manipulate language. The trick is to define a concept with a value-laden connotation in a manner that often bears little relation to ordinary usage—the so-called persuasive definition.[5] Marx's key persuasive definition was that of the word "exploitation"—so defined that any enterprise that pays a worker a wage, and makes a profit, necessarily exploits him.[6] This is similar to the neo-Marxist definition of "unequal exchange," which according to one definition arises whenever countries with equal profit rates exchange products of equal market value that, however, are produced with unequal amounts of current labor.[7] As Samuelson remarks, "It is tautologically a restatement of the fact of assumed wage differentials."[8] But clearly the phrase "unequal exchange" carries the overtone that such exchange is unjust. What is worse is that it might carry for some the further implication either that such trade should be stopped or that real wages should be equalized by raising the lower rate.

This implication, seized on by some trade unionists in rich countries, would be disastrous for the developing countries.

Another feature is the frequent use of value-laden descriptions. Thus, any foreign business is invariably (with some authors) described as a foreign monopoly, whether in fact it operates under monopolistic, oligopolistic, or highly competitive conditions. One result of this linguistic manipulation is that the possibility of serious analysis is greatly reduced. For the purpose of analysis, it is necessary to define the school's terms, neutralize their value-content, and distinguish what has been confused.

In seeking to define terms in a manner that makes analysis possible, one cannot avoid doing some violence to the ways in which some of the authors use them (that is, implicitly define them). The ways in which a country may, or may not, be dependent on foreigners cannot be analyzed, if "dependency" is used to mean nothing more or less than trading with, or receiving investment from, a specified list of other countries. Yet this is how one of the most acclaimed of the "underdevelopment" theorists uses the term. Thus, by definition, any "peripheral" country that trades with, for example, Israel or South Africa, is dependent. By definition, no country is dependent on the USSR.

We shall *not* concern ourselves with the dependence of being unwillingly ruled by foreigners, or of being subject to extortionary raids by a more powerful state or tribe. This is not to say that past colonization is not still casting its shadow on many economies and on many minds. The point is rather that this form of dependency on the Western powers hardly exists today, and that the theory of underdevelopment, insofar as it is relevant to the analysis of existing conditions or to policy, is specifically concerned with neocolonialism or neoimperialism—that is, with the supposedly malign influence of the Western developed powers that does *not* depend on rule or force of arms, or even threats of such.

Moreover, we shall note only in passing the phenomenon of forced trade. The controlled monopolized trade of the mercantilist era was closer to rape than to free trade between consenting adults. Some colonial powers continued such trade even into the second half of the nineteenth century, but it was largely superseded by the British style of open door "free" trade—free in the sense of not being limited by quotas and tariffs, but not free in the sense that it was a free choice of the colonial territories. It was dependent free trade.[9] Since, however, free trade could now be chosen by LDCs, we shall examine the question of whether such a choice would be likely to lead, in any sense, to dependency.

Nor shall we be concerned with strategic dependence, even though it is the most pervasive and powerful form of dependence. Almost all countries in the world could be regarded as dependent for their existence on a world order that is precariously maintained by great power rivalry. One of the main limitations on the room for maneuver of a poor or small state is that it cannot easily make war, or defend itself even against a similar state, without the connivance of a developed country that supplies arms. This may be a reason for a country to try to create its own armaments industry—even though none except the superpowers can be remotely self-sufficient in this respect.

The kind of dependency with which we are concerned is not forced upon a country. The head of state may proclaim, "We are forced to accept aid if we are to prevent starvation, grow, etc." But this use of the word "force" points to cause and effect, not to coercion. The country could retreat into its shell, albeit probably at great cost to other aims than independence.

We shall distinguish three different areas of economic dependency: trade, transfers, and technology. Under technology we include entrepreneurial and managerial dependency.

Trade Dependency

Starting with trade, we make a further tripartite classification into (1) competitive, (2) private noncompetitive, and (3) state noncompetitive. This classification is to some extent arbitrary. In particular, there is no clear dividing line between "competitive" and "noncompetitive." The test is whether any single buyer or seller (or any coalition of them) can exercise significant market power—say, change the price by as much as 10 percent in the long run. But it is often very hard to determine whether such a test would be satisfied.

In one important sense of "dependence," there is never any dependency in *competitive* trade or exchange, whether for a country or an individual. One is not dependent on any individual, organization, or institution. There is no question of being "taken for a ride"—nor does it matter much if any particular person or institution vanishes. One is dependent on no one. But there is another meaning of "dependent" that has nothing to do with the exercise of market power or the threat of coercion. Thus, it makes good sense to say that Ghana is very dependent on cocoa, even if the cocoa market is highly competitive. We may call this "competitive market dependency." It is not a simple concept. There are at least three dimensions to it: (a) the proportion of trade to gross national product, (b) the concentration of trade on one or on a few commodities (commodity concentration), and (c) the concentration of sales or purchases on particular national markets (market concentration).[10] A country is often said to be highly trade dependent if either (a) is high, or (a) is significant while either (b) or (c) is high. The trade dependency of the Third World as a whole is often exaggerated, though many very small countries are highly trade dependent.[11] But for the present argument that is irrelevant, for "competitive market dependency" has nothing to do with the meaning of dependency as used by the underdevelopment school. For instance, India would be classified as a dependent economy, although trade has been only about 6 percent of GNP and is divided between many commodities bought and sold in many markets. It would probably be better if "dependency" were not used in this context at all. We can simply speak of "high-trading" and "low-trading" countries, with high or low commodity and market concentration.

We approach, however, part of the meaning of dependency as we turn to noncompetitive trade. In this context "noncompetitive" means that the dependent economy can be significantly affected by the decisions of a single foreign person or firm, or government agency. There are degrees of dependency in this sense that can be subjectively defined as the expected value of the difference such foreign decisions may make. The dislike of dependency may be that there is expected harm, or risk of harm, as compared with some (difficult to define) independency. Dependency on a certainly benign being, God, perhaps, may be welcome. But some people may resent dependency even if assured that it is benign.

PRIVATE NONCOMPETITIVE TRADE

Many LDC citizens believe that, in the past, they got less than they should for agricultural and mineral exports as a result of the monopolization of trade or of the industry using their exports. In principle, since we are considering only trade at this point, we must abstract from cases such as copper and oil, and some plantations, where production as well as trade was controlled by foreigners. Where production was in the hands of many local producers, unintegrated with downstream industry and usually in several or even many countries, it is very unlikely that purchasers, even when there were fairly few of them, could or did keep the price down significantly by restricting their purchases—simply because the supply was highly elastic. The case is different with mineral production, where the number of mines in developing countries was sometimes small, and where they were often owned and operated by companies engaged in downstream activities or in distribution (there were some cases of this with agricultural products also—especially bananas). In these cases, which involve not merely trade but also transfers of capital and profits as well as technology, the "host" country and the company would have the same interest in a high price. Interests differ mainly on the share of the spoils (that is, the profits of the integrated operation).[12] The host country's bargaining position will depend on the possibility the operator has of producing elsewhere, the richness of the mine, the sunk capital, and the possibility the host country has of operating successfully if the existing owner-operator is expelled. This is an area and type of dependency that has been historically very important, and perhaps it is no accident that the doctrine of dependency originated in Chile, where three United States companies dominated Chile's production and exports of copper until they were expropriated in the early 1970s.

Times have changed, partly as a result of the activities of nationalists and radicals. LDC governments now either own or control production and sales in most of the important minerals, oil, iron ore, copper, and bauxite.[13] Export supplies of these and other raw materials are now rarely, if ever, derived solely from the behavior of atomistic competitors; even if governments do not own the resources, or exercise surveillance over foreign contracts, they intervene through the medium of marketing boards or the imposition of export taxes. The situation is often one of bilateral oligopoly between a few LDC governments and a few large corporations. There is usually some exercise of market power on both sides, and the situation is then clearly one of *interdependence*. We can make no attempt here to assess the division of the spoils. Indeed, no one can as yet, for, apart from the conceptual difficulties, there has been too little research on the workings of these markets, other than for oil.

The imports of LDCs of primary products from more developed countries is not, so far as I am aware, significantly subject to private monopoly (diamonds are an exception if South Africa is counted as an MDC). But any dependence here is dwarfed in importance by dependence on food imports (see below).

We turn to the manufactured exports of LDCs. Is there a case for saying that monopsonistic buyers hold down prices? This must occasionally happen. For instance, if a Western enterprise, whether a manufacturer or very large retail organization, arranges for production abroad (international subcontracting), it may be able to exercise some market power, since alternatives for the supplier may be limited.[14] I am not aware of much work on this subject. But some light is thrown by Westphal, et al., in the case of Korea, which is one of the few great exporters of manufactures to MDCs.[15] They report:

> Successful exporting does not require widespread and close integration more or less directly with the operations of firms overseas—of the sort epitomized by international sub-contracting and similar operations of MNCs [multinational corporations]. This impression is buttressed by the fact that most exporters sold to a

number of buyers, not just to one or two. Of eighty-seven firms that responded to a question about the importance of individual foreign buyers, fifty-nine indicated that at least one foreign buyer normally accounted for more than 10 per cent of their export sales. But the share of a firm's exports accounted for by any one such "large buyer" typically was less than 20 per cent.

Finally, it should be noticed that within a country one does not necessarily bewail the fate of a subcontractor.

As with exports, some imports of manufactures are certain to be at monopolistic prices. For instance, A. J. Yeats found that European Economic Community associated countries, mostly ex-French colonies, paid higher prices for steel than other countries. Reverse preferences, as well as history, tended to tie these countries to French producers. When other EEC countries also received preference after 1966, reducing the French monopoly, the price differential was also reduced.[16] It has also been shown that aid tying raises import prices.[17] These are cases where noncompetitive prices, although privately set, are encouraged by governmental relationships. Of course, there are other monopolies not thus aided and abetted. Pharmaceuticals have attracted particular attention and is one of the relatively few cases where the monopoly position is protected by patents, but then patent monopolies are in practice necessary for the development of new methods and products. Whether the world, or the Third World, would be better off if the pharmaceutical industry had to operate with much lower margins on its successful drugs is questionable. International cartels are quite rare (nickel and aluminum may be exceptions), and competition even where oligopolistic is often fierce (as in the automobile industry). For a great many products, therefore, there is a large number of suppliers from as many as a dozen countries. I doubt if LDCs suffer significantly from the monopolistic supply of imported manufactures. Profit margins on exports are frequently reported to be very low. Competition in many industries has increased in the past twenty years, despite increasing concentration within industrialized countries, because of the industrial growth of Japan and Continental Europe, as well as some LDCs. I believe that trade dependence on private foreign corporations is insignificant compared with trade dependence on foreign governments.

GOVERNMENT TRADE, AND MANIPULATION OF PRIVATE TRADE

Trade with the Communist countries, on both the import and export side, is necessarily dependent, since these countries trade through state monopolies. (Some LDCs also use state trading corporations, but not in all sectors.) In practice, however, their power to influence prices is often limited, since they have to compete with the capitalists in countries that are not themselves Communist. But this does not always apply in primary markets where transactions may be very large, sudden, and unpredictable. The most notorious case was the USSR wheat purchases in the early 1970s.[18] This United States-USSR deal contributed to starvation in Bangladesh.

MDC governments also intervene extensively in trade. The EEC effectively controls imports of most competing agricultural products by import levies. Government or government-induced stockpiling can cause or reinforce large price fluctuations (for example, the large Japanese stockpiling of materials in 1974). Exports have been restricted to limit domestic price increases (for example, United States restrictions on soybean exports). Quota restrictions, or other nontariff barriers, have been arbitrarily imposed on imports of clothing, shoes, television sets, steel, etc., under the so-called new protectionism of the second half of the 1970s. These are interventions for commercial reasons. But there are also interventions for political reasons. There have always been restrictions for long-run strategic reasons: all countries restrict exports of armaments, and of technology of strategic interest, to political enemies. Attempts to prevent nuclear proliferation fall into the same category. But trade interventions are also used for more particular foreign policy reasons. There are the United States embargoes on trade with Cuba, and more recently the United States limitations on wheat exports to the USSR imposed to punish the Russians for the invasion of Afghanistan. Then there were also trade sanctions against South Africa, and

Rhodesia before it became Zimbabwe, and so on. Finally, the special intervention of establishing preferences in favor of LDCs, both those of the EEC for their associates and generalized special preferences (GSPs), must be classed as trade intervention for political reasons.

The LDCs behave in the same way. Since 1945, their general import restrictions have been far more extensive than those of MDCs. As we have seen, LDC governments now very generally control exports of primary goods, trying, where they can, to raise prices. Brazil, like the United States, has banned exports of soybeans, and India has often limited exports to reduce domestic price rises. On the political front, the oil exporters have been active in trying to influence other countries' policies toward South Africa and Israel, by using or threatening to use the weapon of an oil embargo.

It might be argued that the existence of sovereign governments, which are free to restrict or subsidize exports or imports in any way they like, implies that there is no such thing as competitive trade, for the action of the government, or an agency of the government, of country A may always significantly affect the economy of country B. There are two important qualifications to this argument. First, there are many governments of countries whose absolute value of trade, both in the aggregate and in any particular important commodity, is too small for them to affect other countries much. This clearly implies that LDCs are in general more dependent on the actions of the governments of large countries, especially the United States and Japan, or of coalitions like the EEC. The exceptions are where small countries can form coalitions, as in oil and bauxite, or where a single LDC is so important in a particular commodity that it can alone make its authority felt; Saudi Arabia is perhaps the only example. The three most potentially damaging North-South economic dependencies in the world are: (1) those of the MDCs, especially Continental Europe and Japan, on the oil exporters; (2) those of the Far Eastern countries whose specialization in manufactured exports, especially clothing, has made them highly dependent on the protective policies of the MDCs;[19] and (3) those of a great many LDCs and Communist countries, whose increasing reliance on cereal imports had made them dependent on the United States, which is the supplier of last resort and whose government intervenes in the grain trade.

The second important qualification is that in the case of countries that are large (overall, or in the market for particular commodities) one must distinguish between different types of behavior and also ask whether interests differ. An extreme, albeit nonexistent, case would be a large country known to be wedded faithfully to laisser faire. For others, this would imply at worst some market dependence, for although there is a potential actor who could make decisions affecting the economies of other countries, he is assumed to take no such decisions. Of course, other countries might well prefer dependence. If, for instance, the large country successfully pursued macroeconomic policies that made it more stable, other countries would probably prefer this, although it would imply that another government was taking decisions that affected them. There are a half-dozen or so countries whose overall trade is so large that their macroeconomic policies, whether traditionally regarded as internal (fiscal and monetary policies) or external (exchange rates, overall levels of protection, etc.), significantly affect most other countries. This is an important area of concern. It is also, fortunately, an area in which there is a good deal of mutual interest. In general, any country would like others to be stable; with perhaps some strategic exceptions, a country also prefers others to grow. But conflict may arise when there is an element of choice between different objectives that are valued differently. Other countries have often wanted Germany and Japan to be more expansionary, eliminating their balance-of-payments surpluses, which would ease those others' problems. The special interest of developing countries in the manner in which these few large countries conduct their macroeconomic affairs is discussed in chapter 18. They are inevitably dependent on this, and also on institutional arrangements (such as the IMF and the Organization for Economic Cooperation and Development) for discussing and mediating these problems of interdependency. Here we will say only that intervention in particular markets on the part of MDC governments, as opposed to macroeconomic management, increases LDC dependency. This would not be the case if such intervention were only for the purpose of reducing the market power of private actors. It is easy for liberal economists and LDC leaders to cry "hands off" where the reasons for intervention are commercial. Where they are political, almost everyone must pause, for almost everyone favors some political interventions and condemns others.

MDC spokesmen who want to counter complaints of dependency, as well as those who like to exaggerate, often in apocalyptic terms, the extent to which problems require global solutions (with increasing hordes of global bureaucrats), have in recent years spoken much of "interdependency." It is not surprising that this irritates many LDCs, for the only important dependency of the MDCs on LDCs derives from "oil power."

SUMMARY

The following propositions summarize the trade reality reasonably well:

1. The greatest source of dependency of LDCs on MDCs stems from the interventionist behavior of MDC governments, whether for commercial or political reasons.
2. The USSR is of lesser direct importance mainly because it trades so little with LDCs. But its competition for North American cereals is a very important indirect threat.
3. In the field of minerals, where the question is, "Who gets the rent?" LDC government intervention has been very important in reducing dependency.
4. Partly as a result of no. 3, monopolistic private trade is a relatively insignificant source of trade dependency.

Dependency on Transfers

Transfers can be divided various ways (see table 12-1). One important distinction is between grants, which gives rise to no future liability, and loans, which do. Another is between concessionary loans, which, like grants, form part of Official Development Assistance (ODA), and nonconcessionary loans. In total, ODA is highly concessionary. In 1979, 77 percent consisted of grants, and the total "grant element" was 91 percent. The three-way distinction that will most concern us is between (a) ODA, or aid, (b) commercial borrowing, and (c) private direct investment.

TABLE 12-1
Net Receipts of LDCs from All Sources
($ billion)

	1970	1979
ODA from members of the DAC (both direct and through multilateral agencies)	$ 6.7	$ 21.8
Nonconcessionary loans from multilateral agencies (mostly World Bank)	0.7	4.2
Private direct investment	3.7	13.5
Commercial credit	6.0	30.6
Total from DAC and multilateral institutions (excluding OPEC-financed contributions)	$ 17.1	$ 70.1
OPEC (including ODA and nonconcessionary finance)	0.6	5.1
CPEs	1.2	1.9
Other (mainly private grants and other small non-DAC countries)	0.3	3.9
Total	$ 19.2	$ 81.0

SOURCE: OECD, *Development Corporation, 1980 Review*, table IV–VIII.

The table shows the magnitude of these transfers from MDCs to LDCs for 1970 and 1979. But for completeness it also includes intra-LDC transfers from the Organization of Petroleum Exporting Countries, and those from the centrally planned economies (CPEs) and other small donors. The enormous increase in commercial credit has resulted largely from a few LDCs borrowing heavily in the Eurodollar market. It should be noted that transfers are net of amortization and capital repayments, but not of interest of dividends.

OFFICIAL DEVELOPMENT ASSISTANCE (OR AID)

Aid comprises all grants and loans on concessional terms from governments of the industrialized and centrally planned economies, and from multilateral agencies (principally the World Bank) to the governments of, or agencies of the governments of, the developing countries. Technical assistance is a form of aid, where the transfer normally takes the form of the direct provision of services and is small in terms of monetary value.

Almost all liberal intellectuals in the industrialized countries have been in favor of aid, and in favor of increasing aid for humanitarian reasons. Most governments have felt the same way, even if only because aid is a foreign policy tool. Although many "underdevelopment" theorists seem to attach very little importance to aid (it does not figure in the index of several of the works I have read), there is a radical fringe that claims that aid, either bilateral or multilateral, is actually harmful to the recipient, and that it is imperialistic in effect, and even in intent.

It is clear that some very poor countries have been, and even are, in need of aid for investment and growth ("development" aid), and even for running a viable administration ("budget" aid). Since there is a limited number of donors and donor agencies, the receiving country becomes (as in any noncompetitive or imperfectly competitive situation) dependent on the decisions of particular foreign agencies. Of course, a government can refuse aid. But the internal cost may be high. Burma is one of the very few developing countries that has refused aid. Clearly LDC governments believe that the benefits of aid outweigh the dependency created, although they would all like to reduce the dependency in various ways—by multilateralization, by creating United Nations capital funds over which LDCs would have control, by persuading bilateral donors to attach no strings, and by claiming that aid should be given and received as of right.

The donors, on the other hand, often want to increase their leverage over the recipient's policies or choice of investment (that is, increase the recipient's dependence). Sometimes this may be for political or strategic ends. But often it is for good economic motives. The donor agency believes it knows more than the recipient about the means of achieving economic progress. But it is hard to separate ends and means. Sometimes the donor may have a different idea from the recipient government as to the meaning of development. Especially in the 1970s, the World Bank, some other United Nations agencies, and some bilateral donors became more radical than most recipient governments concerning the pattern of income growth—they wanted to see development more slanted toward the poor. This presented dependency theorists with a difficulty. Increased dependency is not supposed to help the poor of the world.

However, I can imagine that their argument might run somewhat as follows (assuming that they do not simply deny that the World Bank, etc., intends to make any serious effort to achieve "redistribution with growth"). The fact that the government of a developing country has to put up with the donor's advice on the shape of its investment plans, use cost-benefit analysis, and even modify its macroeconomic policies, whether in the name of redistribution or not, is quite a trivial sort of dependency. The real "imperialism of aid" lies elsewhere. It lies in the support it (Western aid) gives to a capitalist world, to the trade of the developed countries, but most especially to private foreign investment (by giant transnational monopolies). It does this in a number of ways. The first and most important is that it helps to support the governments to which it is given, and these tend to be right wing. Second, it is used to further the causes of mining, cash crop agriculture, and open trading policies, which suit the capitalist economies of the center (and probably improve their terms of trade). Third, it helps to lay the foundations for private investment by providing the physical infrastructure required—the roads, ports, and power supplies. In itself it shares some of the evils of private investment (see below). Moreover, it tends to perpetuate itself, and consequently dependency. Thus, it may reduce the domestic savings ratio (for it provides not merely balance of payments but budgetary support to governments and so makes them less inclined to raise taxes). Also, a country in the end must always pay back more than it borrows, and in this way, also, aid tends to perpetuate itself (though this is untrue of bilateral ODA, which is mostly granted).

The above paragraph is a tissue of truth, half-truth, and misleading insinuation, an easy tissue to weave, this being the reason why one can find similar paragraphs in hundreds of articles and books. First, it is true that most aid goes to predominantly capitalist countries, including those that proclaim themselves socialist. This could hardly be otherwise, since most LDCs are more or less capitalist. It is also true that foreign policy considerations are important in determining the distribution of bilateral aid and that bilateral donors will not usually give to countries that are allied to or clearly aligned with the USSR. But it does not follow that aid is given to promote capitalism: it would be difficult to reconcile this with the fact that socialist Tanzania gets much more than capitalist Kenya. It must also be remembered that the World Bank extends loans to its members, including Algeria, Yugoslavia, Romania, and Vietnam; and no doubt large loans will go in time to China. It is finally true that aid goes to some nasty repressive regimes, some of which are socialist.

The second and third arguments, which suggest that the kinds of projects and policies that aid donors favor are designed to further the capitalist cause, are very thin. At one time, the World Bank and other donors did eschew aid for public sector projects in areas that were usually a private preserve, but this has not been true for many years. Concentration of the World Bank on physical infrastructure has also greatly diminished. The idea that the new shift in emphasis toward agriculture (including support for small farms), toward education, and in favor of more open trading policies is designed to favor world capitalism rather than to promote a more equally shared growth, can have no plausibility except for those with a chronic tendency to believe in occult forces. This is not to deny that aid may on balance work in favor of private enterprise. But this is not the point of the attack of dependency theorists, which is rather that aid promotes a stunted peripheral form of capitalism, associated with dualism and inequality. Here I would argue that one cannot ignore the genuine effort of aid donors to ensure, with some success, that aid projects have high *social* returns (not merely private or public profit) and that they benefit the mass of the people. Aid donors have been more in favor of poverty-oriented projects than most recipient governments.

The third argument, that aid discourages local efforts, especially savings, and hence perpetuates itself, has no good empirical support. It is based on cross-country correlations that show that those who save less get more aid. It should be needless to add that this does not show that more aid causes less savings. Country-level case studies lend no support to the argument; indeed, they go a long way toward refuting it.[20]

To summarize, aid is undoubtedly a dependency relationship in which the existence and stability of part of a country's resources become dependent on foreign or international agencies. But it is not a dependency relationship in the sense of dependency favored by the radical theorists.

COMMERCIAL BORROWING

In the 1950s and 1960s, commercial borrowing by LDC governments or agencies consisted largely of suppliers' credits, an expensive form of finance that has led a few countries, such as Ghana, into unmanageable debt situations. In the 1970s, a few LDC governments or central banks borrowed very heavily in the Eurocurrency market (that is, from private banks using oil exporters' and other deposits). This seems to have been a fairly competitive market; but it was not a perfectly competitive one, and many countries were, and still are, unable to borrow money in it, being thought to be credit unworthy at any price the banks could be seen to be charging. Despite much alarmism, and heavy indebtedness on the part of a few countries, there has been no collapse (see chapter 17). But aid agencies' loans are still much in demand, even by those countries that can and do borrow commercially, because they offer better terms (longer maturities in the case of IBRD loans).

Provided the debt can be serviced, commercial borrowing does not automatically involve a dependency relationship. As with trade, it does so only to the extent that lenders are monopolistic or oligopolistic. However, if a country fails to be able to meet its commitments, it will usually get its debts rescheduled, by a meeting of creators organized by the IMF or the IBRD; and it is then in a position of dependence. In this connection, it is the IMF that receives the strongest criticism because the IMF's conditional loans are those of last resort. No responsible person can suppose that the IMF's loans should not be conditional, for clearly no country should expect unlimited unconditional support from others. The IMF has earned much hostility by its supposed harshness, and there is a widespread dislike of becoming dependent on the IMF (see chapters 15 and 17).

DIRECT PRIVATE INVESTMENT

This is the bête noire—the most awful species in the bestiary of underdevelopment. As opposed to portfolio investment, the transfer of capital is for the purpose of creating or buying control over real assets in the "host" country. Such investment almost invariably encompasses all three of the possible forms dependency may take: trade, monetary transfers, and technology.

We have already considered the economic analysis of private foreign investment (see chapter 10) and we shall defer further consideration of dependency and the transnational corporations until we deal with the transfer of industrial know-how and technology, which some believe to be the main reason for accepting foreign investment (despite the net transfer of some $13.5 billion in 1979).

Industrial Dependency and Independence

In recent years, there has been much discussion of technological independence. But first it is useful to distinguish industrial independence or self-reliance—a more basic concept than technological independence.

In a strict analogy with trade, we would say that a country was a case of competitive industrial dependence if all its enterprises were owned by foreigners, and if there were a high degree of competition, so that no one foreigner could significantly affect the economy. Since this is clumsy, we shall use the word "independence" simply in the sense of not relying on foreigners, whether in the form of transnationals or not. However, the seriousness of the dependence still relies a lot on the element of competition.

Ownership is not the most critical factor. A country may insist on majority ownership by its own nationals. But if nationals are incapable of successfully making the important entrepreneurial and managerial decisions, there is still reliance on foreigners. Entrepreneurship is more important than management. For instance, in the beginnings of Indian factory industry, Parsee cotton merchants began textile production using British spindles and looms while also employing British managers. Similarly, when J. D. Tata began to produce steel, he used foreign processes and management. No one would suggest that this was not Indian industry. The final decisions on what to make and how to make it, and whether to invest further, etc., were Indian decisions. Again, for many years the Japanese used foreign managers and technicians as they successively began to make products demanding more complex production processes. Yet high-level management is also of some importance. Even if all entrepreneurial decisions were finally made by nationals, one would still not want to speak of full industrial independence if these decisions depended too much on foreign management of production. For instance, a public firm run under a foreign management contract goes some way, but not the whole way, toward industrial self-reliance (we are taking it for granted that lower-level management is indigenous).

We shall say that a country is industrially independent with respect to a particular industry if both the following conditions are satisfied. First, its own nationals must be capable of initiating and sustaining production, either profitably or (if in the public sector) according to some social criteria of efficiency; this is to be understood to involve making rational investment choices from a range of available alternatives. Some degree of technological knowledge is required for this criterion of independence to be satisfied. How much depends on how much effective product choice, and choice of production techniques, there is. The entrepreneur does not have to be a scientist or technologist himself. He can hire advisers, just as a finance minister need not be an economist or an accountant. These advisers can even be foreigners without creating industrial dependency, provided such foreigners are competitively available and are themselves independent of the suppliers of technology. Second, the techniques and the technological knowledge should also be competitively available.

How easily these conditions are fulfilled depends greatly on the industry. In many, the techniques are incorporated in the machines (for example, sewing machines, looms, and lathes). It is easy to acquire a knowledge of the technology, that is, of the available range of techniques, or machines. Often a full knowledge of the technology is not required to make a sound choice. For instance, a small textile manufacturer does not need to know about the latest automatic Western looms. The factory or workshop layout is simple, and, if necessary, the machine supplier will probably advise. The training of operatives is also rather easy. Machine operators and assemblers do not need the skills of craftsmen. At worst, if no local training center can be used, or foremen found locally, workers can be sent abroad or trainers temporarily hired from abroad. An intelligent person with no more than secondary school education who is allowed access to books, catalogs, foreign salesmen, and perhaps travel (which may include work in a firm abroad) can go a long way. In any case, in all but the most industrially backward countries, many of these simple skills and training facilities are already available locally.

In the beginning, if there is no domestic industry other than handicrafts, it is probably impossible to get started without some learning by foreign contact. This might be accomplished by working abroad, in a local transnational corporation in a foreign local enterprise that is not a transnational corporation, or by working in a public turnkey factory where foreigners initially provide training and management under contract. But this stage need last only a very short time for the simple factory industries—baking, brewing, brick-making, canning, cloth, clothing, plywood, furniture, simple metal products such as tools and toys, light electrical products, and so on. Technology is free and easily acquired in all the industries needed for satisfying the wants of the poorer people. Naturally, difficulties multiply as a country embarks on more complex products and processes.

We can illustrate the points made in this section by some quotations from the already cited work on Korea, of Westphal, et al.:

> Korea's strategy to gain industrial competence has thus relied heavily on indigenous effort through various forms of learning by doing and emphasized transactions at arm's length in the use of foreign resources.[21]
>
> Many of the principal industries in Korea's past industrialization—such as plywood or textiles and apparel—use techniques that can be characterized as mature, in that the mastery of well-established and conventional methods embodied in equipment readily available from foreign suppliers is sufficient to permit efficient production.[22]
>
> In the context of calls for a "new international economic order" it frequently is alleged that international markets are noncompetitive and that developing countries either are denied access to technology and export markets in unbundled form or are given access only on highly unfavorable terms. It often is further asserted that foreigners necessarily play the leading role—through the transfer of technology—in the acquisition of technological capacity, and—through the initiative they exercise—in the organization of export activity. If true, both characterizations imply a severe constraint on industrial development. But, far from supporting these characterizations, Korea's experience shows them to be false for many of the industries whose development was important for its achievement of semi-industrial status.[23]

But we should add a final quote:

> If any element in Korea's past situation is unlikely to be widely duplicated, it probably is Korea's abundance of entrepreneurial resources, which in effect removed a major advantage of DFI [direct foreign investment]: the possibility of substituting foreign for domestic entrepreneurship.[24]

It is a lack of indigenous entrepreneurial (and managerial) skill that, together with government policies, leads to industrial dependence, not the fact that the technology used has its origins almost wholly in the West.

The fact that Korea (and Taiwan), and Japan in the days when she was an LDC, have relied rather little on transnational corporations does not, however, imply that a quite high proportion of transnational corporations in an industry constitutes industrial dependence in any threatening sense, or is anything but beneficial for the country and the mass of its people. If local firms exist and can compete successfully, there is a clear sense in which the country is not dependent on the foreigners.

Technological Dependency

An analogy of technological dependency with trade dependency takes one a long way. All countries import foreign manufactures. But they are not dependent in any significant sense if the supply is competitive. Technology is imported in machines and equipment, and the know-how that goes with them. If the supply is competitive, where, one may ask, is the dependence?

We have seen that for many industries most of the technology, and certainly the labor-intensive end of the technology (that is, the spectrum of techniques) is competitively available. It is also free, in the sense that there is no payment for any proprietary knowledge. This is true not only for most of the range of consumer goods, but also for much of the equipment required to make intermediates—for example, steel and cement—and even for that required to make machines themselves (complex specialized machines are made by simple general-purpose machines).

As an industrializing country moves into more complex, up-to-date, and differentiated processes and products, however, suppliers become fewer, and even if there is still quite a number to choose from, each may have some salable knowledge and so require some payment for the transfer of its know-how. If there is any monopolistic element in the price of a company's product, which depends on others not being able to copy it and make it as cheaply without their assistance, then the company will require payment for helping another company to produce (or allowing it to do so, in the case of patents). The newness of a process or product is often more important than its complexity. Patents run out. Moreover, whether protected by patent or not, an innovation is usually successfully copied by other firms, often in other industrialized countries, within a few years.[25]

Finally, a company may refuse to sell a license or to assist foreign producers in any way. This reduces the range of products that the LDC can make, unless perhaps the foreign company and the host government can agree on terms that permit production by a subsidiary of the foreign company or by a joint venture. Permitting the entry of a transnational corporation may thus sometimes be the only way in which production can be achieved.

It is clear that the more complex and recently contrived the processes and products, the more dependent will a country become that insists on producing them. This is especially the case for smaller countries and for products with strongly increasing returns to scale. It can then, or anyway should, enter into a licensing or technical cooperation agreement with only one or a few foreign companies, or similarly accept only one or very few subsidiaries of foreign companies. But it could have imported the product, or very similar products, from a great many sources.

In most cases, the complex and most recent products are highly capital intensive, so that technological dependency and capital intensity are associated—for instance, petrochemicals, man-made fibers, and motorcars (once the mere assembly stage is passed). Similarly, the more complex processes generally use automatic specialized machinery, rather than the more labor-intensive general-purpose machinery. The complaint that technological dependence is responsible for the excessive capital intensity of industry in LDCs is the exact reverse of the truth. It is the choice of excessively capital-intensive products and techniques that causes technological dependency.

Nationalists, Marxists, and neo-Marxists have always laid great stress on the need for a country to have its own heavy industry and capital goods industry. This was particularly the case in India (see chapter 3), where nonreliance on imports of "basic" goods was the main element of self-reliance—self-sufficiency in food coming nowhere by comparison.[26] Many tendentious arguments were used, such as the need to save foreign exchange which, however, in no way distinguishes such industry from any other production of tradable goods.

It is not easy to give a rational explanation of this "basic" industry fundamentalism. Admittedly, LDCs had been starved of capital equipment during both World Wars I and II. The argument that no future war could last long might, I suppose, be countered by the argument that the MDCs and their technology might vanish in the holocaust. The argument from inappropriate Western technology and Western products was not applied to heavy industry.[27] Indeed, there was often confusion between capital goods industry and heavy industry. Cement, steel, nonferrous metals, fertilizers, and petrochemicals are not capital goods. Prestige is often assumed to be the explanation, but I do not rule out the influence of false arguments (that is, simple economic irrationality).

The neo-Marxists who support a very broadly based industrial development, which amounts to as much industrial autarchy as possible, contradict themselves in that they are also often proponents of the view that one of the main distortions of development is the excessive capital intensity of industry. A plausible argument can be made for local production of some capital goods, but that is very different from a broad-based industrial development of the capital-intensive producers' goods mentioned above.

Is not indigenous research and development essential for healthy growth in which production is suited and adapted to the factor proportions, indigenous materials, and special needs of the people? Essentially this is a dynamic form of the argument from inappropriate technology. Appropriate technologies cannot be created once and for all but must be continuously improved and recreated as conditions change. Original indigenous appropriate research and development cannot be carried out if there is no capacity to make experimental instruments, equipment, etc. This is an argument for an engineering industry, especially, perhaps, mechanical engineering, and not for the manufacture of a wide range of capital goods. The engineering is first needed only in support of the research and development. Once more appropriate capital goods have been developed to the point when they are (socially) better than imports, then they need to be made and marketed. However, in this connection it should be noted that most of the capital goods now made in developing countries are copies of those available abroad. From the point of view of "appropriateness," the country is just as "technologically dependent" if its own capital goods industry turns out copies. The fact that there are a number of examples where research has shown this not to be the case only proves the rule. Much more needs to be changed if domestic engineering is to produce more appropriate technology. This includes the attitudes of government and engineers toward "modernity," changes in labor laws to make employment more attractive for employers, and reforms of the price mechanism to make capital-intensive methods appropriately expensive.

There is another argument that is independent of, and could even conflict with, the need for developing appropriate techniques. Indigenous technology development is good business, at least in the long run. Why should not LDCs begin to capture some of the rents that attach to innovation? S. Lall has developed this theme in several articles.[28] Both arguments point to the desirability of an innovative engineering industry, rather than simply the manufacture of machinery, although the latter, even if based on MDC designs, may also be within the range of comparative advantage of the semi-industrialized LDCs (machinery tends to be more skill intensive than capital intensive).[29] At the same time, some warnings would seem to be appropriate. First, it is a stage that is a long way down the road for most LDCs. Second, the contribution to a more equal and labor-intensive development may be minimal; Lall commends India for its far-sighted encouragement of indigenous technological capacity—but India has one of the most capital-demanding industrial developments in the world. Third, the initial transfer of technological and industrial know-how is more difficult in the engineering industries than in many others. Fourth, there may well never be any reduction of dependence on foreign designs and innovations. The case of Japan is worth citing here:

> While restricting foreign direct investment, Japan, as in the prewar period, aggressively sought out advanced foreign technology. Between 1950 and 1968 Japanese firms signed over 9,800 licensing contracts with foreign firms, for which they paid a staggering sum of $1.46 billion.[30]

This does not appear staggering as compared with the 1970s. From 1973 to 1975, Japan paid over $2 billion. West Germany was not far behind. Brazil is much the largest among LDCs with a payment of $272 million in 1976, about a third that of Japan. India paid a mere $24 million (in 1973). Only the United States has a large positive balance of fees and royalties.[31]

The literature on this subject is still resounding. Two main themes can perhaps be detected. The first is the question whether capital goods production merits special encouragement.[32] The second, which may not seem to harmonize with the battle cry of technological independence, concerns the best ways of assimilating technology from MDCs.[33] If one had to give an interim view, it would be that for most LDCs the priority is to improve knowledge of the range of world technology and so to improve the choice of techniques, for there is no doubt that many poor decisions have been made from ignorance. Such knowledge also lays the basis for adaptation and even innovation. Some engineering capacity is surely complementary, though that does not imply that any large-scale production of capital goods is a sine qua non.

For the sake of completeness, the subject of patents and trademarks must be broached, albeit very briefly. It is one part of the range of complaints in the context of the New International Economic Order and hence pursued by the United Nations Conference on Trade and Development, that the MDCs exploit the LDCs through their monopolistic possession of proprietary knowledge, by charging too much or by setting conditions to its acquisition, or both.

Behind this is the idea that knowledge is the property of mankind. This is either metaphysical or false. Provided there were no change in the flow of innovations, mankind would no doubt be better off if every innovation were publicly proclaimed. In a system of private enterprise, an innovator has a monopoly position and will usually do his best to sell his new knowledge or exploit it himself. If, as in a fully socialist society, the private exploitation of new knowledge is made illegal, then the system must rely on public laboratories, supplemented perhaps by a system of prizes. One must wonder whether the technological backwardness of the USSR (except maybe in armaments and space research) is not a result. In capitalist systems, the monopoly position is recognized, approved of, and somewhat strengthened by patent law. One is dealing with an essentially monopolistic area.

A case can be made for some LDCs refusing to subscribe to international conventions for the protection of industrial property. They have few if any patents themselves that could be exploited abroad. Their own market is too small to affect the incentives for innovators in the MDCs. Why not then be a free-rider? The case against it is that piracy already takes place, and is seldom pursued in the courts. Besides, it is not easy to pirate and little more could be done. The country could lose because the climate for the transfer of knowledge would worsen, and eventually the country might want the recognition of its own patents. It can also be argued that anyway the subject is a storm in a teacup. Except for pharmaceuticals, patents are unimportant compared to unpatented know-how and secret processes; and in such cases industrial espionage is the only way to avoid payment or get around a refusal to sell.

Payments for the use of trademarks have also excited attention and are closely related to the subject of "inappropriate" consumption goods because trademarks apply mostly to things bought by the relatively well-off. In a monopolistic market, it may pay a domestic producer to buy a foreign trademark; but there can nevertheless be a loss to society. A foreign payment to permit marketing of the twentieth brand of toothpaste in India is hard indeed to justify. The associated advertising also comes under attack, as a waste of resources, especially if the advertising is done by a transnational corporation. However, trademarks (including foreign trademarks) do benefit consumers by helping to ensure that they know the quality of their prospective purchases. No easy line can be drawn. It should, however, be emphasized that trademarks are certainly valuable for LDCs' exports. For instance, "of the surveyed firms that were exporting wigs, shoes, clothing, table-ware, sporting goods, and electronic products, nearly all sold a sizable fraction—in most cases more than three-quarters—of their exports under foreign brand names."[34]

Restrictive conditions in licensing agreements, especially bans on exports, have also received much attention. Again, this is no black-and-white issue. The analogy with attempts to enforce internal competition in MDCs, and to present this as a simple case of undesirable restrictive practices, breaks down because the very point of patents and trademarks is to create an exploitable element of monopoly. Moreover, such restrictions protect other licensees, and the more the purchaser of a license is likely to have to pay, the wider is his franchise.

Most LDC governments in fact regulate and control the registration of foreign patents, and the acquisition of licenses, and may ban the acquisition of licenses with restrictive conditions. They need break no international convention in so doing:

> A few international conventions have existed on the subject, notably the Berne Convention for the Protection of Industrial Property. But contrary to the general impression the constraints imposed by such conventions by and large have been of minor significance. The conventions have left enough leeway, for example, that countries can refuse to issue patents on certain types of products such as drugs, can fix the life of a patent as they choose, can subject an application to search or not, can define the terms that represent "abuse" of a patent, and can limit the rights of the abusing patent-holder. The developing countries, therefore, are not seriously restrained from following a wide range of policies to hold down the windfall profits of foreigners and to prevent the use of patents or trademarks that contribute to product proliferation.[35]

Whether such regulation and control is always beneficial is another matter. It is easy enough to show that royalty payments can be reduced. The corresponding harm, in the form of reducing the value of the transfer of knowledge or goodwill, is impossible to measure. In this connection it should be noted that the transfer of technology can be costly.[36]

The role of nonindustrial imported technology must be examined briefly before reverting to the relationship between transnational corporations and technology. The largest area (in terms of GNP) is agriculture. Foreign technology has played a large part in high dam building, mechanization, new seeds, fertilizers, and pesticides. Although a considerable part—perhaps as much as half—of the increased agricultural output from LDCs in the postwar period can be traced to new techniques, which themselves are largely foreign, it is still possible to complain of the effects. The "green revolution" technology, with its package approach of irrigation, new seeds, and fertilizers, benefited large farmers more than the small, initially at least. However, the consensus now seems to be that all farmers—except those in some dry areas in South Asia—have benefited to some extent.[37] Nonfarm consumers also surely benefited, and here the poor would benefit more than the rich from food prices being lower than they otherwise would have been. The new technologies may have additional effects. Increased profitability of farming could result in increased concentration of operational holdings, and hence an increase of "capitalistic" farming, which might (or might not) result in less demand for labor.[38] There has been no lack of authors deploring at least some aspects of the green revolution. Although they seldom or never go so far as to say that it would have been better if it had never occurred, the impression is left that this might be so. Mechanization (with usually, but not always, foreign machinery—India and other LDCs make tractors) can be attacked on the ground of displacing labor, though the debate still rages (see chapter 10) as to whether on balance it does or does not.

In Latin America, many voices complain about foreign-owned "agribusiness." Yet on the whole, the accusation that reliance on foreign techniques distorts development or creates "underdevelopment" is less often heard in the case of agriculture than industry. The reason, no doubt, is that the foreign technology is not usually introduced via transnational corporations. It has to be transferred to indigenous and often small operators. Moreover, in the case of agriculture it is more obvious that mainly domestic policies determine the agricultural techniques in use. None of this makes any difference as to whether a technical change is beneficial, but it does make a difference as to whether foreigners can plausibly be blamed for any ill effects there may be.

The third area in which foreign technology has made an enormous difference to the developing world is medicine. There have been complaints about the cost of drugs, but not of the effects of Western techniques as such. The benefits have perhaps been too obvious in terms of life expectancy and some improvement of health during life. Yet the case is analogous to the green revolution, for the rich have benefited most. But here again it is implausible to blame transnational corporations. Finally, there is family planning, with modern Western techniques of contraception. Cries of imperialism have at times been loud, and can be partly blamed on the crudity of some Western enthusiasts. But all governments in the more crowded LDCs have adopted programs, sometimes using methods Western liberals regard as excessively draconian. And no one can plausibly suggest that reduced population growth will be a cause of inequality.

SUMMARY

All countries rely on capital goods imports. A very high degree of reliance does not constitute dependency in any threatening sense, or in the sense of being exploited, if they are competitively available; this seems to be the case except perhaps for some very specialized plant. A country does not become less dependent by making its own equipment; indeed, it may increase its dependency if it thereby reduces the number of foreign firms on which it relies for know-how and design.

The argument that countries will obtain more appropriate (that is, labor-intensive) techniques if they have their own capital goods industry is weak. In general, indigenous capital goods industries make equipment that is little different from what could be imported, although there are some examples of more labor-intensive LDC machinery. But the argument is weak primarily because there is a great deal of room for making production more labor intensive in other ways. In most industries there is already a wide choice of techniques, but the choice is strongly biased in favor of capital intensity by a mystique on the part of local politicians, and local and foreign engineers and managers, favoring the latest thing. Also, many governmental policies distort prices and labor costs in favor of capital intensity; and, possibly most important, LDC governments show a strong preference for industries that are highly capital intensive.

Knowledge is important in the *selection* of technology. Such knowledge is easy to acquire in the case of most of the more labor-intensive industries, producing the simpler and most essential consumer goods. Difficulties mount as a country embarks on more sophisticated capital-intensive products. But they can be exaggerated. Several LDCs, for example, have been able to "unbundle" and put together efficient steel plants using equipment from several different foreign firms and countries. Foreign consultant engineers may be used, but this is unlikely to be a perfect substitute for good indigenous knowledge, the lack of which has resulted in some inefficient and excessively capital-intensive "unbundling." The acquisition of the technical knowledge required to choose well does not, however, presuppose that any of the equipment need be indigenous. Notwithstanding the possibilities of "unbundling," the more sophisticated the industries a country wants to see on its own soil, and the faster it wants to achieve this, the more will it have to rely on private foreign investment.

Capital goods must be distinguished from the products of "basic" industries. The former run from hammers and sickles through sewing machines and lathes and on to rolling mills and giant generators. Many capital goods are relatively labor intensive, unlike metals and chemicals. A country does not have to travel far down the industrialization road for it to have a comparative advantage in making many kinds of capital goods. But production of capital goods is certainly not a sufficient condition for technological development and innovation, though it may be necessary. There is probably some force to the arguments that engineering has externalities and that indigenous research and development is worth subsidizing.

Private foreign investment is almost wholly irrelevant to technological independence. A country with less foreign investment in industry is more industrially independent; after all, fewer foreigners are making decisions. But there is no reason to suppose that this makes the country less reliant on foreign technology in the processes of production or the design of the product. It is no accident that with a lull in the storm over the multinationals, the clouds gathered over licensing, patents, and trademarks, threatening another storm in a teacup.

Transnational Corporations and Dependence

If it is not technological dependency that creates an industrial structure thought to be inappropriate, either because it is very capital intensive or because it is very trade dependent (though these tend to be mutually inconsistent), it may yet be transnational corporations, not as unique purveyors of modern methods but for other reasons.

A common argument relating to "peripheral" capitalism runs as follows. Inequality results in a relatively high demand for hard consumer durables. These can be manufactured only in capital-intensive ways. High wages and salaries, and probably high profits, go with such manufacture, which therefore causes inequality, which in turn results in high demand. This is an example of what is sometimes called circular causation. Although there may be something in this argument, it is very weak. The weakest link is the presumption that the demand of the relatively rich is for goods and services that are produced in relatively capital-intensive ways. It has some plausibility insofar as the poor do not buy cars, etc. But the argument requires that a higher proportion of the expenditure of the rich is on capital-intensive things, which is not very plausible (given their high demand for services). Statistical investigation of the supposed linkage has shown it to be weak or nonexistent. The second link, that capital-intensive production helps to cause inequality, is stronger, for enterprises with high labor productivity usually pay, whether voluntarily or under pressure, relatively high wages and salaries.

Granting some validity to the above argument, the question arises as to how transnational corporations enter the picture. Starting with inequality, it can be argued that the resultant demand for hard consumer durables can be satisfied only by letting in, or inviting in, transnational corporations to make them. But, first, this is false in the case of most countries, as we saw in the previous section. Second, the demand could anyway be satisfied from imports (and severely limited by indirect taxation). So the essential decision that completes the inequality-generating chain is the decision to implement domestic production. Since ex hypothesi, the products under discussion are capital intensive and the domestic market is small (in all except a handful of relatively large or rich LDCs), they will require protection, so that domestic production is in part a government decision. Thus, if transnational corporations enter the picture at all, it is not as cause but as the result of a double governmental or local policy decision: (a) to protect the domestic market for such "luxury" products, and (b) to permit transnational corporations to make them (for, in virtually all LDCs, there is control over the entry of transnational corporations).

Suppose next that we do not start with inequality but simply with the permitted entry of transnational corporations. A lot now depends on why they come in. Without protection, they would not come in to manufacture in a capital-intensive manner, unless possibly to process a local mineral or agricultural product for the export market. For them, at least, the comparative advantage of poor countries is their cheap labor, or some indigenous material or tropical agricultural product that it is economical to process in situ, even capital intensively, because of transport costs or spoilage. Thus, private investment in manufacturing before World War II went into cotton textiles, tea processing, and jute manufactures for export, and to a limited extent into some labor-intensive or transport-protected products for the home market (for example, cement, beer, etc.). The hard consumer durables and producers' goods were imported. Since World War II, transnational corporations have risked unprotected production in LDCs only to manufacture highly labor-intensive products for export—the assembly of electronic equipment mainly in Southern Europe, East Asia, and the border zone of Mexico. In order to produce relatively capital-intensive products for small domestic markets, they had to be enticed in by protection; and it was indeed (and, to a slightly lesser extent, still is) the policy of the governments of many LDCs, especially in Africa and Latin America, to induce such "tariff-jumping" industrialization. It was once held to be one of the merits of tariffs that they caused foreign corporations to supply the host country market by production rather than by trade.

The kind of industry that will be created and the methods of production used by foreign enterprises are thus mainly governed by the protective structure of the host country, for that determines what is profitable. On top of this, most LDCs have excluded foreigners from certain, often quite large, sectors of the economy in order to protect the nationals who have entered them. These include public utilities and the more labor-intensive and simpler manufacturing sectors. Sector by sector, there is nothing to choose between foreign and local industry so far as capital intensity goes.[39] The alleged feedback mechanism—transnational corporations → capital intensity → inequality → transnational corporations—is a seminar debating point, not a significant reality. However, even without the feedback to inequality, excessive capital intensity is one of the major development problems. And clearly, the finger of blame should be pointed at host governments, not at transnational corporations.

We now come to the heart of the argument. It will be said that the foreign companies persuade host governments to choose industries that suit them. The industries that suit them are, so the argument runs, typically consumer goods industries, catering to the better-off sections of the population. It is in the interest of the transnational corporations that income distribution should be unequal, so that there is a demand for cars, air conditioners, cosmetics, and bottled beverages. It is also in their interests to advertise and distort the tastes of local people so that they will starve themselves to buy inappropriate products. To complete the malign circle, all these industries should be especially capital intensive (which they are not), and they should pay high wages and make vast profits.

Much has been written on the determinants of private direct manufacturing investment overseas.[40] Much of such investment comes from oligopolistic industries in which a few companies dominate. "Oligopolistic" usually implies that firms have some particular property in the form of a process or product, as a result of which they can earn rents in a new market. Such industries are often also research and development intensive, so that again extension into a market enables this overhead to be spread. These are conventional profit-making reasons. A different kind of reason is managerial megalomania: a specialized company cannot expand in its home market without either driving down profits or driving out a competitor (which may bring antimonopoly legislation into action or be otherwise expensive). This, plus the fact that diversification is risky, also makes overseas expansion attractive. Such reasons for expanding overseas are not limited to the kind of consumer goods industries the argument requires. They are also valid for companies in producers' goods industries such as petrochemicals, fertilizers and industrial chemicals, computers, and automatic machine tools. But more damaging to the argument is the fact that the reasons given are merely reasons for wanting to supply that market. Unless they are discouraged or excluded by tariffs or controls from exporting to the market, they will want to enter only if the production conditions, the size of the market, and transport costs would make it more profitable to produce there rather than supply from some other base.

It may have happened, but I guess it is rare, for a foreign corporation to approach an LDC government with the request, "Put up a tariff, so that we can profitably produce in your country rather than export to you." It is a possibility if combined with the rider, "And, having done so, give me a monopoly of your market as well." Of course, once local production has been decided on, it may make good sense for the host country to create a monopoly if the potential market is small and economies of scale are significant. But, in general, host countries have been chary of creating such monopolies, and it is common to find many absurdly small-scale plants.

The argument that transnational corporations have seriously influenced the pattern of industrialization in favor of what they were good at producing is not one that can be sustained. Either host governments have particularly wanted the industries in question (for example, automobiles), or they have instituted controls or tariffs for balance-of-payments reasons or as part of a general policy of import substitution. These measures made local production profitable, and transnational corporations would then tend to dominate in sectors where their advantages over local businessmen were greatest (if they were not excluded from them). It is probably true that they have on occasion helped to persuade local governments, sometimes by bribery, to give them such heavy protection that the country suffered as a result. But such persuasion is not the prerogative of transnational corporations. The demand for protection is just as strong in countries such as India, where they play only a small role and have no influence on industrial policy.

Against the above, it may be argued that transnational corporations are usually large and powerful, while local entrepreneurs are puny. Although this is often true, it does not imply that the foreign corporation can dominate the host government. Some dependency theorists are fond of pointing out that General Motors (GM) is bigger than most LDCs. This is irrelevant. Any LDC, however tiny, is sovereign over its own territory. It can let GM in or keep it out. If it lets it in, it has the whip hand, for GM has sunk some capital that is irremovable. If it expropriates GM, the company can try to organize some punishment through the United States government (which, however, has become increasingly chary of thus supporting overseas investors) or privately through its friends in the business world. In that event, the size of GM may have some importance, but not its size relative to the LDC, for it has no gunboats. That transnational corporations dominate by their very size accords ill with the facts of expropriation, which are given in the next section. While a transnational corporation cannot dominate, it can admittedly bribe. But it is then the corruptibility of the host that is the worm in the bud.

Despite the above, there is no doubt that almost all the excessive protection of industry in LDCs has arisen either as a by-product of the LDCs' foreign exchange and payment regimes or because the government became convinced that rapid industrialization was the royal road to progress and must be promoted at any cost. Dependency theorists might concede all this but claim it to be irrelevant because LDC governments, leaders, and bourgeoisie have become so entangled with foreign capitalism that there is an identity of interest that is in conflict with that of the mass of the people. They do not explain how a broadly based modern industry, which they believe in, could have developed rapidly without such entanglement.

Collaborating Elites, Trade, and the Transnational Corporations: Contact and Contagion

Transnational corporations are one form of contact with Western capitalism. The idea that such contact is pernicious precedes this new phenomenon, going back to the days when (for Latin America, China, Thailand) trade was held to be the uncivilizing force. The local inhabitants who specialized in liaison between the (free-trading) foreigners and the indigenous economy were known to old China hands as "compradors." Compradors rank second only to Kulaks in the human demonology of neo-Marxism. This class has been broadened and promoted into that of the "collaborating elites."

Despite the fact that Westerners managed to keep in their own hands a disproportionate amount of the profitable trading and commercial links with LDCs,[41] even with those that were not colonies, international trade inevitably created a set of local people who gained from that trade. It does not follow from this that such people were politically powerful. This was the case where those who gained most from trade were large landowners. Then there is an association of trading interests with conservative and inegalitarian tendencies in the LDCs. This has been typical of

Latin America. Trade can hardly be said to have created the Latin American oligarchies that were based on extremely unequal land ownership. This inequality was established centuries before agricultural trade become important as a result of European growth and the transport revolution in the second half of the nineteenth century. It may, however, be true that trade has helped to preserve the wealth and political influence of these landed interests. A community of interests between rich local landowners and foreign traders was not typical of Asia or Africa. There (apart from Liberia, Ethiopia, Japan, China, and Thailand) it was the colonial relationship of delegated government and the influence on education—including the enlarged possibilities of education in the ruling country—that were mainly responsible both for collaborating elites and for revolutionary leaders (sometimes later "collaborating" after independence).

We must remember that we are now looking for some sociological or political feature of the *trading* contact that can, at least partly, explain some or all of the alleged features of a "dependent" development, especially its dualism, its inequality, and perhaps the reliance on foreign managers and advisers. Except possibly for the Latin American case outlined, I find it hard to discern. Indeed, it is easier to argue the reverse case. In India it has been the trading community that largely developed indigenous industry and that, even after acquiring great industrial wealth, remained less important politically than one might have expected. The private corporate sector lobby in India, judging by results (that is, the political treatment of private industry and trade), must have been one of the weakest in the world.

In recent years, as we have seen, it is the contact with subsidiaries of foreign-based companies, more than the trading contact, which has excited the opposition of those who fear dependency. Dependency and neocolonialism seem to carry the same meaning, although the latter concept is mostly used in an African context. One definition from a student of Kenya, which might be widely accepted on the left is, "Neo-colonialism, in its essential meaning of a system of domination of the mass of the population of a country by foreign capital, by means other than direct rule. By its nature, such dominance requires the development of domestic class interests which are allied to those of foreign capital, and which uphold their joint interests in economic policy and enforce their dominance politically."[42]

Foreign capital used to go predominantly into infrastructure and plantations (before 1914) and into minerals (1914-60, say). There is no doubt that, as in the case of trade, collaboration between local interests and foreign interests occurred. So long as domestic producers were uncompetitive, because they had not yet learned modern technology (this applies mainly to minerals), there was in turn little opposition. But as soon as it appeared that local competition might be viable, that nationals could now run the mines and sell the output, foreign capital rapidly found that it had as many local enemies as friends; and it did not usually take long for the enemies to gain the upper political hand.[43] From about 1960 onward, the LDCs have rapidly increased their bargaining power and have shown little sign of being inhibited from breaking and renegotiating contracts.[44]

Nationalization has been very extensive. Between 1956 and 1972, the book value of assets nationalized (in the following "old" sectors of investment) by LDCs, relative to the stock at the end of 1967, has been estimated to be:[45]

Oil	17 percent
Minerals	49
Agriculture (plantations)	81
Utilities and transport	76
Banks	48
Total for all sectors	30

Compensation paid for the assets nationalized was estimated to be about 40 percent of book value. The low figure for oil has been dramatically raised from 1972 to 1976 with expropriations in Ecuador, Iran, Libya, Saudi Arabia, Abu Dhabi, Kuwait, Nigeria, and Qatar (to mention only United States companies). Other mineral takeovers from 1972 to 1976 include copper in Peru, iron ore in Gabon and Venezuela, and bauxite in Guyana and Jamaica.[46] Perhaps enough has been said to show that collaborating elites have not always, or even usually, collaborated very effectively with transnational corporations.[47]

We may now turn to transnational corporations in manufacturing, which have in recent years excited most attention, accounting as they do for the bulk of new investment. The contact involved in a million dollars' worth of local manufacturing production by a foreign corporation is usually much greater than in the case of an equal amount of trade. Whatever the case earlier, it is now unusual to find more than a handful of expatriate managers in a foreign subsidiary (in the more advanced LDCs the managing director is usually local). The transnational corporation will often send staff, including even blue-collar workers, abroad for training. It will usually buy some of its tradable inputs locally, thus increasing the dependency of local enterprises. It may even assist subcontracting enterprises with designs, quality control, etc., in order that they can supply efficiently. Finally, joint ventures with both private and public interests have been much favored by LDC governments. This inevitably helps to create a national haute bourgeoisie whose interests become to some extent intertwined with those of foreign industry.

In the past it was the alleged lack of intimacy between foreign enterprises and the local concerns that evoked the criticism of economists, sociologists, and politicians—the enclave. Almost everywhere, the policy of LDC governments was to promote greater intimacy, to make rules concerning the employment and trading of local managers, to insist on increasing indigenization of the product (that is, the local purchase and manufacture of components), to encourage the involvement of local entrepreneurs and capital in joint ventures. This is all in aid of the transfer of technology and management know-how. There is thus a conflict between those who want to maximize the learning externality of transnational corporations and those who fear the creation and contamination of a bourgeoisie, which acquires along with some new skills a taste for Western methods, patterns of consumption, and perhaps even Western ideals.

We have already dismissed the idea that manufacturing transnational enterprises can directly distort the pattern of industrial growth against the will of the government. They are just one of the vehicles for achieving the host government's aims. But the contention we are dealing with must be that, in alliance with a domestic class with similar interests (which they partly create and which may include members of the government and the civil service), the foreign corporations contrive a situation in which the government wants what they want—that is, a lopsided industrial development by means of which the mass of people is dominated.

What constitutes this new collaborating domestic elite? Foreign business will always have some friends. Prima facie, however, it seems the friends might be rather too mixed a bunch to constitute a class: the relatively highly paid employees, local suppliers of services, and corrupt officials and politicians. But one has to have classes to see the world in terms of their alliances and conflicts.

An important question is whether indigenous capitalists are friends, as well as being weak and subservient; they must be the latter because otherwise it is not *foreign* capitalists who dominate and "underdevelop" the economy. (We shall ignore actual partners in joint ventures because they are very much the product of LDC governments; foreign capital, especially that of the United States, has often had to be browbeaten into joint ventures, itself nearly always preferring wholly owned subsidiaries.) A priori one would expect as much hostility as friendship, with ambivalence on the part of some. There is some evidence of this, apart from casual empiricism, which also confirms it. M. Kidron writes of India with considerable supporting evidence, "During the half century before Independence, Indian business had set into an attitude of hard hostility towards foreign capital." One official report of 1946 stated, "It seems to us preferable that the goods which the country cannot produce at present but would be in a position to produce later on, should continue to be imported from other countries rather than that their local manufacture should be started or expanded by foreign firms."[48] This continued after Independence, but politicians were soon to take a different view, and to urge that foreign capital was useful for development. Later industrialists came to accept this, provided that it was controlled, which meant that it should not be allowed to compete with existing medium- and large-scale "organized" industry. They were much in favor of technical cooperation agreements, but not foreign competitors. The picture in Mexico seems to be similar though perhaps a little more favorable to foreigners.[49] In neither country can one properly speak of an alliance,[50] nor is it plausible to suggest that foreign capital exercises a large or undue influence on government, for government imposes restrictions on foreign corporations, favoring the domestic over the foreign in many ways.

A few orders of magnitude may be useful to enable the reader to grasp the possible extent of domination of the masses by foreign industrial capital in various parts of the world. A United Nations report[51] gives foreign percentage ownership shares of manufacturing for some countries, but for only a few does it state the coverage (that is, all enterprises, or only those over a certain size) and the criterion for foreign ownership used. The figures are thus very unsatisfactory and of highly dubious comparability.[52] For what they are worth, the proportion of sales attributed to foreign companies suggests the following comparisons (for various dates between 1968 and 1974). In the high league (> 33 percent) we have Canada, Australia, Belgium, and New Zealand among the MDCs; and Nigeria, Ghana, Brazil, and Peru among the LDCs. Canada is champion with 56 percent. In the 20-33 percent range come the Central American Common Market (CACM) countries (on average), Argentina, Austria, France, Germany, Mexico, and Singapore. The United Kingdom is among the lowest in Europe (14 percent), but below her comes India, Korea, and Hong Kong (the last based on employment, not sales). The proportion of foreign-controlled firms among the largest is certainly higher, and this is likely to be true everywhere. Estimates of around 50 percent have been made for the largest three hundred firms in Brazil and Mexico.

It is evident that there is not much difference between MDCs and those LDCs for which there is any information. Clearly the relatively great fuss made in LDCs about transnational corporations, and the far greater degree of control exercised over them, stems from the fact that the foreign investors come mainly from large, powerful countries, and also perhaps from a belief that their own nationals cannot compete. These fears are exaggerated and have been played upon by radicals. But another and more justifiable reason for the controls exercised is that excessive protection has resulted in LDC consumers heavily subsidizing production; and it is less attractive to subsidize foreigners than domestic producers, even if many of the latter are also large and rich. "Consider a mental experiment: suppose that part of US agriculture, say one-fifth, were owned by foreigners (Frenchmen or Japanese perhaps). No doubt this would make US agriculture subsidies less popular, but would it lead to their abolition? In all likelihood the subsidies would stay, and new foreign investing in this industry would be tightly controlled."[53]

The Meaning of Underdevelopment and Its Real Causes

Since Gundar Frank launched his particular concept of "underdevelopment,"[54] rifts have opened up in the neo-Marxist literature.[55] We cannot expect to achieve a clear definition acceptable to all on the left.[56] As I understand it, one takes the worst features of LDCs and ascribes them to the intrusion of capitalism and to the integration of LDCs with the "world capitalist system." Thus, "underdevelopment" is not just a state of affairs, but one caused in a particular way.

The description of the state of affairs hardly varies from that of conventional economists, especially those (like myself) who have stressed the evils of excessive industrial protection through import controls and high tariffs. For example, Colin Leys approvingly quotes:

> It would seem safe to predict that the present strategy of development incorporates the necessary and sufficient conditions for the following characteristics to emerge within the next 25 years:
> (a) agricultural stagnation resulting from adverse terms of trade, urban migration, and low rates of surplus and reinvestment, leading to urban food shortages and structural inflation;
> (b) continual balance of payments crises requiring dependence upon foreign finance to a growing degree, and perhaps to repeated devaluation;

(c) non-competitive domestic industrial sector with powerful trade unions, resulting in employers and unions forcing up import and food prices, further feeding inflationary tendencies; and

(d) increasing urban migration as agricultural terms of trade deteriorate, resulting in explosive growth of shanty-towns around Nairobi.

In brief, the present strategy provides the ingredients for secular stagnation, and must be seen as an underdevelopment strategy. It seems quite possible that Kenya can achieve this state much more rapidly than Latin American countries have managed to do.[57]

Dependency theorists conveniently forget that favoring industry and squeezing agriculture by high tariffs and import controls, favoring capital-intensive basic industries in the name of independent growth, and favoring capital intensity in general for its often illusory contribution to savings, and hence growth, were the policies recommended by most unconventional leftist economists until the middle 1960s, policies to be swallowed happily by both left and right nationalist governments. We have seen that it is probably a mistake to rate the influence of economists very highly. They were to a considerable extent rationalizing these essentially nationalist policies favored by LDC leaders. The policies themselves were, in some cases at least (for example, India), derived directly from the USSR.

Apart from the fact that I would not say that it was safe to predict anything in the field of economic or political development, I might have written most of the above-quoted passage myself.[58] But to call the Kenyan strategy an underdevelopment strategy implies that it is a necessary consequence of trade and investment contacts with capitalist countries. That it is not a necessary consequence is proved by the performance of the "baby tigers." These are among the highest trading economies in the world, and, since they adopted "outward-looking" trading policies, have been the fastest growing. Hong Kong has always been as pure laisser faire as conceivable; the others are far from laisser faire but adopted virtually free-trade policies for exporters in the early or mid-1960s. They all welcome foreign investment and permit free transfer of profits; but, except in the case of Singapore, it is far from dominant.[59] Although much less modern industry is foreign than is the case in the largest countries of Latin America, there is no doubt that by the criteria of dependency theorists these are very highly dependent economies. They are also highly capitalist by any definition. They exhibit none of the characteristics of underdevelopment.

The figures suggest that the distribution of income in Taiwan is the most equal of all LDCs.[60] South Korea is among the most equal. City-states are not very comparable, but Hong Kong, probably the least equal of the four, is certainly not among the more inegalitarian LDCs. But it is not just a matter of Gini coefficients (the most commonly used measure of inequality) or the share of the poorest 40 percent of the population. Consider the four characteristics of the quotation in the previous paragraph. These countries do not have agricultural stagnation or continual balance-of-payments crises. Their net dependency on foreign finance is falling, and is nonexistent in Taiwan and the city-states. Large parts of their industries are so highly competitive that North America and Western Europe are running for cover. Nor are they among the more inflationary economies. Of course, there has been plenty of urban migration (from Mainland China in the case of Hong Kong); and there are shanty settlements (but many of the shanties in Taiwan, as I know from visiting them, have television and refrigerators, some even telephones). Yet most of the characteristics of "underdevelopment" as laid out in the quotation might have been, indeed were, predicted twenty-five years ago, for South Korea and Taiwan at least. But they changed their policies, independently, but not without foreign pressure on the part of the Agency for International Development, the IMF, and some neo-classical Chinese-American economists.

Communists and socialists are reluctant to accept that the mass of the people have benefited enormously from a peripheral, technology-dependent, trade-dependent, mainly capitalist development. Their massive exports, dependent on cheap docile labor, are regarded as the apotheosis of exploitation and unequal exchange.[61] No doubt one can find similar techniques in use in Japan and Korea, with profits higher and wages lower in the latter: this apparently merits the use of such phrases as "unequal exchange" when the products are exported, and also "superexploitation." These economies are also criticized as "shallow," meaning that light industry has grown relative to "basic" or "heavy" industries, which in turn implies that industrialization has been labor demanding. These critics thus implicitly show deep unconcern for the proletariat, which has come to enjoy full employment and rapidly rising consumption as a result of being superexploited. Apart from this inhumanity in pursuit of preconceived theorizing, the theorizing itself is remarkably static (remarkably, since Marxists pride themselves on their magnificent dynamics). To quote S. Amin:

> In other words, the new division of labor would perpetuate and worsen unequal exchange. Furthermore, this unequal division of labor would perpetuate the distorted pattern of demand in the peripheries to the detriment of mass consumption, just as in the previous phases. Therefore, the development of the world system would remain fundamentally unequal. So external demand would still be the main motive force propelling this still dependent type of development.[62]

By Amin's own definition, unequal exchange is becoming more equal. Real wages are rising fast, inducing more capital intensity, just as orthodox capital theorists would predict. The standard of living in town and country is being equalized (in Taiwan and Korea). Literacy is as high as in the United States. Food intake is sufficient. No economy of the center, not even Japan, ever achieved such rapid increases in welfare and in the skills of the population, from very low levels, as have these peripheral economies. Now, after fifteen to twenty years of labor-intensive development, they have also traveled quite a way along the road of making more skill-intensive and more capital-intensive products. This progression is not admitted, because a tenet of some but not all dependency theorists is that no existing state of development in a peripheral economy can be seen as a stage on the road to a mature autonomous capitalism (whatever that means).[63] The doctrine is that peripheral capitalism cannot develop into "autocentric" capitalism.[64]

Although contact with capitalism has led in other countries to many undesirable features, that is not the same as saying that capitalism is the cause. The chief causes have been, in some, the extreme inequality of land ownership,[65] which preceded any capitalist industrial development, and, in most, a neglect of agriculture combined with a forced import-substituting industrialization, with emphasis on modernity and capital intensity—the very kind of industrialization that the radicals proclaim to be most essential for independence. India has pursued these policies of emphasizing a very broad-based import-substituting industrialization, with almost all new basic industry reserved for the public sector. One consequence has been low exports (and imports)—that is, very low trade dependency. She has permitted only a very limited and controlled influx of private capital. She has emphasized trade with socialist countries and built many turnkey plants with assistance from the USSR and Eastern Europe. She has borrowed little on the world's capitalist markets. She has striven, but failed, to do without aid—which is, however, very low in relation to GNP. She has encouraged science and local engineering, and research and development, and has controlled the import of foreign technology. The mass of the people have benefited very little. No radical would, I suppose, allow India to be called even a semisocialist society; but her policies have been similar to those advocated by the supporters of "selective delinking" from the world capitalist system.[66]

Not all countries could benefit as much as the "baby tigers" from high trading along the lines of comparative advantage. But the labor intensity and relative equality of their development is far from being attributable to high trading alone, although that was an important factor.[67]

Dependency and Capitalism

No facet of dependency reliably separates LDCs from MDCs, or the better from the worse performers among LDCs. This has led some radical critics to suggest that "dependency" is a useless analytic tool[68] and further to suggest that it is capitalism that is the foe, and not especially dependent or peripheral capitalism. Thus, "Primary emphasis on dependence (however it is defined, and especially if it is not defined clearly) tends to reinforce the erroneous view that a shift from a dependent to a more independent form of capitalism would significantly improve the pattern of development in third world countries.... There is little hope of overcoming the multidimensional condition of underdevelopment unless a reduction in dependence is combined with fundamental changes in the whole socio-economic order."[69]

It seems to be implied that what is required is a revolution against capitalism. One can certainly agree that in some countries fundamental changes in the socioeconomic order may be necessary (but not sufficient) for a sustained improvement in the lot of the mass of the people. But I believe that the hallowed capitalist-socialist dichotomy is a bad guide as to where such changes are required. It is in any case unclear which countries are capitalist and which are not. Critics refer to the USSR as state capitalism since the means of production are controlled by a minority class, the state bourgeoisie. And surely one has to admit that noncommunist countries may be more or less socialist and more or less capitalist. It might be better to discuss desirable socioeconomic orders in terms of equality, liberty, concentration of power, and potential for growth, rather than toying with one-word descriptions of widely ranging and multifaceted systems.

PART V

Description and Record of Less Developed Countries

Chapter 13

Description and Record

The Structure of LDCs and Structural Change

There is no one definition of less developed countries. The United Nations includes all recognized countries, except those of North America and Europe, Australia, New Zealand, and the centrally planned economies. The CPEs are the Communist countries, except for Cuba, Kampuchea, Laos, and Vietnam. Taiwan and South Africa are not recognized. We shall, however, most often use World Bank figures, which include the poorer Southern European countries (except Albania) as well as South Africa and Taiwan, but exclude Cuba which is placed among the CPEs. Sometimes we exclude Europe, except for Turkey. Little difference is made to our generalizations. We shall occasionally include China, which is normally excluded by virtue of being a CPE: this does make a difference.

We attempt only a vignette. For more, the reader can conveniently refer to World Bank Development Reports, and World Tables 1980, for the figures and sources. There is also an assessment of the record of development in many of its aspects by D. Morawetz.[1] This chapter therefore stresses only a few features of LDCs and their growth, particularly features that are often

Description and Record of Less Developed Countries

underemphasized or even misrepresented. It ignores facts about poverty, within-country income distribution, and instability, subjects that are considered in other chapters.

THE SIZE INEQUALITY OF LDCS

Today, there are over 150 countries, and about 120 are thought of as "developing." Excluding China, the total population of these LDCs is 2,250 million, a little over half the world total. Including China, the total is 3,200 million, four fifths of the world total.[2]

Thirty (that is, one quarter) of the LDCs are the size of towns, and their population amounts to less than 15 million people. These are excluded from most of our figures because they make no difference to any generalization. Moreover, several of the town-sized countries are very rich, and very few are very poor.

Excluding China, India alone accounts for 30 percent of the population of LDCs, and the five largest (Bangladesh, Brazil, India, Indonesia, and Nigeria) for almost a half. If China were included, the two largest (China and India) would account for a half. The smallest half of the LDCs includes only 5 percent of the total population excluding China, and 3 percent with China. Excluding China, only seven large LDCs have populations exceeding 50 million.

The importance of these skewed figures is that it makes a difference whether one thinks in terms of people or countries. If policies toward, or simply thoughts about, the Third World are intended to reach out to the mass of the people, then most of the countries scarcely count. But small countries have a disproportionate diplomatic weight. This is most clear in the General Assembly of the United Nations, where representatives of 5 percent of the world's population could command a majority. It also appears to be the case in the counsels of the Third World itself (that is, the "Group of Seventy-seven"). A prime example is that the chief plank of the New International Economic Order, commodity stabilization, could benefit only a very small fraction of the people of the Third World.[3] It has an influence also among aid donors, for small countries get relatively much more aid per head than large countries. It counts to be a country.

THE REAL INCOME INEQUALITY OF LDCS AND THE WORLD

The inequality in per caput income among LDCs is much greater than among more developed countries. World Bank figures for income per head range from $90 (Bangladesh) to $15,000 (Kuwait). For the more developed countries, the range is from $3,500 (Ireland) to $12,000 (Switzerland). While a range extending from the poorest to four times as much income per head easily includes all the MDCs, it includes only one third of the LDCs. Most of the rich LDCs are small, but two of the large ones, Brazil and Mexico, have per caput incomes over $1,250, more than ten times that of the poorest countries.[4] Half of the LDC population lives in countries with per caput incomes of less than $250. Table 13-1 gives Gini coefficients[5] for the world (excluding CPEs): for ninety-six LDCs and for twenty MDCs.[6]

TABLE 13-1
Gini Coefficients for Per Caput Incomes

	Unweighted		Population Weighted	
	1958	1978	1958	1978
96 LDCs	0.49	0.58	0.41	0.54
20 MDCs	0.22	0.16	0.33	0.13
Total	0.58	0.64	0.65	0.67

The unweighted figures are of interest only to those who think in terms of interstate inequality. The weighted figures would measure personal inequality if everyone had the average per caput income of his country. Inequality as between LDCs has increased a lot. MDCs have become much more equal until they are now remarkably homogenous as compared with LDCs. Adding the MDCs to the LDCs does two things: it adds a block of countries that are much more equal, but it also adds a set of large differences between pairs of MDCs and LDCs. Inequality is thereby increased, but less in 1978 than in 1958. "World" inequality (excluding the CPEs) has slightly increased.

It is interesting to analyze the changes in terms of the change in inequality within each block and the relative "gap" in mean income between the blocks. This cannot be precisely done using the Gini coefficient, which is not thus "decomposable." For this purpose we use the Theil L. Index,[7] which permits world inequality to be expressed as the sum of LDC and MDC inequality, plus the contribution of the "gap," which is what the index would show if each MDC and each LDC had the same per caput income. We give unweighted and population-weighted figures. (See table 13-2.) As with the Gini, the weighted figures would measure interpersonal inequality if every citizen had the mean income of his country. The weighted gap would measure interpersonal inequality if every LDC and MDC citizen had the mean LDC and MDC income, respectively. The Theil index has no upper bound, and so one cannot compare the increases in equality shown respectively by the Gini and Theil indices.

TABLE 13-2
Theil L. Indices (percentages)

		World		LDC Contribution		MDC Contribution		Gap Contribution	
Unweighted	1958	0.62	100	0.34	54	0.02	3	0.27	43
Unweighted	1978	0.91	100	0.52	57	0.01	1	0.38	42
Population weighted	1958	0.87	100	0.19	21	0.07	8	0.62	71
Population weighted	1978	1.13	100	0.38	34	0.01	1	0.73	65

The contribution of the gap has increased absolutely but declined relatively. The contribution of within-LDC inequality has increased, both absolutely and relatively. The contribution of MDC inequality is small and has declined absolutely and relatively. One can also calculate the percentage contribution to the changes in inequality as in table 13-3.

TABLE 13-3
Contributions to Changes in Inequality, 1958–78 (percentages)

	World	LDC	MDC	Gap
Unweighted	100	+63	−3	+40
Weighted	100	+77	−23	+46

POPULATION DENSITY

The population/cultivable land density of LDCs varies enormously. Apart from the city states, Taiwan and South Korea are the densest, with around eighteen persons per cultivable hectare. Egypt has fourteen and Bangladesh ten. At the other end of the scale, Botswana has nearly two hectares per person. South and Central America, Africa, and the Near East are lightly populated (2.4–2.8) relative to South Asia (4.0) and the Far East (6.9). This says a lot about attitudes toward family planning (see chapter 10). The MDCs vary even more, from the United States (1.0) to Japan (23.3). Other natural resources also vary greatly. A lot of minerals and a few people yield high per caput incomes. But the world's most successful performers in the Far East have very little land, and almost no minerals.[8]

TRADE DEPENDENCY

Turning to trade, it is a common misconception that LDCs are very trade-dependent compared to MDCs. The reverse is true, both for countries and persons. (See table 13–4.) A higher proportion of MDC countries are more export dependent at all levels of dependency.

TABLE 13-4
Export Dependency[a]

Percentage of Exports to GDP (X)	Percentage of countries with $X_i > X$		Percentage of total population in countries with $X_i > X$	
	LDCs	MDCs	LDCs	MDCs
40	8	17	2	4
35	10	17	6	4
30	18	22	9	5
25	27	50	11	24
20	42	78	25	39
15	58	83	34	47
10	78	94	44	67
5	95	100	97	100
0	100	100	100	100

SOURCE: *World Development Report 1980*, Tables 1 and 8.
[a] Countries with less than one million persons and the five "capital surplus oil exporters" are excluded.

Description and Record of Less Developed Countries

These figures exclude the town-sized countries. But this exclusion makes no difference to the figures concerning population (columns 4 and 5). A higher percentage of the MDC population lives in more trade-dependent countries at all dependency levels except 30–40 percent. The average LDC person lives in a country with 13 percent export dependency; his MDC counterpart lives in a country with 17 percent export dependency.

LDC exports are divided among agricultural primary goods; minerals, metals, and fuels; and manufactures in the proportion 27-41-31. There have been large changes since the 1960s, when the proportions were 54-31-15.[9] The rise in minerals, etc., is not due only to oil: it has risen markedly for both low- and high-income countries, even when the major "capital surplus" oil producers are excluded.[10] The fall in the land-based primary exports is very general and caused largely by the low agricultural growth rate in LDCs. The doubling of the proportion of manufactures was largely due to the sensational growth from Korea, Taiwan, and Hong Kong. These three countries exported about $24 billion of manufactures and accounted for more than three-quarters of the exports of manufactures of non-European LDCs (in 1977). However, in the 1970s many other countries had very rapidly increased manufactured exports, though from a small base. Seven others exported more than $1 billion of manufactures in 1977.

On the import side, there has been little change, manufactures constituting about 63 percent in 1977, as in 1960. Fuel has risen from 11 percent to 18 percent at the expense of the other categories.

The other great changes in trade have been in oil and cereals. The oil story is too well known to need mention here (see discussion in chapter 16). Cereals are not quite so fully publicized. The changes in net exports (+) and imports (−) by major regions are shown in table 13-5.

The rapidly rising dependence on North America speaks for itself. The LDCs of Africa and Asia, and the Communist countries, have increased their deficit from 20 million tons to 77 million tons in fifteen years.

TABLE 13-5
Net Exports (+) and Imports (−) by Major Regions (million tons—all cereals)

	1963	1971	1978
United States and Canada	+48.7	+53.8	+113.0
Australia and New Zealand	+5.2	+11.1	+13.6
South and Central America	−0.2	+4.4	−4.2
Africa	−1.1	−3.9	−11.0
USSR and Eastern Europe	−3.0	−2.4	−28.3
Near East	−3.6	−8.2	−13.9
China	−4.9	−6.6	−12.3
Far East (excluding Japan)	−7.9	−8.2	−11.1
Western Europe	−25.5	−26.1	−20.0
Japan, others, and errors	−8.3	−13.8	−25.8

SOURCE: *Food and Agricultural Organization Trade Statistics,* various years.

PRODUCTION

The share of agriculture in value added has been much reduced. For LDCs as a whole it is now about 20 percent. By region, it varies from 41 percent for South Asia, 28 percent for Africa south of the Sahara, 23 percent for East Asia, and 13–14 percent for Southern Europe, the Near East, and South and Central America.

Manufacturing has a slightly higher share than agriculture for LDCs as a whole. It is much higher in South and Central America and Southern Europe, slightly higher in North Africa and the Middle East, and lower in other regions.

In countries with incomes exceeding $360 per head at 1978 prices (the World Bank "middle income" countries), the share of manufacturing is very little lower (at 25 percent) than in the "industrialized" countries (27 percent). The share of manufacturing in Argentina, Brazil, Egypt, Hong Kong, Israel, Mexico, the Philippines, Singapore, Taiwan, and Uruguay is now higher than it is in the United States. Evidently manufacturing is not the key either to wealth or a broadly based development.

Industry includes mining, and for this reason many more LDCs are relatively highly industrialized. Twenty-six out of ninety-one LDCs listed by the World Bank (excluding Southern

Europe and South Africa) are more industrialized than the United States.

The share of the service sectors is very roughly correlated with income per head. In the poorer third of all countries, services account for around 40 percent of gross national product, in the middle-income countries for around 50 percent, and in the richest for around 60 percent. But there are very wide variations, which have not been well analyzed. The tendency is to treat them as dependent on the other sectors, but this is not satisfactory—there are clearly important "exogenous" influences, such as the size of government and the armed forces, the importance of tourism, and international commerce. It is clear, for instance, that tourism has been one of the "engines of growth" for some LDCs.

THE STRUCTURE OF EMPLOYMENT AND LABOR PRODUCTIVITY

Everywhere agriculture accounts for a much higher proportion of employment than value added. This gap between labor productivity in agriculture and industry and services is common to nearly all countries, but it is much more pronounced—and indeed has widened—in LDCs. Thus, the decline in the share of agriculture in value added is greater than the decline in the share of employment; and in some countries (for example, India) there has been virtually no decline. This shows up in the relative changes in productivity in the three major sectors: agriculture, industry, and service. In table 13-6, we lump industry and services together as nonagriculture, since there is little recorded difference in productivity between them. It shows the changes between 1960 and 1978, for low- and middle-income LDCs and the MDCs.[11]

These figures are rough, but nevertheless they tell a story. Relative agricultural productivity, already low, has fallen even further in the poorer LDCs. In the middle-income LDCs, where it was even lower in 1960, it has increased a little. It has increased dramatically in the MDCs, where the percentage of the agricultural labor force has fallen far more steeply than in the LDCs, from 17 percent to 6 percent. The high rate of population growth, and rapidly increasing labor productivity in industry,

TABLE 13-6
Relative Agricultural Productivity[a]

	1960			1978		
	(1) Agri-culture	(2) Nonagri-culture	(3) (1)÷(2)	(4) Agri-culture	(5) Nonagri-culture	(6) (4)÷(5)
Low-income LDCs	0.65	2.17	0.30	0.53	2.21	0.24
Middle-income LDCs	0.38	1.86	0.20	0.36	1.53	0.24
MDCs	0.35	1.13	0.31	0.67	1.02	0.66

SOURCE: *World Development Report 1980.*

[a] $\frac{\text{Value added in agriculture}}{\text{Employment in agriculture}} \div \frac{\text{Total value added}}{\text{Total employment}}$; and similarly for nonagriculture.

has resulted in the poorer LDCs reducing the proportion of people working mainly in agriculture only from 77 percent to 72 percent, and in the richer LDCs from 58 percent to 45 percent. The comparative neglect of agriculture has also played a part.

Growth

GNP PER HEAD, 1960-78

Before embarking on a description of this later period, a word is in order about the period from 1945 to 1960. Figures for the earlier period are more unreliable, and often nonexistent. National income accounting was still in its infancy, especially in Africa. Morawetz has conveniently assembled figures for the 1950s.[12] Comparing the longer period (1950-75, in Morawetz) with them suggests that growth accelerated in all regions except South Asia, and possibly Africa (the figures for Africa are too unreliable to say anything).

Table 13-7 gives regional figures of growth in per caput income for 1960 to 1978. We have carved out one unconventional region, the Mediterranean Littoral. Countries included in this region all benefited from their proximity to Europe in terms of tourism, labor exports, and lower transport costs, and most from relatively high aid flows per caput.

TABLE 13-7
Growth in GNP Per Caput—Percent per Annum

		Index of 1978 (1960 = 100)
Latin America and Caribbean	3.4	182
Mediterranean Littoral[a]	4.1	206
Other Africa	1.8	137
South Asia	1.3	127
East Asia[b]	4.5	220
Capital Surplus Exporters[c]	7.1	343
All LDCs	2.6	159

[a] The countries are Greece, Portugal, Spain, Turkey, Yugoslavia, Israel, Egypt, Tunisia, Algeria, Morocco, Syria. Countries with fewer than one million people are excluded (Malta, Cyprus). Albania is excluded as a centrally planned economy. Libya is excluded as a "capital surplus oil exporter." Portugal is deemed to be washed by the Mediterranean for convenience. Lebanon is excluded for a lack of figures, resulting from warfare.
[b] East Asia excludes Laos, Kampuchea, and Vietnam for lack of figures. This is just as well, since their performance would be marred by warfare.
[c] Iraq, Iran, Libya, Saudi Arabia, Kuwait.

These growth rates are measured in terms of constant prices (that is, ignoring price changes). This would make little difference to such broad averages except in the case of the five capital surplus oil exporters, where the growth rate of purchasing power has been much higher than shown. Thus, except for these latter, the external terms of trade of LDCs scarcely changed from 1960 to 1978. They improved from 1960 to 1973 and then worsened—especially in the case of the middle-income LDCs.[13] The terms of trade of the capital surplus oil exporters almost quadrupled.

We saw earlier that LDCs had become much more unequal. This suggests, though it does not imply, that initially the poorer countries grew less fast than the richer countries. The World Bank's figures show that low-income LDCs' per caput income grew at only 1.6 percent per annum, while that of middle-income LDCs grew at 3.7 percent per annum. But this is misleading, since the high-low classification is based on 1978 figures, and not those of 1960.

I made a less misleading test of the relation between initial wealth, and subsequent growth, which shows that there is no relationship whatever between income and growth in either Latin America and the Caribbean or in Africa. The strong positive relationship in Asia comes entirely from the fact that East Asia outgrew South Asia and started better off.[14] That Latin America outgrew Africa would also contribute to the slight overall positive correlation. Interregional differences other than per caput income, which might account for different performance, are so numerous that it is proper to conclude that there is no evidence that differences in initial real incomes have any effect. So much for the poverty trap!

The aggregate figures show clearly enough that the sluggish regions are South Asia and Africa south of the Sahara. But they cannot show the great range of experience. Per caput incomes fell in six African countries, and in Bhutan and Bangladesh. They rose at more than 6.0 percent per annum in seven countries—Korea, Taiwan, Hong Kong, Singapore, Iran, Libya, and Saudi Arabia.

Although MDCs continued to outperform LDCs on a per caput basis up to 1973, this was then reversed as MDC growth slowed, partly because of the oil price rises but mainly because they could not control inflation without depressing demand and creating unemployment. Per caput real product in LDCs rose at an annual rate of 3.1 percent from 1970 to 1979, against 2.5 percent per annum for the MDCs.

For the past twenty-five to thirty years, growth of per caput incomes has been much higher for most LDCs (and MDCs) than in any other historical period. Nearly all have raised investment levels (with some support from foreign savings) and have improved the skill levels of their working force. Some have benefited greatly from rapidly rising world demand for energy and some other primary products. A few have benefited dramatically from exploiting their comparative advantage in labor-intensive manufactures, seizing the opportunity of the increased openness of the MDCs. Even so, the results are surprising in the light of two considerations. First, there has been much wasted investment, mainly but not wholly in inappropriate industrialization, and, second, there has been much damage caused by widespread civil and international warfare.[15]

It is thus pertinent to ask whether the figures are not optimistically biased. There is one good reason for thinking so: the prevalence of excessive protection that has certainly resulted in some industrialization showing up in the figures as an exaggerated rise in productive potential. The extreme example is when a project results in negative value added at international trade prices, thereby reducing the power of the economy to supply final goods, while yet showing up as an increase owing to the divergence of domestic prices from prices that reflect trading opportunities. Little, Scitovsky, and Scott recalculated growth rates of gross domestic product (or production potential) for six countries, using trade or "border" prices instead of domestic prices. The most heavily protected of these was Pakistan, and the growth rate for the period 1950–52 to 1964–66 was reduced from 3.8 to 3.2 percent per annum. Pakistan was an extreme case. For the much more industrialized Argentina, the reduction was from 3.2 to 3.0 percent per annum. Guessing wildly from this calculation, which has not to my knowledge been updated or extended to more economies, one might surmise that growth rates of the more heavily import-substituting economies are on this account exaggerated, but probably by less than half a percent per annum. The overall performance would remain impressive.

EXPORT GROWTH

From 1950 to 1959, dollar export earnings of LDCs grew at 3.8 percent per annum. Those of non-oil-exporters fared worse, with a growth rate of 2.1 percent per annum. This together with the a priori expectation that food and raw materials faced a low import elasticity of demand in MDCs explains the export pessimism that prevailed well into the 1960s and helped to create the United Nations Conference on Trade and Development.

In the 1960s (1959–69), it was different. LDC dollar export earnings rose by 6.6 percent per annum, and those of non-oil-exporters by 6.2 percent per annum.[16] This was faster than the 6.0 percent per annum stated at UNCTAD I in 1964 to be required if the United Nations GNP target of 5.0 percent per annum were to be achieved. It did not require the major changes in policy by MDCs, which were claimed as essential at UNCTAD I in 1964. This acceleration was certainly helped by more rapid growth in the MDCs. Nevertheless, earnings from primary product exports, especially agricultural primary products, grew quite slowly, with LDCs losing their share of world trade in most commodities, mainly due to supply limitations.[17] What had happened was that exports of manufactures took off, albeit from low levels, and grew at 15 percent per annum, faster than the growth in world trade in manufactures.

Table 13-8 gives UNCTAD figures for the purchasing power of exports for the whole period 1960–79.[18] In view of the sharp break in the performance of different LDCs occasioned by the oil price rises of 1973–74, and the much slower growth of MDCs since then, it is useful to separate the period 1973–78. There is a further break in 1978–79 as a result of further oil price rises. So we give the periods separately.

TABLE 13-8
Growth Rate of Purchasing Power of Exports
(percent per annum)

	1960–79	1960–73	1973–78	1978–79
All LDCs[a]	7.8	7.1	9.0	9.4
Major petroleum exporters[b]	11.4	9.3	15.1	20.4
Other	5.1	6.0	4.2	−1.5

SOURCE: United Nations Conference on Trade and Development, *Handbook of International Trade and Development Studies*, 1980.

[a] UNCTAD excludes Southern European LDCs and also Israel and Taiwan—among the most successful countries.

[b] Algeria, Angola, Bahrein, Brunei, Ecuador, Gabon, Indonesia, Iran, Iraq, Kuwait, Libya, Nigeria, Oman, Qatar, Saudi Arabia, Trinidad and Tobago, United Arab Emirates, and Venezuela. These are the countries for which petroleum and petroleum products accounted for more than one-half of total exports.

Table 13-9 gives terms of trade figures. The sharp effect on non-oil-exporting LDCs of the oil price rises in 1973–74 and 1978–79 is very clear from these tables.

TABLE 13-9
Terms of Trade (unit value of exports ÷ unit value of imports)

	1960	1973	1975	1978	1979
All LDCs	62	65	100	97	96
Oil Exporters	33	36	100	94	114
Other	108	109	100	98	90

SOURCE: United Nations Conference on Trade and Development, *Handbook of International Trade and Development Studies, 1980.*

PART VI

International Systems and Confrontation

Chapter 14

The Old International Economic Order— The Trade Regime, 1945-73

From the Civil War until about the mid-1930s the United States tended toward isolationism in the spheres of politics and international political economy, and was in fact highly protectionist. But the sauve qui peut disorder of the 1930s convinced American statesmen, first and foremost Cordell Hull, of the need for international agreements that would produce a worldwide set of rules and conventions both to promote prosperity and to prevent countries and blocs of countries from creating competitive hierarchical subsystems that would damage general prosperity and might well result in war. Peace was as much emphasized as prosperity. The German system of bilateral trading agreements with the Balkan countries and Japan's so-called co-prosperity sphere were seen as part of the causes of war, as well as preparation for it. The British system of imperial preference was fervently disliked, although it was not seen as being aggressive in the manner of the German and Japanese arrangements.

It is remarkable that the United States and the United Kingdom devoted so much attention to designing a postwar trade and payments system in the middle of a world war that they were still in danger of losing. The Bretton Woods monetary system was successfully negotiated in 1944. Although trade negotiations came later, we shall deal with them first, since a payments system is but the servant of a trading system; also, trading arrangements proved more difficult to negotiate than monetary arrangements—indeed they proved impossible.

Post-1945 Trading Rules

Almost as soon as hostilities ceased, the United States attempted to establish, almost single-handedly, a free-trading nonpreferential world system. At the first meeting of the Economic and Social Council of the United Nations in February 1946, a preparatory committee for an International Trading Organization was set up. Its mandate included the request that the organization should take account of "the special conditions which prevail in countries whose manufacturing industry is still in its initial stages of development, and the questions that arise in connection with commodities which are subject to special problems of adjustment in international markets."[1] The preparatory committee included five less developed countries (Brazil, Chile, Cuba, India, and Lebanon) and ten developed countries, as well as China, Czechoslovakia, and South Africa. The essence of the United States position was that most-favored-nation treatment should apply to tariffs, that quota restrictions and export subsidies should be outlawed, and that all countries should commit themselves to a program of reciprocal tariff reductions. The United States proposals made a disastrously self-serving and short-sighted exception for agriculture, where import quotas were to be permitted if domestic output were also restricted; this vitiated the liberal principles inspiring the rest of the American position. The general feeling was that, if the Americans needed to support their farmers' standard of living, they could surely afford to do so without restricting imports.

The United States proposals produced a storm of opposition from the LDCs, though with significant support from several more developed countries and other countries on particular points, both in the preparatory committee and at the full Havana Conference, which included fifty-six countries of which thirty-three were LDCs (eighteen from Central and South America). What is perhaps most remarkable is that almost everything that has since been demanded by LDCs was demanded in 1946. Virtually nothing has been added (except the link, and specific aid targets) and nothing dropped.

Rejecting the MFN principle, LDCs demanded the right to create new preferences: there was a general desire to retain the right not merely to form customs unions but generally to give or receive preferences that might be based on geographical, political, or ethnical considerations. Lebanon, for instance, argued on behalf of the Arab League for preferences that would allow Arab countries to coordinate their economic policies.

The LDCs argued that quotas were essential for development. This did not refer only to the temporary use of quotas for balance-of-payments reasons. Quotas that might discriminate between countries were desired by India, especially as a matter of long-term policy; and this position was supported by some developed countries; for example, the United Kingdom and New Zealand.[2] It was argued that quotas would not restrict trade. This anticipated the Prebisch contention that LDC imports are governed by exports, whose level is exogenously given for the LDCs (see chapter 4). Beyond quotas, the LDCs wanted recognition of their right to use any and every form of protection, including raising tariffs and imposing various internal regulatory devices, such as "mixing requirements" (for example, no more than 25 percent foreign flour in bread). They rejected any obligation to negotiate tariff reductions.

The reaction to the American loopholes for agricultural quotas was not to block them, but to extend them to include manufactures and to provide support for commodity prices. Neither then nor since have LDCs taken the line that if the United States believed in liberal trading principles, it should stick to them.

A code on commodity stabilization was to be included. The LDCs wanted *just* prices, and resisted the United States formula referring to "long-term equilibrium prices." The United States saw commodity agreements as exceptional adjuncts to a free-trading system, the LDCs and others as the keystone to a fair trading system.

The LDCs also wanted special access to capital, and referred to the duty of developed countries to extend loans and their right to receive them. There was the same emphasis on sovereignty, as in the New International Economic Order three decades later. Their right to exclude foreign investment was to be recognized, and also their right to expropriate foreign investments and pay compensation in local currency.

Finally, it was argued that the Havana Charter should recognize that the industrialization of LDCs, and a reduction of the structural disparities between them and the industrialized countries, was as much the purpose of the ITO as the expansion of trade.

The United States proposals shocked the Latin American countries, which had already begun a process of import substitution behind trade restrictions in the 1930s. Factories established during World War II would also need protection, perhaps increased protection. India's belief in planning was already strong (see chapter 3), extending to detailed physical planning of foreign trade. The United States, so recently converted to free trade (except for agriculture), found itself confronted by a world whose equally recent conversion to planning and organized trade was apparent. She found only fractured and varied support even from Europe.

The upshot of this conference was that so many qualifications were accepted that the ITO would have been little short of a charter to "do as you please." It was so clear that Congress would not ratify such an agreement that the Truman administration never even submitted it for approval. Congressional opposition would have come both from protectionists, who were against the free-trading philosophy of the proposed charter, and from liberals, who saw the exceptions and loopholes as effectively undermining that philosophy.

The conflict has never died away. The United States administration wanted overall trading rules that would apply to all: except for some agricultural products of interest to them, there should be open-door free-trading rules with reciprocal tariff reductions. The LDCs were so convinced that free trade would harm them that they wanted any such rules to apply at most only to the developed countries; but they preferred trade by arrangement, in commodities and even manufactures. They believed, with justice, that the United States pressed for international rules only where it was thought that the United States would benefit—trade in goods and services. The movement of capital and people was not to be covered by the ITO. The LDCs did not, however, recognize or believe that what would be good for the United States (or General Motors) might also be good for them, or that the Americans believed this. Since 1948, the reservations of the European countries to the American position have largely fallen away, least so in France. A handful of LDCs might now also subscribe to the United States-Havana position with few reservations. But the conflict between what is now known as the North and the South is essentially unchanged.

The General Agreement on Tariffs and Trade rose like a phoenix from the ashes of the ITO, although the atmosphere in Geneva (and the Calvinist tradition) is not conducive to such pagan events. The GATT, which emerged out of a Tariff Conference in Geneva in 1947, incorporated many of the commercial policy provisions of the ITO draft charter and was amended in 1948 in accordance with the Havana Conference. However, it essentially dealt only with the commercial chapter of the ITO draft, and thus left out much that was dear to the LDCs (for example, the objective of economic development, control over restrictive business practices, and, above all, commodity agreements). It excluded capital movements and other monetary phenomena (deemed to be for the International Monetary Fund) and also invisibles.

After the Geneva Conference, which succeeded in arranging large tariff cuts,[3] the participating parties* signed GATT in 1948, something the United States president could do under the Reciprocal Trade Agreements Act without reference to Congress, which has never approved GATT.

GATT started as, and at least until the 1970s remained, essentially an instrument for tariff reduction by reciprocal bargaining. The mercantilist conception underlying reciprocity needs no stress. But in a period when there was great reluctance to change exchange rates, reciprocity could find support even among those who recognized the benefits of unilateral tariff reduction or elimination. Moreover, reciprocity has political attraction: when attacked for sacrificing jobs in one industry, a government can point to gains elsewhere.

The procedures for reciprocal tariff reduction involved bargaining with one or more principal suppliers in order to limit the free-rider benefits from the MFN clause. The clause forced a tariff reduction to be applied across the board, even to those who did not reciprocate, since they were not involved in the bargain, and often applied even to nonmembers of GATT.

There were no procedures for dismantling nontariff barriers (NTBs); they were supposed to have been abolished anyway, apart from nondiscriminatory quotas for balance-of-payments reasons (Article XVIII), or to prevent market disruption under Article XIX.[4] In fact, the freeing of intra-European trade from quotas occurred outside GATT, and in a context of the Organization for European Economic Cooperation, largely as a result of the Marshall Plan. However, NTBs were not fully abolished, especially for extra-European trade in agricultural products. The United States obtained a broad waiver for agriculture in 1955.[5] After general European convertibility in the late 1950s, many European agricultural quotas dating from the 1930s could no longer be justified on balance-of-payments grounds, and some further waivers from GATT rules were obtained. Most European countries, however, maintained some quotas throughout, often in defiance of GATT rules.

---

* A dozen of the original thirty-three participants were LDCs. The participation of Europe was helped by the initiation of the Marshall Plan.

The provisions of GATT became increasingly permissive as far as LDC behavior was concerned. Early on, Article XVIII was amended to make inadequacy of reserves a reason for quota restrictions on imports. In 1960, the MDCs agreed to eliminate export subsidies, but it was explicitly recognized that LDCs might use them, in view of their overvalued currencies. In 1963, nonreciprocity for LDCs was conceded (it had not in fact been usually demanded), and in 1964, it was written into the constitution under the new Part IV. Apart from a few tariffs that were bound before 1960, the behavior of LDCs who were GATT members was never significantly restricted.

Prima facie GATT rules seem to be highly favorable to LDCs. Under the rules, MDCs reduce tariffs on an MFN basis. Their use of quotas is severely restricted. Export subsidies are outlawed. But LDC members can virtually do as they please; and in practice they use quotas and export subsidies very extensively and have very high tariffs: they need not reduce these restrictions in order to benefit from MDC concessions. Nevertheless, GATT has always been much abused by the LDCs (although membership had increased from twelve originally to about forty by the end of the Tokyo Round in 1979). Before investigating the reasons for this, let us briefly consider the actual gains that have accrued to LDCs via GATT negotiations.

Until the Kennedy Round (1964–67), LDCs gained very little directly.[6] The primary reason for this was that MDCs are usually the principal suppliers of commodities, and therefore "concessions were negotiated primarily with other industrial countries on goods traded primarily among industrial countries."[7] It is possible that the pre-Kennedy GATT rounds contributed to the fact that tariffs on manufactures were relatively high for those typically exported by LDCs. Prior to the Kennedy Round, MDC tariffs on total manufactured imports averaged 11 percent but were 17 percent on those from LDCs.[8] Such considerations, together with the fact that GATT was inactive in agricultural commodities where MDCs were most restrictive, resulted in the second half of the 1950s in efforts to make GATT more relevant for LDCs. The Haberler Report was commissioned in 1957, and as a result the GATT initiated an action program in 1958, which recommended

291

that MDCs unilaterally reduce taxation and trade barriers on some items of particular interest to LDCs—but with little effect. More was achieved in 1963 when the LDC member countries initiated an action program aimed at removing trade barriers: there was some progress in removing quotas and reducing or eliminating tariffs on some tropical products, especially tea and tropical timber. But further progress was hampered by the preferential margins for associates of the European Economic Community—which would thereby be reduced—and by the Brasseur Plan for general preferences in favor of certain LDC exports. To quote K. Dam, on whose work the above sketch is largely based:

> It is a curious point of history that at the end of 1963 when the LDCs urged the MDCs to commit themselves to a GATT type barrier-lowering approach to the problems of the LDCs, the developed countries were unable to give them full satisfaction because some of the MDCs were already interested in more radical ideas that had been advanced by some less developed countries within the GATT and that were to become the platform of the less developed countries at the United Nations Conference on Trade and Development (UNCTAD) the following year.[9]

The Kennedy Round changed things. Bilateral negotiations gave way to "across-the-board" negotiations, which resulted in tariff reductions in the major industrial countries of about one third on about two thirds of their dutiable imports.[10] Although tariff cuts were still somewhat concentrated on items of great interest to MDCs,[11] the gains of the LDCs were important, for tariff reductions were made on products for which LDC exports to MDCs totaled over $2 billion.[12] It has been suggested that the consequent increase in exports from LDCs to MDCs was of the order of $1 billion per annum.[13] It must be added that, while the Kennedy Round gave important absolute benefits to LDCs, MDC tariff levels remained as discriminatory against LDCs as before.

The early 1960s also saw the advent of the Long Term Arrangement on Cotton Textiles (LTA), which lasted from 1962 to 1973. Most MDCs had begun to restrict trade in cotton textiles. Market disruption was sometimes claimed under Article XIX of GATT; more often, so-called voluntary export restrictions (VERs), over which GATT had no control, were used. The aim of the LTA was to regularize and legitimize these restrictions and, it was hoped, to make them less restrictive by guaranteeing a minimum annual rate of increase of imports (5 percent). The determination of what constituted "disruption" was left entirely to the importer. A major loophole that LDCs took advantage of was that the LTA related only to items with over 50 percent cotton content. The dollar value of LDC exports of textile fabrics to MDCs rose at a rate of 8 percent per annum in the 1960s, and of clothing by 22 percent per annum.[14] There was in consequence a renewed growth of unilateral discriminatory quotas and VERs in the late 1960s and the 1970s. The new Multi-fiber Textile Arrangement (MFA) of 1973 resulted. These two arrangements may have prevented worse from happening, though this is impossible to say for sure. What is sure is that they did not prevent an extremely rapid rise of textile and clothing imports from LDCs, even after the MFA, but before "the new protectionism" began to bite after 1975. Thus, as Keesing notes, "Most European countries did not fully use their powers under the MFA, but allowed a rapid increase in imports. Even in the USA ... a considerable increase took place in the value of imports of textiles and clothing, despite serious quota regulations."[15]

From the mid-1950s until the mid-1970s, NTBs were of little importance for manufactures other than textiles and clothing. To quote Keesing again,

> By 1975, not only tariff barriers, but also non-tariff barriers were weak. In the developed countries as a group, outside textile products, about 1½ percent of all imports of manufactures (narrowly defined) from developing countries were subject to quantitative import restrictions. In leading industrial countries, protective non-tariff barriers were practically absent (with only minor products affected) except for a residual of administrative and special obstacles which were most serious in Italy and France.[16]

The Kennedy Round was a triumph for GATT, and an important benefit for LDCs. This triumph was tempered by GATT's inability to control, on a nondiscriminatory basis, the growth of NTBs. This failure, however, was not in practice serious for

LDCs, at least until the mid-1970s. More serious was GATT's irrelevance so far as agricultural protection was concerned. Later on, it became clear also that GATT's concern only with the right to sell, and not at all with the right to buy, was another important weakness. Apart from GATT's weaknesses in these areas, there were also many other forces at work undermining the idea of a general market-oriented, noninterventionist, nondiscriminatory trading system (for MDC trading behavior—the LDCs having accepted neither the theory nor the practice). These stemmed from the creation of common markets, free trade areas, and UNCTAD; from the extension of European and other preferences that were contrary to the spirit and even the letter of GATT; and from an increased use of government trading and government fiat in international economic transactions.[17]

The Creation of UNCTAD and the Undermining of GATT

Reciprocity, or rather nonreciprocity, is close to the heart of the matter. In exactly the same way as the MDCs, the LDCs wrongly regard reductions of trade barriers as concessions; that is, as damaging unless reciprocated. The latter believes that it is up to the developed countries alone to make concessions. Thus, it was thought that the freeing of trade should be one-sided—analogous to aid. But the GATT was not conceived as a forum, like UNCTAD, where demands for unilateral concessions were made. As soon as the Pyrrhic victory of nonreciprocity was achieved in GATT, the participation of the LDCs was almost anomalous. They could sit on the floor and wait for the crumbs to drop from the rich man's table. Even if the crumbs were palatable and the posture self-imposed, this was invidious.

The presence of members who were mainly demanding exceptions to rules may also have weakened the authority of GATT as a rule-creating body: in the late 1960s, the MDCs increasingly began to circumvent and even ignore GATT, which was a serious matter even if the resulting protection did not in practice become very restrictive until the second half of the 1970s.

The unwillingness of the MDCs to allow GATT to limit agricultural protection was another important reason for many LDCs to regard it as irrelevant to their problems. It is ironical that it was the United States that initially led the way, ironical because United States protection of agriculture by quotas is dwarfed by that of Europe and Japan, and because the United States is a major opponent of the EEC's Common Agricultural Policy (CAP).

Moreover, the GATT is not the ITO. There are matters of importance to LDCs that are not in its terms of reference. Perhaps the most glaring omission from the LDC point of view is the subject of commodity prices and stabilization. But invisibles are also invisible, and there is no code concerning cartels or other restrictive business practices, which even when privately organized are fostered and supported by governments. There is a code for state-trading enterprises, but it makes little sense. This is, however, more of a worry for MDCs than LDCs.[18] Finally, there are other matters that seemed unimportant in 1947 but may require international conventions today, such as control and ownership of the seabed.

The GATT is not the ITO, because agreement on liberal trading rules could not be reached in 1947. The philosophy of GATT is still largely that of the United States conception of an ITO: that governmental interference with the workings of the price mechanism, where it seriously affected international transactions, should be quite strictly limited by international agreement. This philosophy stemmed partly from faith in the beneficial working of the price mechanism, and partly from the experience of competitive and oligopolistic interventions by major powers between World War I and World War II. Many LDCs have not accepted this philosophy since the 1930s. This, despite green lights for their own interventions, is the basic reason for distrust of GATT and for the creation of UNCTAD, whose philosophy favors direct regulation of all international transactions rather than the design of a framework within which most transactions can be left to the market. This is all easy to understand. It is harder to

International Systems and Confrontation

understand why so many LDC leaders believe that such direct regulation will benefit them and not lead to increased dependence.

Common Markets, Free Trade Areas, and Related Preferences

Old preferences were permitted to linger under GATT rules. British imperial preferences were the most important, although they withered throughout the postwar period and finally fell to the ground when the United Kingdom joined the EEC in 1973.

New preferences were permitted in the Havana Charter and GATT (Article XXIV) only if they resulted from the formation of a Common Market or Free Trade Area. The EEC dwarfs others in importance and did even when there were only six members. The Yaoundé Convention of 1964 associated eighteen ex-European, mostly ex-French, colonies with the EEC.[19] These countries received duty-free access for industrial products, and any agricultural products not covered by the EEC's CAP. They also received some preferences under the CAP variable levy, but with tariff quotas (that is, quantities receiving preferences were limited). Furthermore, the agreement involved reciprocity. Thus, there were so-called reverse preferences, and the associates agreed not to discriminate between the Six; but reciprocity could still be rejected on grounds of development or revenue needs. Aid from the European Development Fund and the European Bank was tied in with the convention.

Between 1962 and 1972, the Six also negotiated preferential agreements with most Mediterranean countries, including Greece, Turkey, Morocco, Tunisia, Malta, Cyprus, Spain, Israel, Egypt, and Lebanon. Some of these envisaged full membership of a customs union, but others appear to be contrary to both the spirit and the letter of GATT. Apart from the absence of any aid commitment, these agreements were generally similar to the Yaoundé agreement, though less favorable in some cases. The Arusha agreement between the Six and Kenya, Tanzania, and

Uganda was signed in 1971 and was similar to the Mediterranean agreements.

With the enlargement of the EEC from six to nine (January 1, 1973), preferences proliferated. The United Kingdom Commonwealth was divided into the associable and nonassociable. The "nons" were Commonwealth Asia (apart from dependencies, excluding Hong Kong) and Gibraltar.[20] The Yaoundé and Arusha conventions were swallowed by that of Lomé in 1975.[21] The "associable" African, Caribbean, and Pacific (ACP) countries now numbered forty-six, more than one third of all LDCs, though covering much less than a third of LDC trade. Lomé was also more concessionary than Yaoundé. It did not require any reciprocity.* There were no ceilings on duty-free entry of industrial products, or on those agricultural products that were not subject to CAP variable levies. It also incorporated a stabilization arrangement—the EEC's Scheme for Stabilization of Export Receipts Fund of $0.5 billion (STABEX), which would be used to support ACP country earnings from the export of a number of major products to the EEC.

The enlargement of the EEC was also the occasion for extending preferences to the rump of the European Free Trade Area (EFTA) consisting of Finland, Norway, Sweden, Austria, Switzerland, Portugal, and Iceland. These sixteen countries became a free-trade area for manufactures, including processed agricultural products, with no restrictions.

Apart from the above special EEC preferences covering in all over sixty countries, there were many other preferential arrangements in force in the early 1970s. These include the Latin American Free Trade Area (LAFTA), the Andean Common Market, Central American Common Market (CACM), the Caribbean Free Trade Area (CARIFTA), the East African Common Market,[22] the Central African Customs Unions (UDEAC), the West African Economic Community (CEAC), and the Association of South East Asian Nations (ASEAN). All of these regional arrangements fall far short of their original intentions concerning regional integra-

---

*This concession was granted largely to permit the forty-six to benefit from United States generalized special preferences.

International Systems and Confrontation

tion, and in some of them virtually nothing has been accomplished. In all of them, except the CACM, intratrade has remained a small part (10 percent or less) of total trade. Only LAFTA and ASEAN cover a large number of people. Even the oldest, LAFTA, did not get very far in liberalizing intratrade, a liberalization that had to be negotiated on a product-by-product basis.

In addition to these regional efforts that either are or have some claim to being free-trade areas or common markets, there have been two nonregional exchanges of preferences which could make no such claim. In 1967 India, the United Arab Republic, and Yugoslavia exchanged preferences on a number of products. In 1971, negotiating under GATT auspices, sixteen LDCs, including the above, did the same. There was no intention of reducing protection: imports were governed by quotas, and most of the items were not manufactured in the importing country anyway. The result may have been some small switch of imports from MDCs to LDCs but could only have been very small, for the value of trade affected was very small. The agreements are worth noting only for their principle, not their importance.

Generalized Special Preferences

GSPs constituted the main plank of UNCTAD's platform in the 1960s. The principle was agreed on at UNCTAD II in 1968, and most developed countries introduced schemes in 1971 and 1972; Canada and the United States followed only in 1974 and 1976. There were fifteen schemes (including Australia, which jumped the gun in the early 1960s) reduced to twelve when the United Kingdom, Ireland, and Denmark joined the EEC. The example that prompted UNCTAD's enthusiasm was probably imperial preference, which had benefited a few United Kingdom dependencies, notably Hong Kong. If so, the point was missed that it was unrestricted access, not tariff preference, which really counted. The Group of Seventy-seven (formed among LDC members of the United Nations in 1963 in the course of the negotiations that led to UNCTAD I) regarded preferences as a right. But this made no difference, because since there was no reciprocity, the MDCs saw their schemes as unilateral concessions rather than the fulfillment of any obligation. Every scheme was designed to see that little trade expansion would result, especially in sensitive areas where domestic industry or employment might suffer, even temporarily. There was discrimination against successful countries or dependencies, especially Hong Kong and Taiwan. Many products were excluded, notably textiles and shoes (or where textiles were not excluded, they were subject to the overriding quantity ceilings of the LTA or MFA). Those not excluded were subject to some quantity limitation beyond which the MFN rather than the GSP rate would apply (traders would often not know when making a contract which rate would apply); and GATT-type safeguard clauses were included in every scheme. No full description can be given here.[23] Two further points, however, need to be mentioned. The EEC scheme was tailored to minimize the erosion of the preferences already granted to some sixty African and Mediterranean countries; it did this largely by excluding products that were of particular interest to the African associates, but also by granting smaller preferences. The United States scheme was designed for use partly as a lever to promote other foreign policy ends. Countries that asked for preferences could be excluded on various grounds (for example, membership in OPEC); the administration, usually more "liberal" than Congress, has generally tried to use this leverage in a restrained manner.[24] The only lever of particular interest in the present context is that countries can be excluded for giving "reverse preferences." The United States has always tried to prevent the emergence of trading blocs comprising parts of the North and the South. Against GSPs from the beginning, the United States apparently gave way partly because it saw them as an affirmation of a worldwide system against the EEC's fostering of European-Mediterranean-African exclusiveness.[25]

GSPs have not served this United States objective very well. The reason is that Lomé and Mediterranean preferences are more favorable than GSPs. Since, as we have seen, the United States provision against reverse preferences was responsible for the EEC not insisting on any reciprocity, this provision was partly responsible for the clear superiority, for the EEC associates, of the Lomé agreement over GSPs. However, the United States did at least succeed in its objective of preventing discrimination by African and Mediterranean countries against itself and Latin American countries being built into the agreements.

The value of the GSPs was eroded by the enlargement of the EEC. Not only were the preferences given by the United Kingdom, Denmark, and Ireland reduced when these countries came to be governed by the EEC scheme, but so also was the value of existing preferences in all sixteen Community-plus-EFTA countries as this free-trading community was widened. For instance, before the enlargement of the Community, GSP countries would have preference over the United Kingdom in Germany or Switzerland; after the enlargement the United Kingdom and Switzerland would have preference over GSP beneficiaries. UNCTAD estimates suggest that only 42–50 percent of the previous non-preferred EEC imports remained so.[26]

There are now, by and large, five preference levels in Western Europe. These are:

1. EEC/EFTA countries
2. Lomé countries
3. Mediterranean Agreement countries
4. GSP countries (other than those also in categories 2 and 3)[27]
5. The rest, consisting of the United States, Canada, Japan, Australia, New Zealand, South Africa, the USSR, and Eastern Europe.

Baldwin and Murray have estimated the effects of GSPs.[28] They put trade expansion at $500 million (using 1971 trade flows and prices) plus a small amount of aid.[29] This was about 4 percent of beneficiaries' trade subject to MFN duties and about 1.5 percent of their total trade. Even this figure, which might without hyperbole be called peanuts, was in the author's view probably exaggerated for two reasons. First, it was assumed that all trade that could benefit would do so; but the complex provisions, especially on rules of origin, have resulted in many LDCs failing to claim GSP treatment. Second, those quota restrictions and voluntary export restraints that were unconnected with GSP schemes, but fell on GSP products, were assumed away.[30]

The Tokyo Round of MFN tariff reductions will have still further eroded GSPs. Any remaining gain must be very small indeed. Taking a broader viewpoint, which admits the possibility that the MDCs might have done a little more in other directions if they had not been able to pride themselves on meeting, in however shadowy and circumscribed a way, the LDCs' urgent demand for GSPs, it is all too likely that UNCTAD's main demand in the 1960s did the LDCs no good at all. Such a view is supported by the association of GSPs with ceilings or quotas, which may have turned politicians' and administrators' minds in the direction of undermining MFN tariff concessions in the same manner.[31] Certainly it would have taken very little aid to equal the welfare effect of a $500 million increase in exports.

It finally has to be noted that GSP benefits go predominantly to the better-off LDCs. Thus, on Murray's estimates, five countries—Taiwan, Mexico, Yugoslavia, South Korea, and Brazil—accounted for two thirds of the industrial trade that benefited from GSPs.[32] Any increased official development assistance would have gone to poorer countries.

The early 1970s saw a new era marked by the breakdown of the monetary system and the emergence of high inflation in the MDCs, by OPEC and the oil price increases, and by heightened confrontation between the industrialized Western countries and the Group of Seventy-seven, with the latter's calls for a New International Economic Order. We have described the evolution of the world trading system, if system it can be called, up to this point.

The play had changed enormously since the early post-World War II years when the United States was a giant and other countries could be regarded as atomistic actors. But they were also sovereign states and, even without cohesion or organization among them, there was no way that the United States could impose a world trading system in the form of an ITO that it would itself accept. In the early 1970s, the cast of MDCs looked very different. There were three prima donnas, the United States, Japan, and the EEC, which fairly effectively coordinated its own position in the GATT and in UNCTAD. The LDCs had about trebled in number, greatly gained in power and confidence, and were organized in the Group of Seventy-seven. Trade negotiations had become far more oligopolistic, and in this sense there was increased interdependence. Industrial protection had been greatly reduced among MDCs—partly from the creation of the EEC and the EFTA, but also, mainly, under OEEC auspices, from the near elimination of quotas, and under GATT auspices from large MFN reductions in tariffs.[33]

The GATT was also beneficial for LDCs. Although the Kennedy Round did not remove effective discrimination in tariff levels against LDCs, it certainly helped LDC manufactured exports, which rose dramatically fast from 1963 to 1973 (21 percent per annum in dollar value). More than a third of this increase was in textiles and clothing—despite the LTA and MFA.[34] GATT's failure to prevent the growth of NTBs was a weakness that did not appear to be a serious impediment to the growth of LDC manufactured exports until the mid-1970s.

The extraordinary increase in manufactured exports, especially of textiles and clothing, and shoes, is the main reason for believing that access to MDC markets was far more important than the effective tariffs that remained after the Kennedy Round (and more important than GSPs). Thus, effective tariffs in the EEC and the United States, for clothing and apparel, and fabrics and clothing, have been estimated as follows:

Sources[35]	EEC	United States
U.S. International Trade Commission "clothing and apparel"	13.1	42.3
A. J. Yeats "fabrics and clothing"	29.1	40.4

Yet United States imports of clothing from LDCs rose in dollar value at 30 percent per annum from 1967 to 1976. Total imports did not rise that fast, but LDCs doubled their share in imports from about 40 percent to 80 percent.[36] The dollar value of clothing imports from LDCs into the EEC and EFTA rose by 24.5 percent per annum from 1963 to 1973.[37]

This does not show that there was not a lot more to go for in reducing tariffs. Even if quantities would not have increased much faster (there could have been a supply problem), prices would have improved. But what it does show is that efficiency wages in the most successful exporting countries of the Far East were low enough for it to be possible to export very profitably in the face of quite high effective protection, and to drive out other exporters. Preferences were neither operative (United States GSPs were initiated only in 1976), nor apparently needed.

In agricultural products, the MDCs were determined to maintain barriers, and GATT was ineffective. Few doubt that LDCs as a whole would benefit from reduced agricultural protection, especially in Europe and Japan, even though their own policies have contributed to the fact that their trade balance in agricultural products has worsened. World prices would rise, and the terms of trade for LDCs would improve. At the same time, the large cereal importers, which include some of the poorest LDCs, would suffer. A selective reduction in protection (excluding cereals) might be best for them.

It is debatable how much better GATT would have served the LDCs if they had played a more active role, which would have involved their accepting some degree of reciprocity. This is still an open question (see chapter 18). Instead, the LDCs put their faith in UNCTAD. One of the consequences of UNCTAD was an extraordinary proliferation of preferences. We have shown that the value of GSPs to LDCs has been very small; and therefore that the enormous negotiation and administrative effort involved could almost certainly have been better used in other ways for the benefit of LDCs.

This proliferation was not due wholly to UNCTAD. The French have always favored a continuation of the mutually preferential arrangements they made with their African colonies. They succeeded, when the EEC was formed, in transferring some of the cost of their African aid-and-trade system to their new European colleagues. The Yaoundé agreement resulted. And when the United Kingdom joined the Common Market, imperial preference was finished, and Yaoundé became Lomé. The French idea of a special European-African relationship prevailed. However, largely as a result of United States influence, the African countries gained, in principle, a system of nonreciprocal preferences.[38] It appears that most African countries have felt unable to reject the bait of the European relationship in favor of a more nondiscriminatory worldwide trading system. Indeed, as we have seen, the EEC tailored their GSP system to preserving special preferences for EEC associates, with no protest from the latter.

Finally, the LDCs themselves remained highly protectionist, although a few among them had evolved a trading system that amounted to free-trade conditions for exporters, and a few others had taken some steps to liberalize imports. Many preferential systems existed among them, but, except for the CACM, these affected only a very small proportion of trade. By the early 1970s, so far as North-South and South-South trade was concerned, there was almost nothing left of the idea of a worldwide MFN trading system. Moreover the idea was also threatened in the area of trade in manufactures between MDCs.

Chapter 15

The Old International Economic Order— The Monetary System, 1944-73

The Bretton Woods Agreement

In 1944, for the first time in history, a monetary system was negotiated for most of the world. Compared with negotiating the International Trade Organization as well as subsequent efforts at monetary reform, it was amazingly easy. During the war, there was a rapport between the United States and the United Kingdom. The chief negotiators, Lord Keynes and H. D. White, succeeded in presenting an agreed scheme (much closer to the United States conception than the British), which was accepted at the Bretton Woods Conference.

There were no serious objections from the other forty-two countries represented. They may have been dazed by the war, by the dominant position of the Allies, and even by the powerful personalities of Keynes and White. But there were probably other important factors. The agreement was much less detailed than the Havana Charter, and the less developed countries were not so frightened by exchange rates as they were by the bogey of free trade. Moreover, all probably expected to gain from the new monetary and banking institutions that were set up—the International Monetary Fund and the International Bank for Reconstruction and Development. Finally, Article XIV gave an apparently indefinite exemption from complying with the requirements of currency convertibility under Article VIII.[1]

The essence of the system was as follows:

1. Gold was the numeraire.
2. Countries would choose a par value in terms of gold, and the actual rate would be maintained within a very small margin of the par value. The United States would comply by dealing in gold. Other countries in fact expressed their par values in terms of dollars (of a fixed gold value) and maintained their rates by dealing in dollars.
3. Currencies were to be made freely convertible for current operations under Article VIII, and there were to be no exchange controls on current transactions. Article XIV gave exemption for a transition period, originally to last five years, but which became indefinite in practice (and was to last the life of Bretton Woods for most LDCs).
4. Par values could be changed by prior agreement with the IMF only if there were an undefined "fundamental disequilibrium."
5. The IMF was supposed to provide support for a currency in temporary disequilibrium. Drawings on the IMF were conditional beyond the "gold tranche" of a country's quota (that is, the quarter of its quota which it paid in gold, or in a currency convertible into gold). In other words, the IMF could exercise some surveillance over a borrowing country's policies.
6. The IBRD was instituted to give long-term loans for postwar reconstruction or development.

For the rest of this chapter we shall divide the discussion into two parts: first, the monetary system in the narrower sense of exchange rates and their adjustment, convertibility, and reserves; and, second, the role of international institutions as lenders.

Exchange Rates, Convertibility, and Reserves, 1944–73

The size of the postwar European disequilibrium had not been anticipated in 1944. Par rates were established, but 1948 saw very large devaluations in Europe and elsewhere. Exchange rates were then stable until France devalued in 1957 and 1958. European currencies remained inconvertible until 1958, apart from the disastrous British attempt at convertibility in 1947. But the dollar shortage was over by 1957, and most European currencies became convertible for nonresidents on current transactions. The full obligations of Article VIII, implying an end to discrimination against the United States, were not, however, generally accepted until 1961.

For almost a decade after 1958, there were no important exchange rate changes among the developed countries,[2] that is, until 1967 when the United Kingdom devalued from $2.80 to $2.40 to the pound. But this stability was achieved only with the aid of massive lending in support of weak currencies, especially the pound and the lira (see below).

A few more LDCs embraced Article VIII. Nevertheless, a two-tier system operated with almost all LDCs maintaining exchange restrictions on current account, which were often in effect discriminatory. In much the same way as under the General Agreement on Tariffs and Trade there was one law for the rich and one for the poor. Under Article XIV countries did have to consult annually on the maintenance of restrictions, and the IMF argued for their removal, but with almost no success. As far as exchange rates were concerned, the IMF put most emphasis on the elimination of multiple rates, or at least on their simplification.[3] As far as the official rate was concerned, the IMF made no objection to any change, even the unconventional trotting peg. Indeed, it encouraged Chile in 1962 to adopt such a system.[4] It even appears to have made no serious objection to the floating rates adopted by Lebanon and Canada.

This system, as it operated during the 1960s, seemed highly favorable to LDCs, and also to the small high-trading European economies. So long as no par value changes were expected, they did not have to concern themselves with the relative values or usefulness of the major currencies they earned, borrowed, and held.[5] If they pegged, as the vast majority did, they were effectively pegged to all major currencies (or gold). But they were not effectively restrained so far as their own payments regimes were concerned.[6] At the same time, the system permitted the more developed countries to liberalize their trade and to avoid any serious recession.

But unfortunately the system had weaknesses that, for political as much as economic reasons, gave it a short life. The three main weaknesses were:

1. The fact that the increases in reserves that countries other than the United States wanted took the form of dollar holdings to a greater extent than they wanted.

This weakness could have been eliminated by the United States increasing the price of gold. But in an inflationary world, quite frequent rises in the price of gold might be needed. In that case, dollars would ultimately cease to be a world currency, and one would end up with a gold standard. In the meantime, the political objections to a system under which one country appeared to determine the level of world reserves would have been as strong as the political objections to the system as it actually developed. The United States, however, was strongly opposed to any rise in the price of gold. Most economists and countries welcomed this opposition, largely because a gold price rise would have benefited South Africa and the USSR, as well as a few large gold holders.

2. A reluctance to change exchange rates, on the part of both deficit and surplus countries.

This reluctance is probably inevitable. Not only does devaluation become a symbol of failure, but governments are reluctant to change the rate in either direction because change always hurts some important section of society. To be forced to devalue is to fail. To revalue without being forced is irresponsible in the eyes of exporters. It should incidentally be noted that much more frequent exchange rate changes would have made the system less attractive for LDCs, and other small countries.

3. The ineffectiveness of controls over capital movements, implying that large speculative flows could take place.

This weakness has to be seen in conjunction with the high liquidity, and disequilibrium exchange rates, arising from the other weaknesses. With more frequent exchange rate changes, including revaluations, which would also have reduced the outflow of dollars from the United States, it is possible that currency speculation could have been accommodated without upsetting the system. It should be noted that one probably cannot have a system of payments on current account free enough not to restrict trade significantly, and at the same time have tight enough control of capital movements to prevent serious speculation when exchange rates get out of line.

Already in 1960, large capital outflows put the dollar on the defensive. A series of devices to protect it against excessive conversions into gold was arranged to prop up the system. They involved discussion and negotiation between the United States and major dollar holders. The result was the creation in 1961 of the Group of Ten and Working Party 3 of the Organization for Economic Cooperation and Development,[7] which was, and is, the main forum in which the balance-of-payments policies of members were debated. This small group became an essential part of the system and was needed for the support of currencies other than the dollar. But this essential element was naturally resented by those IMF executive directors who were not members of the club. However, as long as the IMF's operations, and indeed the viability of the Bretton Woods system itself, might be dependent on the willingness of a minority of members to lend, it is difficult to see that this minority can, or even should, be denied an exceptional influence.

By 1963 many economists had come to believe that the monetary system suffered from serious defects and that governments should alter the basis of reserve creation within it. Early on, the problem was seen mainly as one of a dollar-gold disequilibrium. This led to schemes for "stretching" gold, such as the French "Collective Reserve Unit," which would have limited reserve creation to a small group of countries, independently of the IMF—a

International Systems and Confrontation

scheme certain, one might think, to infuriate LDCs and the smaller OECD members.[8] But many academics, and then the United States and other governments, insisted that the real problem was an actual or potential *global* liquidity shortage. Although this diagnosis was wrong, it led to politically more acceptable schemes for reserve asset creation under IMF auspices.[9]

It was extremely difficult to get a decision even though only a few countries—the Group of Ten—were effectively involved in most of the discussions.[10] France was the most dissident member. More nationalist than other European countries, France was happy neither with the IMF (which was seen as an Anglo-Saxon organization) nor with the United States ability to run deficits as a result of the dollar being a world currency. Apart from embarrassing the United States by converting dollar reserves into gold, General de Gaulle called in 1965 for a return to the gold standard. However, a new reserve asset, called a special drawing right (SDR),[11] was finally approved in 1967, and the agreement ratified in 1969. The French, in opposition almost to the end, finally succumbed. Nine billion dollars of SDRs were issued from 1970 to 1972, but thereafter none until 1979.

Prior to the SDR negotiations, the monetary reforms of the 1960s totally excluded the LDCs (and indeed the smaller OECD countries). As these reforms were intended to prop up the Bretton Woods system, which LDCs favored, this hurt their pride, not their pockets. Indeed, it could be argued that it was to the advantage of small countries to keep quiet; they were interested in a few major currencies being convertible, and maintaining fixed rates; and in the prosperity of the leading countries that issued these currencies, and in their maintaining open trading positions. Since this was exactly what the leading countries were trying to achieve, why complain at not having a seat at the table? Since agreement is normally easier in a small group, they might even have argued that the Group of Ten was too big.

The idea that fiduciary reserve assets should be created altered the picture, especially when it came to be believed that the new assets should substitute for reserves in general, and not just for gold. That a new asset should be created and credited in some manner to LDCs was an idea that preceded other post-Bretton Woods discussions of monetary reform. It is normally attributed to Maxwell Stamp,[12] although John Williamson traces it to Keynes and the original British Bretton Woods proposals.[13] The Stamp plan was that a prospective shortage of world liquidity, and of aid flows,[14] should be simultaneously solved by the IMF creating "fund certificates," which would become reserve assets by agreement of major central banks to accept them, and which would be first channeled to LDCs via the IBRD. It was assumed that a high proportion would be spent by LDCs, and that the certificates would settle in MDC central banks.

This seemed to many development economists to be a good idea.[15] Opponents said that one should not muddle up the problem of aid with that of increasing international liquidity. Supporters thought that one could kill two birds with one stone. The species, comprising the Stamp plan and any of its subsequent variations, came to be known as "the link"—that is, a link between aid and asset creation.[16]

Given that the receipt of a fiduciary asset is a help (in the general sense of "benefit"), it is an illusion to suppose that aid and the distribution of fiduciary assets can be kept apart. The object of the creation of such assets is to prevent either a general deflationary influence or competitive devaluations, which would occur as a result of countries in the aggregate trying to acquire more reserves than were available. This might suggest that new assets should go to those countries that felt they wanted them and therefore would not spend them. This has indeed been suggested as a "neutral" principle.[17] But it is neutral neither in an economic sense nor a moral sense. Suppose all countries are happy with the level of their reserves, except the United Kingdom, which is about to try to earn more reserves by deflation or devaluation. If the United Kingdom alone received some SDRs, a change would have been inhibited, and so economic neutrality cannot be claimed. On the moral plane, why should not the United Kingdom have had to earn the increased reserves it wanted from another country or set of countries that instead received the SDRs? The truth is that if an international agency is empow-

311

ered to issue fiduciary assets, an inescapable moral problem arises as to how the benefits should be distributed among the members.

If this argument is accepted, even the meaning of "the link" is called in question, for there is no form of new asset distribution which is not "aid" to some country. For practical purposes, one has to take the link as meaning some principle of assets distribution more favorable to LDCs than that actually adopted (that is, distribution in proportion to IMF quotas). The link received support from the United Nations Conference on Trade and Development, but the LDCs achieved no more than their right to a quota-based share. Most MDCs were firmly against the link at the time of the SDR negotiations. Moreover, the LDCs had not formulated an agreed position as to what form the link should take. They pressed for the link more strongly in the negotiations on monetary reform after the breakdown of Bretton Woods (see chapter 17).

SDRs came too late to make much difference to the monetary system. In the early 1970s, the United States overall deficit greatly increased as a result of deficit financing of the Vietnam War.[18] It is arguable whether other countries wanted the increased reserves that resulted. They certainly did not want them in the form in which they came. They were locked into a dollar, not a real gold exchange, system, for they had more dollars than they wanted but could not convert to gold without destroying the system. Yet they did not want the reality of a dollar system, which seemed too one-sided and which seemed to imply too much political power and economic freedom for the United States. It is arguable, though, how far the country that provides a world currency can really determine its own balance of payments; and whether it gains significantly from running the system—certainly, since the 1950s, other countries have tried to opt out of the dubious advantages of providing an international currency. The United States believed it could not devalue (except against gold), and other countries were unwilling to revalue enough to relieve the United States deficit. The pretense of a gold exchange system was ended in August 1971 by the United States "closing the gold window."

If gold convertibility is regarded as the keystone of the Bretton Woods system, it had collapsed. The end of the system of adjustable-peg exchange rates soon followed. The new "Smithsonian" set of par values arranged in December 1971 did not last long. During 1972 and 1973, every major currency was floated—just in time for the Yom Kippur War and the oil price rises. The immediate cause of collapse was the huge volume of currency speculation. The speculation can in turn be blamed on a failure to adjust exchange rates, and discordant monetary policies. We cannot enter into a debate as to whether the adjustable peg can ever again be made to work. It surely cannot in a world of high and differing rates of inflation. Perhaps, however, what is most important for LDCs and others is that the mutual convertibility of the major currencies was retained, and their convertibility into other financial assets, and commodities, was hardly impaired.

The end of the system of pegged rates had been preceded by the formation in July 1972 of the Committee of Twenty (one member for each of the constituencies represented by an executive director of the IMF). Although the immediate cause of the formation of the Committee of Twenty was probably United States dissatisfaction with the Group of Ten in which it increasingly found itself isolated, it also came to be recognized that the Group of Ten could not alone create a new system within the framework of the IMF, if only because the LDCs had enough votes to block the amendments of the IMF articles that would be required.[19]

The International Monetary Fund As Lender, 1947–73

Technically, when using its ordinary facilities, countries do not borrow from the Fund; they pay "charges," not interest. But it is not misleading to speak of lending, borrowing, and repaying, just as if the IMF were a bank.

The ordinary facilities of the Fund[20] can be briefly described as follows. A country paid up its quota, 25 percent in gold and 75 percent in its own currency. If it "borrowed" its own "gold tranche" of 25 percent, the Fund would hold its currency as to 100 percent of quota. This borrowing was effectively unconditional. The country could further acquire other currencies—against surrender of its own currency up to 100 percent of its quota (that is, to the point where the Fund's holding of its currency was 200 percent of quota). This potential credit was divided into four tranches. The credit was conditional, and the severity of the conditions that the Fund imposed increased from tranche to tranche. Borrowing in excess of 100 percent of quota was possible and at first quite frequent for countries with very small quotas—but it required a formal waiver of the rules. Interest rates ("charges") were low—far below commercial rates.

The original objective of IMF lending was quite clear. It was to assist a country to survive a temporary overall balance-of-payments deficit—that is, a deficit that involved no "fundamental disequilibrium"—without devaluing or introducing import restrictions; alternatively, if it were agreed that a devaluation was called for, Fund lending could tide over the period required for the devaluation to be effective. There was no question of such lending being in aid of development, except to the extent that the easing of short-term difficulties must have long-run beneficial effects. IMF loans can therefore best be thought of as cheap but conditional reserve supplements—or as an overdraft facility.

Standby arrangements were introduced in 1952 in order to avoid tranche-by-tranche negotiation. Under a standby, the member is assured that it can draw up to the agreed amount provided that certain quantified performance criteria, which are part of the standby agreement, are met. Most credit tranche drawings have subsequently been under standby arrangements.

In the first decade, up to 1957, the Fund's facilities were hardly used by LDCs,[21] Brazil being the only credit tranche borrower. Then in 1957 Argentina, Brazil, and Chile all borrowed significant amounts. It was these borrowings that first led to the sometimes hysterical criticism of the IMF's conditions. India joined the large borrowers with a $200 million drawing in 1957. In that year, total LDC drawings were just under $400 million. Total (gross) use of the Fund thereafter, until 1973, fluctuated greatly (depending on whether the bigger countries borrowed or not), from about $100 million to about $800 million. However, the number of countries using the Fund greatly increased in the 1960s (partly because the number of countries and IMF members increased). Thus, in 1959, eleven LDCs used the Fund, of which eight were Latin American or Caribbean; in 1969, twenty-eight used it, twelve Latin American or Caribbean, ten African, and six Asian.

The Fund's facilities were small, relative to the size of the balance-of-payments emergencies. For example, India incurred a severe balance-of-payments deficit during the Second Five Year Plan from 1956 to 1958. In 1957 she borrowed $200 million from the IMF (half her quota). But aid increased from about $90 million per annum in 1955–56 to about $660 million per annum in 1958–59, and this increase was in response to India's balance-of-payments problem. But although not true of the Indian case cited,[22] the receipt of other loans has often depended, especially in Latin America, on the Fund's appraisal of the situation and the willingness of the country to take the Fund's advice; this could be true of both bilateral aid agencies and commercial lenders. Although aid is supposed to be for development, and to consist of long-term loans or grants, a timely increase in its availability can make an important difference in a crisis. Moreover, some countries have contrived an inflow of private direct investment when in critical balance-of-payments trouble; and private direct investors are unlikely to be forthcoming if the country is at loggerheads with the IMF.

A balance-of-payments crisis is almost synonymous with a country being forced to rely on new foreign credits. The other possibilities are not to service past credits, or to force traders to default on payments for imports, or to cut imports so much as to create internal disruption of a magnitude that the government dare not contemplate. In a crisis, the foreign creditor is the lesser evil. How much of an evil he is seen to be depends on the severity of the loan conditions imposed. It is not surprising that the conditions of a creditor, as essential as the IMF has been to many countries, should come in for much criticism.

The most vociferous criticism came from Latin America; but

other LDCs, and developed countries such as the United Kingdom and France, have also complained, and reform of the IMF has become part of the New International Economic Order platform. The Fund is held to have been addicted to shock treatment and excessive enthusiasm for the price mechanism, to have caused unnecessary loss of output, and to have been insensitive to the political repercussions of its medicine. The structuralist-monetarist debate discussed in chapter 5 was closely associated with IMF prescriptions in Latin America. But a proper audit of IMF conditions is not possible. No full comparative account of them, how they vary from case to case, how they have evolved, has been made. The exact role of the IMF will never be known because the degree of agreement and disagreement between it and the government is secret at the time and is by now in many cases probably forgotten. Comparative studies of the associated changes in policy and their alternatives (for some change in policy was clearly essential in most cases) have begun to appear only recently. This past neglect is an aspect of the more general absence of studies of actual and desirable year-to-year macroeconomic management in LDCs, which is the other side of the coin of excessive emphasis on five-year plans and long-run structural change.

Nevertheless, the role of IMF lending in an optimum world must be considered—and we shall risk some views on this subject in chapter 18. First, it is necessary to clear the ground by distinguishing some different situations that give rise to balance-of-payments problems.

One must distinguish between the short and the long run. There is no such thing as a long-run balance-of-payments problem. Foreign exchange is always scarce, and countries have to develop within the limits of the likely long-run supply that comes from exports, from grants, and from long-term loans.[23] The official price of foreign exchange in a country—that is, the official exchange rate—often understates its scarcity. This implies an excess demand for foreign currency, but that is not the same thing as a balance-of-payments problem. It just means that the country has opted to control the use of foreign currency.[24] Most LDCs have operated in this way for many years. If the controls are very effective, such a country cannot have a balance-of-payments crisis in the sense that reserves can uncontrollably vanish.

Despite the above, it is clearly true, in some sense, that many LDCs are chronically short of foreign exchange. One must distinguish two varieties of this ailment. First, a country may be so poor that it cannot produce enough even to feed its people adequately, let alone have enough of a surplus to develop. There is a sense in which it needs more foreign exchange, to buy food or some capital goods. But this is not a balance-of-payments problem. There may be no shortage of foreign exchange, either in the sense that there is an excess demand for it or in a sense that implies the country should try to export more or even borrow more. Such a country needs gifts. Its problem has nothing to do with the world's monetary system. Unless the IMF is to be changed into a development institute, it should not be concerned.

Second, some LDCs, as often relatively rich ones as the very poor, have got themselves into a position we shall describe as "import starvation." By this we mean that such a country cannot pay for enough imports to keep its productive capacity going, and so maintain industrial employment, and may even be unable to pay for enough food imports. If imports were further restricted, there would be a severe internal crisis. The demand for imports is thus highly inflexible because there are so few of them. Such a country may always be hovering on the point of crisis. The dangers are magnified if it has low reserves and has already borrowed as much as it can (further borrowing will in any case exacerbate the long-run problem). It is clear that such a country must export more. As a result of policies to reduce imports by excessive import substitution, and in some cases as a result of inflation, the exchange rate is too unfavorable for exports; also, domestically produced inputs into exports are above the world prices paid by competitors. Traditional exports lose ground (and their share of world markets) as there is insufficient incentive to produce and invest. New exports, especially of manufactures, are unprofitable.

This second stereotype applies now, as it has for years, to a good many developing countries. This is by now widely recognized in these countries. A major change of policies is called for. This will include devaluation, and import liberalization—familiar elements of a typical IMF package. It may also include tariff reform and some subsidization of exports, or the introduction of other devices to offset the high cost of domestically produced inputs.[25] It is to be noticed that a devaluation in such circumstances is not always made to improve the balance of payments. The most obvious example is India's devaluation of 1966. There was no payments crisis. The devaluation was partly in order to simplify the complex tax-subsidy system, and partly to improve export earnings so that the chronic import suppression could be relieved. The major foreign role was on this occasion played by the IBRD, not the IMF.

In other cases, indeed usually, resort to the IMF (or other potential creditors) occurs when there is a crisis. If imports are less effectively controlled than in India, or too many licenses have been issued as a result of foreign exchange availability being miscalculated, then reserves may be slipping away, and there is a more or less conventional payments crisis. But the crisis may also take the form that the government realizes that any further cut in imports would be intolerable. If it is already heavily indebted (and many governments have tried to fend off increasing import starvation by borrowing), it will then appeal for debt rescheduling or further loans.

But the fact that a crisis was the reason for recourse to the IMF, or other lenders, does not alter the fact that what is needed in such circumstances is a major reform of the trading regime, permitting a large increase in imports. Any short-term lending that is not accompanied by the appropriate long-term measures would only force further import suppression (or possibly a unilateral debt repudiation).

When the old trading system has been in force for years, prices and incentives are likely to have become badly out of line, and many vested interests have been created. The danger of a political backlash overthrowing the reform or even the regime may be great. In such circumstances, there is clearly a strong argument for gradualism, especially under a political system that permits effective protest. Consequently, there is also a strong argument for longer term support than the IMF normally gave in the past.

If a country is suffering from chronic inflation, as was the case with many Latin American countries, then there are two major problems to solve. It may be possible to tackle the problem of import starvation without curing the inflation, or trying to cure it only slowly, but only if a floating rate or a trotting-peg system is introduced. This was not sufficiently realized until gradualist attempts to solve both problems were made with some success by Brazil in the mid-1960s.[26] If, unlike in Brazil, the new exchange rate, after a devaluation, is supposed to stick, then clearly the inflation has to be eliminated. The deflationary policies that were so unpopular were designed to stabilize prices. They are not needed to cure the problem of import starvation.

A desirable comprehensive reform may involve elements that are excluded from the IMF's sphere of interest. It is notable that the IMF did not in the 1950s and 1960s apparently attempt comprehensive solutions to the problems caused by excessive industrial protection, which can arise as much from tariffs as from quota restrictions. Finally, it has to be noted that such reforms will not stick unless the LDC government is fully convinced and determined, and is not succeeded by another government that thinks differently. If the lender fears this is not the case, then there is a serious dilemma—whether to let the crisis develop or to lend and expect a more serious crisis later.

It was not envisaged by its founders that the crises the IMF would be called upon to resolve might be the result of a long period of policy-induced bias against exporting and of excessive borrowing to support import substitution; nor did they envisage situations of chronic inflation. They envisaged temporary disequilibria that would sort themselves out without any fundamental change of policy, that is, the typical eventuality for which countries held reserves. Thus, Fund drawings were to be a supplement to reserves, albeit conditional.[27]

Short-term disequilibria may arise for a variety of reasons. First, mistakes may be made in the management of demand. Second, a country is liable to experience various kinds of unforeseen shocks. These may be internal: harvest failure or a major, but temporary, dislocation of industrial production is an obvious example. On the external side, there may be a recession in a major trading partner or a large change in the terms of trade. These are reversible situations, which either require a rather routine adjustment of taxes, money supply, or government expenditure, or which may require no action at all. Of course, there is no clear line between short and long term. For instance, a movement in the terms of trade may be expected to be temporary but turn out to be long lasting. The country concerned then has to adjust to the deterioration in its situation, unless it can get more long-term aid. A shock may occasionally be seen to be almost certainly irreversible—the obvious example being the oil price rises of the 1970s. In either case, if the Fund continues support for more than a limited adjustment period, it is clearly getting into the aid business. Whether this is undesirable, or unavoidable even if undesirable, is a problem we can approach only after the events of the 1970s have been surveyed.

Let us try to summarize this preliminary look at official IMF lending to LDCs. No problems really arise when the Fund is giving balance-of-payments support in the face of short-term fluctuations or when the cause of the trouble is recognized to be excess demand.

But the Fund was asked to lend in situations where severe and long-standing disequilibria was evident, at least to itself, and usually to the LDC as well. These disequilibria lay in the real structure of the incentive system. With effective exchange and trade controls, the crisis, when it came, often took the form of "import starvation" or a threat to default on debt service.

Much experience has shown that it is very difficult to emerge from such a situation, especially where it is compounded by rapid inflation. The needed change of direction is certain to be painful both from a political and economic viewpoint. Moreover, there can be legitimate and quite wide differences of opinion as to appropriate measures and their timing, even when the diagnosis is agreed on, which is also not always the case. Foreign or international conditional loans in such circumstances nearly always result in xenophobic outbursts (which are sometimes deliberately contrived). It is almost inevitable that the conditions will be felt to be too harsh.

But external finance can greatly ease the adjustment. It can permit imports to be expanded before there is a response in export earnings. Such an expansion helps to limit inflation. Alternatively, it limits the depth of, or avoids the need for, a recession to reduce imports and control inflation. Furthermore, in severe cases of import starvation, an increase in imports may be necessary for export expansion.

The most serious problems arise when there is no meeting of minds as to what policy changes can and should be made. One thing is certain. Foreign loan finance has to be limited by the prospects for servicing the debt. In many cases this implies that the borrower must be required to take effective measures to increase export earnings. In principle, of course, from a debt servicing point of view, it is as good to save as to earn foreign exchange. But, as we have seen, attempts to save foreign exchange by industrial import substitution have gone too far in most LDCs; the main exceptions are thus where import substitution in food production is likely to be socially profitable.

Contrary to what was widely preached in the 1950s and early 1960s, I doubt if there has been a case in which a sustained improvement in the incentive to export has not resulted in an important rise in export earnings. In many instances, the response has been dramatic, indeed almost unbelievable.

Chapter 16

Distributive Justice and the New International Economic Order

The New International Economic Order makes many claims for transfers of resources from more developed countries to less developed countries, and for arrangements that are intended to increase the benefits LDCs derive from trading and other contacts with MDCs.[1] These claims are made in the name of justice; and it is argued that commodity prices should be just prices. Understanding the meaning of justice in an international and worldwide context[2] is thus a necessary step to understanding the New International Economic Order.

Voluntary Transfers

Commutative justice must be distinguished from distributive justice. The former is concerned with the equal application to persons of the rules of a society: we need not concern ourselves with any elaboration or analysis of the concept. Distributive justice is more contentious. Some consider that the problem is to define what is a fair distribution of income or assets, or both; and that what is fair is independent of how the distribution comes about. All that counts is the upshot of economic transactions, the "end-state." Two chief variants are utilitarianism and Rawlsianism.[3] The former says that a just distribution is one that maximizes utility (this need not be equality in any definable sense, even apart from the vexed question of the need for incentives). The latter defines a just distribution as that which maximizes the welfare of the least advantaged group in a community. But there is another school of thought, which denies that distributive justice can be defined in terms of end-states, independently of the deserts and rights that are satisfied. Robert Nozick presents a strong version of this school, claiming that any distribution is just if it comes about as a result of transactions that people are entitled to make.[4] He would deny that a state has any right to infringe individuals' natural rights (for example, property rights) for the purpose of income or asset redistribution. The only just redistributions would be those that rectified past transactions that people had not been entitled to make.[5]

Political philosophers seem to be silent about the rights and obligations of states to persons who are not members. Under Social Contract theories, the government and the members of a state remain in a "state of nature" with noncitizens.[6] Nozick argues that no state has a right to tax some citizens to benefit others; a fortiori it cannot have a right to redistribute between those in a state of nature who are not members of one community or body politic. Furthermore, the state has no right to intervene in private international transactions made under the laws of nature, unless they transgress or threaten the natural rights of some of its own citizens. If it does so in good faith, has it an obligation to compensate the noncitizens whose natural rights are infringed?

Vijay Joshi has argued "Yes," in the following terms:

> The US Government ... has enacted immigration laws which infringe the natural rights of Indians to live in the US and the natural rights of US employers and Indian workers to enter into

323

International Systems and Confrontation

voluntary contracts.... It would follow from Nozickian principles that US employers and Indian workers must be paid compensation adequate enough to induce them not to undertake these contracts. Of course, many questions remain. For example, who should be taxed? How should compensation be divided between US employers and Indian workers? The principle, however, is clear enough and provides an argument for increased foreign aid based on an entitlement theory of justice.[7]

This is the thin edge of a huge wedge. All governments, MDC and LDC alike, control immigration, and some control emigration. All, and especially LDCs, control and thwart private international transactions of every kind, and LDC governments are particularly insistent on their right to do so. There is no logical reason for singling out (potential) immigration from LDCs to MDCs. It is appealing only because the potential immigrants are poor, but then that is not an appeal based on entitlement. Since there could be no question of compensating individuals (could all individuals in the world claim that their right to become United States citizens was thwarted and demand compensation?), and since aid is a government-to-government relationship, it is not clear that a theory based on the abrogation of individual rights can provide an argument for aid, as Joshi claims.[8]

The USSR asserts that only ex-colonial powers have an obligation to aid, regarding this as compensation for past evils. This could perhaps be regarded as an extension to the international sphere of Nozick's argument for rectification. Here again we have the difficulty that if any compensation is due, it is due to individuals. The closer analogy may be with reparations, which aggressive countries that lose wars are forced to pay, since reparations have been mainly government-to-government transactions and can be justified as such to the extent that the aggressor is guilty of offending against commutative justice governing the behavior of nations. But since the ex-colonies have no power to exact reparations, the analogy has no value unless sufficient people in the ex-colonial powers believe their ancestors were guilty and that they should pay for it.

The trouble with all arguments for international transfers that are neither forced nor self-interested is that they are futile unless they appeal to the moral sense of the potential donors. There is no world distributor. Thus, it seems to me that any acceptable idea of distributive justice requires at least a moral community, in which individuals accept some mutual obligations, for it would be futile to say that the distribution of wealth between a set of wholly isolated Crusoes, who happen to have landed on islands of different fertility, was unjust. Even if they formed a mere system[9] by becoming aware of one another and having some occasional contact, but still not entering into obligations or having any way of settling disputes, etc., it would still be close to futile to talk of distributive justice. If, in such circumstances, one Crusoe made demands in the name of justice, he would be presuming, perhaps hoping to create, a community that did not exist but that, if it did exist, would perhaps recognize an obligation to aid him. We must therefore ask what kinds of community exist in the world—and perhaps what sort is embryonic if not born.

A community of states exists, in that many claims to commutative interstate justice are both made and recognized. Most discussions of interstate justice have been concerned with sovereignty, with the right to conduct wars claimed to be just, with equality of treatment in international organizations, and under international law, and so on. Compensation for transactions that transgress the rules may be provided for in international agreements. Such transfers depend on a system of rules, and are part of what Professor R. W. Tucker refers to as "the old equality."[10]

But LDC claims to transfers of resources, and to special treatment in trade, are made in the name of *distributive* justice. Nevertheless, there seems to be no doubt that the political leaders of LDCs are primarily demanding justice as between states. Many still lack confidence that their sovereignty is secure and believe that they are excessively dependent. So they are demanding greater equality of liberties and equality of respect. They want to be more powerful and better able to exercise the right to defend themselves. Most of this can come only with an increase in wealth. So greater material equality is closely bound up with the aspiration to be able to play a more significant role in the world political order. This is also no doubt a large part of the reason why so much stress is put on industrialization and why there is a lingering belief that more people is no bad thing.

Equality of states, not people, is what the New International Economic Order is about. This is implied by the tremendous stress on sovereignty in the various declarations of the New International Economic Order. It is also the reason why LDCs enthusiastically accepted the declaration of the New International Economic Order but were lukewarm or cold toward the basic needs strategy of the World Employment Conference, which was telling them to look after their poor better (see chapter 11). Since then, many LDC spokesmen have said that international conferences should make proposals only about interstate relations. The substance of the New International Economic Order (see chapter 17) also shows that it was formed with little concern for personal poverty.

But none of the reasons produced by political philosophers as to why some should have their liberties restricted in order to benefit others apply to states. With utilitarianism, it is the utility of individuals that is the final arbiter. Utility cannot be enjoyed by states. For nonutilitarians, redistribution is justified by giving the status of a right to adequate access to the means of securing health, etc. Again, it is human beings who are deemed to have such rights. Commutative justice is a different matter. It constitutes an attempt to create an ordered society of states in which differences can be settled agreeably. Thus, states (and other collectives) admit to moral rights and duties by seeking to justify their actions, both in terms of international law and international justice.

The value of an individual's political and legal rights increases with his wealth. There is an apparent analogy in this respect between individuals and states. Formal equality in terms of international law is already granted to states, but substantive equality in the exercise of these rights demands material equality. Substantive equality would require that all states had nuclear weapons, and so were equally capable of fighting a just war. But redistribution between states on such grounds is not accepted as part of international morality, which implies, of course, that the desirability of substantive equality of states in the world order is not admitted either. Not only is it not admitted; the very idea of substantive equality of states is in conflict with that of nation-states and the idea of self-determination. The analogy breaks down. There is normally no compelling reason why any one person should not be as wealthy as any other. But divergence of numbers is a compelling reason why the Welsh cannot be equal to the Russians.

A strong claim that a community of states exists, among which distributive justice might be said to apply, has been made by Professor Ali Mazrui. To quote:

> The Nuremberg trials helped to redefine aspects of morality and give coherence to the idea of "crimes against humanity." The formation of the United Nations signified that new global institutions were needed. The anti-colonial movements in Asia and Africa heralded new triumphs for the principle of self-determination. And racism based on color all over the world found itself increasingly on the defensive. We were witnessing the birth pangs of a new international moral order.
>
> It is partly on the basis of that moral order that we now hear demands for a new international economic order. Indeed the latter hardly makes sense without a redefinition of international morality itself. The demand for a new international order is a culmination of a quest for appropriate norms to govern relations among collectivities—a quest that goes back to the Treaty of Augsburg of 1555 and far beyond.[11]

I believe that this passage confuses two different concepts, a universal humanistic morality and interstate morality. The Nuremberg trials were based on the concept of humankind. Since only the defeated suffered for their crimes against humanity, the trials have also to be seen as emanating from great power politics; but nevertheless the morality claimed was humanitarian and universalistic. The issue of racism is similarly based on the idea of equality of rights. But self-determination is about the creation of nation-states (a nation being, ex ante, any community that has claims to be a state, and, ex post, any community whose claims have succeeded). The twentieth-century idea that those particular communities that can be deemed to be nations should be self-governing can certainly be seen as a change in international morality, although this morality is overlaid with the expedien-

327

cies of power politics, which often determine whether a claim to nationhood is recognized. In any case, the stress is on nations, not persons. The political rights of persons may (or may not) be better served in a world of nation-states—and this possibility may have supported the change in international morality; nevertheless, distributive justice has very little to do with the ideal of self-determination.

It is thus difficult to see that those parts of the New International Economic Order that are concerned with distributive justice are based on such developments as those described by Mazrui. If they were, it would not be true (as it is true) that the New International Economic Order "hardly makes sense without a redefinition of international morality itself." But this redistribution would consist of a set of imperatives obliging richer states within a society of states to help poorer states, without questioning their behavior toward their own citizens or toward those of other countries.

I can see no moral theory backing up the development of such obligations. Still less can one say that they are now accepted by the richer states. Developed countries have, with reservations, accepted aid targets, thereby putting themselves in a position in which they can be rightly berated for their failure to realize their stated intentions. But what sort of obligation have they accepted? Certainly not to give regardless of the recipients' behavior. The assumed obligation is only to transfer a certain volume of purchasing power to developing countries in general. This is no different from some rich men accepting that they ought to give so much to charity or to charitable organizations of whose policies they approve. They are far from accepting any such notion as an interstate income tax. A state does not tax its own citizens in order to help their enemies. These transfers are essentially political, although helping the poor can and does enter as another objective. International order comes before international justice or at least has a bigger weight.[12]

Most Western liberals are treading a different path. Tucker refers to the "regnant intellectual elites" and calls the movement "the new political sensibility." There is a continuous stream of books and articles aiming to arouse the conscience of people in the West toward the crushing poverty of hundreds of millions of people in the developing countries. Their appeal is universalistic and in the name of humanity. Many liberals would claim that Western governments have a duty to support basic needs and to reduce inequality in the world.[13] If governments do not fully accept this, it is because they dare not spend much on programs that have little popular appeal. And that they have little popular appeal is an unfortunate fact. Sympathy depends on knowledge, contact, and familiarity. Many intellectuals, but few of the electorate, travel to developing countries. To this extent, the regnant intellectual elite seems to be appealing to a community that hardly exists. Some of the same elite try hard to create a sense of community by stressing "growing interdependence," a phrase that is seldom given a factual content. Some authors have expected that the concept of the welfare state would spread outward to embrace mankind. This may be true of Scandinavia, which is a relatively generous donor despite its minimal political interest in aid; elsewhere, egalitarianism at home, implying high taxation, seems to be as competitive with as complementary to the idea of helping foreigners.

Humanitarian appeals tend to ignore many difficulties. Most particularly, they tend to ignore the fact that states (or, more strictly, the changing governments of states) come between the donor and the recipient, or they assume that donors can impose conditions that will ensure that poverty will be reduced. If the appeal is humanitarian, there must be an assurance that the aid reaches the poor to a reasonable extent. This assurance has been undermined in recent years by exaggerated, even false, statements to the effect that the mass of the poor has gained little, or even lost, as a result of the growth of the developing countries (see chapter 11).

The international organizations tend to fall into the same category as Western liberals. Thus, the International Labor Organization submission to the World Employment Conference is entitled *Employment, Growth and Basic Needs*, with the subtitle *A One World Problem*. The delegates' declaration of principles included ensuring "full employment and an adequate income to every inhabitant of this one world in the shortest possible time." Since this could be read as implicitly going over the heads of nation-states, it contributed to the cool reception that was noted above. Any idea of making aid dependent on human rights gets a worse reception. The World Bank has come to include the concept of "basic needs" in its policy utterances, and Robert MacNamara has been emphatic in his appeals to increase aid and to direct it, and development in general, toward the mass of the poor. He has spoken of "a global compact." Similarly, the Development Assistance Committee of the Organization for Economic Cooperation and Development has endorsed the idea that basic human needs should be a central purpose of development cooperation. These appeals to "one world" and "global compact" are, I think, attempts to create a moral community that transcends national sovereignty.

It is not only political leaders and foreign service spokesmen in developing countries who think differently. Even very Westernized and liberal academics from developing countries are usually nationalists first and egalitarians second. They may be very concerned about inequalities and poverty in their own countries; but, not surprisingly, they may at the same time get irritated when Westerners criticize the leaders of developing countries both as self-serving and as more interested in nationalistic objectives than in the poor. Few, I suspect, would support a compact of increased aid if it went with an effective surveillance of policies to ensure (suppose this were a possibility) that development was widespread and human rights respected.

A serious conflict of values has thus become evident. It has often, in the past, been argued by liberals that one of the defects of aid was that MDC governments tended to impose their values on LDCs, and thus distort their development plans. The implication was that the values of LDCs should be respected. I never thought that this was a very serious argument: the conflict of values was exaggerated, and the fault of donors lay more in such matters as aid tying, which had nothing to do with values. But now that "the development community" is promoting the idea of redistribution, and human rights, there is a serious conflict. Both equality and liberty are Western ideals; very few developing countries have embraced that of equality, and still fewer both ideals. If the DAC countries, or the World Bank, proceed very far in the direction of trying to impose redistributive policies, or refusing aid to countries whose policies do not seem to be directly poverty-regarding, conflict will be exacerbated.

The Exercise of State Monopoly Power

The LDCs make strong claims in the name of sovereignty, stronger than most MDCs, which are more willing to surrender some sovereignty to international tribunals. But all states reserve the right to exercise monopoly power and in general to control international transactions (including immigration). If they do not do so, it is in the belief that they will gain by a world trading system under which they accept limitations on the use of such powers. But some countries may gain by opting out of any system, whether or not they are permitted to be free-riders.

We have argued, in the context of aid, that the idea of a distributive justice that transcends frontiers depends on the fragile existence of a worldwide moral community. This carries over to the exercise of monopoly power. One may feel that a rich country is not justified in the exercise of such power on the grounds that it favors the rich at the expense of the poor, and vice versa for a poor country. The argument from Pareto-optimality has no force in this context. Maximizing the value of world output regardless of distribution can have no appeal, especially as there is no world government to influence the distributory outcome.

The exercise of sovereign economic power might be carried to the point where it was so disruptive of another economy that it threatened world order. I leave it to the reader to decide whether under any circumstances economic action would amount to a case for a just war.

International Systems and Confrontation

SUMMARY AND CONCLUSIONS

Individuals have some rights and deserts that the state should not transgress. Therefore, one cannot fully endorse any purely end-state notion of distributive justice. But the state can with justice limit the exercise of some people's property rights for the benefit of others. This depends on a moral consensus operating within a moral community. To the very limited extent that the world is a moral community, such a consensus among the citizens of one nation can justify aid for the poor of other nations (or the acceptance of special trading or other arrangements favoring the poor of other nations at the expense of its own richer citizens).

Aid justified on the above grounds requires an assurance that it benefits the poor to some sufficient degree. This demands surveillance, which may be little more than nominal if the recipient government pursues policies that cause economic benefits to be widely spread. If this is not the case, aid can be justified only with strong surveillance. Strong surveillance offends against an international order based on national sovereignty. There is then a danger of serious conflict between justice and order.

LDC governments and spokesmen claim transfers and favors on grounds of interstate distributive justice. The question arising is whether rich states, or their rich citizens, have an obligation to increase the economic strength, and hence military strength, of weak states, independently of the poverty of individuals. I have some limited sympathy with LDC leaders in their pursuit of such objectives. But I do not think that any moral consensus exists in MDCs in favor of transfers in pursuit of such nationalistic or collective objectives. If interstate distributive justice were admitted as a valid concept, the question of a conflict between justice and order could come up in another form. It may not be orderly to increase the power of weak states.

The upshot is that I remain in favor of aid. But I think that donors have the right not to extend aid to governments whose policies they believe to be excessively inegalitarian. I also think that they have an obligation to exercise surveillance if they give aid; but in exercising surveillance, they should be cautious, for surveillance may result in conflict, and the end result could be worse than no aid. The great differences of wealth are also relevant. Even if only a small part of aid "trickles down," that may be enough to justify it. Finally, in judging between the different demands of LDCs for transfers and favors, I believe that MDCs have an obligation to consider the extent to which poverty is likely to be relieved.

Chapter 17

The New International Economic Order and the Events of 1973-80

Introduction

The New International Economic Order was ignited by the oil price rises of the autumn and winter of 1973-74. Contributing factors to the explosive mood of the Group of Seventy-seven were the failure of confrontation since 1964 to produce much benefit, and the world boom and inflation of the early 1970s, of which only the disadvantages tended to be appreciated.

The New International Economic Order was not a response to the partial breakdown of the old order, described in chapters 14 and 15. It did not analyze or suggest changes that might be required as a consequence of the severe disequilibria created by the oil price rises; nor was it a response to increasing radicalism or concern for the poor shown by the development establishment.

It was rather that the success of the Organization of Petroleum Exporting Countries (OPEC) in causing a transfer of some $60 billion per annum—several times larger than total aid—created a euphoric determination to do likewise. There was almost no new content to the demands of less developed countries. Virtually everything had been on the agenda since the United Nations Conference on Trade and Development I, and most of it since the 1940s. All that was really new was the increased stridency, together perhaps with the increased use of the General Assembly as a forum for economic demands. There was, however, some change of emphasis, also clearly caused by the OPEC success. This was the stress on LDCs' "inalienable right" to sovereignty over materials and their concern to ensure "just" prices for their exports.

As the later 1970s unfolded, there were only slight further changes of emphasis. The New International Economic Order, acquiring the character of Holy Writ, remained largely unaffected by major events, and did not much influence them either.

The General Content of the New International Economic Order[1]

Some of the principles appealed to by the New International Economic Order are those of commutative justice. Sovereignty, especially over natural resources, is stressed again and again; and greater participation in international decision-making and strengthening of the United Nations is called for. But most of the Program of Action appeals to distributive justice, to aid, to just prices for commodities, and to "preferential and non-reciprocal treatment for developing countries, wherever feasible, in all fields of international economic cooperation, whenever possible." We shall call this the principle of "aid with everything." Special discrimination in favor of the least developed countries, the most seriously affected (MSA) by the oil price rise, land-locked and sea-locked countries, was also called for.[2] Self-reliance, including mutual preferences, was stressed. A notable omission is any reference to migration. The sea—"the common heritage of mankind"—also went unmentioned.

We shall confine ourselves to those calls for action that were contained in or resulted from the Program of Action. Some of these were in the field of ongoing programs, and the demand was for extension and improvement (aid and special preferences). In the field of aid, there was a call for debt relief. In the monetary field, the attachment to a special drawing right system and "the link" was reemphasized. This had been and was being considered by the Committee of Twenty. The main features, which would involve new arrangements, understandings, and institutions, were in the field of commodities and food. More minor matters were calls for codes governing liner shipping, transnational corporations, and the transfer of technology. We first consider these features and then turn to monetary reform, International Monetary Fund reform, and the Tokyo Round of multilateral trade negotiations, subjects that are less intimately related to the New International Economic Order.

The Integrated Program for Commodities

The initial idea was that just ("stable, remunerative, and equitable") prices should be established between primary commodities and the manufactures that LDCs mainly imported.[3] This implied raising and maintaining the prices of those commodities with worsening terms of trade. The sovereign right to form cartels was emphasized, and UNCTAD began working on "indexing" commodity prices to the prices of manufactured exports from more developed countries. Both raising and stabilizing prices was the objective. The Common Fund for buffer stocks was mooted. Gradually it came to be recognized that "indexation" was not merely a nonstarter but would inhibit development in the long run. Improved compensatory financing was a substitute. Thus, by the 1976 Nairobi meeting of UNCTAD, it was stabilization of ten core commodities by buffer stocks, and a Common Fund to support the individual schemes, that was emphasized. However, UNCTAD and many LDCs no doubt hoped and expected that the schemes would somehow help to encourage participating LDCs to restrict output and raise prices. Since attempts to stabilize commodity prices by buffer stocks were already venerable, UNCTAD's mast flew the Common Fund flag, which became a symbol of the success or failure of the Nairobi meeting in 1976.

I was at a meeting in April 1975 of the United Nations Committee for Development Planning, when a high-level UNCTAD team was introduced and sought our endorsement of the integrated program for commodities. I was the only member to protest. We had not studied the scheme, and I could vaguely remember that there were grave, possibly irremovable technical difficulties, which UNCTAD's team did not seem to have thoroughly considered. To endorse a huge investment in a still halfbaked and understudied project, in an area where past failure was the rule, appeared irresponsible. I did succeed in introducing an element of ambiguity and meaninglessness into the committee's expression of approval.[4]

BUFFER STOCKS

Since then, independent academic assessments of the value of the UNCTAD scheme, whether for LDCs or MDCs, have been almost wholly unfavorable. A good survey is that of Karsten Laursen.[5] Certain theoretical considerations, already known in the earlier literature on the subject, had been forgotten or ignored. Among them, the following should have tempered enthusiasm, pending serious study: buffer stocks may destabilize prices if they are not very large; stabilized prices may destabilize producers' incomes; producers' long-run incomes may be reduced. Much depends on the supply and demand elasticities, and on whether the source of instability is supply or demand. Quite different results may obtain for different commodities. Finally, there is no evidence that instability reduces growth, rather the reverse (see chapter 9).

One of the most favorable assessments made on the basis of a set of econometric simulation models of the period 1963-72 is that of J. R. Behrman.[6] He analyzed eight of the UNCTAD core

337

commodities (coffee, cocoa, tea, rubber, jute, sisal, copper, and tin; sugar and cotton were excluded), with the following results:

1. First consider the eight stabilization schemes as an ordinary investment. Much depends on the highly uncertain value of the final commodity stocks which the schemes would have accumulated. Behrman writes, "It appears to be almost certain that the present discounted [at 2 percent and 5 percent real rates] values of buffer stock operations for most of these commodities (but perhaps not for coffee, cocoa and wool and for the sums for the core and for all thirteen commodities) are negative." To sum up a very speculative discussion, it seems fair to say that the schemes can be taken as having zero value as an ordinary investment; and can be judged as an investment in stabilization and transfers alone.
2. Stabilization (within a band of ±15 percent of trend prices) would have significantly reduced fluctuations in producers' incomes in the case of cocoa, rubber, and sisal; there would have been little or no change for the other commodities.
3. Behrman believes that the chief value in commodity buffer stocks is that they would reduce inflation in MDCs by eliminating the "ratchet" effect, by which commodity price rises are supposed to raise other prices, while commodity price falls do not reduce them. If Behrman were right, the MDCs should be enthusiastic supporters. I believe this is a highly speculative effect, and in any case it would have to be assessed in the context of a government's whole approach to macroeconomic and stabilization policies. Since this putative gain accrues mainly to MDCs and does not serve to convince them, it is irrelevant to my assessment except insofar as LDCs would gain by the consequentially reduced inflation (or the same inflation, and higher employment) in MDCs. This, in my opinion, gets too remote and uncertain to consider even as a qualitatively significant consideration for LDCs. LDC users of the commodities might gain a little by price stabilization, but this is also a negligible consideration.
4. There would have been a significant income transfer to producers in the case of coffee, cocoa, and rubber; a negligible difference for tea and sisal; and a transfer from producers for copper and tin. The jute scheme would have made no transactions in its ten-year life. Aggregating, there would have been a transfer to producers equivalent to $700 million per annum, 46 percent of which would have come from the financial capital. Assuming (in conformity with [1], above) that final stocks

could be sold to replenish the capital, the $700 million would have come from consumers, about 90 percent of which would be in MDCs or centrally planned economies. Cline takes a figure of $600 million (at 1976 prices) as the transfer to LDC producers.[7]

5. The capital required would be at least $10 billion (at 1970–74 prices) for all ten core commodities, much larger than estimated by UNCTAD ($6 billion).
6. Apart from wheat (which we deal with below), buffer stock schemes for the noncore commodities (rice, wool, bauxite, and iron ore) have no attraction for LDCs as a whole.

To sum up Behrman's results from the point of view of LDCs, a real investment in stocks, which could have risen to $10 billion (1970–74 prices), would have resulted in income stabilization for producers of cocoa, rubber, and sisal.[8] It would have transferred $600 million per annum to LDCs as a whole. Large exporters of coffee, cocoa, and rubber would have made important gains; and of tin and copper considerable losses; with transfers negligible in the case of tea, jute, and sisal. However, it does not require a large investment in stocks to make transfers.

The distribution of gains needs to be considered. It is not necessary to produce precise figures for it to be obvious that the bulk of the $600 million would go to middle income countries such as Brazil, Colombia, Malaysia, and the Ivory Coast.[9] Admittedly, coffee is an important part of the exports of several very poor countries—for example, it accounts for over a third of the exports of Ethiopia, Haiti, Rwanda, and Uganda. But increasing the coffee incomes of the world's producers is a very cost-ineffective way of helping such countries. Finally, it must be noted that there is no guarantee that the poor peasant producers would benefit. In most countries, governments divorce world prices from farm prices via marketing boards, special exchange rates, and export taxes. Countries themselves can and do protect small producers in periods of very low prices. Moreover, a high proportion of the output of the core commodities is produced on large plantations or by mining companies.

We have examined Behrman's estimates at some length because they seemed among the most favorable to the UNCTAD scheme, even though in his opinion the main benefit goes to the

MDCs. But they are, as he would admit, highly speculative; and they may be badly biased in an optimistic direction. After laying out some of the assumptions on which his econometrics is based, he concludes that they probably result in an underestimate of the cost.[10] I concur and would emphasize the following. First, the managers are assumed to, but do not, know the price trend. Second, private stocks are assumed to be unchanged, which is surely wrong, since private speculation would be less worthwhile and the buffer stock would have to absorb some private speculative stocks; this would not be a real cost, but it would imply substituting some relatively scarce public savings for private savings. Third, the buffer stocks are assumed to start with only just enough money not to run out; yet if they came close to running out, private speculation against them would be likely to start. Fourth, there is no positive supply response, which is a likely result of stabilization; this would alter the price trends in a direction unfavorable to producers.

Some commodity agreements would nevertheless make sense for some LDCs. Coffee, cocoa, and rubber are the main candidates if Behrman's analysis stands up. Sugar might be added. A sugar agreement was actually made in 1977, which included quotas to help support the floor price. For nearly two years, however, the price remained below the floor; then it soared far above the ceiling. A rubber agreement was concluded in 1980. Negotiations on coffee, tea, and cocoa continue; it seems that there is some chance of a buffer stock only for cocoa. Negotiations on cotton have broken down.[11]

THE COMMON FUND

This was envisaged by the Group of Seventy-seven as a large ($6 billion) new international institution that would encourage the creation of, and finance, international buffer stocks, but which would be empowered to do much else besides, such as encourage cartels, support national stock-holding, promote diversification and research. Many of the functions would duplicate those of other agencies. The narrower economic justification—that, since some buffer stocks would be selling while others were buying, there would be a financial saving—is feeble. There are many financial institutions in the world, including the IMF, which the buffer stock agencies could lend to or borrow from.

The MDCs eventually and reluctantly accepted the principle of a Common Fund (at the Paris Conference on International Economic Cooperation [CIEC], which ended in June 1977). They then concentrated attention on watering it down in both scale and function. Finally, agreement was reached in June 1980 to establish a $750 million fund divided into two parts. The first ($470 million) is to support buffer stock agreements, which, however, must clearly provide most of the capital independently;[12] similar support is available from the IMF. The second ($280 million), financed by voluntary contributions, is to finance commodity research and development. Ratification is still, however, awaited at the time of writing (May 1981). The second part is just another small aid agency. Its function could be carried out by the United Nations Development Program (UNDP) or other agencies.

The MDCs accepted this tame version for political reasons. They were not convinced that many buffer stock agreements could be negotiated, or that they would do anyone much good if they were. The discussion of the previous section strongly suggests that they were right. Enthusiasm has waned among LDCs also. Attempts to form new commodity agreements have shown that important LDC producers, whose support is essential, may opt out when faced with reality.

The integrated commodity program has been referred to as "the very cornerstone of the programme which constitutes the NIEO."[13] And the Common Fund was the core of the cornerstone. On a political and emotional plane, it is easy to see why. There were the OPEC success, and the exceptional turbulence of commodity prices in the period 1970–75. The UNCTAD program, originally for seventeen commodities, was designed to be as wide as possible in order that as many countries as possible might think there was something in it for them. There was an "aid window," from which others might believe they would get something (or some compensation if they lost out under the program). LDCs always tend to believe that another aid window implies more aid, although this is doubtful. On an economic plane, the inclusion of many of the commodities made no sense.

341

Even for the ten core commodities, only a minority hold out hope of significant gain for LDCs, most of which would go to middle-income countries. For the majority of countries, and the vast majority of people, there would have been nothing—not even stabilization, let alone transfers. It is reasonably certain that any amount spent on stocking commodities could be better used to relieve poverty in the world. Yet it was for this that innumerable and costly meetings for more than five years, and a major exacerbation of North-South relations, took place. (For an account of these negotiations and UNCTAD's role see Christopher P. Brown, *The Political and Social Economy of Commodity Control*.)

Food

FOOD SECURITY

The food grain trade was a less salient feature of the New International Economic Order than commodities, of which LDCs were net exporters. Wheat and rice were included in UNCTAD's integrated program, though not in the core. Throughout most of the postwar period, the prices of cereals were very stable, held so by the huge United States stock which resulted from their farm support program. Then a change in United States policy, together with large sales to the USSR (at a low price) in 1972, virtually exhausted North American reserves. Consequential panic buying, together with the boom conditions of 1972–73, resulted in a near trebling of the wheat price by early 1974. There was no real shortage, for 1973–74 was a record production year. Since then the price has fallen back to approximately the 1972 level.

Stabilization of wheat prices[14] has to be looked at differently from stabilization of materials or beverages. The structure of trade is different, and so may be the welfare implications. Supply comes predominantly from North America, and to a much smaller extent from Australasia and Argentina, the latter being the only large LDC supplier. Demand is from the USSR, Japan, China, and most developing countries. Production is much more unstable in the USSR, China, and India than in North America, so that there is a potential for large variations in import demand. The USSR and China refuse to disclose figures, which increases the uncertainty. The USSR in particular has gained greatly by this secrecy, since it was able to buy cheaply before the world market could assess the position.

Governments in all countries control the grain trade, partially or wholly insulating domestic prices from international prices. This reduces supply and demand elasticities and exacerbates price movements, in the absence of large reserves. Even within countries (for example, India until recently) internal grain movements have been controlled, so that in difficult periods a well-off state would limit its exports to a deficit state. It is arguable whether there would be even a prima facie case for more than working reserves, if trade were free. But free trade in a world of nation states that feel bound to take responsibility for "adequate" food supplies at "reasonable" prices (whether or not they can meet this obligation) is probably a pipe dream.

Actual inability of a country to buy food, or a lack of enough foreign exchange to buy it at prices that have suddenly doubled or trebled, can cause starvation. This suggests a strong case for price stabilization. But food security could be achieved in other ways. The major wheat suppliers could guarantee that supplies would be available to any LDC with some predetermined shortfall below trend production.[15] This would ensure actual availability of a high proportion of normal supplies. Any exceptional cost of food imports could be covered by an insurance scheme, which would operate in the event of either a local shortfall in production or exceptionally high grain prices.[16] An IMF food facility has been suggested in this connection, which would go a long way to meet the criticism that the Compensatory Financing Facility covers only export shortfalls.[17] An international buffer stock may still be desirable to the extent that it would cut off the peaks in prices (which would be exaggerated by the existence of a food facility, or other insurance scheme), and the cost to suppliers of meeting their guarantees.

Sarris, Abbott, and Taylor argue for a small international buffer stock of 10–15 million tons with a wide price band.[18] The essential aim would be to prevent a replay of 1973. Storing wheat is very costly, and any buffer stock is almost certain to lose money; if this were not the case, it could be expected that private stocks would suffice. But losses do not imply that it would not be worthwhile, for the market value of the wheat sold may be less than its welfare value. The size of a desirable buffer stock would be further reduced if considered in conjunction with a financial scheme.[19]

The events of 1973 led to the World Food Conference of 1974. The resulting "Undertaking on World Food Security" concentrated on the idea of building national stocks with exchanges of information on quantities and policies, and periodic consultation. It appears that little progress has been made, and the USSR and China held that the "Undertaking" violated their national sovereignty.[20]

Discussions on an international reserve scheme also proceeded under UNCTAD auspices. The focus was on a 20–30 million metric ton reserve, double the size calculated by Sarris et al., to provide reasonable security, even without an insurance scheme. Negotiations lasted over a year and broke down in 1979, mainly over North-South issues. The LDCs wanted lower price triggers than exporting countries believed realistic, and a narrow spread, which would imply a very large buffer stock. They also wanted special assistance for stock acquisition and holding, preferential access to world stocks, and a subsidy on stocks released to them.[21] In this connection, it should be noted that Sarris et al. show convincingly that a wheat buffer stock would in any case benefit importers. The LDCs were apparently applying the New International Economic Order principle, "preferential and non-reciprocal treatment for developing countries, wherever possible, in all fields of economic operation, whenever possible"—in short, "aid with everything." It is a principle that may wreck many potential agreements of advantage to LDCs.

A breakdown of negotiations may have been a blessing in disguise. Physical buffer stock schemes should not be considered independently of financial schemes that may be able to provide the security required more cheaply. Emergency relief arrangements need to be considered in the same context.[22]

FOOD AID

Food aid is a long-standing affair, largely independent of the New International Economic Order and food security. For the most part it has to be considered as a continuing flow, whereas food insecurity arises from unforeseen fluctuations and crises. To deal with the latter a stock, or a fund, is required—although this is not to say that temporary relief may not also be made on concessionary terms.

There is a large literature on food aid. Opponents claim that it discourages production in LDCs. This will not happen if either food aid results in no additional imports of food (full fungibility, which heartens those who fear its effects on local production and disheartens those who hope that food aid improves nutrition) or if it induces the recipient to take measures to twist domestic demand toward food (heartening everyone). The empirical evidence is inconclusive. But it appears that food aid has been mainly fungible in many LDCs; that a few have twisted demand in favor of food; and that where, nevertheless, grain prices have suffered, the total loss of agricultural output may have been negligible.

From the LDC point of view there can be no reason for this sort of aid in kind, unless it increases the total amount of aid. But this it probably does, especially when it helps donors to solve their own surplus problems.[23] Food aid, which is quite popular with many recipients, is organized under the Food Aid Convention, and commitments in 1980 amounted to 7.5 million tons of cereals. Thus far, the debate has failed to show that food aid should be opposed in the interests of LDCs.

Debt and Debt Forgiveness

There was a rapid rise in the nominal value of debt of the LDCs starting in the early 1970s. It rose rather steadily at 21 percent per annum from 1970 to 1977, reaching a total of $260 billion.[24] The main reason was the desire to maintain the growth of imports in the face of worsened balances of payments caused initially but temporarily by grain price increases, then by the increased cost of oil imports, and by more sluggish exports resulting from the slower growth of the MDCs. But there were other reasons for the increase. Increases in reserves from 1970 to 1977 amounted to 40 percent of the rise in medium- and long-term debt.[25] Net exporters of oil, not ranking among the major oil exporters, borrowed heavily, although they did not lose by the oil price rise.[26] Finally, the magnitude of the increase was amplified by world inflation, which also increased the need for reserves.

The real rate of increase was about 9 percent per annum.[27] A corollary of this is that the ratio of debt to gross national product rose from 1970-77, but not dramatically, from about 16 percent to 21 percent. The ratio of debt to exports actually fell from 88 percent to 83 percent.[28] The debt service ratio (interest plus amortization as a percentage of exports) rose slightly from 10.6 percent to 11.8 percent because a higher proportion of the debt was nonconcessionary with shorter maturities and higher interest rates;[29] from 1969 to 1977 official credit grew at 16 percent per annum, and private credit at 25 percent per annum.[30]

INFLATION AND DEBT REDUCTION

The unexpected acceleration of inflation implied a large gain for the debtor LDCs. The real present value (at a discount rate of 10 percent) of the debt service payments on the 1972 debt of nonoil LDCs was reduced by $18 billion (from $46 billion to $28 billion) by the inflation of 1973-76 alone (using dollar export prices as deflator).[31] This is a considerable understatement, since inflation continued after 1976.

The rapid, but by no means alarming, rise in the average indebtedness of LDCs may be seen partly as a function of interest rates. Real interest rates have turned out to be low and have remained so through the 1970s. Apart from suppliers' credit, the most expensive nonconcessionary finance is from the Eurocurrency market. From 1974 to 1979, the average interest cost of these loans was 10.2 percent per annum.[32] The average rate of inflation of nonoil LDCs' exports and imports was 8.3 percent per annum.[33] Even including fees, the real rate of interest cannot have been much over 2 percent per annum. Calculations over the longer period 1972–80 suggest lower, indeed negative, real rates—the dollar values of nonoil LDC exports and imports rose by 15–16 percent per annum from 1972 to 1980.[34] Furthermore, nearly three-quarters of LDC debt was on concessional terms. The average rate of interest paid by twenty-two non-oil LDCs in 1975 was 6.1 percent.[35]

The New International Economic Order Program of Action expressed concern at inflation, required monetary reform to protect the real value of LDC reserves, and referred to the burden of debt contracted under hard terms. The reference to reserves ignored the fact that LDCs' debts were double their reserves. The fact that inflation had greatly reduced the debt burden, and made even commercial borrowing cheap, was apparently not appreciated. The next move on the debt front was to ask for debt forgiveness. A moratorium on debt service payment was proposed for MSAs, and even all LDCs. This was perhaps the strangest LDC proposal—and the least likely to result in any additional aid. Aid donors budget aid on a net basis. Debt forgiveness would thus simply constitute aid. The richest LDCs had contracted most debt and would be most aided. Moreover, they (for example, Brazil and Mexico) did not want this concession, which might have prejudiced their future credit-worthiness. Even a reduced proposal referring only to the official debt of MSAs appears as an inequitable use of aid. First, MSAs include some better-off LDCs and do not include all poor countries. Relating debt relief to MSAs is confusing a possible need for rescheduling debt, which need not reduce the present value of debt, with forgiveness, which does so reduce the debt, and where poverty should be the criterion. Second, even among the low-income LDCs, debt relief represents a highly arbitrary allocation of aid. For example, official debt per head is less than $10 for Ethiopia, Burundi, Chad, Lesotho, and Rwanda; and over $50 per head for Afghanistan, Pakistan, Benin, Somalia, and Tanzania.[36] However, debt relief on a selective basis can be a sensible way of giving aid. The great attraction from an LDC point of view is that aid in this form is untied, both as to source and as to end-use. That aid should not be source-tied is commonly accepted by economists and has long been urged. End-use tying is a different matter. Whether or not it is desirable depends largely on one's view of the value of surveillance (see chapter 16); but there is the additional point that forgiveness, or a moratorium on debt service, makes foreign exchange available very quickly. Several donor countries have recently extended debt relief to the "least developed countries" (a category that excludes India and Pakistan).

THE DEBT BURDEN AND RESCHEDULING

Countries complain if they cannot borrow and complain of the burden when they have borrowed. The long-run cost of debt is the interest, and the benefit is the real rate of return on the increased investment that the borrowing permits. Since the interest is a foreign exchange cost, the real rate of return of the investment must be calculated at world prices.[37] There is probably no country that cannot find investments with a greater real return than 2 percent, which has been the real commercial rate of interest.

Money illusion is still quite prevalent. A country paying a nominal 12 percent on a debt of $100, with inflation running at 10 percent, may feel that it is paying an exorbitant rate of interest. This is an illusion. The real value of its debt in one year's time will be only $90 (assuming no nominal amortization). It will thus, in real terms, have amortized $10 and paid $2 in interest. If it does not want to bear the balance-of-payments cost of this amortization, it should borrow another $10 to keep the real debt intact.[38]

The above suggests that the real debt problem is that most LDCs have not borrowed enough, some because they have not been able to. But it is also true that some LDCs have used loans to increase consumption, buy armaments, or make investments with a zero or negative rate of return. In these cases, borrowing has reduced national income and has been a burden in this sense.

A debt problem, from an international viewpoint, arises when a country threatens default. This happens when the amount of debt service, which in such cases is predominantly amortization, puts an unbearable strain on the balance of payments. Much debt is normally rolled over, in which case amortization is not a problem. So default usually threatens as a result of excessive use of suppliers' credits, which are not rolled over, or because the country has become a bad risk, possibly as a result of an external shock but more often as a result of an internal crisis, or for all these reasons.

Reschedulings have occurred throughout history; a dozen LDCs have been involved since 1945. Most have included some relief (reduction in the present value of the future services) as well as rescheduling. This relief may be forced (always the case with private creditors) in that creditors do not see their way to getting more. But in the case of official loans, the relief may amount to a deliberate increase in aid, possibly because a change of regime has increased the political value of such aid.

An unsuccessful attempt was made at the Conference on International Economic Cooperation to formulate guidelines for debt renegotiations. In view of the great differences in the circumstances, this is not surprising. But creditor countries should try to avoid the great differences in generosity of treatment which were accorded to Ghana and Indonesia in 1970.[39]

Since the early 1970s, there has been considerable alarm. We have seen that the overall debt service ratio, the most commonly used indicator of potential trouble, rose only a little. But the overall ratio is of little consequence. The main fear is that the debt, especially the private debt, is heavily concentrated in a few middle-income countries, some of which have reached very high debt service ratios; and that major defaults could threaten the international banking system. The alarmists have thus far proved to be wrong.[40]

Our discussion has taken no account of the further major rises in oil prices in 1978–80, which are estimated to increase the surplus of the major oil exporters to $115 billion in 1980. The growth prospects of the MDCs have worsened again. The debt service ratio of the nonoil LDCs may reach 15 percent in 1980. The deficit of the low-income oil importers is expected to reach 7 percent of their GNP.[41] But the direct contribution of oil price increases should not be overestimated. Energy imports of low-income LDCs constitute well under 2 percent of gross domestic

349

product, and averaged (in 1977) 16 percent of merchandise exports, compared with 23 percent for MDCs.[42]

Liner Conferences

"Freedom of the Seas"—that is, an absence of any governmental barriers to the freedom of choice of any shipper as between any ship of any flag (except for coastal trade)—was the order from the mid-nineteenth to the mid-twentieth century. The United States was always an important exception and used subsidies and cargo reservation to protect its merchant marine. France also protected shipping to some extent.

The increased protection introduced by the United States in the 1950s became a model for the LDCs, especially Brazil, which has since led the drive for a new international shipping order.[43] Flag discrimination soon came to be practiced by most LDCs, which have aimed thus to establish their own merchant shipping. The United States and some Latin American countries collaborated in exclusive fifty-fifty reservation of their mutual trade. UNCTAD has been active in promoting these LDC aims since 1964. The New International Economic Order confirmed the demand for an "equitable" participation in world shipping tonnage in 1974.

The idea of sovereignty has played a large part. The right of a country to exploit its materials is first extended to a right to process them, and then to a right to carry them. Historically, control of shipping has always loomed large in mercantilist philosophy. But these notions may conflict with the LDCs' own economic advantage. The UNCTAD has, however, claimed economic advantage also, on the grounds of foreign exchange saving. The LDCs, and UNCTAD in particular, have often confused foreign exchange saving with net benefit, as if foreign exchange were the sole scarcity.[44] But foreign exchange saving is itself often wrongly calculated and overestimated. It needs only a little reflection to see that virtually all costs and benefits in shipping are

THE NEW INTERNATIONAL ECONOMIC ORDER AND THE EVENTS OF 1973-80

in foreign exchange, whether the ship is owned at home or abroad. The ship is imported (and even if a country builds its own ships it can sell them for foreign exchange). The fuel, whether bunkered at home or abroad, costs foreign exchange even if the country is a fuel producer. Even the labor costs are partly foreign exchange, for a country's sailors would often have been employed on foreign-owned ships, and they have to be allowed to spend foreign exchange. The only significant foreign exchange saving would arise if foreign-owned shipping were making monopoly profits (see below). Some LDCs, but only some, may nevertheless have a comparative advantage in shipping, despite its being a very capital-intensive activity. In short, whether or not ships are a good investment can only be determined by proper cost-benefit analysis, which has played almost no part in the argument.

The New International Economic Order and UNCTAD have achieved a political success. It appears that the UNCTAD Convention on liner shipping will enter into force. Liner shipping that deals mainly with general cargo is distinguished by its provision of regular services. It is also distinguished by a large cobweb of small international cartels, known as conferences, which regulate tariffs and schedules on different routes.[45] They do their best to restrict entry by means of loyalty rebates to shippers. That regular transport schedules may be desirable, and competition unable to provide them, is a hoary truth in transport economics.[46] Monopoly (or public subsidy) may be required to garner the consumers' surplus that may make the scheduled run desirable. Monopoly in such cases does not imply that any monopoly profits are earned.

The UNCTAD Code proposes to divide 80 percent of the liner cargo shipped from any port equally between the national shipping lines of the exporting and importing country. The consequences have been analyzed by Per M. Wijkman.[47] It would imply a transfer of 10 million gross registered tonnage (grt) from LDCs to MDCs (out of a gross total of 71 million grt). The jokers in the pack are the "open registry" or "flags of convenience" LDCs.[48] They would lose 13 million grt, almost all their registered tonnage. Other LDCs would gain 3 million grt (an increase of 24 percent in their general cargo grt, and of 11 percent in their total tonnage) of which 2 million grt would go to South American countries. Ownership is different. Presumably much of the open registry tonnage is owned by MDC nationals. The required transfer to national shipping lines need not mean full change of ownership, for national shipping lines could charter ships, and joint ventures might be formed.

Since there is no evidence of monopoly profit, the only remotely calculable effect of the change is that taxes and fees would rise (largely because the open registry countries charge so little). Wijkman suggests that MDC governments gain $576 million, and "closed registry" LDCs $70 million. Which countries gain or lose on balance, LDCs or MDCs, is anyone's guess. Some loss of efficiency in world shipping is certain. Wijkman says, "Even assuming that all companies perform shipping services equally efficiently, application of cargo reservation would increase the cost of transport services by converting liner traffic from a multilateral pattern to a bilateral one."[49] Reduced transport efficiency is likely to harm LDCs. Intra-OECD trade will not be affected, since the acceptance of the European Economic Community was conditional on this and on the Community being treated as a unit for purposes of cargo reservation in trade with LDCs.

There may be a good case for some international supervision of conference arrangements to ensure that LDCs are not discriminated against, either in rates or as a result of exclusion. This is more likely to be to their advantage and is on the agenda. Non-liner shipping, mainly tankers and bulk carriers, is reckoned to be highly competitive; UNCTAD will doubtless press for cargo reservation for these also.

Transnational Corporations and the Transfer of Technology

The New International Economic Order and UNCTAD call for an international code of conduct for transnational corporations. We have dealt at length with the relations between transnational corporations and host governments. Different LDCs want to treat transnational corporations differently, and the same LDC wants to treat transnational corporations differently in different sectors. A general international code would surely be a lowest common denominator, involving a great waste of international time and temper to no purpose.

The relationship between governments and transnational corporations is of international concern only when there is a conflict of jurisdiction. From a dependency point of view, the LDC host has more to fear from the home government's interference with the transnational corporation than from the latter itself. Conflicts have occurred over antitrust policy. The United States government has prevented subsidiaries in Third World countries from trading with the enemy (of the United States). Home governments on occasion have demanded more repatriation of profit, while the host government was trying to prevent it, etc.[50] There may be a case for an international convention on home government regulations that affect the operations of transnational corporations in other countries. This could, positively, attempt to discourage international restraints on trade (which might require some loss of sovereignty to another country or to international jurisdiction) as well as, negatively, limit the power of home governments over foreign subsidiaries. But this is a difficult area; it also has nothing to do with the New International Economic Order, which seeks to control companies, not governments.

An international code is also demanded for the transfer of technology. Much the same applies. I find it impossible to believe that any such code would result in LDCs obtaining more appropriate technology or getting it cheaper. Where they pay too much, this arises from monopoly. But the national regulation of monopolistic practices in another country, or international regulation, would require some loss of sovereignty, which does not appear to be the way that UNCTAD is heading. An UNCTAD Code for technology, and for transnational corporation behavior, would certainly try to incorporate the principle of "aid with everything."[51]

The Group of Seventy-seven achieved a small political success in the technology field at the 1979 World Conference on Science and Technology. A new United Nations Centre was set up, with a new voluntary fund for technology development to be administered by the UNDP, with a $250 million target. By March 1980, pledges of $36 million had been made. The Group of Seventy-seven had proposed a new Special Agency, reporting directly to the General Assembly, to administer financial assistance of $2 billion, rising to $4 billion by 1985, on the basis of mandatory contributions.

International Money

We left the money story in chapter 15 with the formation of the Committee of Twenty for international monetary reform. The thrust of their unsuccessful attempts was to reconstitute a system of relatively fixed rates of exchange, with a greatly enhanced role for an international monetary asset managed by the IMF. The LDCs were in accord with these aims, except that they wanted full convertibility plus fixed exchange rates for the major world currencies while preserving their own options to practice exchange controls (on both current and capital account), and to adopt devices such as trotting pegs where this would help them. Their early reaction to floating rates for major currencies was one of shock and bewilderment.

The Group of Seventy-seven preference for an SDR system is partly political. A dollar system symbolized dollar hegemony, and was resented for this reason, whatever the economic advantages or disadvantages. This also applied to some MDCs, especially France. The LDC position was complicated by the demand for favorable treatment in the issue of SDRs—the link.

An SDR is a right for a central bank to acquire internationally usable money from other central banks. Its value is that of a "basket" of five currencies, with weights of forty-two for the dollar, nineteen for the mark, and thirteen each for the yen, franc, and the pound.[52] Interest is paid or received on the difference between holdings and the cumulative total of allocations. The interest rate was initially 1.5 percent but is now 80 percent of the average short-term basket rate of interest in the United States, United Kingdom, France, Germany, and Japan.[53] Nine billion SDRs were issued from 1970 to 1972; and then none until 1978-80, when 12 billion were issued. Even after the latest issues, SDRs remained as a small percentage of world reserves (3-7 percent, depending on whether gold is included).

All issues of SDRs have been made proportionately to IMF quotas. In effect, the link has come to mean any principle of direct distribution to LDCs more favorable than IMF quotas.[54] There is no fully objective way of determining a neutral distribution (see chapter 15). But it has become conventional to refer to such a more favorable distribution as aid. If made very favorable, so that there were, say, large distributions to poor countries, which would clearly be passed on, and not held as reserves, then the use of the word "aid" becomes realistic.

There is a conflict between a desire for SDRs as aid and the desire to see them substitute for the dollar as the backbone of the world's monetary system. If MDC or OPEC central banks are to be willing to hold SDRs in their portfolios in sufficient quantity to permit their use by LDCs, they must bear an attractive interest rate relative to national currencies.[55] But then they become unattractive as a form of aid, even given that such aid is untied. So, at the Committee of Twenty discussions, the LDCs argued for low interest rates. A second inconsistency in the LDC position was their insistence on their freedom to invest reserves in the high-interest Eurocurrency market. This would undermine the control of international liquidity, which would have to be a feature of an IMF-based world currency system.[56]

Although none of the usual arguments against the link is convincing,[57] it is also true that it was not worth worrying about. The old 1960s arguments for increasing world liquidity had died with floating rates, and so there was at the time no prospect of an issue of SDRs (at an interest rate of 1.5 percent). But taking a longer view, and assuming a steady issue of SDRs, does not eliminate the charge of essential irrelevance. The following example underlines this. Four billion of SDRs were issued on January 1,

1981. Tanzania received 5.6 million.[58] Now suppose that under a link scheme Tanzania's share would be doubled (at the expense only of MDCs). The grant element of SDRs is 20 percent (and might have to be zero under a full-fledged SDR system), so Tanzania would get SDR 1.4 million grant equivalent aid (that is, about $1.75 million). In 1979, Tanzania received $719 million of grant equivalent official development assistance. If 20 billion SDRs were issued annually, the aid thus received by poor aided countries would still be insignificant. The story is a little different for a relatively rich country that gets little ODA (for example, Chile). Chile would have received "link aid" of $5.5 million, against ODA grant equivalent aid of $50 million. Still![59]

The "aid with everything" principle did not kill world monetary reform. It did not need the LDCs to do that. Nevertheless, the LDCs were not helpful. To quote Williamson:

> Since the developing countries were only too conscious that the feedbacks from their own individual actions to the behavior of the system as a whole were negligible, it was no doubt difficult for them to realize that collectively this was not true and that an agreed system required that they shoulder obligations as well as collect benefits. This failure to accept the need to undertake responsibilities all too often reduced the developing countries to a position that looked more like begging than bargaining, while some quite valuable bargaining counters (such as an offer to accept limitations on reserve placements in the Euro-markets) were never exploited to advance their particular demands (such as the link).[60]

So there was no world monetary reform. Exchange rates of the major currencies fluctuated, sometimes quite violently. The LDCs' initial fears, however, proved groundless. We have already shown that the fall of the dollar, as well as general inflation, relieved them of debt more than it devalued their reserves. The further claim that it worsened their terms of trade can also be dismissed.[61]

Another fear was that trade would be lost as a result of greater uncertainty, which would especially apply to LDCs because of the lack of insurance provided by forward markets in their own currencies. In fact, traders can use foreign forward markets to transform, say, a yen risk into a dollar risk. This would not insulate them from variations in their own currency against the dollar, but that risk was always there. As far as exports are concerned, their own central bank can without much risk provide forward cover in any currency.[62] These risks and impediments were exaggerated, not only by LDCs, but also by the IMF, which early in the 1970s was still keen to find arguments against floating rates. There is no empirical evidence that fluctuating rates have caused a reduction in trade, though admittedly that would be hard to detect unless it were large.[63]

LDCs have adopted a variety of policies vis-à-vis the fluctuating majors. Forty Fund members have tied to the dollar; fourteen to the franc; and four to other currencies.[64] Fifteen have linked to the SDR, and seventeen to other currency baskets. Twenty-eight have "other arrangements" (that is, floating, trotting, or managed pegs).[65] An increasing number have moved from the passive reaction of tying to their largest trading partner, or to the SDR, to either a basket of their own choice (which may be more appropriate than the SDR basket) or to the more active alternatives of managed floating or trotting. Analysis of the best policies for individual LDCs is the subject of continuing and as yet inconclusive recent work.

The failure of world monetary reform was both inevitable and a blessing in disguise. The world became a more uncertain place in the 1970s for reasons that are independent of international monetary reform. No system of fixed rates could have weathered the storms. The nonsystem was legitimized at the Jamaica Meeting of the Fund in 1976. Subject to seemingly rather toothless surveillance by the IMF, countries could now do as they pleased, except to peg to gold, which was demonetized. Since their agreement was required to amend the Fund's articles, the LDCs made significant bargaining gains. Their share of total quotas was raised from 26 to 32 percent, and the credit tranches were increased by 45 percent. A further success was the agreement to sell by auction one-sixth of the Fund's gold and use the profit for the benefit of LDCs. As a result, $4.6 billion accrued directly to

LDCs, the rest forming the basis for a revolving loan fund.[66] Another one sixth was restituted to members at $35 an ounce, so that two thirds of the Fund's holding remains in limbo.

Since 1971, gold holders have made enormous, though largely unrealizable, capital gains. About 90 percent of this gain accrued to MDCs, many of whom had maintained the proportion of gold in their reserves since the 1940s, while the LDCs had, ill-advisedly as it turned out, much reduced the proportion, mainly because they preferred not to forgo interest. Three points need to be made. First, only a small part of the subsequent rise in the price of gold was the direct consequence of the removal of the ceiling provided by the United States authorities. At the time of the Smithsonian agreement, the price had risen only to $43. It rose rapidly during and after the inflationary outburst of 1973 and generalized floating of the major currencies but fell again in 1975 and 1976 to about $100. Much the largest part of the huge rise since 1971 occurred in the late 1970s, long after gold had become a highly speculative market which any person or government could play (in relatively small amounts). Second, the gain cannot be represented as a transfer of real resources to the North, for it is impossible to imagine a situation in which a Northern deficit was significantly financed by a transfer of gold to the South at the going price. Third, the fact remains that a very large, and largely unanticipated, increase in reserves has paradoxically resulted from the demonetization of gold. However, this increase in reserves cannot be taken at face value (which experience has shown can double or halve in less than a year), because gold reserves are no longer fully liquid. A country such as France, let alone the United States, could not sell gold to meet a large deficit without driving down the price. The main real beneficiaries are the producers and the few small countries, such as Portugal, which held a high proportion of gold in their reserves.

Part of the New International Economic Order agenda was a "Review of the Methods of Operation of the IMF, in particular the terms for both credit repayments and 'standby' arrangements, the system of compensatory financing, and the terms of the financing of commodity buffer stocks, so as to enable the developing countries to make more effective use of them." In this area, there have been considerable successes, which are described in the next section, since they have to be seen also as a response to the large payments imbalances caused by oil price rises.

The Dance of the Deficits, 1973–80

With the oil price rises of 1973–74, it was obvious that some oil exporters could not spend enough to prevent massive surpluses building up. Some countries had to run corresponding deficits. A more Keynesian way of stating the problem is that there would be an increase in world savings. Investment elsewhere would have to rise, or savings be reduced. The new savings-investment equality might come about through a reduction in incomes elsewhere, which would cause the required fall in savings. If a deep depression were to be avoided, spending might have to be stimulated, and those who were willing to spend must be able to obtain the money required.

The problem was quickly understood; there was no deep depression, but recession in the MDCs was not avoided. Among the MDCs there was no "recycling" problem. MDCs which were willing to take counterrecessionary action could quite easily borrow to finance deficits (the borrowing was automatic for those countries where surplus OPEC funds were deposited). The IMF oil facility 1974 and 1975 and the OECD "safety net" (a $25 billion Financial Support Fund) were organized to help ensure that this was the case. The basic reason for the 1975 recession, and sluggish subsequent recovery (and the 1980 recession), was inflation.

Inflation among the MDCs had already been accelerating before 1973. The oil price rise exacerbated the problem in two ways. First, it raised some prices directly; and second, and more important, it caused a fall in real income. These effects amounted to only a few percentage points of GNP. But the effect of even a small fall in real income, when people are used to steady increases, has a large inflationary effect if income recipients can successfully demand nominal pay increases in a futile effort to avoid the real effects. Thus, most MDCs showed themselves to be inflexible in meeting an external shock.

As a group, the MDCs did not incur current account deficits in the period 1974–78. An initial deficit of about $12 billion in 1974 was transformed to a larger surplus in 1975. In 1976 and 1977, the MDCs were in balance, and then in large surplus in 1978, by which time the oil exporters' surplus had become quite small. The upshot was that on balance it was the non-oil LDCs (NOLDCs) that borrowed and used the oil exporters' surpluses. In these five years, their current account deficits averaged $36 billion.[67] The NOLDCs were more willing to borrow for several reasons. First, the "development imperative" made them more willing to take risks. Second, a number were more habituated to inflation, and did not therefore feel constrained from increasing demand. Third, several were able to reduce an imported inflation without much loss of output or employment and quickly resume growth because their internal prices and wages were more flexible than in the MDCs (Taiwan and India are examples). The consequence was that many, especially the middle-income LDCs, fared much better than the MDCs.

Probably no one in, say, January 1974 would have expected such an outcome. Many thought that new institutions and financial instruments would be needed to channel oil exporters' savings to other countries (and to persuade the oil exporters to sell as much oil as they did). No one would have guessed that the NOLDCs would end up by being the only net borrowers, or have imagined that this would be financially possible.

How was the $36 billion financed? Thirteen-and-a-half billion dollars were covered by financing which did not increase the debt.[68] The net figure of $22.5 billion was increased, by additions to reserves, to an average annual borrowing of $31 billion. The $31 billion was financed as shown in table 17-1.

This table makes clear the dominant role of the banks in "recy-

TABLE 17-1
The Financing of Non-Oil Less Developed Country Deficits

	1974–78	1973–78
	Average Percentage Shares of Different Forms of NOLDC Borrowing	Growth Rate % per annum
ODA Loans	24	18.7
Official Long-term nonconcessionary[a]	13	20.6
Private Banks	41	37.0
Bond Issues	5	43.1
"Reserve-related credit" (mainly IMF)	6	18.5
Other and Errors	11	16.5

SOURCE: Calculated from *IMF Annual Report 1980*, Table 10.
[a] Less than 25 percent grant element.

cling" to LDCs. Despite its quickly organized Oil Facility, which channeled about $3 billion to NOLDCs in 1975 and 1976, the IMF played a small role. The reasons for this are discussed below.

The enormous increase in private bank lending was concentrated on a few middle-income LDCs. Thus, in 1978 Brazil and Mexico alone accounted for 28 percent. The five largest (including Spain and Venezuela) accounted for 44 percent; and the twenty largest for 83 percent.[69] Two concerns arise from this. First, there is the widely expressed fear that the banks have been unwise in assessing risks and overextending themselves. Second, the poorer, least credit-worthy LDCs are left out in the cold.

As was noted in section 5 above, there was much alarm over alleged overcommitment of the banks in the middle 1970s, which has so far proved to be groundless. The world would have been a much worse place if the banks had not accepted the risks of transforming short-term borrowing originating largely from oil-surplus countries into longer-term loans to LDCs.

In the words of the Managing Director of the Fund, M. de Larosière:

The typical current account deficit among industrial and non-oil developing countries in the early 1970s was of the order of 3 per cent of GDP. In 1974–75 this figure rose to over 6 per cent of GDP, and in 1980–81 it is estimated to be over 7 per cent. In order to sustain their imports, countries in deficit have had to borrow massive amounts of capital. The international financial system has shown extraordinary adaptability in meeting these demands. Indeed, the inventiveness, the sophistication, and the efficiency displayed by financial intermediaries in response constitute one of the most remarkable phenomena of recent economic history.[70]

The 1978–79 oil price rise has, however, again given rise to similar fears, either that the banks cannot again perform the same function or that there will be trouble if they do. Some believe that the foreign operations of national banks, and of the Eurocurrency market, should be subject to greater control and supervision.[71] M. de Larosière has commented soothingly on the banks' overall exposure, while also remarking that "bank financing has flowed in substantial and rapidly increasing amounts to countries whose capacity to manage debt on commercial terms was quite limited."[72] I am in no position to judge the adequacy of existing supervision of bankers' international lending, and have to leave the question open. But supervision could certainly go too far, from the point of view of LDCs.[73]

The IMF is taking steps to play a larger role in the recycling game, which will somewhat reduce that of the private banks. Its past role was limited despite liberalization measures taken in the 1970s. The Extended Fund Facility was established in 1974, and permitted longer disbursements (three years), slower repayments (four to eight years) as well as larger drawings relative to quotas, than the normal drawings. It was intended for LDCs with difficult adjustment problems, and thus involved the IMF in supply-side economics to a greater extent than previously. It has been very little used, presumably because LDCs disliked the conditions imposed. The Compensatory Finance Facility, which was little used from 1963 to 1975, was liberalized in the latter year, and was then extensively used, to the amount of SDR 4 billion by March 1980, making it the second largest "window" for Fund credit (after the normal credit tranches). It was further liberalized in 1979, making it possible to draw 100 percent of a member's quota within a year. Since the facility is designed to compensate export shortfalls beyond the borrowing countries' control, it is not subject to conditions other than the calculated shortfall itself, and its use does not count against the quota-related limitations on other drawings.[74] A Buffer Stock Financing Facility came into operation in 1970 to assist members to make contributions to any approved scheme. Drawings have been insignificant, which is not surprising in view of the dearth of such schemes.

The above facilities are dependent on quota subscriptions. IMF quotas have signally failed to keep up with inflation and the expansion of world trade. In 1965, they were 12 percent of world imports and only 4 percent in 1980. As a result, LDCs became increasingly reluctant to accept IMF conditions, in view of the relatively small drawings that were possible. Two Fund sources of finance that were dependent on borrowing or gold sales—the Oil Facility and the Trust Fund—and that were nonconditional were fully used. Two thirds of the Fund's finance used was associated in the middle 1970s with little or no conditionality.[75]

The Fund extended its activities in 1977 by borrowing almost SDR 8 billion to form the Supplementary Financing Facility,[76] thus entering the recycling game on a significant scale. This facility was quota related and conditional. Interest rates were governed by the rates at which the Fund had been able to borrow but were below commercial rates. The facility was exhausted by March 1981. Turkey and Yugoslavia had each borrowed close to SDR 1.5 billion, and three other countries over SDR .5 billion. Meanwhile the Fund's maximum holding of a member's currency had been raised to 600 percent of quota (reduced to 450 percent when quotas were raised by 50 percent in December 1980). In contrast with the middle 1970s, three-quarters of Fund finance was available only under programs of high conditionality.[77] The Fund intends to maintain this enlarged access by borrowing and in 1981 announced both a doubling of Saudi Arabia's quota to SDR 2 billion, and an agreement to borrow from her SDR 4 billion in each of the next two, and possibly three, years.

The Fund has been under pressure to extend medium-term finance and has responded, though doubtless not enough for some critics. It recognizes that "adjustment" is at least a medium-term business. But what does adjustment mean? It means that policies must be such as to ensure that the country remains credit-worthy, and ideally that it should remain credit-worthy at as high a level of borrowing as possible. If it borrows to increase the level of investment, and if such investments have a real yield of even, say, 5 percent per annum at *world prices*, there is no limit. The twin dangers are a fall in domestic savings and unwise or inappropriate investment (an important cause of the latter being excessive protection as a result of which apparently profitable investment yields little or nothing at world prices). A considerable number of countries has failed to avoid these dangers.[78] The first is a traditional IMF concern. The second has been more the World Bank's business. However, as the IMF moves into medium-term "adjustment" loans, it will have to concern itself more with "supply-side" problems, something de Larosière recognizes:

> In blending demand and supply policies, and addressing structural problems, the Fund must take into account considerations that are on the borderline of its traditional competence. It has therefore intensified its collaboration with the World Bank to ensure that its adjustment programs are supportive of the investment priorities of member countries.[79]

It continues to be denied that the IMF provides development finance: but nevertheless the Fund has moved closer toward being a development agency.

We next turn to the problem of the low-income LDCs, including those left out in the cold by the private recycling of the 1970s (and by direct foreign investment), and then again hit by the recent doubling of oil prices. Among low-income countries, only Indonesia, Zaire, and Sudan have been able to borrow large amounts. NOLDCs suffered a $36 billion increase in their oil import bill from 1978 to 1980. The problem for the lower-income group ($<$ \$450 per head in 1978) is more manageable than that of the NOLDCs as a whole, the increase in their oil import bill being about \$5 billion.[80] It is widely accepted that the low-income countries should receive top priority in the distribution of ODA.

The Development Assistance Committee ODA grew at about 16 percent per annum from 1973 to 1979, barely increasing its value to NOLDCs in real terms.[81] It remained at a level of about 0.35 percent of DAC GNP, half the target level. Most DAC countries increased the percentage (Denmark, the Netherlands, Norway, and Sweden exceeding the target level), but the total was held down to 0.35 percent largely because of the United States.

The low-income NOLDCs still receive a little less total ODA per head than the middle-income group. (If India were excluded, the reverse would be true.) But ODA was in 1979 4.8 percent of their GNP as compared with 1.8 percent for all LDCs; and 29 percent of their 1978 imports were aid financed, against 9 percent for all LDCs.

An increase in ODA, and a further reorientation toward the poorest countries, is the only way to help them significantly. No other elements of the New International Economic Order could do much for them. This applies to freer imports by MDCs, to extension of generalized special preferences, to easier access to capital markets, to commodity price stabilization, and to the link. If MDCs regard concessions in these other areas as competitive with ODA, then ODA could be reduced below what it otherwise would have been, to the detriment of the poorest countries and the poorest people.

The Group of Seventy-seven has adhered to the New International Economic Order principle of "aid with everything," thus trying to multiply the forms of aid—the GSPs, the link, and aid associated with commodity price stabilization are examples. They have also favored the multiplication of new special funds (for example, for agriculture, commodities, and technology). In large part this is probably because LDCs have a greater say in the management of new United Nations funds. But they also, presumably, believe that new forms and new funds increase the total amount of aid, that they are "additional."

The share of multilateral ODA in total ODA increased in the 1970s. The financial institutions with weighted voting (the World Bank group, the regional banks, and the International Fund for Agricultural Development [IFAD]), received 82 percent of the increased multilateral ODA from 1974 to 1978–79 (average). Except for IFAD, these are old agencies. Since 1970, contributions to them have increased faster than total ODA. Total contributions to United Nations agencies have increased more slowly, but also faster than total ODA. Contributions to the "old" UNDP program rose more slowly than total ODA. There is no way of determining from these changes to what extent, if at all, the mostly small new funds, and new concessions, have reduced bilateral ODA or contributions to the UNDP below what they otherwise would have been. It seems quite probable, however, that they have increased the total a little while also reducing the flow through the older aid channels. In contrast, the preference of donors for the financial institutions is obvious. The capital of the World Bank has recently been doubled, which should permit it to continue to increase its lending in real terms. It promises to embark on "structural adjustment" programs, involving nonproject aid, that may be difficult to distinguish from the new IMF programs.[82]

Trade, the New Protectionism, and the Tokyo Round

Since 1973, the growth in the purchasing power of NOLDCs' exports has declined (see chapter 13). But this was due to the oil price rises. One would expect the volume to have been affected rather by the slower growth of the MDCs since 1973 and by the resultant growth of protectionism. From 1960 to 1973, the volume of their exports rose at 5.8 percent per annum. From 1973 to 1975, there was no growth, although the "new protectionism" had not begun to bite significantly, so that this must be attributed mainly to the 1975 recession. From 1975 to 1979, the volume of their exports rose at a rate of 10.3 percent per annum.

The new protectionism affects only manufactures. Taking the UNCTAD category of "fast growing exporters of manufactures" (which excludes Taiwan, but otherwise includes countries accounting for a very high proportion of LDC manufactured exports), we find that the volume grew from 1960 to 1973 at 7.4 percent per annum, stagnated from 1973 to 1975, but grew at 16.3 percent per annum from 1975 to 1979. The new protectionism was discriminatory and was aimed at these countries, especially Korea and Hong Kong (and Taiwan). It is evident that it was not very effective overall. It is also evident that the rate of growth of the MDCs' GDP is not the most important factor in determining their imports of manufactures from LDCs. More important is the increase in the latter's share of the consumption of manufactures in MDCs, termed the degree of "penetration." Between 1970 and 1979, penetration doubled from about 1.7 percent to 3.4 percent, a rate of growth of 8.1 percent.[83] Penetration was below average in North America, Japan, and France. In particular products, high penetration (> 25 percent) was achieved in only a handful of very minor products. For the most important group of products, clothing of all kinds, penetration was 14 percent.

The above does not imply that the new protectionism is not to be feared—far from it. By far the most important element for LDCs is quota protection against textiles and clothing. Protectionism for textiles is an old habit (see chapter 14). But it did not begin to bite very seriously until 1977, when the Multi-fiber Arrangement was modified and permitted "reasonable departures" from its rules. The EEC was in the lead; and within the EEC, the United Kingdom and France. D. B. Keesing and M. Wolf have said, "What has since been in effect has been a departure from a departure—waiving of the provisions of an agreement which itself was a derogation from GATT principles."[84] In terms of volume, the effects have been dramatic. EEC imports from LDCs were actually reduced from 1976 to 1978; while Greece, Portugal, and Spain, the EEC aspirants, gained. The United States, Hong Kong, Taiwan, and South Korea lost out, although other LDCs gained (the quotas are often highly discriminatory). In terms of value, the "baby tigers" continued to gain by trading up and raising prices (helped in the latter case by the quotas themselves).

The long-run effects, if the MDCs continue to permit no more volume penetration of their markets, are shocking to contemplate. The effects on the three big suppliers, Hong Kong, Korea, and Taiwan, will not be too serious, for their wages have risen dramatically, and their comparative advantage in clothing is due to disappear. What the new protectionism will do is to ensure that there can be no more miracles like Hong Kong, Korea, and Taiwan. Other LDCs, through their home-market biased policies, were very slow to take any gains from their enormous comparative advantage in clothing. Now the gains from doing so will be severely limited unless far more favorable arrangements can be negotiated.[85] No doubt, manufactured exports will grow rapidly, but the MDC protection of labor-intensive activities (including also footwear) will help to shift the LDCs into more capital-intensive activities, with less demand for labor generated. Admittedly, as we have seen, the leaders in most of them favored capital intensity anyway. It is as if there were a conspiracy between the garment workers of the West and LDC leaders to reduce the demand for labor in LDCs. But some LDCs were beginning to move in the direction of exports of labor-intensive manufactures, and they will be discouraged. The MDCs will also be harming themselves. It is not as if they were merely trying to minimize adjustment costs by slowing the rundown of the textile and clothing industries, in many parts of which they have a comparative disadvantage; they are striving to maintain or even increase production, though employment will in any case fall with rising productivity (itself partly induced by the protection).[86]

So-called voluntary export restraints, which evade GATT rules, have been quite widely used to limit imports from LDCs in other manufacturing sectors. Shoes, cutlery, bicycles, electronic components, and television sets have been among those affected—items of special interest to a number of LDCs. International cartelization, formal or informal, as well as voluntary exports restraints and other devices, are being used to control trade in steel, ships, and cars. Export and production subsidies have become prominent methods of competitive protection in these and other industries.[87] But in these latter industries only a few of the richer LDCs are interested (for example, Korea, Taiwan, and Brazil).[88]

The long, drawn-out Tokyo Round of multilateral trade policy negotiations begun in 1973 finally ended in 1979. Reduction of tariffs was not the main point. Tariffs were already rather low. Even where they were still quite high, especially for textiles and clothing, LDC exporters had shown that, with their formidable comparative advantage, they could step over them. The main point was to reassert an international trade order in which countries' use of policy instruments to solve internal problems would neither preclude structural change due to shifts in comparative advantage nor in the shorter run unduly disturb other economies. The MFA, due to be renegotiated in 1981, lay outside the negotiations.

The negotiations failed to achieve a new code (that is, a reform of Article XIX) governing the use of safeguards to prevent domestic damage arising from very rapid increases in imports. Such safeguards should be subject to evidence of substantial damage, should be for a limited period (while the affected country adjusts by redeploying its resources with limited human hardship), and, in accordance with GATT principles, should be nondiscriminatory. This failure implies that the authority of GATT has not been reasserted. No serious attack on the new protectionism, which evades the existing GATT Article XIX, has been made. It appears that the EEC countries are most adamant in demanding a selective use of safeguards, so that they can discriminate against the LDCs, whose possible retaliation is not a serious threat. The LDCs very rightly opposed such selectivity. They also argued that any code should be biased in their favor, so as to make it more difficult for MDCs to invoke safeguards on exports of interest to them, and that they should be compensated if restrictions were applied.[89] A selective use of safeguards, legitimized under a new GATT Article XIX, would harm LDCs. Protectionist MDCs would then use them instead of VERs, which at least give the exporting LDCs compensation in the form of higher prices (even in cases where the word "voluntary" is a mockery).[90]

Nevertheless, there were a number of achievements. Codes of conduct on export subsidies and countervailing duties, on technical barriers to trade, on government procurement, on import licensing procedures, and on customs valuation were negotiated.

The codes have been reviewed from the point of view of the LDCs by Ginman et al., and by Balassa.[91] Unless one adopts the most pessimistic view that they will turn out to be meaningless (and some suggest that their ambiguous drafting will have this result), there is every reason for LDCs to subscribe. In view of the very general reservations made in favor of LDCs, there is a little to gain and virtually nothing to lose (though even nonsignatories would benefit from some of the codes). Moreover, by not subscribing LDCs would miss the opportunity of participating in the work of the committees set up to monitor adherence to the codes and to settle disputes, and more generally to influence the case law which will have to develop under the codes.

Only a minority of LDCs belong to GATT. About one third of LDCs participated in the negotiations. Disappointed with the results, which did not, in their view, give the LDCs sufficient of the special and differential treatment promised, all (except Argentina) initially refused to sign. Subsequently (by the summer of 1980), some twenty LDCs had subscribed. As a group, the Seventy-seven are reluctant peripheral members of GATT. It is almost as if the multinational trade negotiations under GATT were a sideshow. The real action and bombast which the diplomats and negotiators like occurs under the big top of UNCTAD or the General Assembly.

It is in the trade field that negotiators traditionally fight a distressing kind of battle. They fight to avoid "concessions," which would benefit the vast majority of their own people. This applies to both MDCs and LDCs. If LDC governments accepted more international obligations, above all in the use of quotas, they would be constrained to run their economies in ways that would benefit the mass of the people, even if some sectional interests lost. Since anything LDCs do has rather little impact on MDC countries, the latter's negotiators are quite willing to let LDCs break the rules, and to manage their foreign trade in ways that have been shown to be detrimental to both growth and equality. Refusing to accept obligations hurts LDCs in another way. They cannot exert so much pressure on MDCs to desist from discrimination, or other action that is contrary to their interests, if they insist on discriminating themselves. As in the monetary reform negotiations, LDCs reduce themselves to a position in which they can only beg. In the trade field it is worse. They beg to be allowed to hurt themselves. It is no consolation that MDCs demand to be able to hurt both themselves and the LDCs.[92]

Chapter 18

International Systems: A Summary View

Introduction

Economic development policies can be analyzed only in terms of the contribution of different policies to different ends. One such end is economic "welfare," which depends on output and distribution. Another end we have examined at length is independence. A third end is participation, which we have so far mentioned only in passing. In calling it an end, we take the view that less developed country leaders do not call for greater LDC control of the World Bank and the International Monetary Fund because they believe this would increase welfare.

We shall examine how differences in world economic arrangements impinge upon these ends. They may do so in different ways in different LDCs. We divide these arrangements into trade, money and credit, and aid. Matters are of world importance only if they seriously concern or affect many countries in different continents. Other concerns, though international, are essentially regional or bilateral; say, cleaning the Mediterranean or using the waters of the Brahmaputra. Some concerns, which have been argued in world forums, are not even international, like the relations between a government and a transnational corporation (which become bilateral and international only if and when the parent government gets involved). In my opinion, much very scarce time available for world concerns is wasted on such matters as transnational corporations, technology transfers, patents and trademarks, and advertising. I shall say no more about them. Individual LDCs have fully adequate power to deal with most of such matters.

Trade

Trade is the easiest subject to deal with because there is no significant conflict between ends. What is often called a Liberal International Economic Order is best for output and for independence, and achieving it requires close participation in the making of trade rules. Only in a few countries is production according to comparative advantage likely to make distribution less equal. More generally, the greater demand for labor, implied by liberal policies, will be equalizing.

To all intents and purposes, LDCs are free to adopt any trade regime they like, including export subsidies, without much fear of retaliation. So the problems are primarily how to keep the more developed countries from using trade restraints, and secondarily to get them to reduce tariffs even further, especially on labor-intensive products. A closely related question is whether LDCs would not be better off if they accepted some constraints on their own trade policies.

This study, like many others, has stressed that there is no economic justification (whether in terms of welfare, or of nationalist objectives) for the highly restrictive trade regimes of most LDCs. That weaker countries should not want stronger countries to control trade is less discussed or recognized but would seem obvious on both welfare and dependency grounds. Yet many LDC demands presuppose or require MDC governmental intervention in trade. This politicization of trade is a game that the strong are likely to win, and only a few LDCs are strong. I believe that many LDC leaders are ill-advised on this score and that their predilection for controlled trade, stemming from colonial days or the 1930s, has served their countries badly. Their enthusiasm for some of the New International Economic Order items seems scarcely explicable, except in terms of bad advice. (They receive good advice, too, but are liable to mistrust it when it comes from the North.)

The International Trade Organization still needs to be created, and it must build on the General Agreement on Tariffs and Trade, not on the United Nations Conference on Trade and Development, for the latter is too wedded to controls and its own devices. These devices have been of very little direct benefit to LDCs, and have probably harmed them on the plausible assumption that more developed countries have used their UNCTAD concessions as an excuse for their own restrictive practices (or for not giving more aid). In this forum, the LDCs could trade off many of their own restrictions for advantages in the trade field. This should be pure gain, for their own restrictions often harm them (some LDCs have reduced restrictions without any bargaining). Such advantages would include a more favorable safeguards clause in GATT, and the dismantling of the Multi-fiber Arrangement.[1] The enlarged GATT/ITO would need to include services, agriculture, and export controls within its purview.[2] It should also include as a subject the control of international cartels (transnational corporations as such are the wrong target for an international code) and restrictive business practices; and its codes on other matters, such as state trading and subsidies, need reconsideration.[3]

The LDCs have been hostile to the idea of graduation, which means essentially that the richer should accept more obligations in international agreements. Graduation unfortunately carries with it the idea that any element of reciprocity is a sacrifice. That is false. The poorest countries could with advantage accept reciprocal trade obligations. That does not mean that LDCs should not seek softer rules, or exceptions applying only to them, in certain fields. An example could be the use of export controls, where

373

International Systems and Confrontation

quotas might be desirable to defend a floor price in a commodity agreement. But LDCs should not demand blanket exceptions or those that do not clearly benefit them. They thereby lose bargaining strength. The less they accept obligations, the weaker is the force of their justified accusation that the MDCs do not play the game according to their own supposed philosophy.

LDC spokesmen often claim they have no bargaining power in GATT. I doubt this and suggest that it could be developed, especially since the old "principal supplier" formula is no longer relevant. Coalitions could be formed, and in an enlarged GATT/ITO one might even get some welcome new coalitions, such as the United States and many LDCs combining to attack the European Economic Community's Common Agricultural Policy. More could surely be achieved if LDCs participated fully in multilateral trade negotiations, and were prepared to threaten and horse-trade, not merely demand an exception to every rule. They need to abandon the New International Economic Order principle of "aid with everything," which manifestly reduces the possibility of mutually beneficial agreements, increases administration costs, and adds little or nothing to total aid.

In order to get the most advantage, it would be necessary to associate aid and trade in a suitable forum. The advantages of an early fulfillment of the Official Development Assistance target would enormously outweigh the benefits derived from generalized special preferences, and all the EEC related preferences. If some way could be found of binding MDCs to the existing or even a higher ODA target, it would be worth the while of most LDCs (excepting only a few of the richest who might get little or no aid) to give up all these preferences. The MDCs should be willing to offer, in terms of additional aid, considerably more than the amount by which preferences benefit LDCs—for the administrative cost and the potential ill-will arising from this complicated discriminatory system is also considerable. A fortiori the preferences could be traded off for gains on both aid and most favored nation trade treatment, since aid and free access to MDC markets are both much more important than preferences.

On every ground LDCs have most to gain from a most favored nation trading system limiting so far as possible MDC governmental trade interventions that serve to prevent LDCs growing in line with their changing comparative advantage and that may be used in a disruptive manner. The MDCs have far more economic power to disrupt, whether intentionally or otherwise, than do the LDCs (apart from the Organization of Petroleum Exporting Countries).

Money and Public Credit

EXCHANGE RATES AND SUPRANATIONAL MONEY

The LDC position (as articulated by the Group of Twenty-four)[4] remains basically that of the Committee of Twenty. They favor moving toward an adjustable peg system in which central banks hold reserves and settle payments imbalances in special drawing rights, which are to be created by the IMF in line with world liquidity needs.

What they should want (by the criterion of our three objectives) is much less clear than in the case of trade. The attractions for LDCs of fixed rates between the major currencies are clear; uncertainty would be reduced, and they would have less complicated decisions to make. But if greater real instability resulted from fixed rates, that would most likely be still more disturbing for LDCs. The unfortunate fact that MDCs cannot handle their affairs in a manner that is best for LDCs (and themselves) has to be accepted. Nearly fixed rates seem to be below the horizon.

It is possible to imagine a system in which national currencies floated against, or were movably pegged to, a world currency, and in which reserves were held and international settlements were made only in this supranational currency. This would imply that central banks were not allowed to settle in national currencies, and even that private persons and institutions would not be permitted to hold foreign national currencies. Certainly the use and holding of such currencies would need to be strictly limited and controlled.

Several advantages have been claimed for such a system, both by LDC spokesmen and others. First, it is hoped that the growth of world reserves would come under control, and world inflation would thereby be moderated. Control over world reserves requires that exchange rates be fixed, or only rarely devalued, for, if not, the IMF would control merely the number of SDRs and not their monetary value. The value of world reserves would still be determined by payments imbalances, and not exogenously.[5]

Countries would have to give up considerable economic sovereignty, both over exchange rates and the form in which they hold external assets, if there were to be any question of a World Monetary Authority influencing the level of world reserves and inflation. For differing reasons many countries, both LDCs and MDCs, have opted for inflation (or against the political and economic costs of reducing it or even keeping it low). They would find it impossible to accept a loss of sovereignty that greatly reduced their domestic room for maneuver in this respect.

In short, while one can imagine the system described, it is impossible to imagine that it would be acceptable in a world of independent nation states. An effective world central bank, which exercised the same control over national central banks as the latter do over the national commercial banks, would require a world government. But short of this, a system in which IMF fiat money largely or almost entirely took the place of the dollar and other national currencies in central bank reserves and settlements is unlikely to evolve, and would do little to reduce world inflation.

Another aim of the Committee of Twenty was to remove the possibility that a reserve currency country, especially the United States, could, at least for a while, finance part of its deficits in its own currency, and so not be subject to the same degree of discipline that the system imposed on others. There was strong opposition to this asymmetry. As it happened, floating rates have largely eliminated the problem. Immediate financial discipline is now imposed by a fall in the value of the dollar, if other countries do not want the extra dollars implied.

A third aim was to see that the benefits of the seignorage, which accrues from issuing international money, were more widely distributed. In effect, this seignorage benefit, accruing mainly to the United States, is the banking profit that arises from borrowing short (since foreign central banks hold their dollar reserves in the form of interest-bearing assets) and lending long. The change to an SDR system would reduce banking profits and benefit LDCs to the extent that the interest on borrowing by using SDRs is less than that on commercial borrowing. This difference was about 2 percent in 1981. But if SDRs are to be fully acceptable in central bankers' portfolios, and so largely take the place of the reserve currencies, the interest differential would have to be much smaller, maybe zero. Even at present rates, the gain to LDCs (or any other country whose currency is not used as a reserve asset) would be very small, as we saw in chapter 17 (in connection with the link). It can be argued that anything is worth having. But the truth is that seignorage benefits are tiny in relation to the benefits of a well-working system under which international transactions can be smoothly and efficiently made.

K. Alec Chrystal has argued convincingly that the SDR as presently constituted has little future and is a bad instrument with which to try to effect a transition to a system in which a supranational money plays a major role.[6] It may be possible to institute a better asset, after years of further international negotiation. But the conclusion would seem to be that this is hardly worthwhile unless one can foresee a reversion to a fixed-rate system, which would require an acceptable supranational asset. Further thinking and research, which needs to absorb the experience of floating rates, should proceed intensively, so that when there is next a widely perceived need to change the system (or create a system to succeed the present nonsystem), the negotiators will have more expert assessments and a better understanding of both the feasibility of different schemes and of their own advantages and disadvantages than was the case in the late 1960s and early 1970s.

In the meantime, what is so wrong with the present nonsystem? We have already seen that LDCs' fears were very exaggerated, to say the least. To say the most, one can argue with Deepak Lal that it is the best system, for them, or would be if combined with free capital movements.[7] This view can be contrasted with that of Vijay Joshi, who takes a more orthodox line.[8] Freedom of capital movements will seem shocking to many LDCs. To permit capital flight when they are capital hungry may seem crazy. The counter arguments are well presented by Lal,[9] and it should be noted that Mexico and Hong Kong have never used exchange controls, and that Indonesia has abandoned them in recent years. We leave the subject open and suggest also that it is unwise for the governments of LDCs to close their minds.

IMF REFORM

The changes that LDCs have achieved in the IMF in the 1970s have been considerable and beneficial, despite the fact that quotas have lagged far behind inflation. Further increases in quotas are clearly in their interest. Besides this, it is more arguable what further reform would be desirable.

The role of the Fund depends on whether or not it is seen as an institution that should evolve toward being a world central bank. Those who press for this improbable end, which include the LDCs, should probably try to prevent it becoming an aid and development agency; we have seen that it has recently moved in that direction. The two functions will be seen as incompatible by the more powerful countries, whose money and support the Fund most needs.

If one expects an indefinite period of floating rates and a minor role for SDRs, then there is less need to worry about the IMF's increasing involvement in the problems of development. Nevertheless, the Fund should remain the main forum in which matters concerning international monetary and credit arrangements are discussed and negotiated.

The main current demands of LDCs (apart from increasing quotas, and increasing issues of SDRs) are for less conditionality and more control. I find it impossible to agree with a blanket demand for weaker conditions. Some LDCs have borrowed too much, and many have used the proceeds unwisely. A few LDCs, especially Brazil, have been able to ignore the IMF, regarding its conditions as too stringent, and to borrow very large, perhaps excessive, amounts commercially with no conditions. This has been used as an argument for softening IMF conditions; but it applies to few countries, and in any case commercial lenders will probably become more circumspect. It hardly needs to be said that IMF conditions should be appropriate to the conditions and possibilities, both economic and political, of the borrower; but it may often be hard to agree as to what is appropriate.

Lastly there is the question of control. The demand for more voting power for LDCs in both the Fund and the Bank is reiterated in many gatherings. It is an aim of the New International Economic Order to increase control of, and participation in, international decision-making in all bodies (except the GATT). Exactly how much more voting power is not usually specified, but the most recent demand of the Group of Twenty-four was that LDC quotas in the Fund, and therefore voting, should be raised from 33 percent to 45 percent of the total.[10] Increased quotas in the IMF effectively support lending by surplus to deficit countries, and it is to be expected that LDCs, except the "capital surplus" oil exporters, will be the borrowers. There is a danger that the MDCs will be even more reluctant to increase quotas, the greater the shares of the LDCs.

Furthermore, the greater the voice of the LDCs in the Fund, the more likely it is that decisions affecting international currencies would be taken outside the Fund, as has indeed happened during the 1970s. A major interest of LDCs is that the currencies of the MDCs, principally the United States, Germany, Japan, France, and the United Kingdom, should remain convertible and fluctuate as little as possible, that assets held in these countries should be safe, and that their economies should be healthy, so that demand rises and protectionism is reduced. The Fund may play only a very small role in achieving such objectives, but it will play none if LDCs gain control. In short, too much voice can be counterproductive. I would agree with Vijay Joshi:

> It is not in the interest of the developing countries to argue for schemes which would cast doubt on the financial viability of the IMF. There is also not much point in the non-oil-producing developing countries pressing to increase their share of decision-making in the IMF. They will almost certainly fail to do so; and even if they succeed, this will merely shift the focus of important decision-making to smaller groups of economically powerful countries.[11]

An increased voice for LDCs in the Fund, and in the World Bank, would make it more likely that existing demands for more staff jobs for LDC residents would be met,[12] and such jobs would doubtless have to be spread among many LDCs. There would be a considerable danger of reducing the very high level of competence and independence of particular country interests, shown by the staff of these institutions, to that of many other international organizations where people owe their jobs to pressure exerted by their own governments.[13] This would not be in the interests of the LDCs or of the poor of the world.

AID

For welfare, the more aid the better. Aid is a dependency relationship, but reducing dependency on aid is not in the interests of the mass of the people. Aid should be in grant form; this objective is close to achievement. It should be untied, and here there is much room for improvement. The LDCs have a strong case to argue against this form of protectionism.

The main issues are surveillance (discussed in chapter 16) and project versus program aid. The LDCs have no right to expect automatic unsupervised aid. In the case of most LDCs it would probably reduce welfare to eliminate surveillance; and less aid would be forthcoming, since donor governments are responsible to their own constituents, who need assurance that aid does good. Project versus program aid is an old topic. Giving project rather than program aid is the main way of supervising it. The argument that this is illusory, because aid is fully fungible, has very limited validity. If donors reject a bad project, it may still, but not always, get done. The projects that donors do support would often not have been done, or not in the same form, because donors promote and improve projects. For long-run development, there is much in favor of project aid, though some nonproject aid may also be required if a country has worked itself into a position of being starved of current inputs and consumption good imports. This verges on aid for adjustment, where a need for rapid disbursement may also require program aid. All this is well understood. Indiscriminate de-projectization, which is what some LDC spokesmen and sympathizers seem to advocate, might further the end of independence, but not of welfare. Lastly, the fragmentation of aid, associated with the multiplication of funds and institutions, has gone too far.

PRIVATE CREDIT

As far as private credit is concerned, it is in conformity with a liberal international order that national capital markets should be fully open for bond issues by LDCs; and, under floating rates, MDCs have no excuse to maintain barriers. The seriousness of the remaining restrictions has, however, been much reduced by the development of the Eurocurrency market. On the question of private bank lending, it is in the interests of LDCs as a whole that excessive lending to a particular country should not provoke a crisis; but excessive regulation could also be against their interests. We can quote the Group of Twenty-four with approval. As reported in a 1980 IMF Survey, "They stressed the need to keep their [MDC] capital markets free from interference and restrictions, by confining regulation to concerns which were truly prudential in nature."[14]

International Institutions and Issues

The very large number of international meetings—about 6000 every year in New York and Geneva—and the connected documentation—about a million pages a year—have put an enormous burden on member governments, particularly the smaller ones, when they try to contribute effectively to international cooperation; and the permanent secretariats of UN organizations have been saddled with burdens which they were not originally called upon to shoulder. The question may validly be asked whether the existing negotiating mechanism serves to facilitate the development or emergence of the political will that is necessary for major decisions.[15]

This quotation puts the point very mildly. Apart from Geneva and London, there is a lot of business in Paris, Brussels, and Vienna. There are the annual meetings of the Fund and the Bank, and biennial meetings of the Interim Committee of the Fund. Around the world there are the UNCTAD meetings, and Group of Seventy-seven and Group of Twenty-four meetings preparatory to these and to other international confrontations. The Industrial Development Organization and other United Nations agencies have their periodic meetings here and there. There were during the 1970s world conferences on the environment, employment, food, population, science and technology, and the sea (and probably others), most of which created new institutions. This is all apart from the countless more technical negotiations on matters arising, such as commodity agreements. Finally, there is a mass of South-South meetings on regional subjects and "self-reliance."

As the quotation indicates, the smaller countries cannot possibly participate effectively—nor can the largest. Even India with its highly developed civil service cannot do so. Sometimes a representative, usually a diplomat not well versed in technical matters, takes a line that is opposed to the policy of his government at home; but frequently the home government has not considered the matter. A handful of the most persuasive LDC spokesmen, often the more radical, sets the tone. The safe line is one that will result in confrontation, for it is primarily confrontation that sustains the solidarity of the South.

The Group of Seventy-seven, which came into being as a result of UNCTAD I, now consists of about 120 countries. It orchestrates "Southern" solidarity. But Group of Seventy-seven countries are very heterogeneous, and there can be no harmony of interests concerning particular interventions by Northern governments in favor of the South, which is what so-called North-South international negotiation is mainly about. What the South demands emerges from no genuine community of interest but as a function of its heterogeneity, and of the fact that confrontation has become institutionalized, originally in UNCTAD but spreading from there to all major well-publicized international meetings.

The heterogeneity of the South is papered over in various ways. First, some of the demands are very general, lending themselves to rhetoric rather than negotiation; the rhetoric is based on dependency theory—that the poverty of the South is the fault of the North, which is a useful line of argument for domestic consumption. Second, many LDCs fear to disturb solidarity even on particular issues because they are persuaded that solidarity in general serves them well. Third, the whole slate of Southern demands tends to be presented on almost every occasion, in order to ensure that there is something written there for every country. This latter feature results in a rigidity in the Southern position, which makes the now triennial UNCTAD meetings unsuitable as negotiating forums. The Group of Seventy-seven position cannot easily be changed without disturbing a fragile equilibrium, and Group of Seventy-seven delegations do not usually refer back to their home governments. In contrast, there is no preconcerted Group B position, and MDC negotiators can refer back home, where there is a well-staffed bureaucracy monitoring the proceedings, which permits a flexibility that very few LDCs can emulate. Given the ways in which Southern demands are organized, the benevolence of the North should not be measured, as it usually is, by the degree to which it gives way, which is not, however, to say that the North would score well on any scale.

Has the South in fact gained anything of value as a result of solidarity and confrontation? The analysis of this book has proclaimed the answer to be "No!" at least so far as trade is concerned. Pressure in non-UNCTAD assemblies, where confrontation is less pronounced, has been more successful. But LDCs have gained most from GATT negotiations in which their participation has been least. (See especially chapters 14 and 17.)

So what should happen to UNCTAD? The Brandt Commission Report, like myself, sees the creation of an International Trade Organization as being eventually desirable. I have argued that this should, in the interest specifically of LDCs as well as MDCs, build on GATT. UNCTAD could wither away, but only if the Group of Seventy-seven changes its ideas concerning reciprocity and the kind of international trading regime that will be of most benefit to LDCs. This is a chicken and egg problem, for UNCTAD promotes the ideas of the Group of Seventy-seven as well as serving them.

A wholly LDC economic organization, paralleling the Organization for Economic Cooperation and Development, has been mooted. UNCTAD is already largely this. If the MDCs withdrew, that would be that, for the centrally planned economies play a very small part. But would this serve LDC interests? The heterogeneity we have described suggests that, with its confrontational role removed, such an LDC club would achieve little. It would appear more promising to build again on the regional United Nations agencies, and other organizations including the regional banks.

A reduction of confrontation would seem to be in the interests of all. Reduction does not mean elimination. But the number of major issues from which the LDCs may profit is limited. The present system is designed to make confrontation almost continuous, and to extend it to issues that are not merely unimportant but that do not even require international, and certainly not global, solutions. When the Brandt Commission says, "The permanent secretariats of UN organizations have been saddled with burdens which they were not originally called upon to shoulder," that is not the whole truth. United Nations agencies themselves play a major role in the proliferation of issues. I am not opposed to the New International Economic Order demand that the United Nations organization should be strengthened. It has been weakened by excessive ramification. It can now be strengthened only by hard pruning.

The nature of the international scene is important for development, but it is not important enough, and does not offer sufficient scope for constructive policy action, to justify the amount of attention it attracts relative to domestic matters.

Notes

Chapter 1

1. The article is a condensed version of his presidential address to the Society for International Development in 1969.
2. I. M. D. Little, *A Critique of Welfare Economics* (Oxford: Clarendon Press, 1950), p. 219.
3. H. Leibenstein, *Economic Backwardness and Economic Growth* (New York: John Wiley & Sons, 1957), p. 9.
4. Strictly speaking, this is wrong. An output index does not have utility implications. See P. A. Samuelson, "Evaluation of Real National Income" (Oxford Economic Papers, 1950).
5. Leibenstein, *Economic Backwardness*, p. 9.
6. In Little, *Critique of Welfare Economics*, I successfully exorcised the word "optimum." No one now uses this word without qualification. They use the phrase "Pareto optimum," which I introduced.
7. G. Myrdal, *Asian Drama: An Inquiry into the Poverty of Nations* (London: Allen Lane, 1968), p. 33.
8. Myrdal in practice fails to do this. Thus, in *Asian Drama* he begins by enunciating a set of rather vaguely worded value premises. But the body of the work is replete with further value judgments, often probably unconscious, which certainly do not derive from his stated value premises.
9. See J. Rawls, *A Theory of Justice* (Oxford: Clarendon Press, 1972).
10. The liberal economists' assimilation of "development" to "welfare" constitutes a persuasive use of language, which is new as compared with the usage of colonial economists and writers before World War II. J. S. Furnivall, in his books on Burma and the Netherlands East Indies, drew a sharp distinction between the two. By "development" he meant opening up a country and subjecting it to the free play of world economic forces so that it began to make some contribution to *world* income. "Welfare" meant, roughly, the standard of living of the natives. He argued strongly that development was usually inimical to welfare. His books are a rich mine for "de-

linkers." In the British Colonial Development and Welfare Acts of the 1930s and 1940s, the two words were probably not thought of as synonymous. Some element of Furnivall's idea of development may still have been lurking. But we can take it that few nowadays would subscribe to such a meaning.

11. We ignore any allowance for changes in the amount of work: this can be allowed for, and is left out only to simplify the prose.

12. W. A. Lewis, *The Theory of Economic Growth* (London: Allen & Unwin, 1955). It should be noted that, in this quotation, Lewis uses "freedom" in the positive sense. Thus, a widening of the range of practically possible choices is regarded as an increase of liberty. See I. Berlin, "Two Concepts of Liberty," in I. Berlin, *Four Essays on Liberty* (London: Oxford University Press, 1969).

13. See A. Nove, *An Economic History of the USSR* (London: Allen Lane, 1969), p. 207.

14. See A. Kahan in *Agriculture in Economic Development*, ed. C. Eicher and L. Witt (New York: McGraw-Hill Book Co., 1964).

15. P. C. Mahalanobis, "Science and National Planning," Sankhya, *The Indian Journal of Statistics* 20 (September 1958): Parts 1 and 2, Statistical Publishing Society, Calcutta, India.

16. M. Lipton, *Why Poor People Stay Poor: Urban Bias in World Development* (London: Temple Smith, 1977).

17. See D. Goulet in *The Political Economy of Development and Underdevelopment*, ed. C. K. Wilber (New York: Random House, 1973).

18. We return to the subject of basic needs in chapter 11.

Chapter 2

1. See W. J. Baumol, *Economic Dynamics, An Introduction* (New York: Macmillan, 1959).

2. H. B. Chenery, "The Structuralist Approach to Economic Development," *American Economic Review*, May 1965.

3. J. B. P. Molière, *Le Bourgeois Gentilhomme*, ed. F. M. Warren (Boston: D. C. Heath & Co., 1899).

4. Chenery, "Structuralist Approach to Economic Development," p. 310.

5. This was the inspiration and purpose of Chenery's many structural studies which sought to chart the future by exploring the present.

6. See J. A. Schumpeter, *History of Economic Analysis* (New York: Oxford University Press, 1959), pp. 464–467.

7. D. W. Jorgenson, "The Development of a Dual Economy," *Economic Journal*, June 1961.

8. See R. M. Solow, *Capital Theory and the Rate of Return* (Amsterdam: North Holland Publishing Co., 1964).

9. The rate of profit, in our story, continues to fall despite the defensive action of inventing and adopting more capital-intensive techniques. This part of the theoretical story may not be historically true. But even if there are other factors maintaining the rate of profit, such as biased technical progress, higher real wages remain as an incentive to finding and using labor-saving techniques.

10. For an understandable and good account of reswitching, see J. Hicks, *Capital and Time* (Oxford: Clarendon Press, 1973), chap. 4.

11. I was in Taiwan at a time when real wages were rising rapidly. Every businessman I asked—about a dozen—had plans to save labor by increasing capital intensity.

Chapter 3

1. A refinement of this, to take care of falling cost industries, is the marginal cost

production rule for public industries, which gave rise to a long controversy, especially in the United Kingdom after the wave of nationalization undertaken by the first postwar Labor Government. (See A. P. Lerner, "Economic Theory and Socialist Economy," *Review of Economic Studies* 2, [October 1934] 51-61.) Such rules cannot be applied to public goods that are not sold to individual consumers or corporations; budgets are required in order to control expenditures in these cases. It should also be noted that a decentralization strategy does not preclude some macroeconomic management.

2. E. Barone in *Collectivist Economic Planning*, ed. F. A. von Hayek (Fairfield, N.J.: Augustus M. Kelley, 1967).

3. O. Lange, "On the Economic Theory of Socialism," *Review of Economic Studies*, October 1936.

4. Lerner, "Economic Theory and Socialist Economy."

5. The fact that future prices are unknown, and futures markets limited, is a much discussed reason why the price mechanism may sometimes work poorly. Indicative planning can be seen as an attempt to reduce this uncertainty, as also can private futures contracts and other methods by which firms seek to reduce uncertainty.

6. E. Devons, *Planning in Practice* (Cambridge: Cambridge University Press, 1950).

7. C. A. R. Crosland, *Britain's Economic Problem* (London: Jonathan Cape, 1953). The first sentence of the concluding chapter reads, "The whole emphasis of this book has been on the structural nature of the economic problems facing the United Kingdom."

8. O. Franks, *Central Planning and Control in War and Peace* (Cambridge, Mass.: Harvard University Press, 1947). For a formidable critique of Franks's views, see J. E. Meade, *Planning and the Price Mechanism* (London: Allen & Unwin, 1948).

9. The main exception was T. Balogh, *Dollar Crisis, Causes and Cure* (Oxford: Basil Blackwell, 1949).

10. Meade, *Planning and the Price Mechanism*; W. A. Lewis, *The Principles of Economic Planning* (London: Dennis Dobson, 1949). A notable article is by Hubert Henderson, "The Price System," *Economic Journal* 58 (December 1948): 467-482.

11. Harrod, *Are These Hardships Necessary?* (London: Hart-Davis, 1947).

12. It is interesting that the more structural planners in Britain later became peers (Balogh, Franks, Kahn), while the price mechanism planners got knighthoods and Nobel prizes (Hicks, Lewis, Meade). Except for Sir Roy Harrod, antiplanners got nothing.

13. P. Rosenstein Rodan, "Problems of Industrialization of Eastern and South Eastern Europe," *Economic Journal*, June-September 1943.

14. T. Scitovsky, "Two Concepts of External Economies," *Journal of Political Economy*, April 1954. Both the Rosenstein Rodan and Scitovsky articles are reprinted in A. N. Agarwala and S. P. Singh, eds., *The Economics of Underdevelopment* (London: Oxford University Press, 1958).

15. A. Hirschman, *The Strategy of Economic Development* (New Haven, Conn.: Yale University Press, 1958).

16. See P. Rosenstein Rodan in *Economic Development for Latin America*, ed. H. S. Ellis (London: Macmillan, 1961).

17. J. E. Meade, "External Economies and Diseconomies in a Competitive Situation," *Economic Journal*, March 1952.

18. Although he might not agree with this sentence, Scitovsky himself came to be embarrassed by what he considered to be the many misuses to which his argument was put. He was horrified to see how often wrong investment decisions were made and justified in less developed countries in the name of correcting the error he had pointed out. (Personal communication.)

19. Most manufacturing firms, even quite small ones, are usually in an oligopolistic situation. There is then little reason to suppose that the market will induce optimum investment decisions (supposing, which is doubtful, that an optimum can be defined). But there is also no reason to suppose that a central decision-maker, who can never know as much relevant detail as to the circumstances of producers or the requirements of users as these latter know themselves, would do better.

20. H. B. Chenery, "The Role of Industrialization in Development Programmes,"

387

American Economic Review, May 1955. Reprinted in *Economics of Underdevelopment*, ed. Agarwala and Singh.
21. Agarwala and Singh, eds., *Economics of Underdevelopment*, p. 451.
22. Ibid., pp. 467-468.
23. Of course, Harrod was neither a Marxist nor a structuralist himself!
24. T. Swan, "Economic Growth and Capital Accumulation," *Economic Record*, November 1956.
25. R. M. Solow, "A Contribution to the Theory of Economic Growth," *Quarterly Journal of Economics*, February 1956.
26. N. Kaldor, "Alternative Theories of Distribution," *Review of Economic Studies* 23 (1955-56).
27. R. S. Eckaus, "The Factor Proportions Problem in Underdeveloped Countries," *American Economic Review*, September 1955. Reprinted in *Economics of Underdevelopment*, ed. Agarwala and Singh.
28. As developed in Hirschman, *Strategy of Economic Development*.
29. A. O. Hirschman, "A Generalized Linkage Approach to Development, with Special Reference to Staples," *Economic Development and Cultural Change* 25, supplement (1977). In this article, Hirschman is, as the title implies, much more concerned with agricultural linkages. Earlier, he had industry primarily in mind.
30. Ibid., p. 81.
31. A. O. Hirschman, *A Bias for Hope* (New Haven, Conn.: Yale University Press, 1971), chap. 1. Hirschman's view seems to have been close to the reality of French planning, as contrasted to the French theory of indicative planning. Also, as we shall see later, recent admiration for Japanese and Korean planning is for their sectoral and project planning, not for their overall consistency planning, which has been as counterindicative as in most other countries.
32. H. B. Chenery and T. Watanabe, "International Comparisons of the Structure of Production," *Econometric*, October 1958.
33. There have been various attempts to test Hirschman's hypothesis, correlating performance with imbalance, using input/output methods. As Leroy Jones has pointed out in "The Measurement of Hirschmanian Linkages," *Quarterly Journal of Economics*, May 1976, input/output tables are far too aggregated to catch the linkages that might exist. Perhaps Hirschman now regrets having inserted his notion into an input/output framework. It is also worth noting that his later development of the "linkage" concept plainly embraces pecuniary effects. (Hirschman, "Generalized Linkage Approach to Development.")
34. Hirschman, *Bias for Hope*.
35. This assumption is also called into question by J. Riedel, "A Balanced-Growth Version of the Linkage Hypothesis," *Quarterly Journal of Economics*, May 1976.
36. Crude criteria may be useful, however, as a rough guide as to where to probe more deeply when searching for desirable projects.
37. W. Galenson and H. Leibenstein, "Investment Criteria, Productivity and Economic Development," *Quarterly Journal of Economics*, August 1955.
38. A. K. Sen, *Choice of Techniques* (Oxford: Basil Blackwell, 1960).
39. A translation was published by E. Domar as "A Soviet Model of Growth," in *Essays in the Theory of Economic Growth*, ed. E. Domar (New York: Oxford University Press, 1957).
40. Various models have been used in Indian planning. See A. Rudra, *Indian Plan Models* (Delhi: Allied Publishers, 1975).
41. A. H. Hanson, *The Process of Planning* (London: Oxford University Press, 1956), p. 38.
42. Ibid., p. 48.
43. Ibid., p. 49.
44. Most notoriously, Daniel Moynihan, *A Dangerous Place* (Boston: Little, Brown & Co., 1978).
45. S. Gopal, *Jawaharlal Nehru—A Biography*, vol. 1 (London: Jonathan Cape, 1975), p. 100.
46. Ibid., p. 202.

47. See W. B. Reddaway, *The Development of the Indian Economy* (London: Allen & Unwin, 1962).
48. J. Bhagwati and P. Desai, *India—Planning for Industrialization* (London: Oxford University Press, 1970), p. 236.
49. See B. R. Nayar, *The Modernization Imperative and Indian Planning* (Delhi: Vikas Publishers, 1972).
50. I. M. D. Little, "The Strategy of Indian Development," *National Institute Economic Review*, May 1960.
51. H. B. Chenery and M. Bruno, "Development Alternatives in an Open Economy: The Case of Israel," *Economic Journal*, March 1962.
52. But I have not done justice to all the work, especially the Indian work, on the economics, politics, and administration of Indian planning in the formative years. Hanson, *Process of Planning*, contains many references. Also see J. Bhagwati and S. Chakravarty, "Contributions to Indian Economic Analysis, A Survey," *American Economic Review Supplement*, September 1969.
53. On early Asian planning, see E. S. Mason, *Economic Planning in Underdeveloped Areas* (New York: Fordham University Press, 1958). On Pakistan, see Mahbub ul Haq, *The Strategy of Economic Planning* (Lahore: Oxford University Press, 1963).
54. But Chilean planning can be traced back to 1939 and the establishment of the National Development Corporation (CORFO). Since then, the process has been very intermittent. See E. Boeninger and O. Sunkel in *The Crisis in Planning*, ed. M. Faber and D. Seers (London: Chatto & Windus, 1972). Mexico, and maybe other countries, also drew up plans in the 1930s, but without allowing for the machinery to implement them.
55. See the remarks of Dr. Pazos in Faber and Seers, eds., *Crisis in Planning*, pp. 160-162.
56. See also, A. Waterston, *Development Planning Lessons of Experience* (Baltimore, Md.: Johns Hopkins University Press, 1965), pp. 36, 67, 103. On Brazil, see Roberto de Oliveira Campos in *The Economy of Brazil*, ed. H. Ellis (Berkeley and Los Angeles: University of California Press, 1969).
57. W. A. Lewis, ed., *Tropical Development 1880-1913* (London: Allen & Unwin, 1970); W. A. Lewis, *Growth and Fluctuation 1870-1913* (London: Allen & Unwin, 1978).
58. United Nations, Department of Economic Affairs, *Measures for the Economic Development of Underdeveloped Countries* (New York: United Nations, 1951).
59. A. Nove, *An Economic History of the USSR* (London: Allen & Unwin, 1969), chap. 7.
60. G. Myrdal, *Development and Underdevelopment* (Cairo: National Bank of Egypt, 1956). These lectures also formed the basis of *Economic Theory and Underdeveloped Regions* (London: Duckworth, 1957).
61. Myrdal, *Development and Underdevelopment*, p. 65.
62. Ibid., p. 68.
63. Ibid.

Chapter 4

1. This debate is described in more detail in chapter 14.
2. For an account of the Australian case and references, see P. A. Samuelson, "Summing Up of the Australian Case for Protection," *Quarterly Journal of Economics*, February 1981.
3. T. Balogh, *Dollar Crisis, Causes and Cure* (Oxford: Basil Blackwell, 1949).
4. G. D. A. McDougall, *The World Dollar Problem* (London: Macmillan 1957).
5. R. Nurkse, *Problems of Capital Formation in Underdeveloped Countries* (Oxford: Basil Blackwell, 1955).
6. Ibid., esp. chap. 6.
7. H. Singer, "The Distribution of Gains between Investing and Borrowing Countries," *American Economic Review*, Papers and Proceedings, May 1950.

8. United Nations, Department of Economic Affairs, *Relative Prices of Exports and Imports of Under-developed Countries* (New York: United Nations, 1949).
9. See also ibid., *The Economic Development of Latin America and Its Principal Problems,* 1950.
10. See chapter 9, notes 47 and 48, for references.
11. We saw in chapter 3 that the LDC ITO negotiators had already used this argument.
12. For an account of ECLA's doctrine and influence, see A. O. Hirschman in *Latin American Issues: Essays and Comments,* ed. A. O. Hirschman (New York: Twentieth Century Fund, 1961), and reprinted in A. O. Hirschman, *A Bias for Hope* (New Haven: Yale University Press, 1971).
13. Excluding oil and nonferrous metals, the share of LDCs in world primary commodity trade fell almost continuously from one half in 1950 to one third in 1971.
14. G. Myrdal, *Development and Underdevelopment* (Cairo: National Bank of Egypt, 1956), chap. 13.
15. Ibid., p. 275. Italics in original.
16. Ibid., p. 283.
17. Myrdal's later treatment of the subject in *Asian Drama: An Inquiry into the Poverty of Nations* (London: Allen Lane, 1968), Appendix 8, is not very different. Linguistically, it sounds more in favor of quantitative planning, but this is because he refers to "planning through the price mechanism" as the use of nondiscretionary controls—so that any tax or subsidy is a nondiscretionary control. Instability of export earnings is no longer stressed as a reason for import quotas. Thus, despite initial appearances to the contrary, *Asian Drama* is to some extent a plea for planning by the price mechanism. On the other hand, his insistence both in *Asian Drama* and the earlier *Development and Underdevelopment* on the need for government to take responsibility for the entire economic development of the country, including changing peoples' attitudes and customs, is not easy to reconcile with the more relaxed posture of a government that sought to steer the economy mainly by monetary incentives.
18. G. Haberler, "Some Problems in the Pure Theory of International Trade," *Economic Journal,* June 1950.
19. He did not put the argument in terms of subsistence minimum, as I have done for the convenience of relating it to the deindustrialization argument. He rather assumed factor price rigidity at some higher level. But formally, there is no difference.
20. T. Balogh, "Welfare and Freer Trade, A Reply," *Economic Journal,* March 1951.
21. For a discussion of the Indian case, see I. M. D. Little in *Essays in Honor of W. Arthur Lewis,* ed. M. Gersowitz (London: Allen & Unwin, forthcoming).
22. P. A. Baran, *The Political Economy of Growth* (New York: Monthly Review Press, 1957). See esp. chap. 5.
23. J. Viner, *International Trade and Economic Development* (Oxford: Clarendon Press, 1953).
24. Ibid., pp. 41–42.
25. Ibid., p. 44.
26. Ibid., p. 51.
27. Ibid., p. 79.
28. Some economists in Latin America also dissented strongly from Prebisch-ECLA views. Hirschman in his "Ideologies of Economic Development in Latin America" (see note 12) cites, for instance, Eugenio Gudin and Roberto Campos, both from Brazil. No doubt there were many others. In other continents, there were in the 1950s few developing country economists to debate such issues. But, as we saw in chapter 3, Indian thinking was quite similar to that of Prebisch.

Chapter 5

1. J. Grunwald in *Latin American Issues: Essays and Comments,* ed. A. O. Hirschman (New York: Twentieth Century Fund, 1961).

2. But there were earlier signs of structuralism in Brazil. See T. E. Skidmore, *Politicas in Brazil 1930-1964* (New York: Oxford University Press, 1967). This work also contains accounts of the relations between Brazil and the IMF.

3. This is not the only reason why inflations tend to accelerate. An exogenous shock (for example, the price of oil) must raise the level of prices, if no prices are flexible downward. In thus raising the level, it necessarily accelerates the rate of inflation of prices, just as a car has to accelerate to go from 30 mph to 50 mph. If wages are geared to past price rises, then the rate of increase of wages also rises; and then the higher rate of inflation becomes perpetual. The combination of external shocks, which reduce national income (and which are inevitable from time to time), and real incomes, which can be compressed only by increases in the rate of inflation, condemns an economy to such increases.

4. This was later brought out with great clarity by Carlos Diaz Alejandro in his analysis of the Prebisch and IMF stabilization attempts in Argentina in the 1950s. See C. Diaz Alejandro, *Exchange Rate Devaluation in a Semi-Industrialized Country* (Cambridge, Mass.: MIT Press, 1965).

5. This list is taken from D. Seers, "A Theory of Inflation and Growth in Underdeveloped Economies Based on the Experiences of Latin America," *Oxford Economic Papers*, June 1962. Seers had nothing to say about what should be done during the many years that must elapse before such measures could be effective.

6. Raouf Kahil writes of Brazil, ". . . no compelling force stemming from structural weaknesses in the economy ever played a significant role in the persistence or aggravation of inflationary pressures. At no time, not even during the severe droughts that afflicted the northeast, or when coffee price-support policies led to government mass purchases of surplus stocks, were public deficits chiefly due to substantial increases in expenditure the government was compelled to incur. Still less were deficits caused by too slow an increase in public revenue in relation to the fast growing economy: quite the contrary, from 1947 to 1960 revenue increased so rapidly in real terms that it almost trebled while GDP only doubled." R. Kahil, *Inflation and Economic Development in Brazil 1946-1963* (Oxford: Clarendon Press, 1973), p. 330.

Kahil concludes that structuralist factors played little part, and that inflation was initiated by exogenous government expenditures that were undertaken largely for political reasons and many of which were of doubtful developmental worth; and also, during the 1950s, by minimum wage increases that were far in excess of the cost-of-living increases and so could hardly be said to be determined by them.

7. See Grunwald in *Latin American Issues*, ed. Hirschman.

8. See R. Campos in *Latin American Issues*, ed. Hirschman. Campos was finance minister of Brazil from 1964-67.

9. D. Felix in *Inflation and Growth in Latin America*, ed. W. Baer and I. Kerstenetsky (Chicago: R. D. Irwin, 1964).

10. The "trotting peg" is a name for a policy of frequent small devaluations. It is distinguished from "floating" in that an official rate is designated.

11. But by 1962, the IMF apparently encouraged Chile to adopt a trotting peg. See J. Williamson, *The Failure of World Monetary Reform, 1971-1974* (New York: New York University Press, 1977), p. 6.

12. This may apply to the IMF, but hardly to Roberto Campos, for example, one of the architects of the gradualist approach in Brazil in the 1960s.

13. For example, Diaz Alejandro, *Exchange Rate Devaluation*; and Felix in *Inflation and Growth in Latin America*, ed. Baer and Kerstenetsky.

14. Diaz Alejandro, *Exchange Rate Devaluation*, p. 145.

15. See Campos in *Latin American Issues*, ed. Hirschman.

16. For an implicit defense of this position in the Brazilian case, see A. Fishlow in *Authoritarian Brazil*, ed. A. Stepan (New Haven, Conn.: Yale University Press, 1973). Brazil achieved approximately 9 percent per annum growth from 1967 to 1973 with "only" about 20 percent per annum inflation. But it is far from clear that this would have been possible without the deflationary period of 1964-67, when inflation was reduced from 100 percent to 8 percent (in one quarter). Subsequently, inflation has risen again to 40-50 percent per annum.

Chapter 6

1. J. H. Boeke, *Economics and Economic Policy of Dual Societies* (New York: International Sectariat, Institute of Pacific Relations, 1953).
2. W. A. Lewis, "Economic Development with Unlimited Supply of Labour," *The Manchester School*, May 1954.
3. This vision of the world was incorporated in the influential UN document, Department of Economic Affairs, *Measures for the Economic Development of Underdeveloped Countries*, 1951.
4. J. L. Buck, *Chinese Farm Policy* (Chicago: University of Chicago Press, 1930).
5. D. Warriner, *Economics of Peasant Farming* (London: Oxford University Press, 1939).
6. These early studies have been reviewed by C. H. C. Kao, K. R. Anschel, and C. K. Eicher in *Agriculture in Economic Development*, ed. C. K. Eicher and L. Witt (New York: McGraw-Hill Book Co., 1964).
7. M. Dobb, *Some Aspects of Economic Development, Three Lectures* (New Delhi: Ranjit Publishers, 1951). The second and most relevant of these lectures is reprinted in M. Dobb, *Capitalism, Development and Planning* (London: Routledge & Kegan Paul, 1967). It is notable that Dobb in this lecture clearly anticipated Scitovsky's pecuniary externality argument.
8. R. Nurkse, *Problems of Capital Formation in Underdeveloped Countries* (Oxford: Basil Blackwell, 1953). This book was mainly based on lectures given in Rio de Janeiro in 1951.
9. Ibid., pp. 36-47.
10. Later, A. K. Sen was to point out that zero marginal productivity of labor was neither necessary nor sufficient for surplus labor. What was required was that the supply curve of labor hours should be perfectly elastic at the going level of earnings; or, in plain language, that the remaining members of the family would willingly do the work the departing member had previously done. See A. K. Sen, "Peasants and Dualism with or without Surplus Labor," *Journal of Political Economy*, October 1966.
11. H. Leibenstein, *Economic Backwardness and Economic Growth* (New York: John Wiley & Sons, 1957); H. Leibenstein, "The Theory of Underemployment in Backward Economies," *Journal of Political Economies*, April 1957.
12. Although permanent "farm-servants" exist—for example, in India—the dominant form of employment of landless laborers is casual. The seasonal nature of agriculture implies that it is unlikely to be profitable for a landowner to secure all his required labor by permanent employment.
13. D. Mazumdar, "The Marginal Productivity Theory of Wages and Disguised Unemployment," *Review of Economic Studies*, 1959.
14. In the same article, Mazumdar, however, points out that if the earnings elasticity of work units were greater than one, then the wage bill would be reduced for an unchanged output. In other words, the total consumption of agricultural laborers would fall, and the consumption of the departing laborers would, in part, be thereby financed.
15. Kao, Anschel, and Eicher in *Agriculture in Economic Development*, ed. Eicher and Witt, p. 141.
16. Lewis, "Economic Development with Unlimited Supply of Labour."
17. But Myint has introduced a different notion of surplus labor that would apply to countries with surplus land, and where the marginal product of labor is certainly not zero and may be presumed to equal the average product. (See H. Myint, "The Classical Theory of Trade and Underdeveloped Countries," *Economic Journal*, June 1958; reprinted in *Economic Policy for Development*, ed. I. Livingstone [London: Penguin, 1971].) In a pretrade situation, one can imagine an equilibrium in which a limited range of consumption goods was a factor in determining a leisurely life. The opening of trade implied that rice, say, could now be exchanged for more kinds of things than previously. A new equilibrium might be established in which the people worked harder and produced more (land being no obstacle). It was argued that only surplus land and human resources could account for the rapid increases of peasant

export production—for example, cocoa in Ghana, groundnuts in Senegal, and rice in Burma—which occurred in the late nineteenth and early twentieth centuries without apparently much or even any fall in production for home use. This idea, which has been found acceptable to some economic historians (for example, A. G. Hopkins, *An Economic History of West Africa* [London: Longman, 1973], pp. 231-236), must be sharply distinguished from the surplus labor concept already discussed. In the latter case, surplus labor also implied that peasants would work more—but there was no increase in the marginal utility of whatever the work was exchanged for to compensate for the rising marginal disutility of work that must surely be assumed.

18. Nor is it a necessary condition. As we have seen, A. K. Sen showed that zero marginal productivity is neither necessary nor sufficient for surplus labor. We may add to this that surplus labor is neither sufficient nor necessary for unlimited supplies of labor.

19. See W. A. Lewis, "Reflections on Unlimited Labor." Whether or not the standard of living of workers rose is hotly contested (see the debate between R. M. Hartwell, *Economic History Review* 13: 397-416; 16:135-146; April 1961, August 1963, and E. J. Hobsbawm, *Economic History Review*, 16:119-134, August 1963). But it is possible that living standards rose even while the real wage was constant.

20. For a strong statement along these lines, see L. Spaventa, "Dualism in Economic Growth," Banca Nazionale del Lavoro, *Quarterly Review*, December 1959.

21. W. A. Lewis, "Unlimited Labor: Further Notes," *The Manchester School* (1958).

22. Ibid., p. 9.

23. N. Georgescu-Roegen in *Agriculture in Economic Development*, ed. Eicher and Witt.

24. The two parts need not add up to the whole. Certain working arrangements, such as worker-controlled enterprises, do not easily fit into the dichotomy.

25. But Dobb in *Some Aspects of Economic Development*, emphasized the marketed surplus more than the labor surplus. However, he did not argue that there was a consequential need to assume agricultural growth, but rather stressed that the marketed surplus depended on institutional and organizational factors, as one might expect of a Communist.

26. W. A. Lewis, *The Theory of Economic Growth* (London: Allen & Unwin, 1955), pp. 277-283.

27. N. Kaldor, *Essays on Economic Growth and Stability* (London: Duckworth, 1960), p. 242.

28. Nurkse, *Problems of Capital Formation*, p. 55.

29. United Nations, *Measures for the Economic Development of Underdeveloped Countries*; also quoted with approval by Nurkse, *Problems of Capital Formation*, p. 53.

30. Lewis, "Economic Development with Unlimited Supply of Labour," assumed Indian population growth to be 1 percent per annum. In both the First and Second Plan documents (1952 and 1956), the Planning Commission assumed 1.25 percent for the 1950s. The 1961 census showed it to have been 2.0 percent. It was only by the time of the Third Plan that projections began to be right, or even a little too high.

31. See F. Dovring in *Agriculture in Economic Development*, ed. Eicher and Witt.

Chapter 7

1. H. Leibenstein, *Economic Backwardness and Economic Growth* (New York: John Wiley & Sons, 1957), chap. 3.

2. H. Myint, *The Economics of the Developing Countries*, 4th rev. ed. (London: Hutchinson & Co., 1973), chap. 7, provides an excellent critique of these theories.

3. To give but one example, W. A. Lewis, *The Theory of Economic Growth* (London: Allen & Unwin, 1955) devoted thirty-three pages to "the will to economize," 106 pages to "economic institutions," and 36 pages to "knowledge" before coming to the subject of "capital" (102 pages).

4. E. Hagen, *On the Theory of Social Change* (Homewood, Ill.: Dorsey Press, 1962).

5. Lewis, *Theory of Economic Growth*, pp. 142-143.

6. Ibid., p. 144.

7. M. Olson, *The Rise and Decline of Nations: Economic Growth, Stagflation, and Social Rigidities* (New Haven, Conn.: Yale University Press, forthcoming).

8. W. Rostow, *The Stages of Economic Growth* (Cambridge: Cambridge University Press, 1960). The main ideas had already been published in Rostow, "The Take-off into Self-sustained Growth," *Economic Journal*, March 1956. Indeed, the notion of "take-off" was adumbrated still earlier. (See Rostow, *The Process of Economic Growth* [London: Oxford University Press, 1953].)

9. S. Kuznets in *The Economics of Sustained Growth*, ed. W. Rostow (London: Macmillan, 1963); A. Fishlow, "Empty Economic Stages," *Economic Journal*, March 1965 (this article reviewed Rostow, ed., *Economics of Sustained Growth*); G. Ohlin, "Reflection on the Rostow Doctrine," *Economic Development and Cultural Change*, July 1961; A. Cairncross, *Factors in Economic Development* (London: Allen & Unwin, 1962); H. J. Habbakuk, "The Stages of Economic Growth" [Review of W. Rostow], *Economic Journal*, September 1961; A. Gerschenkron in *The Economics of Take-Off into Sustained Growth*, ed. W. W. Rostow.

10. Rotation is when the pilot pulls back the joystick (this old-fashioned name for the control column seems appropriate), and the aircraft changes its altitude.

11. Rostow, *Stages of Economic Growth*, pp. 52–57.

12. Fishlow, "Empty Economic Stages," p. 122.

13. Anyway, a production impetus given merely by increasing demand (for example, for iron) does not constitute a linkage.

14. Cairncross, *Factors in Economic Development*, argued that it was not large enough! Anyway, wherein lay the externalities? This was probably what worried Rostow.

15. See C. Eicher and L. Witt, eds., *Agriculture in Economic Development* (New York: McGraw-Hill Book Co., 1964).

16. D. Warriner, ibid; W. A. Lewis, ibid.

17. Excluding work on foreign trade in agricultural products, and on price stability, which was considerable.

18. P. C. Joshi, *Land Reforms in India* (Delhi: Allied Publishers Private, 1975), which contains a large bibliography on land reform and related matters; or J. Bhagwati and S. Chakravarty, "Contributions to Indian Economic Analysis, A Survey," *American Economic Review* Supplement, September 1969, and Delhi: Lalvani Publishing House, 1971.

19. B. Johnston, "Agricultural Productivity and Economic Development in Japan," *Journal of Political Economy*, December 1951.

20. Arthur Lewis was the exception. See, for example, his short but enlightening section on agriculture in Lewis, *Theory of Economic Growth*.

21. See T. Killick, *Development Economics in Action* (New York: St. Martin's Press, 1978), pp. 188–195.

22. U. Lele, *The Design of Rural Development, Lessons from Africa* (Baltimore, Md.: Johns Hopkins University Press, 1975).

23. G. Ohlin, *Population Control and Economic Development* (Paris: Organization for Economic Cooperation and Development, Development Centre, 1967).

24. Lewis, *Theory of Economic Growth*, p. 314.

25. For example, P. Streeten in *Towards a New Strategy for Development*, ed. P. Streeten (New York: Pergamon Press, 1979).

26. A. Coale and E. Hoover, *Population Growth and Economic Development in Low Income Countries* (Princeton, N.J.: Princeton University Press, 1958).

27. Simon Kuznets has argued (in "Population Change and Aggregate Output," an essay originally published in 1960 and reprinted in S. Kuznets, *Economic Growth and Structure* [London: Heinemann, 1965]) that population growth may increase output per head, but he did not think that his arguments applied to developing countries. Characteristically, A. O. Hirschman argued in *The Strategy of Economic Development* (New Haven, Conn.: Yale University Press, 1958) that population growth might constitute a challenge that would produce an overcompensating response.

28. Optimum population is normally defined as that level that maximizes income per head. But this level is not uniquely defined by natural endowments and technology. It will, for instance, depend on the distribution of wealth, especially land.

Moreover, from an ethical point of view, it is not clear why the optimum population should be so defined. Another attractive definition would be that the optimum population is that which results from people having the number of children they want.

29. For example, in R. Titmuss and B. Smith, *Social Policies and Population Control in Mauritius* (London: Methuen, 1961) and P. Newman, *Malaria Eradication and Population Growth* (Ann Arbor, Mich.: University of Michigan Press, 1965).

30. For instance, Ohlin's bibliography for *Population Control and Economic Development* contains nearly nothing dating from the 1950s. He saw a remarkable volte face beginning in the early 1960s.

31. U. Tun Wai, "Interest Rates Outside the Organized Money Markets of Underdeveloped Countries," International Monetary Fund, *Staff Papers*, 1957-58.

32. G. Rosen, *Industrial Finance in India* (Bombay: Asia Publishing House, 1962).

33. Banks were never mentioned in Indian plans until after Mrs. Gandhi nationalized them in 1969.

34. An early discussion of selective credit controls is I. G. Patel's "Selective Credit Controls in Underdeveloped Countries," International Monetary Fund, *Staff Papers*, September 1954.

35. An exception was J. G. Gurley and E. S. Shaw, "Financial Aspects of Economic Development," *American Economic Review*, September 1955.

36. See B. F. Kiker, "The Historical Roots of the Concept of Human Capital," *Journal of Political Economy Supplement*, October 1966.

37. See, for example, M. Blaugh, *An Introduction to the Economics of Education* (London: Penguin, 1970), chap. 1.

38. D. C. McClelland, *The Achieving Society* (Princeton, N.J.: D. Van Nostrand, 1961).

39. Hagen, *On the Theory of Social Change*.

40. For the argument that political idealism better explains American foreign policy than does self-interest, see S. Krasner, *Defending the National Interest* (Princeton, N.J.: Princeton University Press, 1978).

41. I. M. D. Little and J. M. Clifford, *International Aid* (London: Allen and Unwin, 1965), pp. 79-83; also see G. Ohlin, *Foreign Aid Policies Reconsidered* (Paris: Organization for Economic Cooperation and Development, Development Centre, 1966), p. 19.

42. Millikan and W. Rostow in U.S. Congress, Senate, Special Committee to Study the Foreign Aid Program, *A Proposal: Key to an Effective Foreign Policy*, 1957.

43. See G. Ohlin, *Foreign Aid Policies Reconsidered*.

44. Ibid., chap. 2, contains a good brief account of aid doctrines in the 1950s and first half of the 1960s, including, besides the United Nations and the United States, those of France, the United Kingdom, the Netherlands, Sweden, Norway, Denmark, Japan, the European Economic Community, and the "Soviet bloc."

45. It is difficult to separate the two: land-settlement schemes may be regarded as local land reforms.

46. United Nations, Department of Economic Affairs, *Land Reform, Defects in Agrarian Structure as Obstacles to Economic Development* (New York: United Nations, 1951).

47. Reprinted with omissions as "Land Reform and Economic Development," in *Agriculture in Economic Development*.

48. Warriner seems to have had a blind spot. Even her 1969 book *Land Reform in Principle and Practice* (Oxford: Clarendon Press) takes no account of them. The Taiwan reforms had been described in a number of publications of the JCRR.

49. R. P. Dore, *Land Reform in Japan* (London: Oxford University Press, 1959).

50. Item 14 in L. J. Walinsky, ed., *Agrarian Reform as Unfinished Business, the Selected Papers of Wolf Ladejinsky* (New York: Oxford University Press, 1977). Ladejinsky also reported to the Planning Commission on Indian land reform in the early 1950s, but these reports were not published. See also Items 18-23.

51. Joshi, *Land Reforms in India*.

52. W. A. Lewis in *Agriculture in Economic Development*, ed. Eicher and Witt.

53. A. Gaitskell, *Gezira: A Story of Development in the Sudan* (London: Faber & Faber, 1959). For a brief account, see A. Gaitskell in *Rural Development in a Changing World*, ed. R. Weitz (Cambridge: MIT Press, 1971).

54. A good reference for contemporary thought on the role of taxation is the

United Nations, Department of Economic Affairs, *Taxes and Fiscal Policy in Underdeveloped Countries*, 3rd ed. (New York: United Nations, 1955). Part I by Walter W. Heller is republished as chapter 1 of R. M. Bird and O. Oldman, eds., *Readings on Taxation in Developing Countries*, 3rd ed. (Baltimore, Md.: Johns Hopkins University Press, 1975).

55. G. M. Meier and R. Baldwin, *Economic Development* (New York: John Wiley & Sons, 1957).

56. Of course, the need for balanced budgets to avoid inflation was preached. But this was more a long-run matter than a transfer of Keynesian demand management to less developed countries.

57. See, for example, the extensive discussion of West African commodity boards in the *Economic Journal* from 1952 to 1954, with contributions by P. T. Bauer and B. S. Yamey, P. Ady, P. Hill, and Milton Friedman.

58. Riots resulted in Ghana and Guiana. Kaldor discusses the fate of his suggestions and defends himself in the introduction to N. Kaldor, *Essays on Economic Policy* I (London: Duckworth, 1964).

59. N. Kaldor, *Indian Tax Reform* (Delhi: Government of India, Ministry of Finance, 1956).

60. Very similar proposals were made for Ceylon, some of which were also legislated.

61. I. M. D. Little in *Pricing and Fiscal Policies*, ed. P. Rosenstein Rodan (London: Allen & Unwin, 1964).

Chapter 8

1. Tony Killick presents Ghana as a case study of the application of the ideas of the development establishment of the 1950s, as the title of his book *Development Economics in Action* (New York: St. Martin's Press, 1978) implies.

2. J. Viner, *International Trade and Economic Development* (Oxford: Clarendon Press, 1953).

Chapter 9

1. One of the latest, N. Caiden and A. Wildavsky, *Planning and Budgeting in Poor Countries* (New York: John Wiley & Sons, 1974), gives a large bibliography.

2. Examples are A. M. Watson and J. B. Dirlan, "The Impact of Underdevelopment on Economic Planning," *Quarterly Journal of Economics*, May 1965; R. Vernon, "Comprehensive Model-building in the Planning Process: The Case of the Less-developed Economies," *Economic Journal*, March 1966; H. Myint, "Economic Theory and Development Policy," *Economica*, May 1967; and S. Wellicz, "Lessons of Twenty Years of Planning in Developing Countries," *Economica*, May 1971.

3. W. A. Lewis, *Development Planning, The Essentials of Economic Policy* (London: Allen & Unwin, 1966). Much of the wisdom in this work still seems to remain unabsorbed. Cookbooks on project planning and programming are referred to below.

4. J. P. Lewis, *Quiet Crisis in India* (Washington, D.C.: Brookings Institution, 1962); A. H. Hanson, "The Crisis of Indian Planning," *Political Quarterly* 34 (1963); P. Streeten and M. Lipton, *The Crisis of Indian Planning: Economic Policy of the 1960s* (London: Oxford University Press, 1969); M. Faber and D. Seers, eds., *The Crisis in Planning* (London: Chatto & Windus, 1972).

5. This was true even of public sectors in India, where state governments were responsible and the center could do little more than preach.

6. There is far more to project planning than the use of shadow prices. There is the identification of promising sectors or subsectors; there is demand analysis and market research, including the supply of imports; there is engineering design, man-

agement, and choice of consultants. The lack of good feasible projects in many less developed countries in many sectors is evidence of a relative neglect of project planning in a broader sense than that of evaluation. I deal exclusively with the latter only because it is the special concern of economists.

7. See chapter 3, above.

8. See M. Bruno in *Planning the External Sector: Techniques, Problems and Policies,* Report on the First International Seminar on Development Planning (New York: United Nations, 1967).

9. A. K. Sen, *Choice of Techniques* (Oxford: Basil Blackwell, 1960).

10. Sen did this later, but in the third edition (1967). Probably, the Cambridge influence of the 1950s made him dislike the notion of even *shadow* prices determining anything!

11. See S. A. Marglin, *Public Investment Criteria* (London: Allen & Unwin, 1967). His *Value and Prices in the Labor Surplus Economy* (London: Oxford University Press, 1976) was available in mimeograph by 1966.

12. I. M. D. Little and J. A. Mirrlees, *Manual of Industrial Project Analysis,* vol. 2 (Paris: Organization for Economic Cooperation and Development, 1968).

13. P. S. Dasgupta, S. A. Marglin, and A. K. Sen, *Guidelines for Project Evaluation* (New York: United Nations Industrial Development Organization, 1972).

14. I. M. D. Little and J. A. Mirrlees, *Project Appraisal and Planning for Developing Countries* (London: Heinemann, 1974).

15. There is a rapidly growing theoretical literature (mainly in the *Journal of Political Economy, Quarterly Journal of Economics,* and *Review of Economic Studies*) stemming from the guidelines that the shadow price of a traded good is its border price (or marginal cost) and that shadow prices for nontraded goods should be derived from their marginal costs in terms of labor and traded goods (or their marginal traded-good productivity). Trade theorists and welfare theorists have been active in subjecting these guidelines to the test of whether they give the correct answer in various general equilibrium models. The guidelines seem to be rather robust, although some theoretical snags are outstanding. The applied economist invariably uses assumptions and makes shortcuts that a theorist could show would lead to a wrong answer in certain precisely defined circumstances. If he did not go to work until his theoretical props were proof against all possible kicks, there would be no applied economics.

16. The best known is L. Squire and H. van der Tak, *Economic Analysis of Projects* (Washington, D. C.: International Bank for Reconstruction and Development, 1975).

17. For an account of this in India, see D. Lal, *Prices for Planning* (London: Heinemann, 1980). In late 1970, I visited India in order to persuade the Planning Commission to create such a division. There were delays as a result of political events; but the idea stuck, and the Project Appraisal Division of the Planning Commission was finally established in 1972.

18. To my knowledge, full sets of shadow prices have at one time or another been worked out for India, Bangladesh, Sri Lanka, Korea, Morocco, Kenya, and Jamaica.

19. Many of the points of this section were already made by Chenery in the 1950s. See H. B. Chenery in *The Allocation of Economic Resources,* ed. M. Abramovitz et al. (Stanford, Calif.: Stanford University Press, 1959).

20. A. S. Manne, *Investments for Capacity Expansion: Size, Location and Time Phasing* (Cambridge, Mass.: MIT Press, 1967). A more recent reference is L. E. Westphal in *Economy-wide Models and Development Planning,* ed. C. R. Blitzer, P. B. Clark, and L. Taylor (London: Oxford University Press, 1975); this contains a bibliography. More recently, the World Bank has sponsored a series of works on industrial investment programs, comprising so far D. A. Kendrick and A. J. Stoutjesdijk, *The Planning of Industrial Investment Programs: A Methodology* (Baltimore, Md.: Johns Hopkins University Press, 1980), and A. M. Choksi et al., *The Planning of Investment Programs in the Fertilizer Industry* (Baltimore, Md.: Johns Hopkins University Press, 1980).

21. S. Wortman and R. Cummings, *To Feed This World* (Baltimore, Md.: Johns Hopkins University Press, 1978), pp. 268, 418.

22. See Little and Mirrlees, *Project Appraisal and Planning for Developing Countries,* p. 380.

23. Development Finance Institutions (DFIs), which are in the public sector but

lend to the private sector, may use shadow prices. Thus, the private sector, although bound to use market prices in the design and operation of its projects, may have them turned down either by a DFI or by the central government, on the basis of a shadow-price appraisal.

24. Blitzer, Clark, and Taylor, eds., *Economy-Wide Models and Development Planning*.

25. Ibid., chap. 8, p. 204.

26. See, for example, P. D. Henderson, *India, the Energy Sector* (Delhi: Oxford University Press, 1975, for the International Bank for Reconstruction and Development).

27. See T. Watanabe in *Economics of Planning* 10, nos. 1-2 (1970). Also see P. H. Tresize and Y. Suzuki in *Asia's New Giant*, ed. H. T. Patrick and H. Rosovsky (Washington, D.C.: Brookings Institution, 1976). These authors also cast doubt on the efficacy of the famed industrial planning of the Ministry of International Trade and Industry.

28. R. Prebisch, *Towards a New Trade Policy for Development* (New York: United Nations, 1964).

29. W. M. Corden, *The Theory of Protection* (Oxford: Clarendon Press, 1971).

30. In reality, it is also hard to measure the effects on traded good prices. Where quotas are in play, the nominal tariff cannot be taken as a measure of the rise in price. Also, tariffs are often partly redundant in the sense that international competition has limited the difference between domestic and foreign prices to less than would be permitted by the tariff. In both cases, foreign and domestic prices have to be directly compared, which is not easy.

31. V. K. Ramaswami and T. N. Srinivasan in *Trade, Balance of Payments and Growth*, ed. J. Bhagwati (Amsterdam: North Holland, 1971); reprinted in V. K. Ramaswami, ed., *Trade and Development* (London: Allen & Unwin, 1971).

32. For an exposition and qualified defense of the effective rate of protection, see I. M. D. Little, T. Scitovsky, and M. FG. Scott, *Industry and Trade in Some Developing Countries* (London: Oxford University Press, 1970), pp. 169-190; also Corden, *Theory of Protection*.

33. R. Soligo and J. S. Stern, "Tariff Protection, Import Substitution and Investment Efficiency," *Pakistan Development Review*, summer 1965.

34. The results are to be found in the companion volumes of the Organization for Economic Cooperation and Development project and in Little, Scitovsky, and Scott, *Industry and Trade in Some Developing Countries*; also in B. Balassa, *The Structure of Protection in Developing Countries* (Baltimore, Md.: Johns Hopkins University Press, 1971).

35. See, for example, Little and Mirrlees, *Project Appraisal and Planning for Developing Countries*, chap. 18.

36. Ibid.; also Bruno, "Optimal Selection of Export Promoting and Import Substituting Projects."

37. A. O. Krueger, "Some Economic Costs of Exchange Control: The Turkish Case," *Journal of Political Economy*, October 1966.

38. An example is J. Page in *Using Shadow Prices*, ed. I. M. D. Little and M. FG. Scott (London: Heinemann, 1976).

39. Little, Scitovsky, and Scott, *Industry and Trade in Some Developing Countries*, pp. 190-197.

40. H. B. Chenery reconciled them at an earlier date in a survey that also emphasized investment interdependencies. Cf. H. B. Chenery, "Comparative Advantage and Development Policy," *American Economic Review* 51, no. 1 (March 1961), reprinted in H. B. Chenery, *Structural Change and Development Policy* (London: Oxford University Press, 1979).

41. Cf. C. Diaz Alejandro in *International Trade and Finance*, ed. P. K. Kenen (Cambridge: Cambridge University Press, 1975), pp. 116-122.

42. M. Singh, *India's Export Trends* (Oxford: Clarendon Press, 1964). See also B. I. Cohen, "The Stagnation of Indian Exports," *Quarterly Journal of Economics*, November 1964.

43. B. A. De Vries, *Export Experiences of Developing Countries*, World Bank Staff Occasional Paper no. 3 (Baltimore, Md.: Johns Hopkins University Press, 1967).

44. H. Lary, *Imports of Manufactures from Less Developed Countries* (New York: National Bureau of Economic Research, 1968).

45. Little, Scitovsky, and Scott, *Industry and Trade in Some Developing Countries*, chap. 7.
46. For example, J. R. Behrman, *Supply Response in Underdeveloped Agriculture* (Amsterdam: North Holland, 1968).
47. R. E. Lipsey, *Price and Quantity Trends in the Foreign Trade of the United States* (Princeton, N.J.: Princeton University Press, 1963).
48. J. Spraos, "The Statistical Debate on the Net Barter Terms of Trade Between Primary Commodities and Manufactures," *Economic Journal*, March 1980. A full bibliography is given. He allows nothing for the quality argument, though his reasons for rejecting it are not wholly convincing.
49. The literature is reviewed in W. M. Corden, *Trade Policy and Economic Welfare* (Oxford: Clarendon Press, 1974), pp. 40–41. Despite earlier snippets, he attributes it first to J. E. Meade, *Trade and Welfare* (London: Oxford University Press, 1955). But the article that first really highlighted the proposition was J. Bhagwati and V. K. Ramaswami, "Domestic Distortions, Tariffs, and the Theory of Optimum Subsidy," *Journal of Political Economy*, February 1963. This has been followed by numerous further contributions by both these authors and by Johnson and Srinivasan. S. P. Magee, "Factor Market Distortions, Production, and Trade: A Survey," *Oxford Economic Papers*, March 1973, has also reviewed the literature on interventions to correct factor market distortions and finds that B. Ohlin clearly recognized the superiority of subsidies in 1931.
50. For fuller discussions of the use of tariffs for revenue reasons, see Little, Scitovsky, and Scott, *Industry and Trade in Some Developing Countries*, pp. 135–144; Corden, *Theory of Protection*, chap. 4; and I. M. D. Little, "Trade and Public Finance," *The Indian Economic Review* 6, no. 2 (1971).
51. An earlier review in 1975 by Diaz Alejandro has already been referred to. Since then, the results of two major research projects have become available, that of the National Bureau of Economic Research in the United States and of the Institut für Weltwirtschaft. The former is discussed below. The results of the latter are summarized in J. B. Donges and L. Müller-Ohlsen, *Aussenwirtschaftsstrategien und Industrialisierung in Entwicklungsländern* (Tübingen: J. C. B. Mohr, 1978). Some of the results of the World Bank project, "Development Strategies in Semi-Industrialized Countries," directed by B. Balassa, are also available and are referred to below.
52. A brief review of the experience of these countries is in I. M. D. Little in *Export-Led Industrialization and Development*, ed. E. Lee (Geneva: Asian Employment Programme, International Labor Organization, 1981). Korea's trade regime is more fully described in C. R. Frank, K. S. Kim, and L. E. Westphal, *Foreign Trade and Economic Development* (New York: National Bureau of Economic Research, 1975); and L. Westphal, "The Republic of Korea's Experiment with Export-Led Development," *World Development*, March 1978. For Taiwan, see M. FG. Scott in *Economic Growth and Structural Change in Taiwan*, ed. W. Galenson (Ithaca, N.Y.: Cornell University Press, 1979).
53. See B. Balassa, "Export Incentives and Export Performance in Developing Countries: A Comparative Analysis," *Weltwirtschaftliche Archiv* 114 (1978); also J. B. Donges, "A Comparative Study of Industrialization Policies in Fifteen Semi-Industrial Countries," *Weltwirtschaftliche Archiv* 112 (1976).
54. Some examples have been found in the case of India and Brazil. Cf. Donges, "Comparative Study of Industrialization Policies in Fifteen Semi-Industrial Countries." The irrationality of Indian export subsidization is discussed in D. Lal, "Indian Export Incentives," *Journal of Development Economics* 6 (1979).
55. For example, in Little, Scitovsky, and Scott, *Industry and Trade in Some Developing Countries*; and Balassa, "Export Incentives and Export Performance in Developing Countries." There is also confirmation in the National Bureau of Economic Research studies discussed below.
56. M. Michaely, "Exports and Growth: An Empirical Investigation," *Journal of Development Economics* 4 (1977). Ratios of exports to gross domestic product are not significant; changes in the ratio are highly significant. Balassa, however, in "Exports and Economic Growth: Further Evidence," *Journal of Development Economics* 5 (1978) finds that both are significant.

57. J. Bhagwati, *Anatomy and Consequences of Trade Control Regimes* (New York: National Bureau for Economic Research, 1978).

58. Westphal, "Republic of Korea's Experiment with Export-Led Development"; R. Banerji and J. Riedel, "Industrial Employment Under Alternative Strategies: Some Empirical Evidence," *Ebenda* 63 (November 1977); W. G. Tyler, *Manufactured Export Expansion and Industrialization in Brazil* (Tübingen: Kieler Studien 134, 1976); I. M. D. Little in *Economic Growth and Structural Change in Taiwan*, ed. Galenson, pp. 491–500.

59. See Little, ibid., on the inappropriateness of such backward linkages; see also J. Riedel, "Factor Proportions, Linkages and the Open Developing Economy," *Review of Economics and Statistics* (1975).

60. G. Ranis, "Equity with Growth in Taiwan: How 'Special' Is the 'Special' Case?" *World Development*, March 1978; I. M. D. Little, ibid.; I. Adelman and S. Robinson, *Income Distribution in Developing Countries* (Oxford: Oxford University Press, 1978); D. C. Rao, "Economic Growth and Equity in the Republic of Korea," *World Development*, March 1978.

61. This assumes that management of the balance of payments is via the exchange rate and use of reserves and borrowing, and not by import quotas or variations in taxes on trade.

62. B. Balassa, "Reforming the System of Incentives in Developing Countries," *World Development* 3 (1975); B. Balassa, *Policy Reform in Developing Countries* (Oxford: Oxford University Press, 1977). S. C. Tsiang reviewed the whole range of incentives in an exemplary manner in a neglected article, "Tax, Credit, and Trade Policies to Promote the Production and Export of Manufactures of Developing Countries," *Journal of Development Studies*, January and April, 1965. I believe that Tsiang had much to do with the Taiwan reforms, which produced an exemplary response.

63. In Little, Scitovsky, and Scott, *Industry and Trade in Developing Countries*, chap. 4. IV; Little and Mirrlees, *Project Appraisal and Planning for Developing Countries*, chap. 5.5; and more fully in Little, "Trade and Public Finance."

64. On petrochemicals in Colombia, see D. Morawetz in *The Choice of Technology in Developing Countries*, Studies in International Affairs, no. 32, ed. C. P. Timmer et al. (Cambridge, Mass.: Harvard University Press, 1975); and D. Morawetz, *Why the Emperor's New Clothes Are Not Made in Colombia: A Case Study of Latin American and East Asian Clothing Exports* (London: Oxford University Press, 1981).

65. A. O. Krueger, "Liberalization Attempts and Consequences" (New York: National Bureau for Economic Research, 1978). The movement toward liberalization is also discussed in Donges, "Comparative Study of Industrialization Policies in Fifteen Semi-Industrialized Countries."

66. Brazil, Chile, Colombia, Egypt, Ghana, India, Israel, the Philippines, Korea, and Turkey.

67. Taiwan liberalized successfully with a fixed rate, but its rate of inflation from 1963 to 1973 was less than the world average, and the Taiwanese dollar was becoming undervalued as productivity rose rapidly. There was also no bias against exports. The case of Singapore is similar.

68. A. I. MacBean, *Export Instability and Economic Development* (Cambridge, Mass.: Harvard University Press, 1966).

69. P. K. Kenen and C. S. Voivodas, "Export Instability and Economic Growth," *Kyklos* 25, no. 4 (1972).

70. C. Diaz Alejandro in *International Trade and Finance*, ed. Kenen.

71. P. A. Yotopoulos and J. B. Nugent, *Economics of Development: Empirical Investigations* (New York: Harper & Row, 1976).

72. I. M. D. Little, "The Strategy of Indian Development," *National Institute Economic Review*, May 1960, p. 24. Since the idea was not incorporated in a model, and appeared in a relatively obscure place, it was hardly noticed.

73. I. M. D. Little and J. M. Clifford, *International Aid* (London: Allen & Unwin, 1965), pp. 141–155.

74. H. B. Chenery and M. Bruno, "Development Alternatives in an Open Economy: The Case of Israel," *The Economic Journal*, March 1962, reprinted in Chenery, *Structural Change and Development Policy*.

75. R. I. McKinnon, "Foreign Exchange Constraints in Economic Development and Efficient Aid Allocation," *Economic Journal*, June 1964.

76. Articles criticizing the foreign exchange gap approach include H. J. Bruton, "The Two-Gap Approach to Aid and Development: Comment," *American Economic Review*, June 1969; and D. Lal, "The foreign exchange bottleneck revisited," *Economic Development and Cultural Change*, July 1972. A geometric exposition and assessment is given in R. E. Findlay, *International Trade and Development Theory* (New York and London: Columbia University Press, 1973), chap. 10.

77. Despite giving rather more credit to the two-gap idea than is given here, a similar conclusion was nevertheless reached in Little and Clifford, *International Aid*, p. 155.

78. This stylized view tends to be one of Asia!

79. D. Turnham and I. Jaeger, *The Unemployment Problem in Developing Countries* (Paris: Organization for Economic Cooperation and Development, Development Centre, 1971). Earlier in the 1960s, there had been country- and continental-level reports and articles that drew attention to the fact that manufacturing employment was, in most countries, growing more slowly than the urban population, with a *presumption* that urban unemployment was growing.

80. A. Berry and R. H. Sabot, "Labor Market Performance in Developing Countries: A Survey," *World Development*, November/December 1978; and L. Squire, *Employment Policy in Developing Countries, A Survey of Issues and Evidence* (London: Oxford University Press, 1981).

81. Turnham and Jaeger, *Unemployment Problem in Developing Countries*, found no such evidence. See also J. Ramos, "An Heterodoxical Interpretation of the Employment Problem in Latin America," *World Development*, July 1974; and D. Morawetz, *Twenty-five Years of Economic Development* (Baltimore, Md.: Johns Hopkins University Press, 1977), pp. 32–37.

82. Morawetz, *Twenty-five Years of Economic Development*, Table X.

83. Some evidence is provided by the Maharastra Employment Guarantee Scheme. It is supposed to guarantee employment at fifteen days' notice at the minimum agricultural wage on local rural works not more than five kilometers from the village. In 1976–77, it was estimated to have attracted 160 million person-days of work, while the rural population was estimated to have 620 million idle person-days, a rate of about 10 percent, well above the all-India average. It can be seen as a wage-support program, enforcing the minimum wage. It is unclear whether the gap between 160 million and 620 million shows that there is no real guarantee, or whether it shows that the "idle person-day" estimate is an overestimate of those willing and able to work more at the prevailing wage within reasonable proximity. For an account of the scheme, see I. Singh, "Small Farmers and the Landless in South Asia," *World Bank Staff Working Papers*, no. 320, February 1979.

84. Recall that we use shadow wages defined with respect to welfare, and not just to national income, which is perhaps the more common usage. Thus, the shadow wage, for us, is the opportunity cost of labor only if dynamic and distributional considerations, and maybe other values, can be neglected.

85. A. K. Sen, *Employment, Technology and Development* (Oxford: Clarendon Press, 1975), argues the case for a "recognition" aspect of employment. For many, no doubt, a job lends self-respect. For others, in less developed countries, it involves a loss of respect.

86. This is the thrust of many articles, and also of such recent surveys as Berry and Sabot, "Labor Market Performance in Developing Countries"; and Squire, *Employment Policy in Developing Countries*.

87. J. Harris and M. Todaro, "Migration, Unemployment and Development: A Two-Sector Analysis," *American Economic Review*, March 1970. As is usual, there are plenty of earlier references in the literature to the distortion caused by high modern-sector earnings, including excessive urbanization. But if not formulated as a model, they do not have so much impact.

88. The model has dramatic implications for the urban shadow wage. If a person is hired from the country directly, the opportunity cost is his rural earnings, that is,

half the urban wage. But if a person is hired from the urban unemployment pool, then two will migrate from the country—and the opportunity cost is equal to the actual wage paid.

89. Berry and Sabot, "Labor Market Performance in Developing Countries."
90. See M. FG. Scott, J. D. MacArthur, and D. M. G. Newbery, *Project Appraisal in Practice* (London: Heinemann, 1976), chap. 4, for an examination of the probability (in Kenya) of such an increase in unemployment.
91. Squire, *Employment Policy in Developing Countries*, pp. 115–6.
92. Berry and Sabot, "Labor Market Performance in Developing Countries," p. 1217; see also Squire, *Employment Policy in Developing Countries*, Table 29.
93. See Berry and Sabot, "Labor Market Performance in Developing Countries"; and Squire, *Employment Policy in Developing Countries*.
94. J. Stiglitz, "Wage Determination and Unemployment in LDCs," *Quarterly Journal of Economics*, May 1974.
95. For references, many in the *Bell Journal of Economics*, see D. Lal, "An Essay on the Study of Labor in Development," *World Bank Studies in Employment and Rural Development*, no. 63, August 1980.
96. Squire, *Employment Policy in Developing Countries*, p. 132.

Chapter 10

1. As already mentioned in chapter 6, there were those who recognized the importance of agriculture for its own sake, notably Lewis and Viner. For an early and powerful comment on the thinking of the 1950s, see W. H. Nicholls, in *Agriculture in Economic Development*, ed. C. Eicher and L. Witt (New York: McGraw-Hill Book Co., 1964).
2. It is much less clear that the first proposition—that little could be done without new inputs—was correct. It appears that improved management and cultivation methods, without new inputs, can both be taught and give important yield and income increases. This is a tenet of the Benor extension system. See I. Singh, "Small Farmers and the Landless in South Asia," *World Bank Staff Working Papers*, no. 320, February 1979; and D. Benor and J. G. Harrison, "Agricultural Extension: The Training and Visit System," Washington, D. C., World Bank, May 1977.
3. This was true of most of the countries studied in I. M. D. Little, T. Scitovsky, and M. FG. Scott, *Industry and Trade in Some Developing Countries* (London: Oxford University Press, 1970), pp. 346–510. Much earlier, Bauer had drawn attention to the way in which marketing boards in Africa were used to tax peasant production heavily. Much subsequent research suggests that "squeezing" agriculture has been part of the policy of almost all African countries. See, for example, S. N. Acharya, "Perspectives and Problems of Development in Low-Income, Sub-Saharan Africa," *World Development*, February 1981.
4. For example, T. J. Byrnes in *Agrarian Reform and Agrarian Reformism*, ed. D. Lehman (London: Faber & Faber, 1974).
5. Raj Krishna in *Agricultural Development and Economic Growth*, ed. H. M. Southworth and B. F. Johnson (Ithaca, N.Y., and London: Cornell University Press, 1967).
6. H. L. Barnum and L. Squire, "An Econometric Application of the Theory of the Farm-Household," *Journal of Development Economics*, March 1979.
7. For a recent account, see E. Thorbecke in *Economic Growth and Structural Change in Taiwan*, ed. W. Galenson (Ithaca, N.Y.: Cornell University Press, 1979).
8. See S. Wortman and R. Cummings, *To Feed This World* (Baltimore, Md.: Johns Hopkins University Press, 1978), pp. 84–94.
9. Ibid., p. 93.
10. Imports of food are most likely to be cut off in wartime. But most starvation has occurred because wars and bad weather have disrupted *domestic* production.
11. A. T. Mosher, *To Create a Modern Agriculture* (New York: Agricultural Development Council, 1971), pp. 78–79.

12. For a bibliography on the adoption of new techniques, see G. Feder, R. Just, and D. Silberman, "Adoption of Agricultural Innovations in Developing Countries: A Survey," *World Bank Staff Working Papers*, no. 444, February 1981.

13. See U. Tun Wai, "Interest Rates Outside the Organized Money Markets of Underdeveloped Countries," *International Monetary Fund Papers*, 1957–58; A. Bottomley, "The Premium for Risk as a Determinant of Interest Rates in Underdeveloped Rural Areas," *Quarterly Journal of Economics*, November 1963; A. D. Chandavarkar, "Comment," *Quarterly Journal of Economics*, May 1965; and A. Bottomley, "Reply," *Quarterly Journal of Economics*, May 1965.

14. Some production cooperatives were formed in India, but on paper only, for the purpose of obtaining the subsidies offered. The Mexican *ejido* seems to be an example of failure. See R. Weitz, *From Peasant to Farmer* (New York: Columbia University Press, 1971), chap. 7, for a valuable discussion of cooperation.

15. See Youngjohn in *Borrowers and Lenders*, ed. J. Howell (London: Overseas Development Institute, 1980).

16. Ibid., p. 79. Disaggregated agricultural sector models, of which there has been a plethora in the past fifteen years, may, however, be of value in suggesting optimum cropping patterns where a distorted price set or market failure implies that actual patterns are suboptimal. They may also be useful in predicting the quantities of outputs, and therefore what complementary facilities should be planned, when a large irrigation system, settlement scheme, or land reform is in preparation.

17. See, for example, G. Hunter, "Management and Self-Management in Economic Development," *Overseas Development Institute Review*, no. 2 (1975), and "Stimulating Local Development," London *Overseas Development Institute*.

18. The main evaluative work to date is U. Lele, *The Design of Rural Development, Lessons from Africa* (Baltimore, Md.: Johns Hopkins University Press, 1975). See also P. Mosley, "Aid for the Poorest: Some Early Lessons of UK Experience," *Journal of Development Studies*, January 1981.

19. The first thorough examination of these questions seems to have been M. Yudelman, G. Butler, and R. Banerji, *Technological Change in Agriculture and Employment in Developing Countries* (Paris: Organization for Economic Cooperation and Development, Development Centre, 1971).

20. I. Singh, "Small Farmers and the Landless in South Asia."

21. A recent review of mechanization studies is H. P. Binswanger, *The Economics of Tractors in South Asia* (New York: Agricultural Development Council, 1978).

22. It is interesting to reflect on why the demand for redistribution of assets in less developed countries focuses always on land reforms that presume that the landowners are severely undercompensated. This offends against "horizontal" equity: businessmen much richer than many landowners are untouched. Business in LDCs is predominantly family owned. Wealth and inheritance taxes, combined with an encouragement of stock markets, can easily produce greater dispersion of ownership of industrial assets. Considerations of equity, vertical and horizontal, suggest wealth and inheritance taxes across the board. Such considerations may, however, have to give way to the peculiar political and emotional values that are associated with land ownership. Yet it is not too early (or is it too late?) for some LDCs to concern themselves more with the dispersion of industrial property ownership.

23. Yudelman, Butler, and Banerji, *Technological Change in Agriculture and Employment in Developing Countries*, pp. 104–119, 171–204.

24. A. Berry and W. A. Cline, *Agrarian Structure and Productivity in Developing Countries* (Baltimore, Md.: Johns Hopkins University Press, 1979).

25. While very plausible, the hypothesis cannot be said to have been empirically verified. For a discussion, see K. Bardhan, "A Survey of Research on Rural Employment, Wages and Labor Markets in India," *Economic and Political Weekly* 12, nos. 27–28 (1977). A recent article examining various hypotheses as to why labor use per hectare is higher on small farms is I. Ahmed, "Farm Size and Labor Use: Some Alternate Explanations," *Oxford Bulletin of Economics and Statistics*, February 1981.

26. An early reference is D. W. Adams, "Agricultural Credit in Latin America: A Critical Review of External Funding Policy," *AJAE* 53, no. 2. (May 1971).

27. See *Rural Enterprise and Nonfarm Employment*, World Bank Paper (Washington, D.C.: World Bank, January 1978). An early article drawing attention to the subject was B. Hansen, "Employment and Wages in Rural Egypt," *American Economic Review* 59, no. 3 (1969).

28. S. Ho, "The Rural Non-farm Sector in Taiwan," World Bank, *Studies in Employment and Rural Development* (Washington, D.C.: World Bank, 1976).

29. H. N. Barnum and L. Squire, "An Econometric Application of the Theory of the Farm-Household," *Journal of Development Economics*, March 1979.

30. For example, P. K. Bardhan and A. Rudra, "Terms and Conditions of Sharecropping Contracts, An Analysis of Village Survey Data in India," *Journal of Development Studies*, April 1980; and F. A. Bray and A. F. Robinson, "Sharecropping in Kelantan, Malaysia," *Research in Economic Anthropology* 3 (1980).

31. S. Cheung, *The Theory of Share Tenancy* (Chicago: University of Chicago Press, 1969).

32. See D. M. G. Newbery and J. E. Stiglitz in *Risk, Uncertainty and Agricultural Development*, eds. J. A. Roumasset, J. M. Boussard, and I. Singh (New York: Agricultural Development Council, 1979).

33. Ibid., p. 338.

34. Macroeconomic and distributional effects of agricultural policies and land reform are considered in G. Pyatt and E. Thorbecke, *Planning Techniques for a Better Future* (Geneva: International Labor Organization, 1976).

35. G. Ranis, "Factor Proportions in Japanese Economic Development," *American Economic Review*, September 1957.

36. A. K. Sen, *Choice of Techniques* (Oxford: Basil Blackwell, 1960).

37. E. F. Schumacher in *Industrialization in Developing Countries*, ed. R. Robinson (Cambridge: Cambridge University Press, 1965). Schumacher founded the London-based Intermediate Technology Development Group.

38. Some evidence is given in L. J. White, "The Evidence on Appropriate Factor Proportions for Manufacturing in Less Developed Countries," *Economic Development and Cultural Change*, October 1978. I have drawn on this extensively. A more recent survey reaching similar conclusions but concerned more exclusively with transnational corporations, unpublished at the time of writing, is V. S. Balasubramanyam, "Multinational Corporations' Choice of Techniques and Employment in Less Developed Countries" (Paper presented to the International Economic Association World Economic Congress, Mexico, September 1980). Another earlier and broader survey is that of S. N. Acharya, "Fiscal Financial Intervention, Factor Prices and Factor Proportions: A Review of Issues," *Bangladesh Development Studies*, October 1975.

39. See chapter 11.

40. For example, J. Gaude in *Technology and Employment in Industry*, ed. A. S. Bhalla (Geneva: International Labor Organization, 1975); D. Morawetz, "Elasticities in Industry: What Do We Learn from Economic Estimates?" *World Development*, January 1976; and Acharya, "Fiscal Financial Intervention."

41. White adds a rider to the effect that "difficult questions of scale, quality, and skill remain." "Scale" refers to the probability that in some industries higher capital intensity and scale economies are associated (but this does not imply that there is zero elasticity of substitution at any scale). "Quality" refers to the fact that high quality and capital intensity are associated in some industries. "Skill" refers to the fact that required operative skills may, in some industries, fall with increasing mechanization.

42. Y. W. Rhee and L. E. Westphal, "A Micro-Economic Investigation of Choice of Technology," *Journal of Development Economics* 4 (1977).

43. S. Morley and G. Smith, "Limited Search and Technology Choices of Multinational Firms in Brazil," *Quarterly Journal of Economics*, May 1977.

44. A brief account can be found in Acharya, "Fiscal Financial Intervention."

45. White, "Evidence on Appropriate Factor Proportions for Manufacturing in Less Developed Countries," gives a limited number of references.

46. Increasing the opportunities for acquiring knowledge of the range of techniques will have a positive payoff, but also some costs.

47. There are always a few exceptions. For example, H. J. Bruton, "Growth Models and Underdeveloped Economies," *Journal of Political Economy*, August 1955, showed concern about the inappropriateness of modern technology.

48. For example, by C. Frank, "Urban Unemployment and Economic Growth in Africa," *Oxford Economic Papers*, July 1968; and D. Turnham and I. Jaeger, *The Unemployment Problem in Developing Countries* (Paris: Organization for Economic Cooperation and Development, Development Centre, 1971).

49. United Nations, Commission on Transnational Corporations, *Transnational Corporations in World Development* (New York: United Nations, 1978), p. 35.

50. Ibid., p. 8.

51. For a good balanced account of Latin American attitudes, see V. L. Urquidi in *Obstacles to Change in Latin America*, ed. C. Veliz (London: Oxford University Press, 1965). For a later account, see C. Diaz Alejandro, in *The International Corporation*, ed. C. P. Kindelberger (Cambridge, Mass.: MIT Press, 1979).

52. S. Hymer, *International Operations of National Firms: A Study of Direct Foreign Investments* (Cambridge, Mass.: MIT Press, 1976).

53. This work is reviewed by C. F. Bergsten, T. Horst, and T. H. Moran, *American Multinationals and American Interests* (Washington, D.C.: Brookings Institution, 1978), chap. 7; and also in Balasubramanyam, "Multinational Corporations' Choice of Techniques and Employment in Less Developed Countries."

54. This is also pointed out by D. Lal, *Appraising Foreign Investment in Developing Countries* (London: Heinemann, 1975), chaps. 1 and 2. He argues that the industrial organization literature, especially the "product cycle" model, was mainly concerned with sophisticated products or techniques; whereas a substantial part of private foreign investment in the least industrialized less developed countries was in simple technology products.

55. G. D. A. MacDougall, "The Benefits and Costs of Private Investment from Abroad: A Theoretical Approach," *Economic Record*, March 1960. Reprinted in *Bulletin of the Oxford Institute of Economics and Statistics* 22, no. 3 (1960), and in American Economic Association, *Readings in International Economics* (London: Allen & Unwin, 1968).

56. MacDougall was writing before the effective protection literature had begun to demonstrate that the benefit to the host country of producing a particular commodity might vary greatly—in other words, the domestic price could not be taken as a measure of benefit.

57. A. O. Hirschman, "How to Divest in Latin America, and Why," *Essays in International Finance*, no. 76, Princeton University (1969).

58. I. M. D. Little in *The Gap between Rich and Poor Nations*, ed. G. Ranis (London: Macmillan, 1972).

59. I. M. D. Little and D. G. Tipping, *A Social Cost Benefit Analysis of the Kulai Oil Palm Estate* (Paris: Organization for Economic Cooperation and Development, Development Centre, 1972).

60. The methodology is well explained, and justified, by Lal, *Appraising Foreign Investment in Developing Countries*, Part 2.

61. S. Lall and P. Streeten, *Foreign Investment, Transnationals and Developing Countries* (London: Macmillan, 1977). See also a review of this book by D. Lal in *Overseas Development Institute Review*, no. 2, 1978.

62. In the case of mining ventures, a scarcity rent may be included in the shadow prices in the case of an exhaustible resource. The lack of such a rent is the basis of most of the complaints of historical exploitation, or "theft," of the raw materials of less developed countries in the past.

63. This can be most vividly seen by imagining an enclave, which sells nothing to the local economy and buys only labor from it. (We can imagine it operating on wasteland, or even on a ship moored offshore.) If labor is surplus, there is a gain to the host country, which has and need have no notion of how the enclave is financed, or what profit it makes.

64. There is evidence on the points in this and the two succeeding paragraphs in, for example, United Nations, *Transnational Corporations in World Development*; G.

Reuber, *Private Foreign Investment in Development* (Oxford: Clarendon Press, 1973); R. Vernon, *Storm over the Multinationals* (London: Macmillan, 1977); and I. Frank, *Foreign Enterprise in Developing Countries* (Baltimore, Md.: Johns Hopkins University Press, 1980). Balasubramanyam, "Multinational Corporations' Choice of Techniques and Employment in Less Developed Countries," also sums up much of the evidence, in the spirit of what is written here.

65. High tariffs also favor underinvoicing of imports, and hence profit transfers to less developed countries. For a review of the fiscal incentives for transfer pricing, see G. F. Kopitz, "Taxation and Multinational Firms' Behavior," *International Monetary Fund Staff Papers*, November 1976.

66. For a review of evidence, see United Nations Conference on Trade and Development, TD/B/C2/167 (1978).

67. Balasubramanyam, "Multinational Corporations' Choice of Techniques and Employment in Less Developed Countries," and White, "Evidence on Appropriate Factor Proportions for Manufacturing in Less Developed Countries," refer to, and briefly review, the evidence.

68. T. W. Schultz, "Investment in Human Capital," *American Economic Review*, March 1961. Professor Strimilin in the USSR was a forerunner in the 1920s.

69. But see A. Maddison, *Economic Progress and Policy in Developing Countries* (New York: W. W. Norton & Company, 1970).

70. Throughout this section I am ignoring the so-called consumption benefits of education. Education as consumption is really a misnomer; it is usually a rather painful *investment* in future consumption or utility. The point is that some, perhaps much, of the value of educational investment lies not in increasing future earnings but in increasing the utility of those earnings, or of other income.

71. Lockheed et al. in "Education and Income," *World Bank Staff Working Papers*, no. 402, ed. T. King (July 1980). See also D. T. Jamison and L. J. Lau, *Farmer Education and Farm Efficiency* (Baltimore, Md.: Johns Hopkins University Press, 1981).

72. D. Wheeler, "Human Resource Development and Economic Growth in Developing Countries," *World Bank Staff Working Papers*, no. 407, July 1980.

73. Based on G. Psacharopoulos in "Education and Income," ed. King; and International Bank for Reconstruction and Development, *World Development Report* (Washington, D.C.: IBRD, 1980), chap. 5.

74. Fields in "Education and Income," ed. King.

75. Berry in "Education and Income," ed. King. This paper is a comprehensive review of the problems discussed in this section.

76. Ibid.; based on D. Mazumder, *Urban Labor Markets and Income Distribution in Peninsular Malaysia* (Baltimore, Md.: Johns Hopkins University Press, 1979).

77. See Mark Blaug in *World Population and Development*, ed. P. N. Hauser (Syracuse, N.Y.: Syracuse University Press, 1979). He also discusses remedies and the problems of curricula and vocational schools, and the efficiency of education in the sense of minimizing the costs of production of particular skills and levels of achievement, quite an important subject for less developed countries given the size of their educational budgets.

78. Ibid.

79. China also in the early 1950s, but the program was then called off and not reconstituted until 1962.

80. W. P. Mauldin and B. Berelson, "Conditions of Fertility Decline in Developing Countries, 1965–1975," *Studies in Family Planning*, May 1978.

81. This implies that the average woman has about 2¼ children in her lifetime—the exact figure dependent on female mortality rates prior to the end of the childbearing period.

82. See N. Birdsall, "Population and Poverty in the Developing World," *World Bank Staff Working Papers*, no. 404, July 1980.

83. India and Nigeria score 19/30 and 2/30, respectively, on the Mauldin/Berelson scale.

84. G. Ohlin, *Population Control and Economic Development* (Paris: Organization for Economic Cooperation and Development, Development Centre, 1967), p. 87. Only in Taiwan was there clear evidence by then of a fall in fertility.

85. International Bank for Reconstruction and Development, *World Development Report* (New York: World Bank, 1980), Table 18.

86. If nothing changed but income, one would tend to expect fertility to rise with income. The contrary expectation implies a belief that children are inferior goods.

87. D. Wheeler, "Human Resource Development and Economic Growth in Developing Countries," *World Bank Staff Working Papers*, no. 407, July 1980, pp. 41–51.

88. Sri Lanka and the state of Kerala are often cited cases where a large fall in fertility is associated with low per caput income but high literacy. However, there are always exceptions. In Taiwan, fertility fell fastest among the least educated women.

89. R. H. Cassen, "Population and Development: A Survey," *World Development*, October/November 1978, stresses the point in this wise study that discusses much more thoroughly most of the points briefly made here. See also M. S. Teitelbaum, "Comment," *World Development*, October/November 1978.

90. One has to assume that the Mauldin/Berelson rankings were objective, that is, not seriously influenced by success. On this, see Birdsall, "Population and Poverty in the Developing World," pp. 62–63.

91. See ibid., Table V-4. The table includes Brazil in the comparison, with similar results.

92. Wheeler, "Human Resource Development and Economic Growth in Developing Countries."

93. For an exhaustive discussion of the Indian case, see R. H. Cassen, *India: Population, Economy, Society* (London: Macmillan, 1978).

94. For a balanced discussion, see ibid.

95. A rare exception is H. Patrick, "Financial Development and Economic Growth in Underdeveloped Countries," *Economic Development and Cultural Change*, January 1966.

96. R. C. Porter, "The Promotion of the Banking Habit and Economic Development," *Journal of Development Studies*, July 1966.

97. R. I. McKinnon, *Money and Capital in Economic Development* (Washington, D.C.: Brookings Institution, 1973); and E. S. Shaw, *Financial Dependency in Economic Development* (New York: Oxford University Press, 1973).

98. For some figures, see V. V. Bhatt and J. Meerman, "Resource Mobilization in Developing Countries: Financial Institutions and Policies," *World Development*, January 1978.

99. McKinnon's figures are ten years old. Since then, M_2/GNP has fallen further in seven of the ten countries examined. In India and Venezuela it rose, and Pakistan is noncomparable. It seems that the repression thesis has not had any impact.

100. Experience in Taiwan was quite similar, except that Taiwan maintained high real interest rates throughout the period 1950-70. Real rates on deposits varied from year to year, but the average was high—about 9 percent. M_2/GNP rose from about 0.10 in the early 1950s to 0.45 in 1974–75. For an account, see E. Lundberg in *Economic Growth and Structural Change in Taiwan*, ed. W. Galenson (Ithaca, N.Y.: Cornell University Press, 1979), chap. 4.

101. M. J. Fry, "Savings, Investment, Growth, and the Cost of Financial Repression," *World Development*, April 1980.

102. Interest rate discussions usually have lenders in mind. But borrowers for whom the substitution and income effects work together may also be affected. Bhalla found that high interest rates (greater than 15 percent) had a positive effect on borrowers' savings in rural India. See S. S. Bhalla, "Aspects of Savings Behavior in Rural India," International Bank for Reconstruction and Development, *Domestic Finance Studies*, no. 31, December 1976.

103. V. V. Bhatt and A. S. Roe, "Capital Market Imperfections and Economic Development," *World Bank Staff Working Papers*, no. 338, July 1979.

104. Ibid., p. 64; Roe develops a model of financial disequilibrium. For another such, see V. Galbis, "Financial Intermediation and Economic Growth in Less-Developed Countries: A Theoretical Approach," *Journal of Development Studies*, January 1977, and Spellman in *Money and Finance in Economic Growth and Development: Essays in Honor of Edward S. Shaw*, ed. R. I. McKinnon (New York: Marcel Dekker, 1976).

Chapter 11

1. D. T. Healey, "Development Policy: New Thinking About an Interpretation," *Journal of Economic Literature* 10 (1972).
2. D. Turnham and I. Jaeger, *The Unemployment Problem in Developing Countries* (Paris: OECD Development Centre, 1971).
3. International Labor Organization, *Towards Full Employment*, report of the first of the ILO missions to promote employment (Geneva: ILO, 1970). The mission to Colombia was headed by D. Seers.
4. In India, the book by V. M. Dandekar and N. Rath, *Poverty in India* (New Delhi: Ford Foundation, 1970), was influential.
5. See M. S. Ahluwalia, "Rural Poverty and Agricultural Growth in India," *Journal of Development Studies*, April 1978. This careful survey is challenged by K. Griffin, "Growth and Impoverishment in the Rural Areas of India," *World Development*, April/May 1979. But Griffin arbitrarily takes a beginning point when the incidence of poverty was least, in order to show an increase. Another careful survey is by R. H. Cassen, *India: Population, Economy, Society* (London: Macmillan, 1978). This, too, is agnostic: "The evidence permits no lucid ringing truths."
6. Cassen, *India*, p. 250.
7. Ahluwalia, "Rural Poverty and Agricultural Growth in India."
8. Undoubtedly, it has increased in the war-torn areas in Southeast Asia, and in parts of Africa in drought years.
9. Most of the other cases (Pakistan, Malaysia, the Philippines, and four Indian states) examined by K. Griffin and A. R. Kahn, "Poverty in the Third World: Ugly Facts and Fancy Models," *World Development*, March 1978, are either inconclusive or are based on a comparison of incomparable surveys (for example, Malaysia).
10. J. Bergsman, "Income Distribution and Poverty in Mexico," *World Bank Staff Working Papers*, no. 395, June 1980 (forthcoming in *World Development*).
11. A brief survey of these cases, as well as India and Pakistan, is in T. N. Srinivasan, "Development, Poverty, and Basic Human Needs: Some Issues," *Food Research Institute Studies*, 1977. For income distribution in Taiwan, see J. Fei, J. Ranis, and S. W. Y. Kuo, *Equity with Growth: The Taiwan Case* (London: Oxford University Press, 1979).
12. See R. Hsia and L. C. Chau, "Industrialization and Income Distribution in Hong Kong 1961-1971" (World Employment Programme Research Working Paper, Geneva, International Labor Organization, 1975, mimeograph).
13. International Bank for Reconstruction and Development, *World Development Report* (Washington, D.C.: IBRD, 1980), Tables 21-23.
14. The problem of defining absolute poverty is touched on when discussing "basic needs" below.
15. S. Kuznets, "Economic Growth and Income Inequality," *American Economic Review* 45, no. 1, March 1955, reprinted in *Economic Growth and Structure* (London: Heinemann, 1965).
16. S. Jain, "Size Distribution of Income: A Compilation of Data" (Washington, D.C.: World Bank, 1975).
17. Cf. M. S. Ahluwalia, "Inequality, Poverty and Development," *Journal of Developmental Economics* 3 (1976). The equation used is: share of quintile = constant + δ log (per caput income) + β log (per caput income)^2. Presumably, other functional forms could give different results.
18. But the relationship has nevertheless been used to project poverty levels. See M. S. Ahluwalia, N. G. Carter, and H. B. Chenery, "Growth and Poverty in Developing Countries," *Journal of Development Economics*, September 1979.
19. There is scattered evidence of willingness on the part of the poor to pay prices at which a service could be provided—for example, people in slums buy water from carriers at a high price. On the other hand, in the poorer less developed countries, the lowest decile, perhaps quintile, could not pay fully for any public service, however low the cost of providing it might be.
20. See, for instance, M. ul Haq, *The Poverty Curtain* (New York: Columbia University Press, 1976), chap. 4.

Notes to Pages 216-222

21. H. B. Chenery et al., *Redistribution with Growth* (London: Oxford University Press, 1974).

22. Realistically, a trade-off with growth has to be faced. A good example of what is suggested for at least the better-off less developed countries is M. Selowsky, "Income Distribution, Basic Needs and Trade-Offs with Growth: The Case of Semi-Industrialized Latin American Countries," *World Development*, January 1981.

23. International Labor Organization and Overseas Development Council, *Employment, Growth and Basic Needs: A One-World Problem* (New York: Praeger, 1977), p. 33.

24. Ibid.; for a valuable account, see Annex A by C. Paolillo.

25. For example, S. Dell, "Basic Needs or Comprehensive Development: Should the UNDP Have a Development Strategy?" *World Development*, March 1979.

Chapter 12

1. It must be distinguished from the Prebisch/Economic Commission for Latin America economic doctrines, although these also employ the center/periphery dichotomy. To quote F. M. Cardoso and L. Faletto, *Dependency and Development in Latin America* (Berkeley and Los Angeles: University of California Press, 1979), p. viii, "ECLA economic theories and critiques were not based on an analysis of social process, did not call attention to imperialist relationships among countries, and did not take into account the asymmetric relations between classes."

2. P. A. Baran, *The Political Economy of Growth* (New York: Monthly Review Press, 1957; New York: Penguin, 1973), p. 402.

3. T. E. Weisskopf, "Dependence as an Explanation of Underdevelopment: A Critique," Center for Research on Economic Development, University of Michigan, mimeograph, February 1977.

4. We give no references. The interested reader will have no difficulty in finding extensive bibliographies.

5. Cf. C. L. Stevenson, *Ethics and Language* (New Haven, Conn.: Yale University Press, 1944).

6. Marx defined "embodied labour" as equal to exchange value. Surplus value is the difference between embodied labor and the wage paid. It thus necessarily arises if there is any gross profit. So labor is exploited by definition in any enterprise that covers its costs, since the rate of exploitation is the ratio between surplus value and wages. It is curious how even Schumpeter did not seem to understand fully the essence of this trick. He wrote: "Even if we do not admit that labour embodied is the 'cause' of exchange value in the ordinary sense, there is no logical rule to prevent us from *defining* labour embodied as exchange value, though this gives another and perhaps misleading sense to the latter term. For, on principle, we may call things what we please." J. A. Schumpeter, *History of Economic Analysis* (New York: Oxford University Press, 1954), p. 598. But he did not go on to say that if people use words without regard to their normal meaning, we had better be on our guard, although he did add in a footnote that "agitatorial glamour" would have been lost if Marx had defined words differently. Of course, the definition of value and surplus value are there to add plausible overtones to the definition of exploitation.

7. This appears to be A. Emmanuel's preferred definition in *Unequal Exchange* (New York: Monthly Review Press, 1972).

8. D. A. Belsey et al., eds., *Inflation, Trade and Taxes* (Columbus, Oh.: Ohio State University Press, 1976), p. 107.

9. In a celebrated article, "The Imperialism of Free Trade," *Economic History Review*, August 1953, John Gallagher and Ronald Robinson argued that there was no deep lull in imperialism during the period of British free trade. Before (but also during) the new colonialism beginning around 1870, free trade was secured, where possible, by informal influence and exercise of power, and only by direct rule if that became necessary and were possible. The United Kingdom imposed free trade or, like the

Godfather, made offers that could scarcely be refused, in order to secure it. But the title suggests that there is something inherently imperialistic, and hence, "exploitative" about free trade. This is not, I think, what the authors meant.

10. But even if, for example, country A sells only to country B, this does not preclude perfect competition.

11. See chapter 13.

12. There can also be conflict concerning employment policy, the amount of processing in the developing country, etc.

13. For the metals, see M. Radetski, "Market Structure and Bargaining Power," *Resources Policy*, June 1978. See also below for some facts about nationalization.

14. If the supplying enterprise is a wholly owned subsidiary, the price does not affect national ownership of the gross profits. There is only a tax issue, which has been dealt with in chapter 10.

15. L. Westphal, Y. W. Rhee, and G. Purcell, "Korean Industrial Competence: Whence It Came From," *World Bank Staff Working Papers*, no. 469, July 1981, pp. 62-63.

16. A. J. Yeats, *Trade Barriers Facing Developing Countries* (London: Macmillan, 1979), chap. 8.

17. See J. Bhagwati in *Foreign Aid*, ed. J. Bhagwati and R. S. Eckaus (London: Penguin, 1970).

18. They rose from 2.7 million tons in 1972 to 8.7 million tons in 1973, and triggered a wheat price rise, which matched that of oil. See chapter 17.

19. I can imagine some spokesman for more developed countries arguing that MDC clothing industries were dependent on the actions of the governments of Hong Kong, Taiwan, and South Korea in promoting exports. This is not really so, for the exports of these countries were fully in line with their comparative advantage, and a mild subsidization of exports (from South Korea and Taiwan, not Hong Kong) did no more than offset the effects of their own protection on the costs of their industries.

20. Radical attacks on aid, starting with K. Griffin and J. L. Enos, "Foreign Assistance: Objectives and Consequences," *Economic Development and Cultural Change*, April 1970, have much in common with the more laisser faire views of Bauer (for example, in P. T. Bauer, *Dissent on Development* [London: Weidenfeld and Nicholson, 1971]). J. Healey and C. Clift defend aid against these attacks in "The Development Rationale for Aid Re-Examined," *Overseas Development Institute Review*, no. 2 (1980). This article gives references to the case studies referred to in the text, as well as to other articles countering the anti-aid arguments. For a fuller account of my own views on most aspects of aid, views which I still subscribe to, see I. M. D. Little and J. M. Clifford, *International Aid* (London: Allen & Unwin, 1965).

21. Westphal, Rhee, and Purcell, "Korean Industrial Competence," p. 65.

22. Ibid., p. 66.

23. Ibid., p. 70.

24. Ibid., p. 69.

25. See E. Mansfield and A. Romeo, "Technology Transfer to Overseas Subsidiaries by U.S.-based Firms," *Quarterly Journal of Economics*, December 1980.

26. Cuba seems to be an exception. I can recall Michael Kalecki passing through Oxford on his return from an advisory trip to Cuba, apologetically telling a seminar that Cuba would have to concentrate on sugar.

27. But it was made. See H. W. Singer, "Problems of Industrialization of Underdeveloped Countries," *International Social Science Bulletin* 6, no. 2 (1954), where the author states: "Modern technology is not compatible with their endowments and their natural requirement.... At some stages it may have been an advantage to be a latecomer in economic development. By now, it is a serious disadvantage."

28. S. Lall, "Transnationals and the Third World: The R. and D. Factor," *Third World Quarterly*, July 1979; S. Lall, "Developing Countries as Exporters of Industrial Technology," *Research Policy* 9 (1980).

29. Exporting machinery is not exporting technology unless some extra element of rent accrues to the exporter as a result of the unique desirability of his product.

India, Mexico, Brazil, Argentina, and Taiwan have, however, exported complete plants, and here a technological element generally enters.

30. M. Y. Yoshino in *The International Corporation*, ed. C. P. Kindelberger (Cambridge, Mass.: MIT Press, 1970), p. 347.

31. United Nations, Commission on Transnational Corporations, *Transnational Corporations in World Development* (New York: United Nations, 1978), Tables III-64, III-68.

32. Many of the lessons are reviewed in J. D. Mitra, "The Capital Goods Sector in LDCs: A Case for State Intervention," *World Bank Staff Working Papers*, no. 343, 1979.

33. There is a large literature on the merits of "unbundling," or buying techniques independently of management and ownership, for example, by licensing and turnkey projects combined with training and technical assistance. There are also those who claim that licensing perpetuates itself and inhibits indigenous learning-by-doing; for example, L. K. Mytelka, "Licensing and Technology Dependence in the Andean Group," *World Development*, April 1978. My knowledge of this literature is too scanty for me to be able to review it adequately. But I suspect the verdict is "unproven" on most issues.

34. Westphal, Rhee, and Purcell, "Korean Industrial Competence," p. 61. For further discussion and illustration of the social benefits of trademarks in the export field, see D. Morawetz, *Why the Emperor's New Clothes Are Not Made in Colombia: A Case Study of Latin American and East Asian Clothing Exports* (London and New York: Oxford University Press, 1981). Morawetz rightly remarks, "... these benefits are almost totally ignored in the symposium on 'Trademarks in Developing Countries' that occupies the entire July 1979 issue of *World Development*."

35. R. Vernon, *Storm over the Multinationals* (London: Macmillan, 1977), p. 167. A short bibliography of the patent and trademark literature can be found in this book.

36. See D. J. Teece, "Technology Transfer by Multinational Firms: The Resource Cost of Transferring Technological Know-how," *Economic Journal*, June 1977.

37. See chapter 10.

38. The borderline between peasant and capitalist farming is unclear. If capitalism in agriculture is defined in terms of ownership of equipment and stock and the use of hired labor, then the evidence suggests that almost all peasant farming is capitalistic (for the operators of even very small holdings, less than a hectare, often hire labor). If this is dismissed as petty or primitive capitalism, a line still has to be drawn. Presumably, it is drawn at the size above which a holding is disapproved of as being too large for private operation, since those who are anticapitalistic cannot allow small holdings, of which they might approve, to be dubbed capitalistic.

39. See chapter 10.

40. See chapter 10.

41. Cf. W. A. Lewis, *Growth and Fluctuation 1870-1913* (London: Allen & Unwin, 1978), p. 222.

42. C. Leys, *Underdevelopment in Kenya* (London: Heinemann, 1975), p. 271.

43. The history of friendship and hostility between various local interests and the copper companies in Chile is told in an enlightening way by H. Moran, *Multinational Corporations and the Politics of Dependence* (Princeton, N.J.: Princeton University Press, 1974).

44. See, for instance, C. F. Bergsten, T. Horst, and T. H. Moran, eds., *American Multinationals and American Interests* (Washington, D.C.: Brookings Institution, 1978), chap. 5; also G. Reuber, *Private Foreign Investment in Development* (Oxford: Clarendon Press, 1973), Appendix A; and T. H. Moran in *American Multinationals and American Interests*, ed. Bergsten, Horst, and Moran; or any one of the many accounts of the oil industry since 1973.

45. M. L. Williams, "The Extent and Significance of the Nationalization of Foreign-Owned Assets in Developing Countries, 1956-1972," *Oxford Economic Papers*, July 1975. The figures given are calculated from Table VI.

46. S. Krasner, *Defending the National Interest* (Princeton, N.J.: Princeton University Press, 1978), Table V-1.

47. For a political analysis of the determination of expropriation, see D. A. Jodice, "Sources of Change in Third World Regimes for Foreign Direct Investment," *Interna-*

tional Organization, spring 1980. This article estimates that 12 percent of the 1967 stock was nationalized from 1968 to 1976. It contains an extensive bibliography of the nationalization literature.

48. Quoted in M. Kidron, *Foreign Investments in India* (London: Oxford University Press, 1965), p. 68.

49. Cf. F. Derossi, *The Mexican Entrepreneur* (Paris: Organization for Economic Cooperation and Development, Development Center, 1971), esp. chap. 2.

50. The word is part of the title of a book about Brazil, which also, however, suggests close parallels in Mexico; cf. P. Evans, *Dependent Development, the Alliance of Multinational, State and Local Capital in Brazil* (Princeton, N.J.: Princeton University Press, 1979). The meat of the book consists of accounts of linkages and cooperation, but also competition and conflict, between the state and public and private industry, both domestic and foreign, in the development of various industries. Such interaction must surely occur in any country, including more developed countries, where there are important elements of both public and foreign ownership. Brazilian industry may well be more monopolistic than most, and has one of the highest proportions of foreign ownership of industry in the world, as well as a strong public sector. But that is not the point. The word "alliance" implies cooperation in pursuit of a common objective. It is clear that the three elements of the so-called triple alliance in fact have different objectives. However, by implication, and only by implication, it is suggested that there is a conspiracy against the mass of the people.

51. United Nations, *Transnational Corporations in World Development*, Table III-54.

52. As an example, take Brazil, which is widely supposed to have the highest foreign penetration of manufacturing among less developed countries. The table cited above gives 29 percent as the 1974 foreign ownership share of assets in the 5,113 largest corporations, but without indicating the criterion of ownership. From Table III-50 in ibid., one can calculate that the stock of foreign capital was $6,889 million in 1976. World Bank Tables 1980 give a figure of $35,629 million for 1976 value added in manufacturing. If the overall capital output ratio were 2:1, a low figure, this gives a total capital stock of $71,258 million, and the foreign share in total assets would be about 10 percent. If all foreign capital were in joint venture with 51 percent foreign ownership (an absurd supposition), the foreign majority ownership of assets would rise to 20 percent. The same calculation for the United Kingdom gives 11 percent foreign ownership of assets in 1974, which accords much better with the 16 percent for foreign majority ownership given for 1971 in the table. But for some other countries, similar calculation yields wide divergencies.

53. Diaz Alejandro in *International Corporation*, ed. Kindelberger.

54. A. G. Frank, *Capitalism and Underdevelopment in Latin America* (New York: Monthly Review Press, 1967).

55. For an account, see A. Foster-Carter, "The Modes of Production Controversy," *New Left Review*, January/February 1978.

56. Some may never have accepted the radical idea of "underdevelopment" at all. For instance, Bill Warren held that a thriving industrial capitalist development, which was both "independent" (that is, broadly based) and even with an independent technological potential, was well under way in the Third World. See his "Imperialism and Capitalist Industrialization," *New Left Review*, September/October 1973.

57. Leys, *Underdevelopment in Kenya*, p. 273, quoted from a background paper by John Weeks, a member of the International Labor Organization Mission to Kenya.

58. Its conformity to the analysis of I. M. D. Little, T. Scitovsky, and M. FG. Scott, *Industry and Trade in Some Developing Countries* (London: Oxford University Press, 1970), is clear.

59. See, for example, Westphal, Rhee, and Purcell, "Korean Industrial Competence."

60. Cf. S. Jain, "Size Distribution of Income: A Compilation of Data," Washington, D.C.: World Bank, 1975.

61. See, for example, S. Amin, "Some Thoughts on Self-Reliance Development, Collective Self-Reliance and the NIEO" (Paper presented to the Conference on the Past and Prospects of the Economic World Order, Institute for International Economic Studies, Stockholm, 1978).

Notes to Pages 264-274

62. Ibid.
63. The word "autonomous" is often used. It is not clear whether it is meant to mean exactly the same as "independent" or not—and, as we have seen above, "independent" has many meanings.
64. This element in dependency theory (held true by Amin and others) would be denied by F. H. Cardoso, who cites as an "erroneous thesis" that "capitalist development at the periphery is not viable." Cf. F. H. Cardoso, "Current Theses on Latin American Development and Dependency: A Critique," *Latin American Research Review*, 1977.
65. In contrast, land ownership is extremely equal in Korea and Taiwan, as a result of land reform in the 1940s and 1950s, and in Singapore and Hong Kong there is almost no land.
66. For a discussion of selective de-linking, see C. F. Diaz Alejandro in *Rich and Poor Nations in the World Economy*, ed. A. Fishlow et al. (New York: McGraw-Hill Book Co., 1978).
67. For an interpretation of the Taiwan case, see I. M. D. Little in *Economic Growth and Structural Change in Taiwan*, ed. W. Galenson (Ithaca, N.Y.: Cornell University Press, 1979); see also I. M. D. Little in *Export-Led Industrialization and Development*, ed. E. Lee (Geneva: Asian Employment Programme, International Labor Organization, 1981).
68. S. Lall, "Is 'Dependence' a Useful Concept in Analysing Underdevelopment?" *World Development*, November 1975.
69. T. E. Weisskopf, "Dependence as an Explanation of Underdevelopment: A Critique," Center for Research on Economic Development, University of Michigan (mimeograph), February 1977.

Chapter 13

1. D. Morawetz, *Twenty-five Years of Economic Development* (Baltimore, Md.: Johns Hopkins University Press, 1977).
2. The figures in this section refer to 1978.
3. See chapter 17.
4. The translation of gross national product into U.S. dollars, using exchange rates, should *at best* be taken to show comparative real income on an ordinal scale. Purchasing power parities show much smaller differences. According to I. B. Kravis, A. Heston, and R. Summers, *International Comparisons of Real Product and Purchasing Power* (Baltimore, Md.: Johns Hopkins University Press, 1978), one should multiply incomes from less developed countries by a factor of about three for the very poorest, and about two for the richer. This would probably make India's absolute GNP larger than Spain's, although the meaning of any such proposition is exceedingly tenuous.
5. The Gini is the best-known measure of inequality. It has a clear intuitive meaning. It is the average difference between all possible pairs of incomes divided by twice the average income. It is zero for complete equality, and approaches 1.00 if all incomes are zero except one. Within countries, Ginis vary from 0.20 to 0.60.
6. All countries are included for which there were 1958 figures in the United Nations *Handbook of National Income Statistics*. Southern European LDCs are included, since they were generally thought to belong there in 1958.
7. Defined as $L = \frac{1}{n} \sum_{i=1}^{n} \log \frac{\mu}{y_i}$, where μ is the mean income. I am indebted to Dr. Sudhir Anand for tuition on the Theil index, and for the inequality calculations.
8. The source for cultivable land is Food and Agriculture Organization, *Production Yearbook 1979*.
9. International Bank for Reconstruction and Development, *World Tables*, 2nd ed. (Baltimore, Md.: Johns Hopkins University Press, 1980), Table V.

10. International Bank for Reconstruction and Development, *World Development Report 1980* (Washington, D.C.: IBRD, 1980), Table 9.
11. Ibid., Tables 3, 19.
12. Morawetz, *Twenty-five Years of Economic Development*.
13. International Bank for Reconstruction and Development, *World Development Report 1980*, Table 8.
14. I regressed growth of real income per caput from 1960 to 1978 (G) on 1958 real income per caput (Y), for the same set of less developed countries as used for the inequality estimates given above. A positive coefficient emerged, the equation being $G_{ALL} = -2.28 + 0.94 \log Y$. But R^2 was only 0.15, so that the fit is very poor. Experimenting, I estimated the same equation for Latin America and the Caribbean (LA), Africa, and Asia separately, with these results:

		R^2	N
G_{AFRICA} =	$1.90 - 0.14 \log Y$	0.00	35
G_{LA} =	$1.88 + 0.12 \log Y$	0.01	21
G_{ASIA} =	$-9.95 + 2.87 \log Y$	0.57	15

The South Asian countries included were Afghanistan, Bhutan, Burma, India, Nepal, Pakistan, and Sri Lanka; and the East Asian were Indonesia, Hong Kong, Korea, Malaysia, the Philippines, Singapore, Taiwan, and Thailand.

15. Our figures leave out Kampuchea, Laos, Lebanon, and Vietnam, but not Bangladesh, Egypt, Ethiopia, India, Israel, Jordan, Nigeria, Pakistan, Uganda, and other African and Asian countries where war or civil war was a significant factor in the late 1960s and 1970s.

16. United Nations, Committee on Trade and Development, *Handbook of International Trade and Development Statistics* (New York: United Nations, 1980). In this period, import prices for less developed countries scarcely rose, so these figures can also stand for real purchasing power.

17. B. I. Cohen and D. G. Sisler, "Exports of Developing Countries in the 1960s," *Review of Economics and Statistics*, November 1971.

18. After 1969, world inflation makes it essential to give purchasing power rather than dollar value.

Chapter 14

1. Cited in W. A. Brown, *The United States and the Restoration of World Trade* (Washington, D.C.: Brookings Institution, 1950).

2. The United Kingdom feared for a loss of reserves in the face of a dollar shortage even if its overall balance of payments was satisfactory. It also used discriminatory quotas to favor the exports of some colonies.

3. At this time, tariffs were not the main barriers to trade; also, many tariffs were higher than needed for protection.

4. Since adhesion to the General Agreement on Tariffs and Trade did not require legislation, the commitment to abolish quotas, except those permitted under GATT, could be overridden by existing domestic legal commitments.

5. Quotas were already permitted if domestic output restrictions were in force. But this covered neither European restrictions nor a new set of quotas required by American law for domestic price support. The European coal and steel community also required a waiver.

6. See J. M. Finger, "GATT Tariff Concessions and the Exports of Developing Countries," *Economic Journal*, September 1974. The main indirect effect is that the General Agreement on Tariffs and Trade's beneficial effect on the Organization for Economic Cooperation and Development's intratrade in the 1960s helped to raise income levels in the OECD, whose prosperity in turn increased demand for less developed countries' exports.

7. K. Dam, *Law and International Economic Organization* (Chicago: University of Chicago Press, 1970), p. 235. See also, on the Brasseur Plan and the origins of the gener-

alized special preference within the General Agreement on Tariffs and Trade, P. Tulloch, *The Politics of Preference* (London: Croon Helm, 1975), chap. 5.

8. See A. J. Yeats, *Trade Barriers Facing Developing Countries* (London: Macmillan, 1979), Tables 4 and 5. The original source is the United Nations Conference on Trade and Development.

9. Dam, *Law and International Economic Organization*, p. 235.

10. J. M. Finger, "Effects on the Kennedy Round Tariff Concessions on the Exports of Developing Countries," *Economic Journal*, March 1976, p. 87.

11. It has been calculated that nominal protection on total imports was reduced by 40 percent, and on imports from less developed countries by 31 percent; for effective protection the corresponding figures were 42 percent and 32 percent. But the absolute reductions were larger for LDCs, and it is far from obvious that the former are more relevant. See I. M. D. Little, T. Scitovsky, and M. FG. Scott, *Industry and Trade in Some Developing Countries* (London: Oxford University Press, 1970), pp. 273–274. Finger, "Effects of the Kennedy Round Tariff Concessions," however, shows proportionate reductions by the United States and the European Economic Community to be greater for LDCs than for more developed countries, although the reverse is the case for Japan.

12. Finger, "Effects of the Kennedy Round Tariff Concessions."

13. In M. E. Kreinin and J. M. Finger, "A Critical Survey of the N.I.E.O.," *Journal of World Trade Law*, November/December 1976.

14. Figures from the General Agreement on Tariffs and Trade quoted by P. Tulloch, "Developing Countries and Trade in Textiles," *Overseas Development Institute Review*, no. 2 (1974).

15. D. B. Keesing, "World Trade and Output of Manufactures: Structural Trends and Developing Countries, Exports," *World Bank Staff Working Papers*, no. 316, January 1979. The omitted part of the quotation refers to a table that shows that U.S. imports of clothing rose in value by 26 percent per annum from 1973 to 1976, and textiles by 8 percent per annum. (The former was by 1976 worth four times the latter.)

16. Ibid., p. 59. Keesing refers also to I. Walter, "Non-tariff Barriers and the Export Performance of Developing Economies," *American Economic Review*, May 1971. But nontariff barriers in Japan were very probably more serious than in any European country, despite the quotation.

17. Many would add the growth of transnational corporations, since these to some extent plan and regulate rather than merely respond at arms' length to market trends. It is not, however, clear that such private planning has increased. The role of the transnational corporations is considered in chapter 12.

18. Recently, 40 percent of U.S. imports have come from, and 30 percent of exports go to, state-controlled enterprises. Of exports to less developed countries, 52 percent were bought by government agencies. See R. E. Baldwin, *Beyond the Tokyo Round Negotiations* (London: Trade Policy Research Centre, 1979).

19. Only Guinea refused to become associated; other French and Netherlands dependencies were covered by a similar agreement.

20. Gibraltar aside, I suppose the real reason for exclusion was their potential or actual trading importance, with Sri Lanka perhaps suffering in order not to make the real reason too obvious. I presume Gibraltar was excluded for some diplomatic reason. On the other hand, no African country, however large—for example, Nigeria—could be excluded. Several non-Commonwealth African countries were roped in (for example, Ethiopia and Liberia), thus making the European Economic Community African coverage complete, apart from South Africa, Rhodesia, and the remaining handful of colonies.

21. Although Lomé was concluded in February 1975, it was substantially part of the scene before the eruption of the New International Economic Order.

22. The odd man out: born 1922, and since deceased. The Latin American Free Trade Area was also wound up in 1980.

23. See T. Murray, *Trade Preferences for Developing Countries* (London: Macmillan, 1977).

24. Ibid., pp. 36–50.

25. Ibid., p. 16. The United States also received little or no support from Europe and probably tired of being a minority of one.

26. Ibid., p. 132.

27. These mostly comprise the Latin American countries, and South and Southeast Asia (with various exclusions depending on the scheme).

28. R. E. Baldwin and T. E. Murray, "MFN Tariff Reductions and Developing Country Trade Benefits under the GSP," *Economic Journal*, March 1977. Also Murray, *Trade Preferences for Developing Countries*, chap. 7.

29. Arising from higher prices on products that hit generalized special preference ceilings.

30. The Baldwin-Murray estimates have been updated to 1974–75 trade flows and prices by T. B. Birnberg in *Policy Alternatives for a New International Economic Order*, ed. W. R. Cline (New York: Praeger, 1979). The updated figure is $1.1 billion, slightly more than 1 percent of the total exports of non-oil-exporting less developed countries. Both these estimates showed that the gain from most-favored-nation tariff reductions under the Tokyo Round for LDCs would far outweigh the loss due to the consequential erosion of preferences by a factor of 10 to 1, or more. The United Nations Conference on Trade and Development had been very suspicious of MFN reductions because of the erosion effect and produced an estimate with the opposite result.

31. So far as I am concerned, the above assessment of generalized special preferences, if it is wise, is not being wise after the event. I told the late C. A. R. Crosland, then president of the U.K. Board of Trade in 1968, before the United Nations Conference on Trade and Development II, that in my opinion the less developed countries were chasing after something that would do them little if any good, and that it would be much better to increase aid. He rightly said that this advice, previously unsought, came too late.

32. Murray, *Trade Preferences for Developing Countries*, Table 7.4. Taiwan alone accounted for 20 percent despite the fact that it was excluded from the European Economic Community's generalized special preferences, since it was not one of the Group of Seventy-seven.

33. In the first decade after World War II, intra-MDC effective protection was very high (as a result of quota restrictions), almost certainly higher than MDC effective protection against LDC exports.

34. R. Blackhurst, N. Marian, and J. Tumlir, *Adjustment, Trade and Growth in Developed and Developing Countries* (Geneva: General Agreement on Tariffs and Trade, September 1978), Table 7. These figures exclude oil-exporting less developed countries.

35. Quoted in D. Lal, "Market Access for Semi Manufactures from Developing Countries" (Geneva and London: Graduate Institute for International Studies, Trade Policy Research Centre, 1979).

36. Keesing, "World Trade and Output of Manufactures," p. 47. During the same period, U.S. clothing prices rose by less than 4 percent per annum.

37. Blackhurst, Marian, and Tumlir, *Adjustment, Trade and Growth in Developed and Developing Countries*, Appendix, Table I.

38. There is, however, some evidence that the African countries, while undoubtedly gaining from their preferences in the European Economic Community, have paid more for some imports as a result of a limitation of competition that may be furthered by this special relation. See Yeats, *Trade Barriers Facing Developing Countries*, chap. 8. In theory, the nonreciprocity of preferences under the Lomé agreement implies that the African countries can trade where they will and should not pay more than world prices. French technical and administrative assistance may, however, preserve informal preferences for some time.

Chapter 15

1. But Mexico and three Central American Republics accepted Article VIII immediately.

2. Germany and the Netherlands had a minirevaluation in 1961.

3. Multiple rates have, of course, their equivalents in terms of trade taxes and subsidies. Economists have consequently often accused the International Monetary Fund of extreme economic naiveté. This is unjust, for there may be a case for limiting trade price interventions to tariffs and subsidies. Although it is also true that there can be legislative or bureaucratic reasons for using multiple exchange rates, I would sympathize with this view. It should be noted that if tariffs or subsidies had been in the purview of the IMF, it would doubtless have argued in favor of simpler and more rational systems.

4. See J. Williamson, *The Failure of World Monetary Reform, 1971-1974* (New York: New York University Press, 1977), p. 6. The "trotting" or "crawling" peg is, strictly, a par value system. It just means that the peg is moved very frequently. The difference between "crawling" and "trotting" is obvious (see also chapter 5 above, note 10).

5. Tied aid is an exception.

6. On the subject of the paragraph, see C. Diaz Alejandro, "Less Developed Countries and the Post-1971 International Finance System," *Princeton Essays in International Finance*, no. 108, 1975.

7. The Group of Ten were those members of the International Monetary Fund who subscribed in 1961 to the "General Agreement to Borrow," which was a general agreement to *lend* their currencies to the IMF in the event of them becoming scarce in the Fund. An expected occasion for this scarcity would be a large U.S. drawing. Working Party 3 of the Organization for Economic Cooperation and Development, also formed in 1961, came to have an identical membership (the ten largest OECD countries).

8. This raises the question as to how far exclusive monetary clubs can legitimately be objected to. Those outside are much less likely to lose than in the case of common markets or free-trade areas.

9. See R. Solomon, *The International Monetary System* (New York: Harper & Row, 1977), chap. 8, for an account of the "Gestation and Birth of the SDR 1965-1969." The influence of the International Monetary Fund was also important. The IMF naturally preferred a more global scheme under its own auspices to a more exclusive club, and this stance was supported by the United States.

10. Less developed countries were marginally involved in that several joint meetings were held between the Group of Ten deputies and the International Monetary Fund Executive Board in 1966 and 1967. See Solomon, *International Monetary System*.

11. The clumsy name was chosen to please the French, who did not want an asset to be created under the International Monetary Fund. So it was not called an asset.

12. M. Stamp, "The Fund and the Future," *Lloyds Bank Review*, October 1958; M. Stamp, "The Stamp Plan—1962 Version," *Moorgate and Wall Street Review*, October 1962.

13. J. Williamson in *The New International Order: The North-South Debate*, ed. J. Bhagwati (Cambridge, Mass.: MIT Press, 1977).

14. The shortage of aid flows could be partly attributed to a shortage of reserves. By 1959 donor countries had already begun to tie their aid in order to try to minimize its balance-of-payments impact.

15. For enthusiastic support of the Stamp plan, see I. M. D. Little and J. M. Clifford, *International Aid* (London: Allen & Unwin, 1965), pp. 241-245.

16. For an excellent account of the species, see Williamson in *New International Order*, ed. Bhagwati.

17. See H. G. Grubel in *Monetary Problems of the International Economy*, ed. R. A. Mundell and A. K. Swoboda (Chicago: University of Chicago Press, 1969).

18. The trade balance had worsened as a result of the Vietnam War in the late 1960s. A consequential worsening of the overall balance was delayed until the early 1970s by tight monetary policies.

19. Williamson, *Failure of World Monetary Reform*, p. 61.

20. By 1980, the Fund had several extraordinary facilities. Two of them, the Compensatory Finance Scheme and the Buffer Stock Financing Facility, were established in the 1960s. But it is more convenient to consider these together with other new

facilities established in the 1970s, in chapter 17. In the 1960s, these new facilities in any case played a very minor role.

21. Nor, as a result of a policy decision, by the Organization for European Economic Cooperation countries during the Marshall Aid period.

22. This was the first Fund loan to India and the first significant loan to any Asian country. The Fund was probably more at sea than the British and U.S. aid agencies and the International Bank for Reconstruction and Development.

23. For a discussion of the "two-gap" model, see chapter 9. The text claims, in the light of that discussion, that a long-run foreign exchange gap is not a tenable concept.

24. There may be trade controls, but no exchange control, as in Mexico. In this case, there will be excess demand for foreign goods, but not for foreign currency.

25. A large number of liberalization attempts have been examined in the ten-country National Bureau of Economic Research study of trade regimes. Some, but not all, of these involved the International Monetary Fund. Two summary volumes are J. Bhagwati, *Anatomy and Consequences of Trade Control Regimes* (New York: National Bureau of Economic Research, 1978); and A. O. Kruger, *Liberalization Attempts and Consequences* (New York: National Bureau of Economic Research, 1978). A very brief summary of these works is contained in I. M. D. Little in *Challenges to a Liberal International Economic Order*, ed. R. D. Amacher, G. Haberler, and T. D. Willet (Washington, D.C.: American Enterprise Institute, 1979).

26. South Korea could also be cited. She devalued frequently rather than adopting a trotting peg. But between devaluations, the authorities saw to it that exporting remained profitable, by increasing the value of various export incentives.

27. But conditionality was not part of the original Articles of Agreement. For an account of the development of conditionality, see S. Dell and R. Lawrence, *The Balance of Payments Adjustment Process in Developing Countries* (London: Penguin, 1980), Appendix.

Chapter 16

1. Formally, the New International Economic Order was born in a declaration of the United Nations General Assembly in May 1974. Most of its substance is quite old. Regarded as a set of economic demands made by a coordinated movement of less developed countries, its roots go back at least to the first meeting of the United Nations Conference on Trade and Development in 1964. For a brief history, see L. Anell and B. Nygren, *The Developing Countries and the World Economic Order* (London: Methuen, 1980).

2. "International" may refer to relations between individuals who are resident in, or citizens of, different countries. Where such relations are between nations or states, we use the word "interstate" or "intergovernmental."

3. J. Rawls, *A Theory of Justice* (Oxford: Clarendon Press, 1972).

4. R. Nozick, *Anarchy, State and Utopia* (Oxford: Basil Blackwell, 1974).

5. My account is brief to the point of absurdity. A longer exposition is I. M. D. Little in *Issues in International Economics*, ed. P. Oppenheimer (Boston, Mass.: Oriel Press, 1978).

6. John Locke, *Second Essay on Government*, ed. J. W. Gough (New York: Macmillan, 1956), chap. 2.

7. Joshi in *Issues in International Economics*, ed. Oppenheimer.

8. Several authors have accused "liberals" of inconsistency in advocating free markets for goods and services, but not for persons. In fact, few liberals claim that governments should never intervene in product or capital markets. Even those who do advocate uninhibited free trade together with control of immigration need not be inconsistent. They are inconsistent only if free migration would serve the same ends as they claim for free trade. A utilitarian would have little difficulty in making a strong case that free migration was unlikely to maximize happiness.

Notes to Pages 325-341

9. For the concept of a system presupposing much less contact and assumption of obligation between members than in a society, see H. Bull, *The Anarchical Society* (London: Macmillan, 1977), pp. 9-15.
10. R. W. Tucker, *The Inequality of Nations* (New York: Basic Books, 1977).
11. A. Mazrui in *The New International Order: The North-South Debate*, ed. J. Bhagwati (Cambridge, Mass.: MIT Press, 1977), pp. 373-374.
12. On order versus justice, see especially Bull, *Anarchical Society*, chap. 4; and Tucker, *Inequality of Nations*, chap. 3.
13. The growing weight of Japan has caused a ninety-degree twist in the perceived development surface of the earth. The reader can substitute North for West whenever it seems more appropriate.

Chapter 17

1. The New International Economic Order is set out in the "Declaration of Establishment of" and "Program of Action on" a New International Economic Order, General Assembly, May 1, 1974. For the detail, and the vast number of subsequent declarations in innumerable meetings and conferences, see E. Laszlo et al., *The Objectives of the New International Economic Order* (New York: Pergamon Press, 1978).
2. This latter concern did not much show up in proposals for action, with the exception of a Special United Nations Emergency Fund for the most seriously affected for a twelve-month period. This fund was duly established on the basis of voluntary contributions. It attracted derisory support.
3. The concept of a just price dates at least from medieval times. It was a form of incomes policy. Artisans should receive prices that would enable them to maintain, but no more, their accepted position in an hierarchical religious society. In a world in which cotton is exported by the United States and Uganda, and coffee by Brazil and Haiti, the concept makes no sense.
4. Committee for Development Planning, Report of the Eleventh Session, April 1975 (paras. 100-101).
5. K. Laursen, "The Integrated Programme for Commodities," *World Development*, April 1978. This also contains a bibliography of post-New International Economic Order literature on the subject. Another rather broader discussion is S. Harris, M. Salmon, and B. Smith, *Analysis of Commodity Markets for Policy Purposes* (London: Trade Policy Research Centre, 1978). The most recent theoretical work is D. M. G. Newbery and J. E. Stiglitz, *The Theory of Commodity Price Stabilization: A Study in the Economics of Risk* (London: Oxford University Press, 1981).
6. J. R. Behrman in *Policy Alternatives for a New International Economic Order*, ed. W. R. Cline (New York: Praeger, 1979).
7. Ibid. Overview chap., Table 1.
8. This ignores the operations of the governments of less developed countries, themselves.
9. These four alone account for about 40 percent of the exports of less developed countries of coffee, cocoa, and rubber. The only poor country with absolutely large exports of the three commodities is Indonesia. If benefits were proportional to exports, then Indonesia would gain about $40 million per annum—rather small beer for her.
10. Behrman in *Policy Alternatives for a New International Economic Order*, ed. Cline, p. 95.
11. For a review of commodity negotiations and agreements, see Food and Agricultural Organization, *Commodity Review and Outlook 1980-81*, March 1981.
12. For an account of the negotiations and further detail, see A. Sengupta, "Issues in the North South Negotiations on Commodities," *Overseas Development Institute Review*, no. 2 (1979).
13. L. Anell and B. Nygren, *The Developing Countries and the World Economic Order* (London: Methuen, 1980), p. 135, quoting M. Perez-Guerrero, sometime secretary-general of the United Nations Conference on Trade and Development.

14. We concentrate on wheat because coarse grains are mainly fed to animals and do not have the same welfare connotations. Rice is very small in international trade; and rice shortages, which can be serious, raise quite different problems. Insecurity of supply is probably an increasing problem because of the desire of many Asian countries to be self-sufficient.

15. See D. G. Johnson in *The New International Order: The North-South Debate*, ed. J. Bhagwati (Cambridge, Mass.: MIT Press, 1977).

16. S. Reutlinger, "Food Insecurity: Magnitude and Remedies," *World Development*, June 1978.

17. A country might be in the position of being unable to afford adequate imports, although both food prices and local food production were normal, as a result of failure of exports. But the Compensatory Financing Facility covers this case.

18. A. H. Sarris et al. in *Policy Alternatives for a New International Economic Order*, ed. Cline. The present section owes much to this article, which also has a bibliography of recent work.

19. Reutlinger argues that an insurance scheme with no physical buffer stock is probably most economical in ensuring any given degree of food security.

20. Sarris et al. in *Policy Alternatives for a New International Economic Order*, ed. Cline.

21. For an account, see D. E. Hathaway, "Food Issues in North-South Relations," *The World Economy*, January 1981. The author concludes that it will be impossible to reach agreement except in a much smaller forum involving only the major exporters and importers, remarking, "I am afraid, however, that many countries would prefer a scheme in which they play a part rather than a scheme that works but does not require their participation."

22. This subject is also dealt with by Sarris et al. in *Policy Alternatives for a New International Economic Order*, ed. Cline. An International Emergency Food Reserve has been created.

23. Recent discussions include ibid.; P. J. Isenman, and H. W. Singer, "Food Aid: Disincentive Effects and Their Policy Implications," *Economic Development and Cultural Change*, January 1977; and S. J. Maxwell and H. W. Singer, "Food Aid to Developing Countries: A Survey," *World Development*, March 1979. These are quite favorable to food aid, a view with which I would concur.

24. J. A. Katz, "Capital Flows and Developing Country Debt," *World Bank Staff Working Papers*, no. 352, August 1979, Table A-2. For the (incomplete) coverage of World Bank debt figures, see this publication.

25. International Bank for Reconstruction and Development, *World Development Report, 1979* (Washington, D.C.: IBRD, 1979), Table 22.

26. This is an International Monetary Fund category of countries comprising Bahrein, Bolivia, Congo, Ecuador, Egypt, Gabon, Malaysia, Mexico, Peru, Syria, Trinidad and Tobago, and Tunisia.

27. International Bank for Reconstruction and Development, *World Development Report, 1979*, Table 2. The question arises as to how to deflate debt. The burden of debt is reduced by inflation to the extent that inflation makes it easier to repay—or pay the interest. Payment can be made by reducing imports or increasing exports. It could therefore be argued that one should deflate by whichever price index rises most. If import prices rise most, and the terms of trade worsen, then it is most desirable to repay by reducing imports. Nevertheless, an average of import and export prices seems more reasonable. Deflating by import prices yields a figure of 9.9 percent, and by export prices 7.6 percent. Inflation in this period was combined with a worsening of the terms of trade of many less developed countries. The two together may increase a country's balance-of-payments problem. But the net result cannot be attributed simply to inflation, or constitute an argument, in the manner of the United Nations Conference on Trade and Development, that inflation may not reduce the debt burden (see United Nations Conference on Trade and Development, Secretariat, "Some Aspects of the Impact of Inflation on the Debt Burden of Developing Countries," *World Development*, February 1979).

28. International Bank for Reconstruction and Development, *World Development Report, 1979*, Table 10.

Notes to Pages 346-354

29. Ibid., Table 15.
30. Ibid., Table 1.
31. G. W. Smith in *Policy Alternatives for a New International Economic Order*, ed. Cline, Table 6. Little difference would have been made by using export prices from less developed countries as a deflator.
32. Calculated from International Bank for Reconstruction and Development, *World Development Report 1980* (Washington, D.C.: IBRD, 1980), Tables 3-5.
33. United Nations, Conference on Trade and Development, *Handbook of International Trade and Development Statistics* (New York: United Nations, 1980), Tables 2-3 and 2-4.
34. See International Monetary Fund, *World Economic Outlook* (Washington, D.C.: IMF, May 1980). Almost all debt from less developed countries is denominated in dollars.
35. Smith in *Policy Alternatives for a New International Economic Order*, ed. Cline, Table 9.
36. Ibid., Table 16.
37. As advocated by I. M. D. Little and J. A. Mirrlees, *Project Appraisal and Planning for Developing Countries* (London: Heinemann, and New York: Basic Books, 1974); and Little and Mirrlees, *Manual of Industrial Project Analysis*, vol. 2 (Paris: Organization for Economic Cooperation and Development, 1968).
38. This point is elaborated in E. L. Bacha and C. F. Diaz Alejandro, "Financial Markets: A View from the Semi-Periphery," Yale Growth Center Discussion Paper, no. 367, 1981, which also illuminates most of the issues discussed in this section, and more.
39. For an account, see A. C. Cizauskas, "International Debt Renegotiations: Lessons from the Past," *World Development*, February 1979.
40. Smith in *Policy Alternatives for a New International Economic Order*, ed. Cline, discusses the prospects for rescheduling with what he describes as "tentative optimism." Since he wrote, there has been a further major increase in oil prices. But it should also be noted that reschedulings do not constitute disaster. The high debt service countries are mostly in Latin America; others include Zaire, Egypt, Zambia, and Algeria. See International Bank for Reconstruction and Development, *World Development Report 1980*, Table 13.
41. J. de Larosière, *International Monetary Fund Survey*, November 10, 1980.
42. International Bank for Reconstruction and Development, *World Development Report 1980*, Table 7.
43. H. Bohme, "Restraints on Competition in World Shipping," London Trade Policy Research Centre, 1978, p. 47.
44. This was, for instance, also evident in the United Nations Conference on Trade and Development's research on transnational corporations. See chapter 10.
45. For some detail, see Bohme, "Restraints on Competition in World Shipping," and also P. M. Wijkman, "Effects of Cargo Reservation," Institute for International Economic Studies, *Marine Policy*, reprint 14, October 1980. These articles contain references to the relevant documents of the United Nations Conference on Trade and Development, and other works of shipping economists.
46. See, for example, R. Turvey, "A Simple Analysis of Optimal Fares On Scheduled Transport Services," *Economic Journal*, March 1975.
47. Wijkman, "Effects of Cargo Reservation." A fifty-fifty division between more developed countries and less developed countries is assumed. The distribution of the 20 percent reserved for "pirates" evidently could not be estimated. But the fifty-fifty division gives a broad idea of the results.
48. Cyprus, Liberia, Oman, Panama, Singapore, and Somalia.
49. Wijkman, "Effects of Cargo Reservation," p. 283.
50. See S. J. Rubin in *The International Corporation*, ed. C. P. Kindelberger (Cambridge, Mass.: MIT Press, 1970).
51. United Nations, Conference on Trade and Development, *An International Code of Conduct on Transfer of Technology* (New York: United Nations, 1975), chap. 10.
52. International Monetary Fund, *Survey*, January 12, 1981. Earlier there was a sixteen-currency basket.

53. Ibid.
54. This is the form of link favored by less developed countries. For a history of the many forms of link proposed, see Williamson in *The New International Order*, ed. Bhagwati; or W. R. Cline, *International Monetary Reform and the Developing Countries* (Washington, D.C.: Brookings Institution, 1976).
55. Almost all less developing countries, except oil exporters, have used special drawing rights. See International Monetary Fund, *Annual Report 1980* (Washington, D.C.: IMF, 1980), Tables 1-17. They have not found the SDR a satisfactory reserve asset, preferring to hold national currencies despite the greater risk.
56. For an account of the Committee of Twenty negotiations, see J. Williamson, *The Failure of World Monetary Reform, 1971-1974* (New York: New York University Press, 1977).
57. See, for example, Cline, *International Monetary Reform and the Developing Countries*.
58. International Monetary Fund, *Survey*, January 12, 1981.
59. The form of the link I favored in 1965 (see chapter 15, note 15) would have had quite different and more relevant consequences—the proposal was that the special drawing rights should go to the International Development Agency. Such a link has not found favor with the Group of Seventy-seven.
60. Williamson, *Failure of World Monetary Reform*, p. 174. The position of the less developed countries is more fully described on pp. 91-95. Williamson's most acid comments on unhelpfulness are reserved for Australia (p. 96).
61. J. Williamson in *The International Monetary System and the Developing Nations*, ed. D. M. Leibziger (Washington, D.C.: Agency for International Development, 1976); also Cline, *International Monetary Reform and the Developing Countries*, pp. 32-34.
62. Cline, *International Monetary Reform and the Developing Countries*, p. 33.
63. See, for example, R. Blackhurst and J. Tumlir, *Trade Relations under Flexible Exchange Rates* (Geneva: General Agreement on Tariffs and Trade, 1980).
64. Only one—the Gambia—to sterling. How the mighty have fallen!
65. International Monetary Fund, *Annual Report 1980*, Table 13.
66. Ibid., pp. 85-88.
67. Figures and groupings from the International Monetary Fund. See International Monetary Fund, *Annual Report 1980*, Table 5. Non-oil less developed countries are all LDCs except Algeria, Indonesia, Iran, Iraq, Kuwait, Libya, Nigeria, Oman, Qatar, Saudi Arabia, the United Arab Emirates, and Venezuela.
68. Mainly grants from Official Development Assistance and direct private investment.
69. International Bank for Reconstruction and Development, *World Development Report 1980*, Tables 3-4.
70. Reported in International Monetary Fund, *Survey*, February 9, 1981. For a private assessment, see S. Griffith-Jones, "The Growth of Multinational Banking, the Euro-currency Market, and their Effects on Developing Countries," *Journal of Development Studies*, January 1980.
71. These matters are discussed in the International Monetary Fund, *Survey*, September 3, 1979; and in the International Monetary Fund, *Annual Report 1980*.
72. International Monetary Fund, *Survey*, November 10, 1980, p. 349.
73. Bacha and Diaz Alejandro, "Financial Markets."
74. See L. M. Goreux, *Compensatory Financing Facility* (Washington, D.C.: International Monetary Fund, 1980) for a full description of the facility.
75. de Larosière, *International Monetary Fund Survey*, April 1981.
76. Of these eight billion special drawing rights, two billion came from Saudi Arabia, and a little over one billion came from other countries in the Organization of Petroleum Exporting Countries (Abu Dhabi, Kuwait, Nigeria, and Venezuela).
77. de Larosière, *International Monetary Fund Survey*, April 1981.
78. B. Balassa, "The Newly Industrialized Countries after the Oil Crisis," *World Bank Staff Working Papers*, no. 437.
79. de Larosière, *International Monetary Fund Survey*, April 1981.
80. Organization for Economic Cooperation and Development, *Development Cooperation* (OECD, 1980), Table 4-6.

81. Using the United Nations Conference on Trade and Development's import unit value index for non-oil less developed countries as a deflator. Ibid., however, states that the Development Assistance Committee, Official Development Assistance grew at about 5 percent in real terms (p. 74) but without stating the deflator used. Organization for Petroleum Exporting Countries ODA grew faster, but little of it goes to low-income countries.

82. On the subject of this paragraph, see ibid., chap. 8.

83. See H. Hughes and J. Waelbroeck, "Trade and Protection in the 1970s: Can the Growth of Developing Country Exports Continue in the 1980s?" *World Economy*, June 1981. This article derives from a large research project on penetration and the roots of protectionism, organized by the World Bank.

84. D. B. Keesing and M. Wolf, *Textile Quotas against Developing Countries* (London: Trade Policy Research Centre, 1980). This is a definitive treatment of the whole subject. For a shorter account, see Keesing and Wolf, "Questions on International Trade in Textiles and Clothing," *The World Economy*, March 1981.

85. For a restrained plea from Sri Lanka, a small, poor country that has rather recently promoted a clothing industry, see L. Athulathmudali, "Forthcoming Negotiations on the Multi-fibre Arrangement," *The World Economy*, June 1980.

86. There are many studies pointing out that rising imports from less developed countries are only a minor cause of falling employment, and that other industries increase employment as a result of higher trade with LDCs. References can be found in Keesing and Wolf, *Textile Quotas against Developing Countries*.

87. Economists laud subsidies as a mode of promoting an industry. But they have in mind subsidies carefully designed to counter defects of the price mechanism. This is very different from subsidization to further sectional interests. On this, see D. Lal, "The Wistful Mercantilism of Mr. Dell," *The World Economy*, June 1978; E. Dell, "The Wistful Liberalism of Deepak Lal," *The World Economy*, May 1979; and D. Lal, "Politicians, Economists and Protection—The Deaf Meet the Blind," *The World Economy*, September 1980.

88. For an account of the new protectionism, apart from textiles and clothing, see L. M. Gard and J. Riedel, "Safeguard Protection of Industry in Developed Countries: Assessment of the Implications for Developing Countries," *Weltwirtschaftliches Archiv* Bank 16, Heft 3 (1980). The authors conclude that "apart from textiles and clothing, recent protectionism in the U.S., E.E.C. and Japan, in the form of *official* changes in import barriers, does not constitute a serious obstacle to continued expansion of LDC exports. However, the difficulty of just documenting informal and unofficial forms of protectionism precludes one from being too sanguine about the recent experience."

89. P. J. Ginman et al., "Mixed Blessings for the Third World in Codes on Nontariff Measures," *The World Economy*, September 1980, p. 231.

90. For an excellent discussion of voluntary export restraints and Article XIX, see B. Hindley, "Voluntary Export Constraints and the GATT's Main Escape Clause," *The World Economy*, November 1980.

91. Ginman et al., "Mixed Blessings"; B. Balassa, "The Tokyo Round and the Developing Countries," *Journal of World Trade Law*, March/April 1980.

92. This section does not do full justice to the problems of trade policy reform in a context of the General Agreement on Tariffs and Trade. During the 1970s, the Trade Policy Research Centre, London, sponsored a large number of works on this subject. These include: P. Lloyd, *Anti-dumping Actions and the GATT System*, 1977; T. E. Josling, *Agriculture in the Tokyo Round Negotiations*, 1977; H. B. Malmgren, *International Order for Public Subsidies*, 1977; D. Robertson, *Fail Safe Systems for Trade Liberalisation*, 1977; S. Golt, *Developing Countries in the GATT System*, 1978; R. E. Hudec, *Adjudication of International Trade Disputes*, 1978; and R. E. Baldwin, *Beyond the Tokyo Round Negotiations*, 1979.

Chapter 18

1. The best way of dealing with textiles and clothing might be to permit an initial increase in tariffs, combined with treaty arrangements to reduce them gradually to an average level (which might be zero) in fifteen years, and to forswear all quotas.

2. On the difficult subject of the control of export controls, see C. F. Bergsten, *Completing the GATT: Towards New International Rules to Govern Export Controls* (London: British-North American Committee, 1974).

3. See the literature cited in note 92 of chapter 17.

4. The Group of Twenty-four consists of eight members each from Africa, Asia, and Latin America, and speaks for the less developed countries on matters of monetary reform.

5. That global reserves have long been endogenous to the system is argued by P. M. Oppenheimer, "International Monetary Arrangements: The Limits to Planning" (Paper presented to the Panel of Academic Consultants, no. 8, Bank of England 1979).

6. K. A. Chrystal, "International Money and the Future of the SDR," *Essays in International Finance*, no. 128, Princeton University (1978).

7. D. Lal, "A Liberal International Economic Order: The International Monetary System and Economic Development," *Essays in International Finance*, no. 139, Princeton University, 1980.

8. V. Joshi, "Exchange Rates, International Liquidity and Economic Development," *The World Economy*, May 1979.

9. Lal, "Liberal International Economic Order."

10. Group of Twenty-four Communique, Annual Fund and World Bank Meeting, 1980, reported in *International Monetary Fund Survey*, October 13, 1980.

11. Joshi, "Exchange Rates, International Liquidity and Economic Development," p. 267.

12. See Group of Twenty-four Communique as reported in *International Monetary Fund Survey*, October 13, 1980.

13. On this point, see P. D. Henderson, "Survival, Development and the Report of the Brandt Commission," *The World Economy*, June 1980, p. 109.

14. *International Monetary Fund Survey*, October 13, 1980, p. 302.

15. Independent Commission on International Development Issues, *North-South: A Programme for Survival* [Brandt Report] (London: Pan Books, 1980), p. 260.

Bibliography

Abramovitz, M., et al., eds. *The Allocation of Economic Resources.* Stanford, Calif.: Stanford University Press, 1959.
Acharya, S. N. "Perspectives and Problems of Development in Low-Income, Sub-Saharan Africa." *World Development*, February 1981.
Adelman, I., and Robinson, S. *Income Distribution Policy in Developing Countries.* Oxford, England, and New York: Oxford University Press, 1978.
Agarwala, A. N., and Singh, S. P., eds. *The Economics of Underdevelopment.* London: Oxford University Press, 1958.
Ahluwalia, M. S. "Inequality, Poverty and Development." *Journal of Development Economics* 3 (1976).
―――――. "Rural Poverty and Agricultural Growth in India." *The Journal of Development Studies*, April 1978.
―――――; Carter, N. G.; and Chenery, H. B. "Growth and Poverty in Developing Countries." *Journal of Development Economics*, September 1979.
Ahmed, I. "Farm Size and Labor Use: Some Alternative Explanations." *Oxford Bulletin of Economics and Statistics*, February 1981.
Amacher, R. D.; Haberler, G.; and Willett, T. D.; eds. *Challenges to a Liberal International Economic Order.* Washington, D.C.: American Enterprise Institute, 1979.
Amin, S. "Some Thoughts on Self-Reliant Development, Collective Self-Reliance and the NIEO." Paper presented to the Conference on the Past and Prospects of the Economic World Order. Institute for International Economic Studies, Stockholm, 1978.
Anell, L., and Nygren, B. *The Developing Countries and the World Economic Order.* London: Methuen, 1980.
Athulathmudali, L. "Forthcoming Negotiations on the Multi-fibre Arrangement." *The World Economy*, June 1980.

Bacha, E. L., and Diaz Alejandro, C. F. "Financial Markets: A View from the Semi-Periphery." *Yale Growth Center Discussion Paper*, no. 367 (1981).

Bibliography

Baer, W., and Kerstenetsky, I., eds. *Inflation and Growth in Latin America*. Chicago: R. D. Irwin, 1964.

Balassa, B. "Export Incentives and Export Performance in Developing Countries: A Comparative Analysis." *Weltwirtschaftliches Archiv*, Band 114 (1978).

──────. "The Newly Industrializing Countries after the Oil Crisis." *World Bank Staff Working Papers*, no. 437 (October 1980).

──────. *Policy Reform in Developing Countries*. London: Oxford University Press, 1977.

──────. "Reforming the System of Incentives in Developing Countries." *World Development* 3 (1975).

──────. *The Structure of Protection in Developing Countries*. Baltimore, Md.: Johns Hopkins University Press, 1971.

──────. "The Tokyo Round and the Developing Countries." *Journal of World Trade Law*, March-April 1980.

Balasubramanyam, V. N. "Multinational Corporations' Choice of Techniques in LDCs." Paper presented to the International Economic Association World Congress, Mexico, September 1980.

──────. *Multinational Enterprises and the Third World*. Thames Essay 26, London: Trade Policy Research Centre, 1980.

Baldwin, R. E. *Beyond the Tokyo Round Negotiations*. London: Trade Policy Research Centre, 1979.

──────, and Murray, T. "MFN Tariff Reductions and Developing Country Trade Benefits under the GSP." *Economic Journal*, March 1977.

Balogh, T. *Dollar Crisis, Causes and Cure*. Oxford: Basil Blackwell, 1949.

──────. "Welfare and Freer Trade, A Reply." *Economic Journal*, March 1951.

Banerji, R., and Riedel, J. "Industrial Employment Expansion under Alternative Strategies: Some Empirical Evidence." *Ebenda* 63 (November 1977).

Baran, P. A. *The Political Economy of Growth*. New York: Monthly Review Press, 1957.

Bardhan, K. "A Survey of Research on Rural Employment Wages and Labor Markets in India." *Economic and Political Weekly* 12, nos. 26–28 (1977).

Bardhan, P. K. and Rudra, A. "Terms and Conditions of Share-cropping Contracts, An Analysis of Village Survey Data in India." *Journal of Development Studies*, April 1980.

Barnum, H. N., and Squire, L. "An Econometric Application of the Theory of the Farm-Household." *Journal of Development Economics*, March 1979.

Barone, E. "Il Ministro della produzione nello stato collectivista." ["The Ministry of Production in the Collectivist State."] *Collectivist Economic Planning*, ed. F. A. von Hayek, New York: Augustus M. Kelley, 1967.

Bauer, P. T. *Dissent on Development*. London: Weidenfeld & Nicholson, 1971.

Baumol, W. J. *Economic Dynamics*. New York: Macmillan, 1959.

Behrman, J. R. *Supply Response in Underdeveloped Agriculture*. Amsterdam: North-Holland Publishing Co., 1968.

Belsey, D. A., et al., eds. *Inflation, Trade and Taxes*. Columbus, Oh.: Ohio State University Press, 1976.

Benor, D., and Harrison, J. Q. *Agricultural Extension: The Training and Visit System*. Washington, D.C.: World Bank, May 1977.

Bergsman, J. "Income Distribution and Poverty in Mexico." *World Bank Staff Working Papers*, no. 395 (June 1980) and forthcoming in *World Development*.

Bergsten, C. F. *Completing the GATT: Towards New International Rules to Govern Export Controls*. London: British-North American Committee, 1974.

──────; Horst, T.; and Moran, T. H.; eds. *American Multinationals and American Interests*. Washington, D.C.: Brookings Institution, 1978.

Berlin, I. *Four Essays on Liberty*. London: Oxford University Press, 1969.

Berrill, K. *Economic Development with Special Reference to East Asia*. London: Macmillan, 1963.

Berry, A., and Cline, W. A. *Agrarian Structure and Productivity in Developing Countries*. Baltimore, Md.: Johns Hopkins University Press, 1979.

Berry, A., and Sabot, R. H. "Labor Market Performance in Developing Countries: A Survey." *World Development*, November-December 1978.

Bibliography

Bhagwati, J. *Anatomy and Consequences of Trade Control Regimes.* New York: National Bureau for Economic Research, 1978.
_____, ed. *The New International Order: The North-South Debate.* Cambridge, Mass.: MIT Press, 1977.
_____. *Trade, Balance of Payments and Growth.* Amsterdam: North-Holland Publishing Co., 1971.
Bhagwati, J., and Chakravarty, S. "Contribution to Indian Economic Analysis, A Survey." *American Economic Review Supplement,* September 1969.
Bhagwati, J., and Desai, P. *India—Planning for Industrialization.* London: Oxford University Press, 1970.
Bhagwati, J., and Eckaus, R. S., eds. *Foreign Aid.* London: Penguin, 1970.
Bhagwati, J., and Ramaswami, V. K. "Domestic Distortions, Tariffs, and the Theory of Optimum Subsidy." *Journal of Political Economy,* February 1963.
Bhalla, A. S., ed. *Technology and Employment in Industry.* Geneva: International Labor Organization, 1975.
Bhalla, S. S. "Aspects of Savings Behavior in Rural India." International Bank for Reconstruction and Development, *Domestic Finance Studies,* no. 31 (December 1976).
Bhatt, V. V., and Meerman, J. "Resource Mobilization in Developing Countries: Financial Institutions and Policies." *World Development,* January 1978.
Bhatt, V. V., and Roe, A. S. "Capital Market Imperfections and Economic Development." *World Bank Staff Working Papers,* no. 338 (July 1979).
Binswanger, H. P. *The Economics of Tractors in South Asia.* New York: Agricultural Development Council, 1978.
Bird, R. M., and Oldman, O., eds. *Readings on Taxation in Developing Countries,* 3rd ed. Baltimore, Md.: Johns Hopkins University Press, 1975.
Birdsall, N. "Population and Poverty in the Developing World." *World Bank Staff Working Papers,* no. 404 (July 1980).
Blackhurst, R.; Marian, N.; and Tumlir, J. *Adjustment, Trade and Growth in Developed and Developing Countries.* Geneva: General Agreement on Tariffs and Trade, September 1978.
Blackhurst, R., and Tumlir, J. *Trade Relations under Flexible Exchange Rates.* Geneva: General Agreement on Tariffs and Trade, 1980.
Blaug, M. *An Introduction to the Economics of Education.* London: Penguin, 1970.
Blitzer, C. R.; Clark, P. B.; and Taylor, L., eds. *Economy-wide Models and Development Planning.* London: Oxford University Press, 1975.
Boeke, J. H. *Economics and Economic Policy of Dual Societies.* New York: International Secretariat, Institute of Pacific Relations, 1953.
Böhme, H. *Restraints on Competition in World Shipping.* London: Trade Policy Research Centre, 1978.
Bottomley, A. *Factor Pricing and Economic Growth in Undeveloped Rural Areas.* London: Crosby Lockwood & Son, 1970.
_____. "The Premium for Risk as a Determinant of Interest Rates in Underdeveloped Rural Areas." *Quarterly Journal of Economics,* November 1963.
_____. "Reply." *Quarterly Journal of Economics,* May 1965.
Brandt Commission Report. *North-South: A Programme for Survival.* London: Pan Books, 1980.
Bray, F. A., and Robertson, A. F. "Sharecropping in Kelantan, Malaysia." *Research in Economic Anthropology* 3 (1980).
Brown, C. P. *The Political and Social Economy of Commodity Control.* London: Macmillan, 1980.
Brown, W. A. *The United States and the Restoration of World Trade.* Washington, D.C.: Brookings Institution, 1950.
Bruno, M. "The Optimal Selection of Export Promoting and Import Substituting Projects," in *Planning the External Sector: Techniques, Problems and Policies,* Report on the First International Seminar on Development Planning. New York: United Nations, 1967.
Bruton, H. J. "Growth Models and Underdeveloped Economies." *Journal of Political Economy,* August 1955.

———. "The Two-Gap Approach to Aid and Development: Comment." *American Economic Review*, June 1969.
Buck, J. L. *Chinese Farm Economy*. Chicago: University of Chicago Press, 1930.
Bull, H. *The Anarchical Society*. London: Macmillan, 1977.

Caiden, N., and Wildavsky, A. *Planning and Budgeting in Poor Countries*. New York: John Wiley & Sons, 1974.
Cairncross, A. *Factors in Economic Development*. London: Allen & Unwin, 1962.
Cardoso, F. H. "Current Theses on Latin American Development and Dependency: A Critique." *Latin American Research Review* (1977).
———, and Faletto, L. *Dependency and Development in Latin America*. Berkeley and Los Angeles: University of California Press, 1979.
Cassen, R. H. *India: Population, Economy, Society*. London: Macmillan, 1978.
———. "Population and Development: A Survey." *World Development*, October-November 1978.
Chandavarkar, A. D. "Comment." *Quarterly Journal of Economics*, May 1965.
Chenery, H. B. "The Role of Industrialization in Development Programmes." *American Economic Review*, May 1955.
———. *Structural Change and Development Policy*. London: Oxford University Press, 1979.
———. "The Structuralist Approach to Economic Development." *American Economic Review*, May 1965.
———, and Bruno, M. "Development Alternatives in an Open Economy: The Case of Israel," *The Economic Journal*, March 1962.
Chenery, H. B., and Watanabe, T. "International Comparisons of the Structure of Production." *Econometrics*, October 1958.
Chenery, H. B. et al. *Redistribution with Growth*. London: Oxford University Press, 1974.
Cheung, S. N-S. *The Theory of Share Tenancy*. Chicago: University of Chicago Press, 1969.
Choksi, A. M.; Meeraus, A.; and Stoutjesdijk, A. J. *The Planning of Investment Programs in the Fertilizer Industry*. Baltimore, Md.: Johns Hopkins University Press, 1980.
Chrystal, K. A. "International Money and the Future of the SDR." *Essays in International Finance*, no. 128, Princeton University (1978).
Cizauskas, A. C. "International Debt Renegotiations: Lessons from the Past." *World Development*, February 1979.
Cline, W. R. *International Monetary Reform and the Developing Countries*. Washington, D.C.: Brookings Institution, 1976.
———, ed. *Policy Alternatives for a New International Economic Order*. New York: Praeger, 1979.
Coale, A., and Hoover, E. *Population Growth and Economic Development in Low Income Countries*. Princeton, N.J.: Princeton University Press, 1958.
Coates, W. L., and Khatkhate, D. R. *Money and Monetary Policy in Less Developed Countries: A Survey of Issues and Evidence*. London: Penguin, 1980.
Cohen, B. I. "The Stagnation of Indian Exports." *Quarterly Journal of Economics*, November 1964.
———, and Sisler, D. G. "Exports of Developing Countries in the 1960s." *Review of Economics and Statistics*, November 1971.
Corden, W. M. *The Theory of Protection*. Oxford: Clarendon Press, 1971.
———. *Trade Policy and Economic Welfare*. Oxford: Clarendon Press, 1974.
Crosland, C.A.R. *Britain's Economic Problem*. London: Jonathan Cape, 1953.

Dam, K. *Law and International Economic Organization*. Chicago: University of Chicago Press, 1970.
Dandekar, V. M., and Rath, N. *Poverty in India*. New Delhi: Ford Foundation, 1970.
Dell, E. "The Wistful Liberalism of Deepak Lal." *The World Economy*, May 1979.
Dell, S. "Basic Needs or Comprehensive Development: Should the UNDP Have a Development Strategy?" *World Development*, March 1979.

Bibliography

———, and Lawrence, R. *The Balance of Payments Adjustment Process in Developing Countries.* London: Penguin, 1980.
Derossi, F. *The Mexican Entrepreneur.* Paris: Organization for Economic Cooperation and Development, Development Centre, 1971.
Devons, E. *Planning in Practice.* Cambridge: Cambridge University Press, 1950.
De Vries, B. A. *Export Experiences of Developing Countries,* World Bank Staff Occasional Paper, no. 3. Baltimore, Md.: Johns Hopkins University Press, 1967.
Diaz Alejandro, C. *Exchange Rate Devaluation in a Semi-Industrialized Country.* Cambridge, Mass.: MIT Press, 1965.
———. "Less Developed Countries and the Post-1971 International Finance System." *Princeton Essays in International Finance,* no. 108 (1975).
di Marco, L. E., ed. *International Economics and Development.* New York: Academic Press, 1972.
Dobb, M. *Capitalism, Development and Planning.* London: Routledge & Kegan Paul, 1967.
———. *Some Aspects of Economic Development, Three Lectures.* New Delhi: Ranjit Publishers, 1951.
Domar, E., ed. *Essays in the Theory of Economic Growth.* New York: Oxford University Press, 1957.
Donges, J. B. "A Comparative Study of Industrialization Policies in Fifteen Semi-Industrial Countries." *Weltwirtschaftliches Archiv,* Band 112, Heft 4 (1976).
———, and Müller-Ohlsen, L. *Aussenwirtschaftsstrategien und Industrialisierung in Entwicklungsdändern.* Tübingen, W. Germany: J.C.B. Mohr, 1978.
Dore, R. P. *Land Reform in Japan.* London: Oxford University Press, 1959.
Dovring, F. "The Share of Agriculture in a Growing Population." Food and Agricultural Organization, *Monthly Bulletin of Economics and Statistics,* August-September 1959.

Eckaus, R. S. "The Factor Proportions Problem in Underdeveloped Countries." *American Economic Review,* September 1955.
Eicher, C., and Witt, L., eds. *Agriculture in Economic Development.* New York: McGraw-Hill Book Co., 1964.
Ellis, H. S., ed. *Economic Development for Latin America.* London: Macmillan, 1961.
———. *The Economy of Brazil.* Berkeley and Los Angeles: University of California Press, 1969.
Emmanuel, A. *Unequal Exchange.* New York: Monthly Review Press, 1972.
Evans, P. *Dependent Development, the Alliance of Multinational, State and Local Capital in Brazil.* Princeton, N.J.: Princeton University Press, 1979.

Faber, M., and Seers, D., eds. *The Crisis in Planning.* London: Chatto & Windus, 1972.
Feder, G.; Just, R.; and Silberman, D. "Adoption of Agricultural Innovations in Developing Countries: A Survey." *World Bank Staff Working Papers,* no. 444 (February 1981).
Fei, J.; Ranis, G; and Kuo, S. W. Y. *Equity with Growth: The Taiwan Case.* London: Oxford University Press, 1979.
Findlay, R. E. *International Trade and Development Theory.* New York and London: Columbia University Press, 1973.
Finger, J. M. "Effects of the Kennedy Round Tariff Concessions on the Exports of Developing Countries." *Economic Journal,* March 1976.
———. "GATT Tariff Concessions and the Exports of Developing Countries." *Economic Journal,* September 1974.
Fishlow, A. "Empty Economic Stages." *Economic Journal,* March 1965.
———. et al. *Rich and Poor Nations in the World Economy.* New York: McGraw-Hill Book Co., 1978.
Food and Agricultural Organization. *Commodity Review and Outlook 1980/81,* March 1981.
———. *Production Yearbook 1979.*
Foster-Carter, A. "The Modes of Production Controversy." *New Left Review,* January-February 1978.

Bibliography

Frank, A. G. *Capitalism and Underdevelopment in Latin America.* New York: Monthly Review Press, 1967.
Frank, C. R. "Urban Unemployment and Economic Growth in Africa." *Oxford Economic Papers,* July 1968.
Frank, C. R.; Kim, K. S.; and Westphal, L. E. *Foreign Trade and Economic Development.* New York: National Bureau for Economic Research, 1975.
Frank, I. *Foreign Enterprise in Developing Countries.* Baltimore, Md.: Johns Hopkins University Press, 1980.
Franks, O. *Central Planning and Control in War and Peace.* Cambridge, Mass.: Harvard University Press, 1947.
Fry, M. J. "Savings, Investment, Growth, and the Cost of Financial Repression." *World Development,* April 1980.

Gaitskell, A. *Gezira: A Story of Development in the Sudan.* London: Faber & Faber, 1959.
Galbis, V. "Financial Intermediation and Economic Growth in Less-Developed Countries: A Theoretical Approach." *Journal of Development Studies,* January 1977.
Galenson, W., ed. *Economic Growth and Structural Change in Taiwan.* Ithaca, N.Y.: Cornell University Press, 1979.
Galenson, W., and Leibenstein, H. "Investment Criteria, Productivity and Economic Development." *Quarterly Journal of Economics,* August 1955.
Gallagher, J., and Robinson, R. "The Imperialism of Free Trade." *Economic History Review,* August 1953.
Gard, L. M., and Riedel, J. "Safeguard Protection of Industry in Developed Countries: Assessment of the Implications for Developing Countries." *Weltwirtschaftliches Archiv,* Band 116, Heft 3 (1980).
Georgescu-Roegen, N. "Economic Theory and Agrarian Economics." *Oxford Economic Papers,* February 1960.
Gersowitz, M., et al., eds. *The Theory and Experience of Economic Development: Essays in Honour of Sir W. Arthur Lewis.* London: Allen & Unwin, forthcoming.
Ginman, P. J.; Pugel, T. A.; and Walter, I. "Mixed Blessings for the Third World in Codes on Non-tariff Measures." *The World Economy,* September 1980.
Golt, S. *Developing Countries in the GATT System.* London: Trade Policy Research Centre, 1978.
Gopal, S. *Jawaharlal Nehru—A Biography,* vol 1. London: Jonathan Cape, 1975.
Goreux, L. M. *Compensatory Financing Facility.* Washington, D.C.: International Monetary Fund, 1980.
Griffin, K. "Growth and Impoverishment in the Rural Areas of India." *World Development,* April-May 1979.
―――――, and Enos, J. L. "Foreign Assistance: Objectives and Consequences." *Economic Development and Cultural Change,* April 1970.
Griffin, K., and Kahn, A. R. "Poverty in the Third World: Ugly Facts and Fancy Models." *World Development,* March 1978.
Griffith-Jones, S. "The Growth of Multinational Banking, the Eurocurrency Market, and Their Effects on Developing Countries." *Journal of Development Studies,* January 1980.
Gurley, J. G., and Shaw, E. S. "Financial Aspects of Economic Development." *American Economic Review,* September 1955.

Habbakuk, H. J. "Review of W. Rostow, The Stages of Economic Growth." *Economic Journal,* September 1961.
Haberler, G. "Some Problems in the Pure Theory of International Trade." *Economic Journal,* June 1950.
Hagen, E. *On the Theory of Social Change.* Homewood, Ill.: Dorsey Press, 1962.
Hansen, B. "Employment and Wages in Rural Egypt." *American Economic Review* 59, no. 3 (1969).
Hanson, A. H. "The Crisis of Indian Planning." *Political Quarterly* 34 (1963).
―――――. *The Process of Planning.* London: Oxford University Press, 1956.
Haq, Mahbub ul. *The Poverty Curtain.* New York: Columbia University Press, 1976.
―――――. *The Strategy of Economic Planning.* London: Oxford University Press, 1963.

Bibliography

Harris J., and Todaro, M. "Migration, Unemployment and Development: A Two-sector Analysis." *American Economic Review*, March 1970.
Harris, S.; Salmon, M.; and Smith, B. *Analysis of Commodity Markets for Policy Purposes.* London: Trade Policy Research Centre, 1978.
Harrod, R. F. *Are These Hardships Necessary?* London: Hart-Davis, 1947.
Hathaway, D. E. "Food Issues in North-South Relations." *The World Economy*, January 1981.
Hauser, P. M., ed. *World Population and Development.* Syracuse, N.Y.: Syracuse University Press, 1979.
Healey, D. T. "Development Policy: New Thinking about an Interpretation." *Journal of Economic Literature* 10 (1972).
Healey, J., and Clift, C. "The Development Rationale for Aid Re-examined." *Overseas Development Institute Review*, no. 2 (1980).
Henderson, P. D. *India, the Energy Sector.* Delhi: Oxford University Press, 1975.
―――――. "Survival, Development and the Report of the Brandt Commission." *The World Economy*, June 1980.
Hicks, J. *Capital and Time.* Oxford: Clarendon Press, 1973.
Hindley, B. "Voluntary Export Restraints and the GATT's Main Escape Clause." *The World Economy*, November 1980.
Hirschman, A. O. *A Bias for Hope.* New Haven, Conn.: Yale University Press, 1971.
―――――. "A Generalized Linkage Approach to Development, with Special Reference to Staples." *Economic Development and Cultural Change* 25, supplement (1977).
―――――. "How To Divest in Latin America, and Why." *Essays in International Finance*, no. 76. Princeton University, International Finance Section (1969).
―――――. *The Strategy of Economic Development.* New Haven, Conn.: Yale University Press, 1958.
―――――, ed. *Latin American Issues: Essays and Comments.* New York: Twentieth Century Fund, 1961.
Ho, S. "The Rural Non-Farm Sector in Taiwan." World Bank, *Studies in Employment and Rural Development*, 1976.
Hopkins, A. G. *An Economic History of West Africa.* London: Longman, 1973.
Howell, J., ed. *Borrowers and Lenders.* London: Overseas Development Institute, 1980.
Hsia, R., and Chau, L. C. "Industrialization and Income Distribution in Hong Kong 1961-1971." *World Employment Programme Research Working Paper.* International Labor Organization, Geneva, 1975.
Hudec, R. E. *Adjudication of International Trade Disputes.* London: Trade Policy Research Centre, 1978.
Hughes, H., and Waelbroeck, J. "Trade and Protection in the 1970s: Can the Growth of Developing Country Exports Continue in the 1980s?" *The World Economy*, June 1981.
Hunter, G. "Management and Self-Management in Economic Development." *Overseas Development Institute Review*, no. 2 (1975).
Hymer, S. *International Operations of National Firms: A Study of Direct Foreign Investment.* Cambridge, Mass.: MIT Press, 1976.

International Bank for Reconstruction and Development. *Rural Enterprise and Nonfarm Employment.* January 1978.
―――――. *World Development Reports*, 1979, 1980.
International Labor Organization. *Towards Full Employment.* Geneva, 1970.
――――― and Overseas Development Council. *Employment, Growth and Basic Needs: A One-World Problem.* New York: Praeger, 1977.
International Monetary Fund. *Annual Reports*, 1979, 1980.
―――――. *Surveys*, various numbers.
Isenman, P. J., and Singer, H. W. "Food Aid: Disincentive Effects and Their Policy Implications." *Economic Development and Cultural Change*, January 1977.

Jain, S. "Size Distribution of Income: A Compilation of Data." Washington, D.C.: World Bank, 1975.

Bibliography

Jamison, D. T., and Lau, L. J. *Farmer Education and Farm Efficiency.* Baltimore, Md.: Johns Hopkins University Press, 1981.
Jewkes, J. *Ordeal by Planning.* London: Macmillan, 1948.
Jodice, D. A. "Sources of Change in Third World Regimes for Foreign Direct Investment." *International Organization*, Spring 1980.
Johnston, B. "Agricultural Productivity and Economic Development in Japan." *Journal of Political Economy*, December 1951.
Jones, L. "The Measurement of Hirschmanian Linkages." *Quarterly Journal of Economics*, May 1976.
Joshi, P. C. *Land Reforms in India.* Delhi: Allied Publishers Private, 1975.
Joshi, V. "Exchange Rates, International Liquidity and Economic Development." *The World Economy*, May 1979.
Josling, T. E. *Agriculture in the Tokyo Round Negotiations.* London: Trade Policy Research Centre, 1977.
Joyce, J. P. "Money and Production in the Developing Economies: An Analytical Survey of the Issues." International Monetary Fund (mimeograph), February 1981.

Kahil, R. *Inflation and Economic Development in Brazil 1946–1963.* Oxford: Clarendon Press, 1973.
Kaldor, N. "Alternative Theories of Distribution." *Review of Economic Studies* 23 (1955–56).
──────. *Essays on Economic Growth and Stability.* London: Duckworth, 1960.
──────. *Essays on Economic Policy*, vol. 1. London: Duckworth, 1964.
──────. *Indian Tax Reform.* Delhi: Government of India, Ministry of Finance, 1956.
Katz, J. A. "Capital Flows and Developing Country Debt." *World Bank Staff Working Papers*, no. 352 (August 1979).
Keesing, D. B. "World Trade and Output of Manufactures: Structural Trends and Developing Countries' Exports." *World Bank Staff Working Papers*, no. 316 (January 1979).
──────, and Wolf, M. "Questions on International Trade in Textiles and Clothing." *The World Economy*, March 1981.
──────. *Textile Quotas against Developing Countries.* London: Trade Policy Research Centre, 1980.
Kendrick, D. A., and Stoutjesdijk, A. J. *The Planning of Industrial Investment Programs: A Methodology.* Baltimore, Md.: Johns Hopkins University Press, 1980.
Kenen, P. K., ed. *International Trade and Finance.* New York: Cambridge University Press, 1975.
Kenen, P. K., and Voivodas, C. S. "Export Instability and Economic Growth." *Kyklos* 25, no. 4 (1972).
Kidron, M. *Foreign Investments in India.* London: Oxford University Press, 1965.
Kiker, B. F. "The Historical Roots of the Concept of Human Capital." *Journal of Political Economy*, supplement, October 1966.
Killick, T. *Development Economics in Action.* New York: St. Martin's Press, 1978.
Kindleberger, C. P., ed. *The International Corporation.* Cambridge, Mass.: MIT Press, 1970.
King, T., ed. "Education and Income." *World Bank Staff Working Papers*, no. 402 (July 1980).
Kopitz, G. F. "Taxation and Multinational Firms' Behavior." International Monetary Fund, *Staff Papers*, November 1976.
Krasner, S. *Defending the National Interest.* Princeton, N.J.: Princeton University Press, 1978.
Kravis, I. B.; Heston, A.; and Summers, R. *International Comparisons of Real Product and Purchasing Power.* Baltimore, Md.: Johns Hopkins University Press, 1978.
Kreinen, M. E., and Finger, J. M. "A Critical Survey of the N.I.E.O." *Journal of World Trade Law*, November–December 1976.
Krueger, A. O. "Liberalization Attempts and Consequences." New York: National Bureau for Economic Research, 1978.
──────. "Some Economic Costs of Exchange Control: The Turkish Case." *Journal of Political Economy*, October 1966.

Bibliography

Kuznets, S. *Economic Growth and Structure.* London: Heinemann, 1965.

Lal, D. *Appraising Foreign Investment in Developing Countries.* London: Heinemann, 1975.

———. "The Foreign Exchange Bottleneck Revisited." *Economic Development and Cultural Change,* July 1972.

———. "Indian Export Incentives." *Journal of Development Economics* 6 (1979).

———. "A Liberal International Economic Order: The International Monetary System and Economic Development." *Essays in International Finance,* no. 139, Princeton University, October 1980.

———. "Market Access for Semi-Manufactures from Developing Countries." Geneva and London: Graduate Institute for International Studies and Trade Policy Research Centre, 1979.

———. "Politicians, Economists and Protection—The Deaf Meet the Blind." *The World Economy,* September 1980.

———. *Prices for Planning.* London: Heinemann, 1980.

———. "Theories of Industrial Wage Structures: A Review." *Indian Journal of Industrial Relations* 15, no. 2 (1979).

———. "The Wistful Mercantilism of Mr. Dell." *The World Economy,* June 1978.

Lall, S. "Developing Countries as Exporters of Industrial Technology." *Research Policy* 9 (1980).

———. "Is 'Dependence' a Useful Concept in Analysis Underdevelopment?" *World Development,* November 1975.

———. "Transnationals and the Third World: The R. and D. Factor." *Third World Quarterly,* July 1979.

———, and Streeten, P. *Foreign Investment, Transnationals and Developing Countries.* London: Macmillan, 1977.

Lange, O. "On the Economic Theory of Socialism." *Review of Economic Studies,* October 1936.

Lary, H. *Imports of Manufactures from Less Developed Countries.* New York: National Bureau of Economic Research, 1968.

Laszlo, E. et al. *The Objectives of the New International Economic Order.* New York: Pergamon Press, 1978.

Laursen, K. "The Integrated Programme for Commodities." *World Development,* April 1978.

Lee, E., ed. *Export-Led Industrialization and Development.* Geneva: Asian Employment Programme, International Labor Organization, 1981.

Lehmann, D., ed. *Agrarian Reform and Agrarian Reformism.* London: Faber & Faber, 1974.

Leibenstein, H. *Economic Backwardness and Economic Growth.* New York: John Wiley & Sons, 1957.

———. "The Theory of Underemployment in Backward Economies." *Journal of Political Economy,* April 1957.

Leipziger, D. M., ed. *The International Monetary System and the Developing Nations.* Washington, D.C.: Agency for International Development, 1976.

Lele, U. *The Design of Rural Development, Lessons from Africa.* Baltimore, Md.: Johns Hopkins University Press, 1975.

Lerner, A. P. "Economic Theory and Socialist Economy." *Review of Economic Studies* 2, no. 1 (October 1934).

Lewis, J. P. *Quiet Crisis in India.* Washington, D.C.: Brookings Institution, 1962.

Lewis, W. A. *Development Planning, The Essentials of Economic Policy.* London: Allen & Unwin, 1966.

———. "Economic Development with Unlimited Supply of Labour." *The Manchester School,* May 1954.

———. *Growth and Fluctuation 1870–1913.* London: Allen & Unwin, 1978.

———. *The Principles of Economic Planning.* London: Dennis Dobson, 1949.

———. *The Theory of Economic Growth.* London: Allen & Unwin, 1955.

———. "Unlimited Labor: Further Notes." *The Manchester School,* 1958.

———, ed. *Tropical Development 1880–1913.* London: Allen & Unwin, 1970.

Bibliography

Leys, C. *Underdevelopment in Kenya*. London: Heinemann, 1975.
Lipsey, R. E. *Price and Quantity Trends in the Foreign Trade of the United States*. Princeton, N.J.: Princeton University Press, 1963.
Lipton, M. *Why Poor People Stay Poor: Urban Bias in World Development*. London: Temple Smith, 1977.
Little, I. M. D. *A Critique of Welfare Economics*. Oxford: Clarendon Press, 1950.
─────. "The Strategy of Indian Development." *National Institute Economic Review*, May 1960.
─────. "Trade and Public Finance." *The Indian Economic Review* 6, no. 2 (1971).
─────, and Clifford, J. M. *International Aid*. London: Allen & Unwin, 1965.
Little, I. M. D., and Mirrlees, J. A. *Manual of Industrial Project Analysis*, vol 2. Paris: Organization for Economic Cooperation and Development, 1968.
─────. *Project Appraisal and Planning for Developing Countries*. London: Heinemann, and New York: Basic Books, 1974.
Little, I. M. D.; Scitovsky, T.; and Scott, M. FG. *Industry and Trade in Some Developing Countries*. London: Oxford University Press, 1970.
Little, I. M. D., and Scott, M. FG., eds. *Using Shadow Prices*. London: Heinemann, 1976.
Little, I. M. D., and Tipping, D. G. *A Social Cost-Benefit Analysis of the Kulai Oil Palm Estate*. Paris: Organization for Economic Cooperation and Development, Development Centre, 1972.
Livingstone, I., ed. *Economic Policy for Development*. London: Penguin, 1971.
Lloyd, P. *Anti-dumping Actions and the GATT System*. London: Trade Policy Research Centre, 1977.

MacBean, A. I. *Export Instability and Economic Development*. Cambridge, Mass.: Harvard University Press, 1966.
McClelland, D. C. *The Achieving Society*. Princeton, N.J.: D. Van Nostrand, 1961.
MacDougall, G. D. A. "The Benefits and Costs of Private Investment from Abroad: A Theoretical Approach." *Economic Record*, March 1960. (Also in *Bulletin of the Oxford Institute of Economics and Statistics* 22, no. 3 [1960].)
─────. *The World Dollar Problem*. London: Macmillan, 1957.
McKinnon, R. I. "Foreign Exchange Constraints in Economic Development and Efficient Aid Allocation." *Economic Journal*, June 1964.
─────. *Money and Capital in Economic Development*. Washington, D.C.: Brookings Institution, 1973.
─────, ed. *Money and Finance in Economic Growth and Development: Essays in Honor of Edward S. Shaw*. New York: Marcel Dekker, 1976.
Magee, S. P. "Factor Market Distortions, Production, and Trade: A Survey." *Oxford Economic Papers*, March 1973.
Malmgren, H. B. *International Order for Public Subsidies*. London: Trade Policy Research Centre, 1977.
Manne, A. S. *Investments for Capacity Expansion: Size, Location and Time Phasing*. Cambridge, Mass.: MIT Press, 1967.
Mansfield, E., and Romeo, A. "Technology Transfer to Overseas Subsidiaries by U.S.-based Firms." *Quarterly Journal of Economics*, December 1980.
Marglin, S. A. *Public Investment Criteria*. London: Allen & Unwin, 1967.
─────. *Value and Price in the Labor Surplus Economy*. London: Oxford University Press, 1976.
Mason, E. S. *Economic Planning in Underdeveloped Areas*. New York: Fordham University Press, 1958.
Mauldin, W. P., and Berelson, B. "Conditions of Fertility Decline in Developing Countries, 1965–1975." *Studies in Family Planning*, May 1978.
Maxwell, S. J., and Singer, H. W. "Food Aid to Developing Countries: A Survey." *World Development*, March 1979.
Mazumdar, D. "The Marginal Productivity Theory of Wages and Disguised Unemployment." *Review of Economic Studies* 26 (June 1959).
─────. *Urban Labor Markets and Income Distribution in Peninsular Malaysia*. Baltimore, Md.: Johns Hopkins University Press, 1979.

Bibliography

Meade, J. E. "External Economies and Diseconomies in a Competitive Situation." *Economics Journal*, March 1952.
———. *Planning and the Price Mechanism*. London: Allen & Unwin, 1948.
———. "Planning without Prices." *Economica*, February 1948.
———. *Trade and Welfare*. London: Oxford University Press, 1955.
Meier, G. M., and Baldwin, R. *Economic Development*. New York: John Wiley & Sons, 1957.
Michaely, M. "Exports and Growth: An Empirical Investigation." *Journal of Development Economics* 4 (1977).
Mitra, J. D. "The Capital Goods Sector in LDCs: A Case for State Intervention." *World Bank Staff Working Papers*, no. 343 (1979).
Moran, H. *Multinational Corporations and the Politics of Dependence*. Princeton, N.J.: Princeton University Press, 1974.
Morawetz, D. "Elasticities of Substitution in Industry: What Do We Learn from Econometric Estimates?" *World Development*, January 1976.
———. *Twenty-five Years of Economic Development*. Baltimore, Md.: Johns Hopkins University Press, 1977.
———. *Why the Emperor's New Clothes Are Not Made in Colombia: A Case Study of Latin American and East Asian Clothing Exports*. New York: Oxford University Press, 1981.
Morley, S., and Smith, G. "Limited Search and Technology Choices of Multinational Firms in Brazil." *Quarterly Journal of Economics*, May 1977.
Mosher, A. T. *To Create a Modern Agriculture*. New York: Agricultural Development Council, 1971.
Mosley, P. "Aid for the Poorest: Some Early Lessons of UK Experience." *Journal of Development Studies*, January 1981.
Moynihan, D. *A Dangerous Place*. Boston: Little, Brown & Co., 1978.
Mundell, R. A., and Swoboda, A. K., eds. *Monetary Problems of the International Economy*. Chicago: University of Chicago Press, 1969.
Murray, T. *Trade Preferences for Developing Countries*. London: Macmillan, 1977.
Myint, H. "The Classical Theory of Trade and Underdeveloped Countries." *Economic Journal*, June 1958.
———. "Economic Theory and Development Policy." *Economica*, May 1967.
Myrdal, G. *Asian Drama: An Inquiry into the Poverty of Nations*. London: Allen Lane, 1968.
———. *Development and Underdevelopment*. Cairo: National Bank of Egypt, 1956.
———. *Economic Theory and Underdeveloped Regions*. London: Duckworth, 1957.
———. *An International Economy*. London: Routledge & Kegan Paul, 1956.
Mytelka, L. K. "Licensing and Technology Dependence in the Andean Group." *World Development*, April 1978.

Nayar, B. R. *The Modernization Imperative and Indian Planning*. Delhi: Vikas Publishers, 1972.
Newbery, D. M. G., and Stiglitz, J. E. *The Theory of Commodity Price Stabilization: A Study in the Economics of Risk*. London: Oxford University Press, 1981.
Newman, P. *Malaria Eradication and Population*. Ann Arbor, Mich.: University of Michigan Press, 1965.
Nove, A. *An Economic History of the USSR*. London: Allen Lane, 1969.
Nozick, R. *Anarchy, State and Utopia*. Oxford: Basil Blackwell, 1974.
Nurkse, R. *Problems of Capital Formation in Underdeveloped Countries*. Oxford: Basil Blackwell, 1953.

Ohlin, G. *Foreign Aid Policies Reconsidered*. Paris: Organization for Economic Cooperation and Development, Development Centre, 1966.
———. *Population Control and Economic Development*. Paris: Organization for Economic Cooperation and Development, Development Centre, 1967.
———. "Reflections on the Rostow Doctrine." *Economic Development and Cultural Change*, July 1961.

Bibliography

Olson, M. *The Rise and Decline of Nations: Economic Growth, Stagflation, and Social Rigidities.* New Haven, Conn.: Yale University Press, forthcoming.

Oppenheimer, P. M. "International Monetary Arrangements: The Limits to Planning." Papers presented to the Panel of Academic Consultants, no. 8, Bank of England, 1979.

⎯⎯⎯⎯, ed. *Issues in International Economics.* London: Oriel Press, 1978.

Organization for Economic Cooperation and Development. *Development Cooperation, 1980 Review.*

Patel, I. G. "Selective Credit Controls in Underdeveloped Countries." International Monetary Fund, *Staff Papers,* September 1954. Reprinted in Coates, W. L., and Khatkhate, D. R., eds. *Money and Monetary Policy in Less Developed Countries: A Survey of Issues and Evidence.* London: Penguin, 1980.

Patrick, H. T. "Financial Development and Economic Growth in Underdeveloped Countries." *Economic Development and Cultural Change,* January 1966.

⎯⎯⎯⎯, and Rosovsky, H., eds. *Asia's New Giant.* Washington, D.C.: Brookings Institution, 1976.

Pearson Commission Report. *Partners in Development.* New York: Praeger, 1969.

Porter, R. C. "The Promotion of the Banking Habit and Economic Development." *Journal of Development Studies,* July 1966.

Prebisch, R. *Towards a New Trade Policy for Development.* New York: United Nations, 1964.

Pyatt, G., and Thorbecke, E. *Planning Techniques for a Better Future.* Geneva: International Labor Organization, 1976.

Radetski, M. "Market Structure and Bargaining Fower." *Resources Policy,* June 1978.

Ramaswami, V. K. *Trade and Development.* London: Allen & Unwin, 1971.

Ramos, J. "An Heterodoxical Interpretation of the Employment Problem in Latin America." *World Development,* July 1974.

Ranis, G. "Equity with Growth in Taiwan: How 'Special' is the 'Special' Case?" *World Development,* March 1978.

⎯⎯⎯⎯, ed. *The Gap between Rich and Poor Nations.* London: Macmillan, 1972.

Rao, D. C. "Economic Growth and Equity in the Republic of Korea." *World Development,* March 1978.

Rawls, J. *A Theory of Justice.* Oxford: Clarendon Press, 1972.

Reddaway, W. B. *The Development of the Indian Economy.* London: Allen & Unwin, 1962.

Reuber, G. *Private Foreign Investment in Development.* Oxford: Clarendon Press, 1973.

Reutlinger, S. "Food Insecurity: Magnitude and Remedies." *World Development,* June 1978.

Rhee, Y. W., and Westphal, L. E. "A Micro-Econometric Investigation of Choice of Technology." *Journal of Development Economics* 4 (1977).

Riedel, J. "A Balanced-Growth Version of the Linkage Hypothesis." *Quarterly Journal of Economics,* May 1976.

⎯⎯⎯⎯. "Factor Proportions, Linkages and the Open Developing Economy." *Review of Economics and Statistics* 57 (November 1975).

Robertson, D. *Fail Safe Systems for Trade Liberalisation.* London: Trade Policy Research Centre, 1977.

Rosen, G. *Industrial Finance in India.* Bombay: Asia Publishing House, 1962.

Rosenstein Rodan, P. "Problems of Industrialization of Eastern and South Eastern Europe." *Economic Journal,* June-September 1943.

⎯⎯⎯⎯, ed. *Pricing and Fiscal Policies.* London: Allen & Unwin, 1964.

Rostow, W. *The Process of Economic Growth.* London: Oxford University Press, 1953.

⎯⎯⎯⎯. *The Stages of Economic Growth.* Cambridge: Cambridge University Press, 1960.

⎯⎯⎯⎯. "The Take-Off into Self-sustained Growth." *Economic Journal,* March 1956.

⎯⎯⎯⎯, ed. *The Economics of Take-off into Sustained Growth.* London: Macmillan, 1963.

Bibliography

Roumasset, J. A.; Boussard, J. M.; and Singh, I. J., eds. *Risk, Uncertainty and Agricultural Development.* New York: Agricultural Development Council, 1979.

Rudra, A. *Indian Plan Models.* Delhi: Allied Publishers, 1975.

Samuelson, P. A. *Evaluation of Real National Income.* London: Oxford Economic Papers, 1950.

―――――. "Summing Up on the Australian Case for Protection." *Quarterly Journal of Economics,* February 1981.

Schultz, T. W. "Investment in Human Capital." *American Economic Review,* March 1961.

Schumpeter, J. A. *History of Economic Analysis.* New York: Oxford University Press, 1954.

Scitovsky, T. "Two Concepts of External Economies." *Journal of Political Economy,* April 1954.

Scott, M. FG.; MacArthur, J. D.; and Newbery, D. M. G. *Project Appraisal in Practice.* London: Heinemann, 1976.

Seers, D. "A Theory of Inflation and Growth in Underdeveloped Economies Based on the Experiences of Latin America." *Oxford Economic Papers,* June 1962.

Selowsky, M. "Income Distribution, Basic Needs and Trade-Offs with Growth: The Case of Semi-Industrialized Latin American Countries." *World Development,* January 1981.

Sen, A. K. *Choice of Techniques.* Oxford: Basil Blackwell, 1960.

―――――. *Employment, Technology and Development.* Oxford: Clarendon Press, 1975.

―――――. "Peasants and Dualism with or without Surplus Labor." *Journal of Political Economy,* October 1966.

Sengupta, A. "Issues in the North South Negotiations on Commodities." *ODI Review,* no. 2 (1979).

Shaw, E. S. *Financial Dependency in Economic Development.* New York: Oxford University Press, 1973.

Singer, H. W. "The Distribution of Gains between Investing and Borrowing Countries." *American Economic Review,* Papers and Proceedings, May 1950.

―――――. "Problems of Industrialization of Underdeveloped Countries." *International Social Science Bulletin* 6, no. 2 (1954).

Singh, I. "Small Farmers and the Landless in South Asia." *World Bank Staff Working Papers,* no. 320 (February 1979).

Singh, M. *India's Export Trends.* Oxford: Clarendon Press, 1964.

Skidmore, T. E. *Politics in Brazil 1930-1964.* New York: Oxford University Press, 1967.

Soligo, R., and Stern J. S. "Tariff Protection, Import Substitution and Investment Efficiency." *Pakistan Development Review,* Summer 1965.

Solomon, R. *The International Monetary System.* New York: Harper & Row, 1977.

Solow, R. M. *Capital Theory and the Rate of Return.* Amsterdam: North-Holland Publishing Company, 1964.

―――――. "A Contribution to the Theory of Economic Growth." *Quarterly Journal of Economics,* February 1956.

Spaventa, L. "Dualism in Economic Growth." *Banco Nazionale del Lavoro, Quarterly Review,* December 1959.

Spraos, J. "The Statistical Debate on the Net Barter Terms of Trade between Primary Commodities and Manufactures." *Economic Journal,* March 1980.

Squire, L. *Employment Policy in Developing Countries, A Survey of Issues and Evidence.* London: Oxford University Press, 1981.

―――――, and van der Tak, H. *Economic Analysis of Projects.* International Bank for Reconstruction and Development, 1975.

Srinivasan, T. N. "Development, Poverty, and Basic Human Needs: Some Issues." *Food Research Institute Studies,* 1977.

Stamp, M. "The Fund and the Future." *Lloyds Bank Review,* October 1958.

―――――. "The Stamp Plan—1962 Version." *Moorgate and Wall Street Review,* October 1962.

Stepan, A., ed. *Authoritarian Brazil.* New Haven, Conn.: Yale University Press, 1973.

Bibliography

Stevenson, C. L. *Ethics and Language.* New Haven, Conn.: Yale University Press, 1944.
Stiglitz, J. "Wage Determination and Unemployment in LDCs." *Quarterly Journal of Economics,* May 1974.
Streeten, P., and Lipton, M. *The Crisis of Indian Planning: Economic Policy of the 1960s.* London: Oxford University Press, 1969.
Swan, T. "Economic Growth and Capital Accumulation." *Economic Record,* November 1956.

Teece, D. J. "Technology Transfer by Multinational Firms: The Resource Cost of Transferring Technological Know-how." *Economic Journal,* June 1977.
Teitelbaum, M. S. "Comment." *World Development,* October–November 1978.
Timmer, C. P., et al. *The Choice of Technology in Developing Countries.* Studies in International Affairs, no. 32, Cambridge, Mass.: Harvard University Press, 1975.
Titmuss, R., and Smith, B. *Social Policies and Population Control in Mauritius.* London: Methuen, 1961.
Tsiang, T. C. "Tax, Credit, and Trade Policies to Promote the Production and Export of Manufactures of Developing Countries." *Journal of Development Studies,* January and April 1965.
Tucker, R. W. *The Inequality of Nations.* New York: Basic Books, 1977.
Tulloch, P. "Developing Countries and Trade in Textiles." *ODI Review,* no. 2 (1974).
_____. *The Politics of Preference.* London: Croon Helm, 1975.
Tun Wai, U. "Interest Rates Outside the Organized Money Markets of Underdeveloped Countries." International Monetary Fund, *Staff Papers,* 1957-58.
_____. "A Revisit to Interest Rates Outside the Organized Money Markets of Underdeveloped Countries." Banco Nazionale del Lavoro, *Quarterly Review,* September 1977. Reprinted in Coates, W. L., and Khatkhate, D. R., eds. *Money and Monetary Policy in Less Developed Countries: A Survey of Issues and Evidence.* London: Penguin Press, 1980.
Turnham, D., and Jaeger, I. *The Unemployment Problem in Developing Countries.* Paris: Organization for Economic Cooperation and Development, Development Centre, 1971.
Turvey, R. "A Simple Analysis of Optimal Fares on Scheduled Transport Services." *Economic Journal,* March 1975.
Tyler, W. G. *Manufactured Export Expansion and Industrialization in Brazil.* Tübingen, W. Germany: Kieler Studien 134, 1976.

United Nations, Commission on Transnational Corporations. *Transnational Corporations in World Development.* New York: United Nations, 1978.
United Nations, Committee for Development Planning. *Report on the Eleventh Session.* New York: United Nations, April 1975.
United Nations, Committee for Trade and Development. *Handbook of International Trade and Development Statistics.* New York: United Nations, 1980.
_____. "An International Code of Conduct on Transfer of Technology." New York: United Nations, 1975.
_____. TD/B/C2/167. New York: United Nations, 1978.
United Nations, Department of Economic Affairs. *The Economic Development of Latin America and Its Principal Problems.* New York: United Nations, 1950.
_____. *Land Reform, Defects in Agrarian Structure as Obstacles to Economic Development.* New York: United Nations, 1951.
_____. *Measures for the Economic Development of Underdeveloped Countries.* New York: United Nations, 1951.
_____. *Planning the External Sector: Techniques, Problems and Policies,* Report on the First International Seminar on Development Planning. New York: United Nations, 1967.
_____. *Relative Prices of Exports and Imports of Under-developed Countries.* New York: United Nations, 1949.
_____. *Taxes and Fiscal Policy in Underdeveloped Countries.* New York: United Nations, 1955.
United Nations, International Development Organization. *Guidelines for Project Evaluation.* New York: United Nations, 1972.

Bibliography

U.S., Congress, Senate, Special Committee to Study the Foreign Aid Program. *A Proposal: Key to an Effective Foreign Policy,* 1957.

Veliz, C., ed. *Obstacles to Change in Latin America.* London: Oxford University Press, 1965.
Vernon, R. "Comprehensive Model-building in the Planning Process: The Case of the Less-developed Economies." *Economic Journal,* March 1966.
———. *Storm over the Multinationals.* London: Macmillan, 1977.
Viner, J. *International Trade and Economic Development.* Oxford: Clarendon Press, 1953.
Visvesvarayya, M. *Planned Economy for India.* Bangalore, India: Bangalore Press, 1934.

Walinsky, L. J., ed. *Agrarian Reform as Unfinished Business, The Selected Papers of Wolf Ladejinsky.* New York: Oxford University Press, 1977.
Walter, I. "Non-tariff Barriers and the Export Performance of Developing Economies." *American Economic Review,* May 1971.
Warren, W. "Imperialism and Capitalist Industrialization." *New Left Review,* September-October 1973.
Warriner, D. *Economics of Peasant Farming.* London: Oxford University Press, 1939.
———. *Land Reform in Principle and Practice.* Oxford: Clarendon Press, 1969.
Waterston, A. *Development Planning Lessons of Experience.* Baltimore, Md.: Johns Hopkins University Press, 1965.
Watson, A. M., and Dirlan, J. B. "The Impact of Underdevelopment on Economic Planning." *Quarterly Journal of Economics,* May 1965.
Weisskopf, T. E. "Dependence as an Explanation of Underdevelopment: A Critique." Center for Research on Economic Development, University of Michigan, Ann Arbor (mimeograph) 1977.
Weitz, R. *From Peasant to Farmer.* New York: Columbia University Press, 1971.
———, ed. *Rural Development in a Changing World.* Cambridge, Mass.: MIT Press, 1971.
Wellicz, S. "Lessons of Twenty Years of Planning in Developing Countries." *Economica,* May 1971.
Westphal, L. "The Republic of Korea's Experience with Export-Led Development." *World Development,* March 1978.
———; Rhee, Y. W.; and Pursell, G. "Korean Industrial Competence: Where it Came From." *World Bank Staff Working Papers,* no. 469 (July 1981).
Wheeler, D. "Human Resource Development and Economic Growth in Developing Countries." *World Bank Staff Working Papers,* no. 407 (July 1980).
White, L. J. "The Evidence on Appropriate Factor Proportions for Manufacturing in Less Developed Countries." *Economic Development and Cultural Change,* October 1978.
Wijkman, P. M. "Effects of Cargo Reservation." Institute for International Economic Studies, Stockholm, Reprint 142. Also in *Marine Policy,* October 1980.
Wilber, C. K., ed. *The Political Economy of Development and Underdevelopment.* New York: Random House, 1973.
Williams, M. L. "The Extent and Significance of the Nationalization of Foreign-Owned Assets in Developing Countries, 1956–1972." *Oxford Economic Papers,* July 1975.
Williamson, J. *The Failure of World Monetary Reform, 1971–1974.* New York: New York University Press, 1977.
Wortman, S., and Cummings, R. *To Feed This World.* Baltimore, Md.: Johns Hopkins University Press, 1978.

Yeats, A. J. *Trade Barriers Facing Developing Countries.* London: Macmillan, 1979.
Yotopoulos, P. A., and Nugent, J. B. *Economics of Development: Empirical Investigations.* New York: Harper & Row, 1976.
Yudelman, M.; Butler, G.; and Banerji, R. *Technological Change in Agriculture and Employment in Developing Countries.* Paris: Organization for Economic Cooperation and Development, Development Centre, 1971.

Name Index

Abbot, P. C., 343
Amin, S., 219, 264
Anschel, K. R., 90
Arndt, H., 35n

Balassa, B., 369
Baldwin, R. E., 300
Balogh, T., 35n, 62, 74, 218
Baran, P. A., 74, 219
Barone, E., 30
Bauer, P. T., 35n
Baumol, William, 18–19
Behrman, J. R., 337–40
Berlin, Isaiah, 20
Bhagwati, J. N., 52, 142, 145
Bhatt, V. V., 205
Blaug, Mark, 193, 194–95
Blitzer, C. R., 135
Boeke, J., 86–87
Bose, Subhas Chandra, 49
Brown, Christopher P., 342
Bruno, M., 53, 135, 148
Buck, J. L., 88

Cairncross, A., 102
Campos, Roberto, 81–82
Cardoso, F. H., 219
Caves, R., 183
Chenery, Hollis, 19, 40, 41, 45, 53, 128, 148
Cheung, S. N-S, 174
Chiang Ching-kuo, 11
Chiang Kai-shek, 11
Chrystal, K. Alec, 377
Clark, Colin, 107
Coale, A., 108
Corden, W. M., 137

Cummings, R. W., 131, 163

de Gaulle, Charles, 310
de Larosière, M., 361–62, 364
Desai, P., 52
De Vries, B. A., 139
Diaz Alejandro, Carlos, 83, 138, 147
Dobb, M., 88
Domar, E., 57
Dore, R. P., 114
Dutt, Palme, 51

Eckaus, R. S., 42
Eicher, C. K., 90, 104
Emmanuel, A., 219

Feldman, 47, 51
Felix, David, 82
Fishlow, A., 102, 103
Frank, A. Gundar, 219, 261
Frankel, S. H., 35n
Franks, O., 36
Furnivall, J. S., 99

Gaitskell, Arthur, 115
Galenson, Walter, 46, 47
Georgescu-Roegen, N., 95
Gerschenkron, A., 102
Ginman, P. J., 369
Gopal, Sarvepalli, 50–51

Habbakuk, H. J., 102
Haberler, G., 73–74, 75, 291

441

Name Index

Hagen, E. E., 18, 100, 111
Hanson, A. H., 49, 50
Harris, J., 155, 157
Harrod, Roy F., 18, 41–42, 57
Healey, D. T., 209–10
Hecksher, Eli, 142–43
Hirschman, A. O., 37, 42–43, 44, 45, 64, 68, 69, 103, 104, 184
Hobson, J. A., 219
Hoover, E., 108
Hull, Cordell, 285
Hymer, S., 183, 219

Jaeger, I., 150, 151
Johnston, Bruce, 105
Jorgenson, D. W., 23
Joshi, P. C., 114
Joshi, Vijay, 323–24, 377, 379
Jourdain, M., 19

Kaldor, Nicholas, 35n, 42, 96, 117
Kao, C. H. C., 90
Keesing, D. B., 293, 367
Keynes, John Maynard, 305, 311
Kidron, M., 259
Kindleberger, C., 183
Krueger, A. O., 144, 145
Kuznets, S., 102, 213

Ladejinsky, Wolf, 114
Lal, Deepak, 377–78
Lall, S., 243
Lange, O., 30
Lary, H., 139
Laursen, Karsten, 337
Leibenstein, Harvey, 4, 46, 47, 89, 98–99, 108
Lele, Uma, 107
Lenin, Vladimir, 218–19
Lerner, A. P., 30
Lewis, W. Arthur, 8, 19, 35n, 54, 86–87, 90–94, 96, 100–1, 108, 115
Leys, Colin, 219, 261–62
Lipsey, Robert E., 139
Lipton, Michael, 11
List, Friedrich, 73–74
Little, Ian M. D., 4, 5, 51, 117, 128n, 129, 138, 139, 141–43, 145–46, 178, 185, 337
Longfield, Samuel M., 22

MacBean, A. L., 146

McClelland, D. C., 111
MacDougall, G. D. A., 62, 184
McKinnon, R. I., 148, 200, 202
MacNamara, Robert, 170, 330
Mahalanobis, P. C., 10, 47, 50, 51, 64
Malthus, Thomas, 87, 99
Mandelbaum, K., 35n
Manne, A., 130
Marglin, S. A., 129
Marx, Karl, 18
Mazrui, Ali, 327, 328
Mazumdar, D., 89
Meade, J. E., 39, 69
Millikan, M. F., 112
Mirrlees, J. A., 128n, 129, 138, 185
Morawetz, D., 269, 277
Morris, Morris D., 14
Mosher, A. T., 163, 168
Murray, T., 300, 301
Myint, Hla, 99
Myrdal, Gunnar, 5–6, 19, 58–59, 72–73, 218

Nehru, Jawaharlal, 49, 50–51, 52
Nicholls, W. H., 163
Nove, Alec, 8–9
Nozick, Robert, 323, 324
Nugent, J. B., 147
Nurkse, Ragnar, 19, 64, 65, 66, 86, 88, 96

Ohlin, G., 102, 142–43, 197

Pack, H., 178
Pigou, A. C., 69
Prebisch, Raul, 19, 70, 71, 74, 83–84, 136, 139, 287

Ramaswami, V. K., 137
Ranis, G., 176, 178
Rawls, John, 7, 323
Ricardo, David, 87
Robinson, E. A. G., 35n
Roe, A. S., 205
Rosen, George, 110
Rosenstein Rodan, Paul N., 19, 35n, 37, 38, 39, 99
Rostow, W. W., 18, 102–4, 112

Samuelson, P., 220

Sarris, A. H., 343, 344
Sau, R., 219
Schultz, T. W., 160, 190
Schumacher, E. F., 176
Schumpeter, Joseph, 18
Scitovsky, T., 37, 38, 39-40, 41, 43, 45, 68, 69, 104, 138, 139, 141-43, 146
Scott, M. FG., 138, 139, 141-43, 146
Seers, Dudley, 3, 82
Sen, A. K., 46, 129, 176
Shaw, E. S., 200, 202
Singer, Hans W., 19, 35n, 70, 71, 74, 139, 218
Singh, I., 170-71
Singh, Manmohan, 138-39
Smith, Adam, 99
Solow, Robert M., 23, 42
Spraos, John, 139
Squire, Lyn, 158
Srinivasan, T. N., 137
Stamp, Maxwell, 311
Strassman, W., 178
Sunkel, O., 219
Swan, T., 42

Tata, J. D., 237
Taylor, Lance, 343
Tinbergen, Jan, 128

Todaro, M., 155, 157
Tucker, R. W., 325, 328
Tun Wai, U., 110
Turnham, D., 150, 151

Vernon, R., 183
Viner, Jacob, 74-75, 96, 120-21
Visvesvarayya, Sir M., 48-49
von Thünen, Johann H., 22

Warriner, Doreen, 88, 114
Watanabe, T., 45
Westphal, L., 225-26, 239
White, H. D., 305
White, L. J., 177, 178
Wijkman, Per M., 351-52
Williamson, John, 311, 356
Wilson, Harold, 48
Witt, L., 104
Wolf, M., 367
Wortman, S., 131, 163

Yeats, A. J., 226
Yotopoulos, P. A., 147

Subject Index

Abu Dhabi, 257
ACP. *See* African, Caribbean, and Pacific countries
Afghanistan, 227, 347
Africa, 115, 194, 252, 256, 315, 327; agriculture, 106, 275; development, 212, 277, 279; employment, 151, 156; planning, 53-54, 166; population, 107, 109, 196, 199, 273; trade, 274, 299, 303
African, Caribbean, and Pacific (ACP) countries, 297, 299-300, 304
Agency for International Development, 263
Agricultural development, 9-10, 55, 102, 104-7, 131, 136, 163-69, 234. *See also* Green revolution
Agricultural labor, 74, 88-97, 105, 149-50, 152-55, 161, 173, 175, 192, 276-77

Subject Index

Agricultural labor *(continued)*
See also Sharecropping
Agricultural mechanization, 106, 164, 171, 179, 247-48
Agricultural products, 61, 224, 227, 233, 251, 256, 274, 286, 297, 303. *See also specific products* (for example, Food, Jute)
Agricultural stagnation, 261, 263, 265
Agricultural surplus, 95-97
Agriculture, 45, 51, 64, 75, 119-20, 159-62, 175-76, 257, 275, 345. *See also* European Economic Community, Common Agricultural Policy; Terms of trade, agriculture and industry
Aid. *See* Foreign aid
Albania, 269
Algeria, 234
Alliance for Progress, 48, 54
Andean Common Market, 297
Appropriate technology, 176, 180-81, 188-89, 242-43, 279, 353
Arab countries, 287
Argentina, 61, 83, 202, 260, 275, 280, 314, 342, 370
Arusha agreement (1971), 296-97
ASEAN. *See* Association of South East Asian Nations
Asia, 46, 115, 194, 252, 256, 297, 315, 327; agriculture, 88, 91, 247, 275; development, 212, 219, 277, 279; employment, 151; planning, 54; population, 107, 109, 196, 273; trade, 274
Asia (baby tigers), 103, 145, 155, 212, 262, 265, 367
Association of South East Asian Nations (ASEAN), 297, 298
Australasia, 342
Australia, 61, 113, 184, 260, 269, 298, 300
Austria, 260

Balance of payments, 36, 60, 63-64, 67, 70-72, 81, 148, 185, 188, 254-55, 261, 263, 290, 312, 315-17, 320, 348, 376. *See also* Current account
Bangladesh, 199, 211, 270, 271, 273, 279
Banks, 32, 109-10, 119, 203-5, 360-61, 362. *See also* Central banks
Basic needs, 15, 173, 209, 214-17, 329
Belgium, 260
Benin, 347
Bhutan, 279
Big push, 38, 39, 94, 120
Bolivia, 114
Botswana, 273
Brandt Commission Report, 383, 384
Brazil, 211, 244, 271, 339; development, 63, 202; industry, 178, 260, 275; inflation, 77, 83, 84, 145, 319; loans to, 314, 347, 361, 378; population, 195, 199, 270; trade, 138, 145, 301, 350, 368
Bretton Woods Agreement, 62, 83, 286, 305-6, 309, 310-11, 312, 313. *See also* International Bank for Reconstruction and Development; International Monetary Fund
Budget, 30, 132. *See also* Public expenditures
Buffer stocks, 337-40, 343-44, 358, 363. *See also* Common Fund
Burma, 203, 232
Burundi, 347

CACM. *See* Central American Common Market
Cambridge school, 22, 24
Canada, 113, 183, 260, 298, 300, 307
Capital, 22-23, 64, 102, 109-10, 116, 154, 200-5, 288. *See also* Human capital; Marginal productivity of capital
Capital goods, 20, 49, 243-44, 248-49. *See also* Technology
Capital-intensive growth, 46-47, 119
Capital-intensive industries, 38-39, 142, 146, 158, 176, 189, 243, 250, 253
Capitalism, 42, 86, 91-93, 94-96, 218-20, 233-34, 250, 255, 263-66. *See also* Marxism
Caribbean Free Trade Area (CARIFTA), 297
Caribbean region, 53-54, 279, 315
Cartels, 295, 336, 351, 368, 373
Central African Customs Union (UDEAC), 297
Central American Common Market (CACM), 260, 297, 298, 304
Central banks, 34, 109-10, 311, 354, 355, 357, 377, 378
Centrally planned economies (CPEs), 33, 231, 269
Central planning, 33-34, 40-41, 44, 46-47, 54, 57-59, 76, 118, 127, 131-34
Cereals, 167, 170, 227, 230, 274, 342-44, 345, 346
Ceylon. *See* Sri Lanka
Chad, 347
Chicago school, 12
Chile, 202, 224-25, 307, 314, 356; inflation, 77, 78, 84, 145; population, 196, 197; trade, 61, 138
China, 234, 255, 256, 269, 344; agriculture, 105, 342-43; population, 93, 195, 197, 270
Classical economics, 18-19, 94. *See also* Neoclassical economics

444

Subject Index

Closed economy, 38, 44, 79-80, 91-92, 97, 129-30, 141, 160
Clothing, 144, 302-3, 367-68
Coal, 36, 103
Cocoa, 223, 338-40
Coffee, 338-40
Collective goods. *See* Public goods
Collectives. *See* Cooperatives
Colombia, 145, 196, 197, 198, 339
Colonialism, 50, 53-56, 68, 87, 111, 199, 221-22, 226, 296, 303, 324, 327. *See also* Imperialism, Neocolonialism
Commodities, 130, 143, 223, 226, 279, 280, 288, 336-37. *See also* Agricultural products; Buffer stocks; Consumer goods; Prices; *specific commodities* (for example, Textiles)
Common Agricultural Policy. *See* European Economic Community, Common Agricultural Policy
Common Fund, 336-37, 340-42
Common markets, 294, 296-98
Communist countries, 196, 227, 228, 274
Commutative justice, 322-23, 324, 326, 335
Comparative advantage, 38, 40, 45, 138, 142, 205, 243, 251, 265, 279, 351, 367-68, 375
Competition, 22, 222-23, 295. *See also* Monopoly
Concessionary loans. *See* Loans
Conference on International Economic Cooperation (CIEC), 341, 349
Consumer goods, 53, 64-65, 148, 245-46, 251-54
Consumption, 6-7, 8-10, 14-15, 47, 72, 88, 116, 129, 211, 213, 264, 367
Cooperatives, 94, 167-68, 204
Copper, 224-25, 257, 338-40
Corporations, 201. *See also* Transnational corporations
Costa Rica, 197
Cost-benefit analysis, 39, 46, 128, 131, 138, 184-86, 190, 192, 233, 350-51. *See also* Social cost-benefit analysis
Cost-push theory, 79
Costs, 4, 68-69, 85, 145, 180, 204, 205, 368. *See also* Domestic resource cost; Marginal cost; Opportunity cost; Social cost
CPEs. *See* Centrally planned economies
Credit, 32, 47, 146, 166, 200-1, 203-5, 235, 314, 349, 358, 364, 371, 381. *See also* Loans
Cuba, 227, 269
Currency convertibility, 62, 290, 306, 310, 312-13, 354
Currency devaluation, 62-63, 81-83, 144-45, 308-9, 312, 314, 318, 356, 376

Current account, 307, 309, 359, 360, 362
Customs unions, 287, 296
Cyprus, 296

DAC. *See* Organization for Economic Cooperation and Development, Development Assistance Committee
Debts, 81, 144, 235, 321, 336, 345-50, 356, 359-66. *See also* Loans
Decentralization, 30, 32, 132, 133
Decision-making, 7-8, 43. *See also* Planning
Demand. *See* Supply and demand
Denmark, 104, 298, 300, 365
Dependency, 12, 52, 108, 209, 218, 220-22, 262-63, 265-66, 325, 353, 383; industrial, 236-40, 254-55; technological, 240-48; trade, 222-25, 228-30, 256, 273-74, 296, 372; on transfers, 230-36, 380
Devaluation. *See* Currency devaluation
Developed countries. *See* More developed countries
Developing countries. *See* Less developed countries
Development. *See* Economic development; Underdevelopment
Development decades, 3, 9
Development economics, 16-17, 120-21, 311
Distribution, 14, 22-23, 126, 157, 170, 213, 216, 331, 355. *See also* Income distribution
Distributive justice, 322-32, 335
Domestic resource cost (DRC), 128, 137, 138
Drugs. *See* Pharmaceuticals
Dualism, 23, 86, 90-95, 214, 234, 256
Dynamic analysis, 18-19

Earnings. *See* Wages
East African Common Market, 297
Eastern Europe. *See* Europe, Eastern
Economic Commission for Latin America (ECLA), 54, 70, 71, 78, 218
Economic development, 209-10; definition, 4, 6-7, 17; measurement, 3-5, 13-15
Economic growth, 4, 17, 23, 41-42, 44, 65, 80, 100-4, 112, 147, 210. *See also* Capital-intensive growth; Labor-intensive growth; Planning; Stagnation
Economic theory, 18. *See also specific theories* (for example, Neoclassical economics)

445

Subject Index

Economic welfare. *See* Welfare economics
Economies of scale, 40, 129-30, 133, 146, 196, 253-54
Ecuador, 257
Education, 75, 81, 96, 155, 158, 189-98, 212, 215-16, 234, 256
EEC. *See* European Economic Community
Effective rate of protection (ERP), 137-38, 140
Efficiency, 12, 82, 83, 116, 176, 179
EFTA. *See* European Free Trade Area
Egypt, 56, 88, 91, 114, 195, 273, 275, 296
Elites, 11, 12, 86, 102, 255-59, 328-29
Employment, 4, 42, 47, 66, 79, 88, 89, 144, 152-58, 209-10. *See also* Full employment; Labor; Underemployment; Unemployment; World Employment Conference
England. *See* United Kingdom
Entrepreneurship, 45, 95, 110-11, 118, 120, 237, 239, 259
Equality, 3, 15, 97, 143, 167, 171, 210, 212-13, 325-27. *See also* Inequality
Equilibrium, 99-100, 101, 108, 137, 144, 319-20, 334
ERP. *See* Effective rate of protection
Ethiopia, 256, 339, 347
Eurocurrency market, 235, 237, 246, 355, 356, 362, 381
Europe, 38, 55, 113, 114, 183, 187, 219, 256, 269, 307; agriculture, 88, 275; industry, 39, 226, 252, 276; planning, 47-48, 78; population, 107, 109; trade, 36, 62, 288, 289, 290, 293, 300, 303
Europe, Eastern, 95, 180, 265, 300
European Economic Community (EEC), 226, 228, 292, 296-97, 298, 299-300, 302-4, 352, 367; Common Agricultural Policy (CAP), 227, 292, 296, 297, 374
European Free Trade Area (EFTA), 297, 300, 302, 303
European Payments Union, 48
Exploitation, 98, 166, 220, 248, 263-64
Expropriation, 143, 187, 254, 257, 288
Externalities, 38-39, 41-43, 45, 68-69, 71, 103, 184, 186, 258, 320

Family planning programs (FPPs), 195-99, 273
Far East, 135, 142, 179, 228, 273, 303
Feudalism, 94-95
Financial institutions, 101, 110, 119, 200, 306, 341, 365-66. *See also* Banks
Fiscal policy, 116, 229. *See also* Central banks; Monetarism

Five Year Plans, 34, 128; Indian, 10, 45, 47, 48-53, 56, 78, 117, 127, 134, 165, 315; Soviet, 8-9, 56
Fixed exchange rate, 83, 145, 310, 354, 375-76, 377
Floating exchange rate, 145, 313, 319, 354, 355, 375-76, 378, 381
Flow of funds. *See* Liquidity
Food, 80, 96, 104, 105, 175, 196, 336, 342-45; prices, 78-79, 161-62, 164, 247, 342-46; supply and demand, 20, 79-80, 81, 162-164, 170-71, 225, 241-42. *See also specific foods* (for example, Rice)
Food and Agricultural Organization (FAO), 163
Foreign aid, 53, 63, 111-14, 118, 126, 147-49, 182-83, 231, 265, 328, 330-32, 335-36, 347-49, 371, 380-81. *See also* Loans; Official Development Assistance
Foreign aid donors, 129, 147, 170, 270, 347-49
Foreign corporations. *See* Transnational corporations
Foreign exchange, 47, 68, 72, 128, 148-49, 186, 242, 255, 316-18, 348, 351, 356-57. *See also* Money; Two-gap theory
Foreign exchange rates, 34, 63, 81, 82, 144-45, 181, 306, 307-13. *See also* Fixed exchange rate; Floating exchange rate; Trotting peg
Foreign investment. *See* Private foreign investment
FPPs. *See* Family planning programs
France, 48, 226, 260; money, 307, 309, 310, 316, 354, 355, 358, 379; planning, 32, 40, 127; trade, 289, 293, 303, 304, 367
Full employment, 23, 55, 56

Gabon, 257
GATT. *See* General Agreement on Tariffs and Trade
GDP. *See* Gross domestic product
General Agreement on Tariffs and Trade (GATT), 62, 289-98, 302-3, 307, 367-70, 373-74, 379
Generalized special preferences (GSPs), 228, 297n, 298-304, 365
Germany, 229, 244, 260, 285, 300, 355, 379
Ghana, 106, 117, 145, 223, 235, 260, 349
Gini coefficients, 263, 271-72
GNP. *See* Gross national product
Gold, 306, 308, 309, 310, 312-13, 314, 357-58

446

Subject Index

Government, 101-2, 120, 194, 201, 233. *See also* Centrally planned economies; Central planning; Industry, and government
Grain. *See* Cereals
Grants. *See* Foreign aid
Greece, 296, 367
Green revolution, 170-71, 247, 248
Gross domestic product (GDP), 15, 33, 349-50, 362
Gross national product (GNP), 9-10, 57n, 192, 202, 210, 223, 247, 265, 276, 277-81, 346, 360, 365
Group of Seventy-seven, 270, 298-99, 301, 302, 334, 340, 353-54, 365, 370, 382-83
Growth, economic. *See* Economic growth
GSPs. *See* Generalized special preferences
Guyana, 117, 257

Haiti, 339
Havana Charter (1948), 60, 61, 75, 288, 289, 306
Havana Conference, 63, 64, 287
Hong Kong, 24, 212, 260, 263, 279; industry, 181, 275; population, 93, 197; trade, 74, 141, 262, 274, 297, 298, 299, 367-68
Human capital, 14, 24, 110-11, 189-93, 195
Hungary, 31

IBRD. *See* International Bank for Reconstruction and Development
ILO. *See* International Labor Organization
IMF. *See* International Monetary Fund
Imperialism, 50, 219, 221, 233, 248
Import controls, 60, 62-63, 67-68, 70, 82, 84, 146, 227, 301, 340
Import substitution, 46, 51, 53-54, 61, 76, 80-81, 118, 128, 136-42, 204, 254, 265, 288
Inappropriate technology. *See* Appropriate technology
Income, 79, 168, 196, 202, 233, 275, 330, 338-39, 359-60. *See also* National income; Per capita income; Wages
Income distribution, 9, 12, 21, 24, 67, 83, 115, 116, 252, 263
Independence. *See* Sovereignty
Indexation, 8, 83, 336
India, 101, 117, 164, 193, 194, 211, 216, 365, 382; agriculture, 105, 166, 169, 170, 276, 343; development, 57, 100, 147-48; industry, 31-32, 33, 178, 180, 243, 247, 254, 256, 262, 265; investments in, 110, 183, 203, 204, 244, 259-60; loans to, 314; money, 119, 145, 244, 318; planning, 109, 114, 126, 129, 130, 204, 288 (*see also* Five Year Plans); population, 93, 195, 197, 199, 270; trade, 138-39, 145, 223, 228, 237, 241, 245, 287, 298, 360
Indicative planning, 32, 37, 40, 127
Indonesia, 195, 197, 199, 270, 349, 364
Industrial Development Organization. *See* United Nations Industrial Development Organization
Industrialization, 33, 37-39, 55, 61, 68-71, 80, 93-94, 96-97, 106, 116, 120, 160, 239, 252, 254-55, 264, 275-76, 280, 288, 326. *See also* Five Year Plans
Industrial planning, 44, 127-30, 136
Industry, 10, 38, 91, 204, 242; and government, 31-32, 37, 44, 54, 68, 146, 353, 372-73; ownership, 236-38. *See also* Capital-intensive industries; Dependency, industrial; Expropriation; Labor-intensive industries; Manufactures; Technology; Terms of trade, agriculture and industry; Transnational corporations
Inequality, 7, 9, 158, 214, 234, 250, 256, 329. *See also* Equality
Inflation, 56, 63-64, 66-67, 71, 79-85, 116, 144-45, 203, 262, 279, 301, 338, 346-48, 359-60, 376
Infrastructure, 78, 81, 166, 233, 234, 257
Institutional economics, 26, 33-34, 95, 100, 101-2, 103, 140, 156, 157
Interest rates, 22, 110, 119, 181, 200, 202-5, 314, 346-47, 348, 354-55
Interindustry transactions, 45, 68, 69, 118
Intermediates, 38-39, 45, 103, 142, 144, 240
Intermediate technology. *See* Appropriate technology
International Bank for Reconstruction and Development (IBRD), 9, 17, 48, 113, 131, 137, 145, 148, 170, 212-13, 215, 231-35, 269, 275, 278, 306, 311, 318, 330, 371, 380-81
International Conference on Underdeveloped Areas, 96
International Fund for Agricultural Development, 365
International Labor Organization (ILO), 151, 177, 209, 214, 216, 329
International Monetary Fund (IMF), 17, 19, 83-84, 145-46, 220, 229, 235, 263, 289, 306, 309-20, 336, 341, 343, 354-55,

447

Subject Index

International Monetary Fund *(continued)* 357-58, 361-64, 366, 371, 375-82
International relations, 11, 325-26, 330, 342
International Trade Organization (ITO), 60, 61, 288, 289, 295, 301, 305, 373, 374, 383
Investments, 9-10, 39-40, 72, 102-3, 118, 120, 127, 129, 133-34, 147, 166, 339, 348. *See also* Private foreign investment; Savings, and investments
Iran, 101, 257, 279
Iraq, 114
Ireland, 271, 298, 300
Iron, 103, 257
Israel, 94, 115, 145, 167, 221, 228, 275, 296
Italy, 40, 41, 293, 307
ITO, *See* International Trade Organization
Ivory Coast, 199, 339

Jamaica, 257
Japan, 33, 107, 111, 114, 187, 227, 256, 264, 273, 285; agriculture, 104, 105, 167, 172; industry, 31, 136, 176, 226, 237, 239; investments in, 10, 67, 244; money, 355, 379; trade, 180, 228, 229, 300, 301-2, 303, 342, 367
Joint Commission on Rural Reconstruction (JCRR), 105, 114
Joint ventures, 187, 241, 258, 259
Jute, 338-40

Kampuchea, 269
Kenya, 234, 262, 296
Keynesian economics, 13, 48, 55, 65, 359
Korea, 24, 114, 129, 151, 172, 260, 263, 264, 279; industry, 31, 49, 143, 178, 181, 239; money, 145, 202, 203; population, 93, 195, 197, 273; trade, 63, 139, 141, 142, 225-26, 260, 274, 301, 367-68
Kuwait, 257, 271

Labor, 22, 41, 129, 183, 264, 279. *See also* Agricultural labor; Employment; Trade unions; Wages
Labor-intensive growth, 13, 46, 264
Labor-intensive industries, 38, 142, 143, 148, 177, 178-81, 240, 251, 279, 368
Labor productivity, 89, 276-77. *See also* Marginal product of labor

Labor supply, 13, 86, 108, 149-50, 153-55, 157-58, 161, 214
Labor surplus, 87-94, 96-97, 99, 105, 118, 120, 147, 150, 152, 159
LAFTA. *See* Latin American Free Trade Area
Laisser faire, 56, 58, 162, 229, 262
Land, 91, 96, 99, 273
Land reform, 81, 102, 104, 114-15, 171-73
Land tenure, 104, 143, 152-53, 174, 255-56, 265
Laos, 269
Latin America, 151, 209, 256, 275, 315-16; development, 262, 279; industry, 252, 255; inflation, 19, 64, 67, 77-78, 82, 83-84, 319; investments in, 127, 183, 184, 247, 263; planning, 54, 56; population, 109, 196, 273; trade, 61, 63, 287, 288, 300, 350
Latin American Free Trade Area (LAFTA), 297, 298
LDCs. *See* Less developed countries
Lebanon, 198, 296, 307
Lesotho, 347
Less developed countries (LDCs), 11, 16-17, 32-33, 269-70. *See also* Group of Seventy-seven
Liberal economists, 12, 17
Liberia, 256
Libya, 257, 279
Linear programming, 40, 57, 134, 135, 136
Liner conferences. *See* Shipping
Linkages, 38, 41-44, 45-46, 103-4, 210, 250-51, 311-12, 336, 355-56, 365
Liquidity, 110, 309, 310, 311-12, 355
Literacy, 192, 198, 212, 264
Loans, 142, 231, 235-36, 313-21, 349. *See also* Debts
Lomé Convention. *See* African, Caribbean, and Pacific (ACP) countries
Long Term Arrangement on Cotton Textiles (LTA), 292-93, 299, 302

Macroeconomic policies, 33, 34, 48, 115, 175, 229, 233
Malaya, 138
Malaysia, 155, 161, 173, 193, 203, 216, 339
Malta, 296
Manpower planning, 193-195
Manufactures, 44, 75, 103, 139, 144, 147, 178, 183, 225-26, 241, 250-54, 258, 274-75, 304, 366-67
Marginal cost, 3, 39
Marginalism, 22, 152

Subject Index

Marginal productivity of capital, 22, 24–25, 57n
Marginal product of labor, 22, 88–92, 94, 109, 149
Market socialism. See Socialist economy
Marshall Plan, 48, 54, 290
Marxism, 50–51, 156, 218, 241, 264. See also Neo-Marxism
MDCs. See More developed countries
Mediterranean countries, 193, 277–78, 296–97, 299
Metal industries, 178, 274. See also Copper, Iron, Steel
Mexico, 144, 117, 198, 211–12, 260, 271; agriculture, 162, 167, 171–72; industry, 138, 252, 275; loans to, 347, 361; trade, 63, 301
MFA. See Multi-fiber Textile Arrangement
MFN. See Most-favored nation
Middle East, 196, 275
Minerals, 143, 224–25, 226, 228, 230, 251, 257, 273, 274
Mining, 143, 224–25, 275
Mixed economy, 31, 41, 201
Monetarism, 19, 78, 80–84, 229, 301, 316
Money, 78–81, 200, 205, 309–13, 354–59, 362, 370, 371. See also Capital, Currency convertibility; Currency devaluation; Foreign exchange; Liquidity; Reserves
Monnet Plan, 48
Monopoly, 22, 25, 43, 85, 101, 140, 166, 183, 205, 224–27, 230, 235, 240, 245, 353. See also Competition; Oligopoly
Monopsony, 22, 125, 225
More developed countries (MDCs), 17, 33–34
Morocco, 296
Most-favored nation (MFN), 60–61, 286, 290, 291, 300, 301, 302, 374
Most seriously affected (MSAs) LDCs, 335, 347
Multi-fiber Textile Arrangement (MFA), 293, 299, 302, 367–69, 373
Multinational corporations. See Transnational corporations

National Bureau of Economic Research (NBER), 144
National income, 12, 13–15, 22, 152, 277, 348
National income per head, 3, 5, 98–99, 107–9, 195, 196, 276
Nationalism, 11. See also Sovereignty
Nationalization. See Expropriation

National objectives, 10–11, 13, 15, 37
Natural laws, 74, 323
Near East, 273, 275
Neoclassical economics, 19, 20, 22–26, 42, 48, 75, 94, 209, 263
Neocolonialism, 221, 256–57
Neo-Marxism, 12, 19, 98, 218–20, 241–42, 255, 261
New International Economic Order (NIEO), 216, 239, 244, 270, 288, 301, 316, 322, 326–28, 334–36, 341–42, 344, 347, 350–53, 358, 365, 372, 379, 381, 384
New Zealand, 260, 269, 287, 300
NIEO. See New International Economic Order
Nigeria, 195, 197, 257, 260, 270
Nonoil LDCs (NOLDCs), 349, 360–61, 364–65, 366, 379
Nontariff barriers (NTBs), 227, 290, 293, 302
North America, 107, 109, 269, 274, 342–43, 367
NTBs. See Nontariff barriers

Objective function. See Welfare function
ODA. See Official Development Assistance
OECD. See Organization for Economic Cooperation and Development
OEEC. See Organization for European Economic Cooperation
Official Development Assistance (ODA), 230–35, 355–56, 364–66, 374
Oil, 38, 224, 225, 228, 230, 274, 346; prices, 279, 281, 301, 334, 335, 349, 359, 362, 366. See also Petrochemicals
Oil exporting LDCs, 65, 228, 278, 349, 360, 361
Oligopoly, 25, 85, 183, 225, 226, 235, 253, 295
OPEC. See Organization of Petroleum Exporting Countries
Open economy, 80, 93, 97, 141, 143, 153, 160
Opportunity cost, 12, 39, 69, 149, 177, 179, 198
Organization for Economic Cooperation and Development (OECD), 129, 137, 163, 193, 209, 229, 309–10, 352, 359, 383–84; Development Assistance Committee (DAC), 113, 330, 331, 364–65; Development Centre, 138, 150, 177, 209, 214
Organization for European Economic Cooperation (OEEC), 48, 290, 302

449

Subject Index

Organization of Petroleum Exporting Countries (OPEC), 231, 299, 301, 335, 341, 355, 359, 375
Organized labor. *See* Trade unions
Overseas Development Council, 14
Overseas Development Institute (ODI), 114

Pakistan, 137, 138, 170, 195, 202, 280, 347, 348
Pareto-optimality, 25, 155, 331
Patents, 226, 240-41, 244-46, 250
Peasants, 20, 89, 99, 149-50, 160-62, 339. *See also* Agricultural labor
Per caput income, 4, 120, 197, 210, 271-73
Peru, 202, 257, 260
Petrochemicals, 38, 144, 241, 253
PFI. *See* Private foreign investment
Pharmaceuticals, 226, 245
Philippines, 138, 145, 167, 203, 275
Phillips curve, 66-67
Planning, 30-33, 35-37, 54-59, 72, 125-27, 135-36; definition, 29-30; models, 134-35. *See also* Centrally planned economies; Central planning; Five Year Plans; Indicative planning; Industrial planning; Manpower planning; Project planning; Sector planning
POI (private overseas investment). *See* Private foreign investment
Politics, 8, 17, 56-58, 112-13, 115, 126, 156, 186-87, 220, 227-28, 232-33, 259, 318, 328, 373. *See also* Elites; International relations; National objectives; Sovereignty
Poor, 49, 119, 175, 233. *See also* Poverty; Rural poor
Population, 92-93, 97, 99, 107-9, 162, 195-200, 270, 272-73, 276. *See also* Rural population; Urban population
Populism, 11, 210
Portugal, 358, 367
Poverty, 3-4, 10-11, 15, 17, 20, 98, 120-21, 151, 158, 209-17, 329, 332-33, 342. *See also* Income; Poor; Standard of living; Wealth
Price control, 67, 85, 373-74
Price mechanism, 25, 30, 39, 58, 62, 65-66, 68-69, 72-73, 78, 80-81, 132-33, 140, 146, 168-69, 194, 243, 295
Prices, 3, 21-22, 175, 280, 287-88, 319, 322, 336-40, 365. *See also* Food, prices; Oil, prices; Shadow prices
Private foreign investment (PFI), 70, 182-86, 231, 233, 236, 239, 244, 249-50, 253, 262, 288, 364. *See also* Transnational corporations
Production, 20, 25, 44-45, 100, 116, 275-76
Production function, 22, 23-24, 150, 176-77. *See also* Substitution
Productivity, 42, 85. *See also* Labor productivity; Marginal productivity of capital
Profit, 22, 68, 156, 188, 253. *See also* Social profit
Progress, economic. *See* Economic development
Project planning, 34-35, 46-47, 54, 65, 127-29, 136, 138
Protectionism, 37, 61, 68-69, 74, 101, 136-38, 160-61, 181, 186, 227, 229, 251-52, 254-55, 261-62, 280, 289, 304, 319, 366-67. *See also* Effective rate of protection; Import controls; Nontariff barriers; Tariff
Public expenditures, 57, 113-14, 115, 133-34, 190
Public finance, 115-16. *See also* Fiscal policy
Public goods, 7, 33
Public health, 109, 189, 195, 196, 198, 215, 248
Public services, 215, 216, 252
Public works, 153, 173

Qatar, 257
Quota restrictions. *See* Import controls

Radical economists, 12, 73, 210, 219, 232, 233-35, 260, 265
Real wage, 13, 22, 24, 91, 92-93
Religion and economics, 100, 101
Reserves, 67-68, 144, 308-12, 314, 317, 336, 346, 354-58, 362-63, 375-78
Reswitching theory, 23, 24, 148
Rice, 161-62, 166-67, 171
Romania, 234
Rubber, 338-40
Rural development, 106-7, 131, 165, 169-70
Rural labor. *See* Agricultural labor
Rural poor, 161, 170, 339
Rural population, 151-52, 161, 170
Russia. *See* Soviet Union
Rwanda, 339, 347

450

Subject Index

Saudi Arabia, 228, 257, 279, 363
Savings, 57n, 81, 108, 112, 118, 201, 203; and investments, 45, 47, 64, 66, 99, 115, 279, 359, 364
Say's law, 38
Scandinavia, 329, 365
SDR (special drawing right). *See* Reserves
Sectoral planning, 35, 54
Self-reliance, 51, 52, 241, 335
Services industry, 13, 45, 65, 276
Shadow prices, 12–13, 39–40, 41, 128, 129, 130, 135, 185–86
Sharecropping, 150, 174
Shipping, 336, 350–52
Singapore, 24, 141, 142, 197, 203, 260, 262, 275, 279
Sisal, 338–40
Sliding peg. *See* Trotting peg
Social cost, 90, 176, 185
Social cost-benefit analysis, 128, 140
Social indicators, 13–15, 212
Socialist economy, 30–31. *See also* Centrally planned economies; State capitalism
Social profit, 12, 68, 234
Somalia, 347
South Africa, 221, 225, 227, 228, 269, 276, 300, 308
South Korea. *See* Korea
Sovereignty, 11, 228, 326, 330, 331, 335, 344, 350, 353
Soviet Union, 66, 105, 111, 164, 221, 234, 265, 308, 324, 344; industry, 55, 245; investments in, 10, 67; planning, 31, 33, 44, 50–51, 52, 262, 266 (*see also* Five Year Plans); trade, 180, 227, 230, 300, 342–43
Spain, 296, 361, 367
Special drawing right. *See* Reserves
Special United Nations Fund for Economic Development (SUNFED), 113
Sri Lanka, 117, 129, 151, 202
Stabilization, 115–16, 144, 338, 340, 343, 365
Stabilization of Export Receipts Fund (STABEX), 297
Stagnation, 71, 98–99. *See also* Agricultural stagnation
Standard of living, 4, 36, 56, 74, 91, 93, 108, 119, 264, 287
State capitalism, 95, 266, 331
Steel, 11, 38, 45, 144, 226, 237, 240, 249
Structuralism, 19–21, 23, 25–26, 31, 36, 40–42, 55, 67, 78–84, 99, 118, 147, 153, 176, 209, 316
Subsidies, 69, 140–44, 146, 157, 167, 175, 215–16, 261, 291, 318, 368
Subsistence economy, 86–87, 91
Substitution, 38–39, 153, 176–81. *See also* Import substitution
Sudan, 364
Sugar, 61, 164
Supply and demand, 21, 25, 38, 40–41, 44, 62, 65, 67, 71–73, 78–79, 84–85, 364. *See also* Food, supply and demand; Labor supply
Sweden, 104, 365
Switzerland, 271, 300
Syria, 151

Taiwan, 24, 114, 151, 156, 212, 263, 264, 269, 279, 360; agriculture, 105, 136, 162, 167, 171–72, 173; industry, 11, 31, 49, 143, 178, 181, 239, 275; money, 202, 203; population, 93, 109, 195, 197, 273; trade, 63, 139, 141, 142, 274, 299, 301, 366, 367–68
Tanzania, 234, 296, 347, 356
Tariff, 62, 65, 69–70, 72–74, 82, 144, 181, 252, 318; reductions, 60, 61, 286, 292. *See also* General Agreement on Tariffs and Trade; Most-favored nation
Taxation, 65, 69, 71, 115–18, 140, 143–44, 161, 169, 185, 187–88, 203
Tea, 338–40
Technical assistance, 231–32
Technical progress, 42, 92, 97, 189
Technology, 78, 178–79, 237–39, 243, 249. *See also* Appropriate technology; Capital-intensive industries; Dependency, technology; Patents
Technology transfer, 236, 239, 244–50, 258–59, 336, 353–54
Terms of trade, 70–71, 74, 139, 278, 281, 320; agriculture and industry, 92–93, 96, 160–61, 262
Textiles, 36, 53, 103–4, 143–44, 164, 176, 178, 237–39, 241, 251. *See also* Clothing; Long Term Arrangement on Cotton Textiles; Multi-fiber Textile Arrangement
Thailand, 155, 255, 256
Theil Index, 272
Third World. *See* Less developed countries
Timber, 104, 292
TNCs. *See* Transnational corporations
Trade, 20, 60, 73, 81–82, 129, 146, 148–49, 209, 221–30, 285–86, 304, 317–19, 371–75. *See also* Dependency, trade; Protectionism; Terms of trade
Trade controls, 63–66, 72–76, 144, 286–92, 373–74. *See also* Import controls

451

Subject Index

Trademarks, 244–46, 250
Trade preferences, 226, 286–87, 296–98. *See also* Generalized special preferences; Most-favored nation
Trade unions, 85, 101, 156, 221, 262
Training, 75, 143, 157, 165–66, 167, 194
Transfers. *See* Dependency, on transfers; Foreign aid; Loans; Technology transfer
Transnational corporations (TNCs), 139, 156, 178, 182–89, 221, 224–27, 239–40, 247–48, 250–61, 352–53. *See also* Cartels; Private foreign investment
Trinidad and Tobago, 197
Trotting peg, 83, 145, 307, 319, 354
Tunisia, 197, 296
Turkey, 117, 170, 198, 269, 296
Two-gap model, 52–53, 147–49, 156–57

Uganda, 297, 339
UNCTAD. *See* United Nations Conference on Trade and Development
Underdevelopment, 218–21, 232, 247, 261–65. *See also* Dependency
Underemployment, 55, 89, 150–52
UNDP. *See* United Nations Development Program
Unemployment, 3, 15, 42, 55, 85, 89–90, 150–51, 153, 155–58, 196. *See also* Employment
UNIDO. *See* United Nations Industrial Development Organization
United Arab Republic, 298
United Kingdom, 11, 66, 93, 260; industry, 104, 143; money, 62, 307, 311, 316, 355, 379; planning, 35, 41, 48, 55; trade, 68, 285–86, 287, 297, 298–99, 300, 304, 367
United Nations, 3, 9, 75, 96–97, 111, 113, 147, 182, 232, 260, 269, 327, 365, 382, 384; General Assembly, 11, 270, 335, 354, 370
United Nations Conference on Trade and Development (UNCTAD), 70, 148, 185, 244, 300–3, 312, 337, 339, 351–53, 366, 370, 373, 382–84; doctrine, 136, 137, 139; I (1964), 280–81, 292, 294–95, 299, 335, 382; II (1968), 298. *See also* Common Fund
United Nations Development Program (UNDP), 341, 354, 366
United Nations Economic and Social Council (ECOSOC), 113, 216, 286
United Nations Industrial Development Organization (UNIDO), 129, 382

United States, 55, 111–12, 113, 114, 163, 187–88, 273, 300, 365; agriculture, 164, 342; industry, 103, 178, 275, 276; investments by, 183, 184, 224–25, 244, 257; money, 36, 62, 307–10, 312–13, 355–56, 358, 376, 379; trade, 68, 227–29, 285–90, 293, 297n, 298–99, 301–4, 350, 367, 374
Urban population, 79, 151, 262, 263
Uruguay, 275
USSR. *See* Soviet Union
Utilitarianism, 7, 12, 323, 325
Utility, 4, 10, 22, 138

Values, 8, 9–10, 11, 13, 15, 22, 99, 330, 331
Venezuela, 257, 361
Vietnam, 114, 234, 269, 312

Wages, 69, 95, 144, 149–51, 155–58, 181, 190–92, 303; rural, 89, 92–93, 149, 152, 173. *See also* Real wage
War, 52, 70, 139, 312, 324. *See also* World War II
Wealth, 121, 325, 326, 333. *See also* Income; Poverty
Welfare economics, 4, 6–9, 115, 120, 155, 329, 371, 372, 380. *See also* Distributive justice; Externalities; Utility
Welfare function, 9, 10, 13, 15, 17, 97, 152, 154
West African Economic Community, 297
Western Europe. *See* Europe
West Germany. *See* Germany
World Bank. *See* International Bank for Reconstruction and Development
World Conference on Science and Technology, 354
World economy, 54–55, 366
World Employment Conference, 214, 216, 326, 329–30
World Population Conference, 199
World War II, 10, 35, 62–63, 66, 285–86

Yaoundé Convention (1964), 296, 297, 303–4
Yugoslavia, 30–31, 234, 298, 301

Zaire, 364

452